1968

RADICAL PROTEST AND ITS ENEMIES

Richard Vinen

HARPER

An Imprint of HarperCollins*Publishers*

HarperCollins books may be purchased for educational, business, or sales promotional use. For information, please email the Special Markets Department at SPsales@harpercollins.com.

Originally published as *The Long '68* in the United Kingdom in 2018 by Penguin Random House UK.

FIRST U.S. EDITION

Library of Congress Cataloging-in-Publication Data has been applied for.

ISBN 978-0-06-245874-2

18 19 20 21 22 LSC 10 9 8 7 6 5 4 3 2 1

For Alex

Contents

List of Tables

List of Chronologies

Abbreviations

BPP	Black Panther Party
CDU	Christlich Demokratische Union Deutschlands
CFDT	Confédération Française Démocratique du Travail
CGT	Confédération Générale du Travail
CIA	Central Intelligence Agency
CSU	Christlich-Soziale Union in Bayern
FBI	Federal Bureau of Investigation
FO	Force Ouvrière
IMG	International Marxist Group
IRA	Irish Republican Army
IS	International Socialists
JCR	Jeunesse Communiste Révolutionnaire
NATO	North Atlantic Treaty Organization
NUM	National Union of Mineworkers
PCF	Parti Communiste Français
PSU	Parti Socialiste Unifié
RSA	Radical Student Alliance
RSSF	Revolutionary Socialist Students' Federation
SDS (Germany)	Sozialistischer Deutscher Studentenbund
SDS (USA)	Students for a Democratic Society
SFIO	Section Française de l'Internationale Ouvrière
SLL	Socialist Labour League

SNCC	Student Non-Violent Co-Ordinating Committee
SPD	Sozialdemokratische Partei Deutschlands
UJCML	Union des Jeunesses Communistes Marxistes-Léninistes

Introduction

This book is about '68', by which I mean the radical movements and rebellion of the late 1960s and early 70s, rather than about the year 1968. 68 is both ubiquitous and remote. The songs of the era can be heard playing in the background at supermarkets, the slogans pop up in advertisements and yet the militants of the late 1960s and early 70s are now past retirement age: pensions are a frequent concern among those who spent years outside the conventional economic system. The 'veterans' (a term that no longer seems as ironical as it once did) are painfully conscious of how the world has changed. Casting his 2012 film on 68, *Après Mai*, Olivier Assayas was struck by the fact that young actors were more interested in the clothes than the politics. Those undergoing his screen tests were mainly united by a common enthusiasm for hair gel.[1]

Whole mountain ranges have disappeared from the political landscape. The image of Chairman Mao is now mainly diffused on banknotes. The collapse of the Soviet Union was an earthquake for orthodox Communists but also for the Trotskyist factions that distinguished themselves from each other by the different grounds on which they denounced the USSR. The kind of working class that once interested parts of the student left has changed beyond recognition. Daniel Rondeau, revisiting his Maoist past in the 1980s, met an old friend who said that returning to Paris in the mid-1970s, after their political group had dissolved itself, felt like coming to a 'museum'. Rondeau himself went back to Lorraine, the industrial area in which he had gone to work as a political missionary in the early 1970s, but it was unrecognizable. The factories had all been dynamited.[2] Anyone visiting the University of Kent near Canterbury in England will still see a university of the 1960s, complete with a college named after Keynes, but who now would believe that there were once coal mines in the English home counties and that the Kent miners were particularly radical in the strikes of the early 1970s?

Sometimes the period from the mid-1960s to the late 1970s seems like a dream, or nightmare, from which the participants eventually woke up. Eleanor Stein was born in 1946. She was the daughter of Communists and her parents were under FBI surveillance from the early 1940s, but the style of her early life was relatively conventional. When she married Jonah Raskin in 1964, he wore a suit and the couple twisted on the dance floor as the band mangled a Beatles song. Five years later, Eleanor was photographed with an Afro haircut giving a clenched fist salute. Five years further on, Jonah Raskin did not even know where his wife was. Their marriage had been pulled apart by the cross currents of sexual and political liberation. She was on the run with the Weather Underground – holed up in New York apartments, living on rice and a Vietnamese fish sauce that radicals affected to like. She had an affair with Jeff Jones but broke up with him and gave birth to their son Thai – named after a Viet-cong leader – on her own. However, by the time the FBI tracked them down in 1981, Jeff Jones and Eleanor were back together – living under false names but raising their child in the way that a young couple of fifteen years earlier might have regarded as normal. When Eleanor got out of prison, she went back to law school and became an adjunct judge specializing in administrative law.[3]

This book is an attempt to reconstruct the world that came and, largely, went in the late 1960s and early 70s. Defining '68' is difficult and the next chapter is devoted to the various ways in which one might do this. It would be useful, however, to begin with some simple points. First, I have distinguished between '1968', by which I mean a single eventful year, and '68' or 'the long 68', by which I mean the variety of movements that became associated with, and sometimes reached their climax in, 1968 but that cannot be understood with exclusive reference to that year. In chronological terms, I have not set precise frontiers. Most of my account concerns events in the late 1960s and early 70s but I have sometimes gone back further in time, especially with regard to America. As for when 68 ends, in the obvious sense that many who were most active in it are still alive, and that a small but significant minority of them reached the apogee of their influence around the end of the twentieth century, 68 goes on for several decades.

In at least one important respect, my approach may seem perverse, and indeed to run counter to my own emphasis on a 'long 68'. I have been influenced by the work of French historians on what they refer to as '*les années soixante-huit*'. By this they mean something similar to what I mean by 'the long 68'. Together with the efforts of French historians to 'decentre' the year 1968 has often gone an effort to 'decentre' the French 68 geographically and to emphasize the role of the provinces rather than focusing on Paris. However, I have come to feel that an approach based on 'the 68 years' sometimes works better for other countries than it does for France itself, or at least that it obscures some aspects of the French experience. I understand the enthusiasm of French historians to escape from a hackneyed view that centres on the boulevard St Michel and to broaden the scope of their analysis. I also appreciate that this broadening of emphasis sometimes goes with a desire to assert the significance of 1968 against those who dismiss it as ephemeral. It seems to me, though, that French historians have become victims of their own originality and sophistication and that they do not give enough weight to the unique drama of France, especially Paris, in May and June 1968 – a time when demonstrations involved tens or even hundreds of thousands of people and when almost 10 million workers were on strike. Even those who were most involved in the radicalisms of the 1970s often explained their action with reference to the high drama of 1968. One recalled: 'we learned more in a month than they [his teachers] had taught us in seven years of study'.[1] For this reason, my chapter on France adopts what would once have seemed a conventional approach – with an almost exclusive focus on the year 1968, especially just two months of that year, and with a heavy emphasis on Paris. I recognize that the French 68 needs to be set in a longer chronological span and a wider geographic view but I have tried to do this in the broad thematic chapters – partly because I wish to take French historians seriously when they talk of setting France in an international context.

More generally, the partly comparative approach of this book may sometimes put me at odds with recent writing. Many historians have tended to play down national peculiarities in their accounts of 68 – either because they have been influenced by 'transnational' approaches that look for links between countries, or simply because they react against the clichés of national self-perception. Putting things in comparative perspective, however, illustrates the fact that clichés usually have some root in reality. Recent American historians have reacted against the notion that the origins of Students for a Democratic Society were marked by an 'innocent' optimism that evaporated with the violence that came around 1968. Well, compared with most of Western Europe, the American student radicals of the early 1960s were innocent and the late 1960s in America were violent. Similarly, some historians of Germany have reacted against the notion that workers played no part in the country's agitations of the late 1960s.[5] Once again, international comparison suggests that German workers were indeed less radical than most of their counterparts elsewhere. The strikes in France in May and June 1968 were so widespread that the government was unable to compute the number of strikers; strikes in Germany in 1968 were so rare that the International Labour Organization did not bother to record them.

In terms of geographical coverage, this book is about the democracies of the industrialized West. I realize once again that this may seem a contrary interpretation of 68. The most momentous events of the period often happened outside Western Europe and North America. The Prague Spring and its suppression, the Vietnam War, the Chinese Cultural Revolution, the violent suppression of protest around the Olympic Games in Mexico City were matters of life and death to millions of people. Clearly, in terms of bloodshed and social upheaval, they were more important than anything happening in the industrialized West. However, for this very reason, I am wary of trying to fit all these different stories together and conscious in any case that I do not have the expertise to do so. My version of 68 is one that involves affluent countries, in which radical protest came up against elected governments. Even, and perhaps especially, those European and North American militants who spent time outside Europe and North America recognized that there was something distinct about 68 in their own countries. Luisa Passerini was in Kenya, Tanzania, Zambia and Egypt during the late 1960s and later recalled: 'While I was taking part in all this in the third world, 1968 was happening in the first world.'[6] The conflicts in Asia, Latin America and Eastern Europe come into my account only to the extent, sometimes considerable, that what happened there, or what people believed to be happening there, influenced Western Europe or North America.

I have devoted single chapters to the United States, France, Germany and Britain. America is important partly because it was the most powerful of the Western democracies. Protesters elsewhere so often looked to it – both because they regarded its government with hostility and because they sought to emulate what they took to be its 'counter-culture'. America illustrates a particular version of 68 – one that was characterized by movements which had already been highly active earlier in the 1960s and that was also marked by a sense of crisis later in that decade, which involved, among other things, a break between the student movement and much of the working class. France is important because it attracted much international attention in 1968 and it offers, particularly because of the alliance between workers and students, an interesting counterpoint to America. Germany is significant because its version of 68 is so often – though, I have come to think, wrongly – seen as the sequel to Nazism and/or the prequel to the terrorism of the 1970s. Britain illustrates another pattern of 68 – one that gained momentum in the 1970s and in which labour often played the most important role.

This book is primarily a synthesis that draws on other people's research. Though I have also done a small amount of archival work in Britain and France, I have used mainly secondary sources and a few published primary ones – the distinction between the two is unusually blurred given the number of academics who were 'participant observers' of 68. Not all of those whose accounts I have used will agree with the interpretations that I have put on their writing. Participants in the long 68 sometimes express their indignation when someone else tells 'their story'. I appreciate that works of contemporary history will often seem strange to those who lived through the events being described, but I see no reason why participants in 68 should claim a special right to be spared the cold scalpel of historical autopsy. Above all, this book seeks to integrate 68 into the broader political history of the period. It argues that one way to understand 68 might be to examine those – in governments, trade unions and established political parties – who opposed protest or who sought in one way or another to manage it.

I

Words and 'the Thing': Defining 68

'Beauty is in the street'. Poster from 1968.

I

The Conservative politician Enoch Powell was a central figure in the British 68. After his 'rivers of blood' speech in April of that year attacking non-white immigration, his presence in universities was the single most common cause of student protest. Powell's own position, however, was strange. He was fiercely anti-American, and his stance on, say, the Vietnam War, sometimes resembled that of his bitterest enemies. Equally, he did not always agree with the numerous admirers who wrote to him. He did not share the view of one correspondent that the spread of Chinese restaurants in English villages was a front for Maoist infiltration.[1] When a worried mother wrote about an article in her daughter's copy of *Honey* magazine that described a girl who found sex, drugs and left-wing politics in the 'Wild Blue Yonder' commune, Powell gently suggested that the article might have been ironical in intent.[2] Powell placed some of the letters he received in boxes marked 'lunatics', but put those that concerned the counter-culture, student radicalism and trade union power in a file that was labelled simply 'The Thing'.

Many observers shared Powell's sense that they knew broadly what a certain kind of radicalism was about while not being able to pin it down in words. There was also a curious symbiosis between 68 and its enemies: both defined themselves in terms of what they opposed, or what opposed them, more than what they proposed. Stuart Hall was the kind of man that Enoch Powell would have identified as part of 'the Thing'. A black cultural theorist, involved in the student occupations at Birmingham University in 1968, and an exponent of what French conservatives would come to call '*la pensée 68*', Hall wrote in 1979 that Thatcherism could be defined in opposition to 'the radical movements and political polarizations of the 1960s, for which "1968" must stand as a convenient, though inadequate notation'.[3] In April 1965, Paul Potter, a leader of Students for a Democratic Society in the United States, gave a speech after a demonstration against the Vietnam War in which he urged his listeners to identify the structures against which they were fighting and to 'name that system'. Some assumed that 'the system' must be capitalism but Potter himself did not use the word. He did, however, like Powell and Hall, seem to feel that the cause for which he stood might best be defined by opposition. He said later: 'The name we are looking for . . . not only "names the system" but gives us a name as well.'[4]

Words – in pamphlets, speeches, slogans and graffiti – were important to 68. A French historian wrote: 'Revolution? May 68 was only one of words and it was first of all because the public was fed up of being governed . . . in the language of Bossuet [the seventeenth-century theologian].'[5] Some in 68 assumed that getting away from formality of expression would itself be a political act. When trying to persuade Pierre Mendès France (born in 1907) to address a rally in 1968, Michel Rocard (born in 1930) offered to translate the speech into 'patois compatible with that of May 68'.[6] Articles in the alternative press in Britain and America made laborious efforts to deploy the language of the street – 'fuzz', 'pigs', 'busted'. In continental Europe, using English (or American) expressions was sometimes a way of marking radicalism. Régis Debray, a Frenchman who regarded his fellow *soixante-huitards* with caustic disdain, wrote that *Cahiers du Communisme*, an old-style left-wing publication, was written in French but that those who wanted to read *Libération*, founded after 1968, 'would need to know American'.[7] The German radical left communicated in a mixture of 'Berlin dialect, American slang and social science jargon'.[8] At the same time, others discussed political theory in a language that seemed ostentatiously inaccessible. A journalist for the underground press complained that the Maoist Progressive Labour Party inhabited 'a Tolkien Middle Earth of Marxist-Leninist Hobbits and Orcs and speaks a runic tongue only intelligible to such creatures'.[9]

The simplest words acquired a political charge in 68. 'Student' was widely bandied about, though the two most important organizations to use this name, Students for a Democratic Society in the USA and the Sozialistischer Deutscher Studentenbund in Germany, had many members who had long ceased to attend university. In Britain, the word implied modernity and was explicitly contrasted with 'undergraduate'. Richard Crossman, a Labour minister and former Oxford don who was bitterly opposed to youthful protest, wrote in March 1968 that the trouble in the 'old universities' sprang from the fact that 'everybody is a student rather than an undergraduate'.[10]

Words that seemed to make sense of 68 – 'multiversity', 'counter-culture' – had often been coined in the 1960s. Some on the left felt that they could name a 'thing' for the first time. The English feminist Sheila Rowbotham recalled, of an American friend, 'Henry had produced a name for all these puzzling difficulties: male chauvinism.'[11] Male homosexuals had used the term 'gay' for a long time, but in the early 1970s it acquired new political connotations. In the 1990s, a historian interviewing veterans of the British Gay Liberation Front (founded in 1971) noted how such men had grown up at a time when 'homophile' seemed the safest term to describe their sexuality. Her interviewees flinched when she used the word that came naturally to an activist of her generation: 'queer'.[12]

Michael Schumann, of a left-wing German student association, said in 1961: 'we belong to the movement, which originates in England under the name "New Left" and in France is called "Nouvelle Gauche"'.[13] The same term was used in the United States, and in 1966 the bulletin of Students for a Democratic Society took the name 'New Left Notes' – revealingly, one student leader believed that the 'new' and 'old' left in America were themselves distinguished by language: 'The old left would have said contradictions, but paradox was an intellectual discovery, not an objective conflict.'[14] The sociologist C. Wright Mills, who inspired much of the student movement in the United States, had expressed his views in a 'letter to the New Left' – which meant in practice a letter to the English *New Left Review*. However, the ubiquity of the term 'New Left' derived in part from the very fact that it encompassed so many different things. A CIA report summed matters up thus:

> Loosely dubbed the New Left, they have little in common except for their indebtedness to several prominent writers such as American sociologist C. Wright Mills, Hegelian philosopher Herbert Marcuse, and

the late negro psychiatrist Frantz Fanon ... (The term New Left, itself, has little meaning – except as a device to distinguish between today's young radicals and the Communist-Socialist factions of the interwar period. It is taken to mean an amalgam of disparate, amorphous local groups of uncertain or changing leadership and eclectic programmes) ... an amalgam of anarchism, utopian socialism, and overriding dedication to social involvement.[15]

One term not much used in 68 was '68'. At the time, those who hoped for revolutionary change assumed that the period in which they were living would be the prelude to something more dramatic. Some French revolutionaries did not bother to fill in their tax returns in the summer of 1968 because they assumed – until the bailiffs took their furniture away – that the bourgeois order was about to collapse. Perhaps precisely because the high drama of May 1968 was followed by a period of peace, the French did begin to talk of '68' relatively early. Pierre Grappin, the dean of the university campus at Nanterre, went to the United States in late 1968 to escape from the student upheavals in his own institution. He returned to find 'a world in which May 68 had become a directing myth'.[16] Elsewhere, revolutionaries remained focused on the future for longer. In 1970 or '71, a group of Italian militants, presumably after an evening of narcotic consumption, held a séance to call up the ghost of Frantz Fanon and ask him when the revolution would come. The date given in reply, 1984, seemed disappointingly distant.[17] The words sixty-eighter or *soixante-huitard* implied the past tense and involvement in something that was now finished.

During 68 itself, some talked as though the mere definition of words might be an act of coercion. An American guide for those who wanted to found communes advised: 'it would probably be a good idea to refrain from giving yourself a name ... you will be harder to talk about without a handle'.[18] When a lawyer at the trial of protesters in Frankfurt in 1968 talked of the 'extra-parliamentary opposition', to which they all professed to belong, the Franco-German student leader Daniel Cohn-Bendit stood up to proclaim that only a 'parliament of students' would have the right to determine who belonged to the extra-parliamentary opposition.[19]

In practice, 68ers, Cohn-Bendit especially, often have been allowed to define themselves. Their accounts revolve around their own friends. Cohn-Bendit's published *We Loved the Revolution so Much*;[20] the American Tom Hayden's autobiography was entitled *Reunion*. Relying on the memories of prominent participants in 68, though, raises problems. Confident and articulate witnesses are not always reliable. Cohn-Bendit was interviewed on French radio in late 2016. He recalled that Sartre had seemed intimidated when the two men met in 1968, which is certainly not how Sartre remembered things.[21] He also believed that Roger Garaudy was the Communist leader chased from Nanterre by *gauchiste* students in 1968 – it was in fact Pierre Juquin.

The leading figures in 68 often had a highly developed sense of themselves as historical actors and as people who would one day be the object of historical research. The Italian guerrilla group Prima Linea dissolved itself in 1983 partly to allow its own members to provide 'a full reconstruction of the history of the organization, its origins, development, aims and activities, to avoid leaving it to others to tell the story of Prima Linea'.[22] In Chicago in February 1970, one of the last acts of members of Students for a Democratic Society who were about to go underground and form the Weathermen was to telephone a member of the State Historical Society of Wisconsin, who turned up with a van to collect the movement's archives.[23] In Paris, two groups of sympathetic historians collected documents relating to the student movement in May 1968.[24]

The historical profession itself had an intimate relation with 68. A relation that is now itself an object of study.[25] Many historians – products of the post-war baby boom and of university expansion – were on the cusp of their academic careers in 68 and sometimes felt, as Geoff Eley put it, 'propelled into being a historian' by their political commitments: 'the possibilities for social history's emergence ... were entirely bound up with the new political contexts of 1968'.[26] In France, Marc Heurgon abandoned his work on the Mediterranean in the age of Napoleon because he preferred to make history as a revolutionary member of the Parti Socialiste Unifié, rather than to write it. But others – Gareth Stedman Jones and Sheila Rowbotham in Britain or Götz Aly in Germany – saw politics and historical research as intertwined. British police archives on American radicals in London refer to Robert Brenner, later professor of history at UCLA, and

Linda Gordon, later professor of history at New York University. Susan Zeiger – who sometimes published in the London underground press under the name 'Susie Creamcheese' – is presumably the same Susan Zeiger who now writes on women's history.[27]

There was a twist, though. The historians most admired by 68ers were probably Eric Hobsbawm (born 1917), E.P. Thompson (born 1924) and, in a more complicated way, Fernand Braudel (born 1902). Braudel, a conservative who addressed the occasional fan letter to Charles de Gaulle,[28] disliked the challenge to academic authority in 1968.[29] Hobsbawm and Thompson were more sympathetic to the protest of their juniors but also felt distant from it. They belonged, in both political and intellectual terms, to a tradition that valued structure, rigour and a degree of intellectual detachment. Hobsbawm was mystified by the significance that radicals in Berkeley and Paris attributed to his own work on *Primitive Rebels* (1959). He had sought to explain 'pre-political' forms of rebellion but not to suggest that such rebellion should be a model for the modern world.[30] Thompson wrote, half seriously, that student radicals would benefit from time in 'a really well-disciplined organization such as the Officers' Training Corps or the British Communist Party'.[31]

Perhaps the gulf between 68ers and those older historians they admired springs in part from the high value that the former placed on subjective experience – particularly their own experience – and this may also explain the gap between 68ers and those much younger historians who now make 68 an object of their own research. Three children of 68ers – Julie Pagis and Virginie Linhart, working on France, and Sofia Serenelli, working on Italy – have noted that the contemporaries of their parents were often only willing to be interviewed on their own terms, as though people who disdained property nevertheless insisted on their 'ownership' of their own stories. When sent a questionnaire, one subject of Pagis's study wrote: 'you think we can be put in files and decoded with statistics . . . I made only one choice to be myself: free and autonomous.'[32]

Oral histories, which have been especially influential for the study of 68, reinforce the sense that 68ers have the right to tell their own story. The subjects of oral history are often members of the same networks and have also often written autobiographies – a veteran of the American SDS drily told a historian who interviewed him in 1997 that he was 'one of the few activists not writing his memoirs'.[33] The result of this is that the same people produce multiple, mutually confirming, accounts. 68ers have a special attachment to autobiography. Some grew up in political milieux that laid a heavy emphasis on the significance that an individual might attach to their own life story, as in the Communist *autocritique*, or the *révision de vie* practised in Catholic youth movements. The widespread resort to psychoanalysis by 68ers in their later life meant, as Julie Pagis noted somewhat wearily, that many *soixante-huitards* had a well-rehearsed account of their life.[34]

Perhaps because they are dealing with an unusually assertive and articulate group of subjects, or perhaps because they feel that a magisterial Olympianism would be inappropriate to the topic, historians are curiously tentative and hesitant in their approach to 68ers. Oral histories often reproduce passages of interviews without putting them into the context that might be provided by written sources, or even by other oral histories. Sometimes simply providing banal factual detail is treated as an act of violence against subjectivity. Consider Nicolas Daum's work on 'anonymous *soixante-huitards*', a category that turns out to mean people who were members of the same discussion group as himself in Paris between 1968 and 1972. Each interview is presented as a separate chapter but none begins with conventional biographical information or with a description of the subject of the interview. Details such as date of birth, profession and family background emerge, if at all, only in the course of interviews. When one interviewee mentions 'our family', Daum inserts a note to reveal that he and the interviewee are distant cousins.[35]

Historians themselves, though, illustrate the dangers of relying on personal memories of 68. Interviewed by younger colleagues, a *chartiste* (trained in the study of medieval documents) gave a vivid account of his experience of France in May 1968. Later he contacted them in some confusion. He had found his appointments diary, which seemed to suggest that he had in fact been in Italy at the time. He thought it possible that the journey to Italy had been cancelled but he was no longer sure of anything.[36]

By the time she published her memoirs in 1991, Annie Kriegel had come to define herself in opposition to 1968. She poured scorn on everything about the student agitation – though she thought that students at the university of Reims, where she taught in 1968, were more moderate and realistic than those at Nanterre, where she took up a chair in 1969. Berkeley, which she visited in the summer before arriving at Nanterre, was a 'bad dream' – the campus being marked not simply by the horrors of 'affirmative action' and 'women's studies' but also by a plague of dogs, abandoned at the end of term, which, she claimed, began to eat each other.[37] Kriegel's account is striking but at odds with those of her academic colleagues, including her own brother.[38] As for Paul Veyne and Maurice Agulhon, two contemporaries of Kriegel's who both taught at the University of Aix-en-Provence, the former recalls 68 as a protest about style of life that had little to do with de Gaulle, whom students found 'fusty and comic'.[39] By contrast, the latter insisted that the movement had concrete and modest aims: university reform and the overthrow of de Gaulle.[40]

An emphasis on those who were most obviously 'actors' in 68 can itself be deceptive. There was a penumbra of political militancy that had an effect on many people whose relations with 68 were more complicated. The career of the film director Louis Malle illustrated a range of ways to be *soixante-huitard*. He played a direct role in 1968 because he was a member of the jury of the Cannes film festival that resigned in sympathy with the students that year, and he was caught up in fighting between students and the police on his return to Paris. However, as early as 1965, he had made a film, *Viva Maria!*, that inspired a faction of the German left – the student leader Rudi Dutschke believed that revolutionaries could be divided into those who resembled the character played by Brigitte Bardot and those who resembled the one played by Jeanne Moreau. In 1974, Malle made *Lacombe Lucien,* a film that was *soixante-huitard* its approach to the Occupation in that it subverted a certain idea of the Resistance. Malle, though still in his thirties, had already been a famous director for over ten years by 1968. His relations with politics were also complicated because he had often been fascinated by figures – such as Drieu la Rochelle – from the extreme right. Finally, in 1990, Malle made a film – *Milou en Mai* – which described the events of 1968 in mocking terms, as seen through the eyes of an eccentric bourgeois family in the provinces. Michel Piccoli, who played the disabused middle-aged hero of *Milou en Mai*, had considered abandoning his acting career in 1968 to devote himself to full-time revolutionary agitation.[41]

Most obviously, in Europe at least, the penumbra of 68 affected the working classes. In France, Italy, Britain, workers went on strike around 1968 and often formed alliances with other kinds of militants. Student activists were enthusiastic to embrace workers as fellow 68ers but, even during the comparatively brief periods when they were on strike, workers were rarely full-time political militants and rarely thought of themselves as being 68ers. They were also less likely than middle-class activists to write autobiographies. Indeed, there are ways in which the burst of autobiographical reflection about 68 by the middle-classes has helped to obscure working-class experience. This is illustrated by the career of the French Maoist intellectual Robert Linhart. He left the École Normale Supérieure and went to work in a Citroën factory in the autumn of 1968. He wanted to help workers make their own revolution. Writing about his experience, he was keen to avoid the self-indulgence of autobiography: 'The bourgeoisie imagine that they have a monopoly on personal histories . . . They have a monopoly on speaking in public, that's all.'[42] However, whether he wanted it or not, Linhart's own life – his psychological troubles, his divorce and attempted suicide – rather than that of the workers he described has been at the centre of public discussion. It has been recounted by his former friends, his daughter and his sister, Danièle, herself an academic who has worked on 1968.[43]

Students in 68 are portrayed in words, frequently their own words, but workers are often remembered in pictures. The strikes and factory occupations that caught the public imagination in France frequently did so because a film crew happened to be present. But audiences learned remarkably little of individuals who were caught on camera. In 1996, Hervé Le Roux (born in 1958) directed a movie called *La Reprise* and subtitled 'journey to the heart of the working class'. It examined an unfinished film made in 1968 about the return to work after a strike at the Wonder battery factory at St Ouen. It featured a woman crying and saying: 'I won't go back, I will not set foot again in this prison, it's too disgusting.' The clip had been widely played in documentaries over many years and Le Roux set out to find the woman. He failed. He established that she had married, given birth to a daughter and left the factory. But he never found out her name.[44]

Even among the wealthy, unexpected people could in some way be touched by 68. Consider William Waldegrave. Born in 1946, he was a student leader in 68 – albeit a leader in the rarefied world of the Oxford Union. He prided himself on his resemblance to Bob Dylan and blended the personal and political in a 68ish way – recalling how he had heard of the death of Robert Kennedy while lying in bed with a girlfriend. As a visiting student at Harvard in 1969–70, he was beaten almost unconscious by the American police when he got too close to a demonstration by the Weathermen.[45] He wrote to *The Times* denouncing the behaviour of these policemen and added that it would shock inhabitants of mainland Britain – but not, he thought, those who had endured the attentions of the B-Specials in Northern Ireland.[46]

Anyone reading what Waldegrave wrote during, or about, the late 1960s might assume that he was a student radical. In fact, he was an ambitious Conservative politician. As president of the Oxford Union, in the summer of 1968 he invited Quintin Hogg – a Tory with a hysterical dislike of left-wing protest – to debate the motion 'This house is not ashamed of the British Empire.'[47] In the 1970s, he was a member of a secret committee that discussed how the 'authority of government' might be restored. He once asked his colleagues how easy it would be in Britain to organize the kind of demonstrations in favour of order that the Gaullists had staged in Paris at the end of May 1968.[48] Waldegrave was not the only Conservative who was in some respect sympathetic to 68. John Scarlett, later to become a diplomat and head of the British Joint Intelligence Committee, was an undergraduate at Oxford in 1968. He wrote to *The Times* – as a 'Conservative who while not agreeing with the American position in the war has very little sympathy for the Vietcong' – to protest against the 'unnecessarily violent' police response to an anti-Vietnam War demonstration that he had attended.[49]

Some readers will object that treating British Conservatives as 68ers implies a definition so broad as to drain all meaning from the term. They should remember that students at the epicentre of the British 68 – the London School of Economics – elected a Conservative, Peter Watherston, as president of their union in 1968 and that Watherston appears to have enjoyed better relations with the most radical students than his predecessor, a member of the Labour Party.[50] More generally, the right was sometimes present in the protests of 68. In Germany, Christian Democrat students had their own version of 68, which was not one of unqualified hostility to left-wing protest.[51] In Italy, some supporters of the extreme right made common cause with student protesters against the authorities.[52] In France, some right-wingers (still bitter over the loss of Algeria) assumed that any enemy of de Gaulle was a friend of theirs – though some young Gaullists (those who took the general's rhetoric on social reform seriously) also sympathized with the protests of 68. In early May 1968, a member of the Gaullist Front du Progrès pinned up a picture of Che Guevara with the caption: 'De Gaulle is a rebel like me'.[53] There were also those (such as Powell in Britain or George Wallace in the United States) who shared the rumbustious anti-establishment feelings of 68 even when they were hostile to it.

68 had so many facets and has been studied in so many different ways that work on one aspect can obscure others. Consider the recent burst of writing on the religious roots of political radicalism in the period. We learn that Tom Cornell, who was to lead anti-Vietnam War protest in the second half of the 1960s, had worked so hard to include an anti-war declaration in the statement of the Second Vatican Council that one bishop had described him as 'an invisible Council Father',[54] that the French Dominican Paul Blanquart helped draft Fidel Castro's closing speech at the Havana Cultural Congress of January 1968[55] or that the Protestant Church of Montreuil was transformed into a political centre.[56] One should, however, remember that there were multiple strands in this process. Those who continued to define themselves as religious were different from those who broke with a religious upbringing. Those who redefined their religion (for example, Catholic priests who married) were different from those who embraced radical politics while staying within the rules of their orders. One thinks of the nun in David Lodge's novel *How Far Can You Go* (1980), who participates in Californian anti-war

demonstrations while believing that the word 'mothers', which protesters use to describe the police, must allude to Mother Superiors.

However, religious believers of any kind were a minority among 68ers, most of whom regarded themselves as irreligious – the role of secularized Jews in France and America was particularly important – and some of whom were positively opposed to religion. A group of progressive Catholics sought to found a new kind of community in the provençal village of Cadanet after 1968 but the other *soixante-huitards* who lived there seem to have regarded them with distaste.[57] In any case, left-wing radicals were a minority in the Churches, some of which moved to the right in reaction against the political culture of the 1960s.[58] Even the embrace of Eastern mysticism by Westerners was not always a sign of counter-cultural sympathies – Christmas Humphreys was England's most prominent Buddhist; he was also a judge who presided over the trial of disorderly students in 1969.[59]

How then is 68 to be defined? It had several components: generational rebellion of the young against the old, political rebellion against militarism, capitalism and the political power of the United States and cultural rebellion that revolved around rock music and lifestyle. These rebellions sometimes interacted, but they did not always do so. 68 often subverted or circumvented existing structures. It emphasized spontaneity rather than formality. The mass meeting and the sit-in replaced formal meetings. Unofficial strikes, factory occupations and attempts to establish worker cooperatives challenged the power of trade unions as well as that of employers. Sometimes, it seemed that 68 subverted itself and that the movements of the early 1970s – women's liberation, gay liberation and some of the organizations devoted to armed struggle – were rebellions against, as well as continuations of, aspects of 68.

WHEN WAS 68?

A musicologist has suggested that '68' is, like 'Baroque', a term that signals a style as much as a period in time. As it happens, Baroque music flourished in the aftermath of 68, partly because the value attached to 'authenticity' contributed to a rise in the use of original instruments.[60] Questions about how to date 68 have come to have special significance in France, where popular recollection has focused on a single year (1968) and indeed a single month (May), in which there was a concentration of dramatic events. A cartoon in *Le Monde* during the fortieth anniversary of the Paris events showed a confused man in a bookshop asking: '*Vous n'avez pas quelque chose sur juin 68?*' However, and perhaps precisely because they wished to escape from the stifling constraints of a focus on one city in one month of one year, French historians have been most wide-ranging in their approach to 68 and most prone to think of that year as having long-term origins and consequences. Since the 1980s, they have used the phrase '68 years' which they usually define as being the period between 1962 (the end of the Algerian War) and 1981 (the advent of the first Mitterrand government).

Curiously, the term '68 years', which was originally coined with reference to France, may have the most important implications when applied elsewhere. Many places look quiet if judged against the high drama of France in the early summer of 1968 but things change if we extend the angle of chronological vision. Some see a European era of protest that began in the late 1960s and extended until at least the Portuguese revolution of 1974. Student protest in Germany peaked in 1967; more militarized political violence did not start until the following decade. Greece was under military dictatorship from 1967 to 1974 – historians talk of a 'pre-1968', which partly provoked the coup, or a 'late 1968', which helped bring the regime down.[61] The Italians talk about the 'hot autumn' that went with strikes in 1969 and that began a new cycle of protest.

Timing matters because interpretations of 68 depend partly on where one stops the clock. One political scientist wrote briskly that 'With the elections of 1976 the Italian 1968 ended';[62] other scholars have seen the 'movement of 1977' in northern Italian cities as the last incarnation of the long 68. An account of Germany that stopped in 1968 would show a student movement that had broken up, one that stopped in the autumn of 1977 would present terrorism as a major legacy of 68, one that stopped ten or twenty years later would concentrate on the origins of the Green Party and a new kind of democratic politics.

WHERE WAS 68?

There was protest across the world in 1968 – a fact that British diplomats recorded in the arch tones that they reserved for the misfortunes of other countries. In Rome, Rodric Braithwaite, a rather bohemian figure by the standards of the Foreign Office, reported that 'with my friends from the Movimento Studentesco' he had been to the occupied University of Rome to hear James Boggs, an American exponent of Black Power. Boggs's southern accent was hard to follow and the audience apparently 'did not understand how uninterested Boggs was in the white revolutionary movement'.[63] Even Iceland was paralysed by a general strike the British ambassador attributed to 'an indifferent herring harvest'.[64] A delegate to a Commonwealth conference on the matter concluded that Western Australia was the only place that was unaffected.[65]

Many saw the long 68 as something that transcended, and perhaps subverted, national frontiers. Police chiefs and conservative politicians were obsessed by the 'international conspiracy' that they discerned behind disturbances in their own countries. Enoch Powell, a rare example of conservative scepticism on this topic, wrote to one of his many correspondents on the matter that he personally had always found it hard enough to launch 'a little local conspiracy'.[66] Raymond Marcellin, the French minister of the interior, wrote a book about the links that he perceived between various movements.[67] The Berne Club, which coordinated the struggle of European governments against terrorism in the 1970s, had been established in 1968 to deal with 'youthful contestation'.[68]

Generally, conspiracy theorists attributed such contestation to left-wing bodies, perhaps supported by Russia or China. French Gaullists – who appreciated that their own foreign policy did not fit neatly into the dichotomies of the Cold War – sometimes advanced more extravagant theories. British diplomats occasionally wondered whether the Gaullists blamed them for supporting the agitation. One reported the opinions of the general secretary of the Gaullist party:

> France was the victim of an international conspiracy. He said he thought that certain foreign powers were involved (... we detected a faint

implication that HMG might be amongst them). When asked to be more specific, he referred to the Israelis and the Americans, both of whom, he said, had a strong interest in getting rid of General de Gaulle.[69]

Touring provincial France in May 1968, the ambassador reported a belief that student agitators had been trained in Berne and Amsterdam, but was relieved to find that no one spoke of London.[70]

Radical students relished slogans that presented themselves as part of a wider international movement: 'Rome, Paris and Berlin, we will fight and we will win'. Some radicals came to feel like foreigners in their own country. Bob Moses, a member of the Student Non-Violent Co-Ordinating Committee, born in Harlem, who went south to help the civil rights movement, remarked that 'When you're in Mississippi, the rest of America doesn't seem real, and when you're in the rest of America, Mississippi doesn't seem real.' Later in the 1960s, especially during the Vietnam War, other activists came to express active distaste for their country. Jerry Rubin, of the Youth International Party, wrote: 'I am an orphan of Amerika. Fuck Amerika.'[71] Misspelling the country's name was itself a political gesture. Black radicals sometimes wrote of Ameri*kkk*a. Perhaps for descendants of Jewish immigrants, such as Rubin, the word 'Amerika' had an additional significance – it recalled the Hamburg-Amerika line that had brought their grandparents to the country into which they were so desperate to integrate. In Britain too, rejection of 'Englishness' was often seen as a badge of radical respectability – though some left-wingers recognized that the most enthusiastic exponents of English values (and bitter opponents of 68) were Jewish intellectuals from Eastern Europe, such as Isaiah Berlin.

Protest was often international. In May 1968, students occupied the British Institute in Paris. The British authorities could not determine whether most of these students were British or French or drawn from further afield – the director of the institute noted bitterly that his office had acquired a large bill for phone calls made to Mexico during the occupation.[72] Embassies were sites of protest and sometimes international encounters. An American marine sergeant standing guard outside the US embassy in London had a brief conversation with two British Black Power activists – he later told the Metropolitan Police: 'I gave them some senseless crap that was more or less polite.'[73]

The CIA reckoned that there were 90,000 foreign students in the United States in the year 1967–8 and 80,000 Americans studying abroad at the same time. Sometimes a brief stay abroad – often recalled in highly coloured terms – formed part of young people's image of themselves as outsiders in their own culture. Gareth Stedman Jones, later an exponent of 'student power', spent ten months in Paris after leaving St Paul's School:

> I went up to Oxford in October 1961, smoking Gitanes and immaculately dressed in the best that could be found on the rive gauche. My time in France reinforced my sense, shared by many of my friends in the early 1960s, of Britain as some sort of ancien régime presided over by a hereditary peer and still clinging to the decrepit trappings of Edwardian gentility.[74]

The number of young French people coming to Britain was higher than the number of British going to France. In July 1968, 100,000 French people, mainly teenagers, undertook language courses in Britain.[75] They rarely discovered political radicalism – one assumes that bourgeois parents were happy to get their children away from the *comités d'action lycéens* and safely installed at an English seaside town – but travel could stimulate reflection in unexpected ways. Guy Hocquenghem, later to found the Front Homosexuel d'Action Révolutionnaire, recalled his *séjour linguistique* taken at the age of twelve in a working-class household at Shoreham-by-Sea, where 'one dined at six' and ate *'haricots rouges sur toast aux petits déjeuners'*.[76]

It was not just the young who travelled. Herbert Marcuse, the German Jewish philosopher born in 1898, had moved to America during the Second World War and was by 1968 holding court at the University of California. Angela Davis was inspired by him to go and study in Frankfurt. Marcuse himself was briefly in Paris in May 1968 around the time when the Communist leader Georges Marchais denounced his malign influence on the young. When Richard Nixon met the British cabinet in February 1969, he suggested, after Richard Crossman had made a characteristically apocalyptic intervention: 'Why don't we have Dick Crossman and we'll send you Marcuse!'[77]

Sometimes nationalities became associated with political tendencies. When a French Communist was described as 'Italian', it might mean that they had been influenced by the writings of Antonio Gramsci or simply that they were more open to reform than their own authoritarian party leaders. European Maoists were described as 'Chinese' – though not all of them felt unqualified admiration for Mao's China. 'American' or 'Californian' was often used as a label for those who invested their energies in new ways of living rather than the political theory that interested some of their European contemporaries. Colin Crouch wrote of his fellow students at the LSE:

> It is desirable here to point out a difference in emphasis on these matters between the old-guard Marxists, who were mainly interested in the developing of their model of direct action, and the anarchists, libertarians and Americans, who were interested in building a community.[78]

Counter-revolution was also frequently described in terms of international comparison. The French political scientist Maurice Duverger called the law forbidding certain political parties 'Greek' – meaning it was the kind of legislation he associated with the Greek dictatorship of the colonels. Gaston Defferre, socialist mayor of Marseilles, said that he feared a 'Greek' dictatorship in his country.[79]

Some European left-wingers joined guerrilla movements in Latin America. Michèle Firk, born in France in 1937 and, like many French Jews of her generation, haunted by the memory of the Second World War, joined the rebels in Guatemala and killed herself after being taken prisoner in 1968.[80] Régis Debray was captured in Bolivia in 1967, after having met, though not fought alongside, Che Guevara. His trial provoked a curious international alliance as Lothar Menne (German), Robin Blackburn (English), Perry Anderson (Irish aristocrat) and Tariq Ali (holder of the only Pakistani passport the Bolivian authorities had ever seen) went to try to extract him.

Debray and Guevara had both spent time in Castro's Cuba, which became an important centre for radicals in 68. It had the advantage of being a Communist country that did not, at least at first, seem to be associated with Soviet orthodoxy. As host of the Tricontinental Conference in 1966, it seemed to stand at the centre of movements in Africa and Latin America. Algeria also illustrates some of the complexities of the relationship between radicals in the industrialized West and the Third World. Events of 1968 in France owed something to the Algerian

War of 1954 to 1962 – though students were less likely to have direct memories of the war than workers, or for that matter Gaullist ministers. After Algerian independence, the Italian director Gillo Pontecorvo, in collaboration with the Algerian government, made a film, *The Battle of Algiers*, that was released in 1966. It was a multinational enterprise made with Algerian and French actors, but also drawing in a ragtag of people who happened to be available – including an English jazz musician busking his way around the world, who got a severe haircut and spent a few weeks as an actor playing a German legionnaire. The film was banned for many years in France but exercised a considerable influence on radicals in Britain and the US.

Large numbers of militants – the so-called *pieds rouges* – went to Algeria after it obtained independence in 1962. It was at an Algerian youth camp that Tiennot Grumbach first met some of the Maoists and Trotskyists with whom he would work in France in 1968. Later, Algeria became a place of refuge for some fleeing the United States – such as Eldridge Cleaver (of the Black Panthers) or Timothy Leary, the proponent of LSD, who had been sprung from a California jail by the Weathermen. By this time, however, many of the European left-wingers had become uncomfortable at the authoritarian aspects of the new state. Boumediene's coup d'état of June 1965 encouraged many *pieds rouges* to leave.[81]

Having said all this, 68, at least in its West European and North American version, cannot necessarily be interpreted as part of 'transnational' or 'global' history. Contact between countries, and particularly between the Western industrialized democracies and the rest of the world, was often more apparent than real and, indeed, it sometimes diminished around 68. The 'hippy trail' – which stretched across Asia – mainly involved stoned Western teenagers talking to each other in a succession of well-established meeting points that took them from the Istanbul Pudding Shop to the beaches of Goa. The Chinese Cultural Revolution – whose image was so attractive to some Westerners – made it less likely that outsiders would actually visit the country or learn anything about it if they did.

Going to foreign countries did not always mean engaging with their populations and some travelling by left-wing activists was little more than tourism. Tariq Ali – who wrote travel articles for a smart

London magazine in his spare time from fomenting revolution – was much given to phrases such as 'Prague is a city for all seasons'. In fact, Prague illustrates the limits of transnational exchange in 68. It is true that the Prague Spring coincided with the peak of many protest movements in the West and it is true too that Western students usually sympathized with their contemporaries in Prague. However, surface similarities between Czechoslovakia and the West could be deceptive. Tom Hayden had a brief fling with a Czech woman during a stopover on his way to North Vietnam. The atmosphere reminded him of Berkeley but the politics were different – he discovered that his lover, like many intelligent Czechs, simply assumed that every word emanating from the regime was the exact opposite of the truth and, therefore, that American intervention in Vietnam must be a good thing.[82]

The Czech Jan Kavan was one of the student leaders who participated – along with Tariq Ali, Daniel Cohn-Bendit and Karl Dietrich Wolff – in a BBC television programme about student revolt in June 1968. But he was able to address a Western audience, and to escape relatively easily when the tanks rolled in, because he had been born in London and had an English mother. As for the most famous of all Czech 68ers, one of Vaclav Havel's biographers describes how he was in Paris, on his way to New York, on 13 May 1968. He had arranged to meet the *émigré* Pavel Tigrid at Paris airport. Havel had no visa to enter France but suddenly airport staff and customs officials walked off the job to join the general strike – leaving him free to enter their country:

> the barriers between East and West collapsed . . . Borders were meaningless. Identity papers were obsolete. Surveillance was just a word. Nobody asked questions. The distinction between citizen and alien, between insider and outsider, was struck down. Everybody was equal.[83]

It is a wonderful story, but it is not true. Havel had already been in New York for three weeks on 13 May.[84]

The rhetoric of global connection could cover activities that were parochial. Richard Neville arrived in London to join his sister Jill after having hitch-hiked overland from Australia. However, Neville's grasp of politics outside west London was sometimes uncertain. He recalled an anti-Vietnam War demonstration of 1969 where he and his girlfriend 'were so baffled by the proliferation of New Left splinter groups [we] joined the ranks of Aussie expats distinguishable by a high-held national flag'. Neville, still sentimental about his native country, was upset when Germaine Greer grabbed the flag and set it alight.[85]

For some, national culture remained important in 68. First there were some radicals who actively embraced national culture. This was true in France, where a specifically French revolutionary tradition was referred to with almost obsessive intensity, and also true, at least in the early part of the 1960s, for some on the American left who were keen to claim connection with native forms of radicalism as an alternative to international Marxism. Even gestures that seemed like rebellions against the nation might take distinctively national forms. The French demonstrators who chanted '*Nous sommes tous des juifs allemands*' were referring to France's experience of occupation, and their hostility to currents that they associated with collaboration was matched by their enthusiasm for those they associated with resistance. To an even greater extent, German radicals had specifically German reasons for rejecting part of their national past.

Sometimes the militants of 68 were preoccupied with communities that were smaller than the state instead of, or as well as, ones that were larger than it. Regionalism was important in western France, especially Brittany. Northern Ireland saw a rising by Catholics who wanted to break with the United Kingdom, as well as by Protestants who wanted to defend their special status within that kingdom. Members of the Front de Libération du Québec (FLQ) rebelled against Anglophone rule in Canada though not all of the members were Francophone, or even Canadian. Until the movement's leaders finally fled to exile in Cuba, the FLQ provided inspiration, and occasionally practical help, to radicals in the United States and France – though one assumes that their notion of anti-imperialism was different from that of Charles de Gaulle, who saluted 'Free Quebec' in 1967 and began 1968 with a mischievous expression of goodwill to the French population of Canada. In Belgium, the University of Louvain was riven by conflict that sprang partly from those who wanted to defend the rights of Flemish speakers.

Even ideas that apparently held international appeal could change their sense as they moved across frontiers. The 'personalism' of the

Catholic philosopher Emmanuel Mounier probably seemed more radical to young Americans than it had done in France, where the Catholic
Church was associated with the political right. Likewise, membership
of the Communist Party meant something different to Europeans, particularly those old enough to remember Stalinism, than it did in the
United States. Edgar Morin, the French author of *Autocritique* (1959),
the classic text by a disillusioned ex-Communist, admired the black
American activist Angela Davis, but her decision to join the Communist Party gave him 'a familiar and painful sense of hypocrisy'.[86]

There was a revealing difference in the reception of Jean-Paul Sartre
and Albert Camus on either side of the Atlantic. Sartre, whose importance had seemed to diminish in the 1960s as structuralism displaced
existentialism in intellectual fashion, shot to new heights of fame during the student protests of 1968. His call for political engagement
suited the mood of the times – and he had the advantage of being
physically present in the Latin Quarter. Camus, on the other hand,
had been killed in a car crash in 1960. His ideas played little role in
the French 68. His reputation on the French left had been damaged by
his reluctance to condemn France during the Algerian War and by the
venomous assault on his philosophical ideas published by Sartre's pro-
tégé Francis Jeanson in the journal *Les Temps Modernes*.

In the United States though the relative prestige of the two authors
was reversed. Sartre was unattractive to those who had not been
brought up on a diet of continental philosophy. Camus had qualities
that particularly appealed to Anglo-Saxon youth. He was, in conspicuous contrast to Sartre, physically attractive, and his early death had
frozen him, like James Dean and John F. Kennedy, into a perpetual
youth. His writing was clearer and more obviously moral than Sartre's.
John Gerassi, the son of a friend of Sartre's who had moved to the US,
began postgraduate research on the Sartre/Camus split at the University of Columbia but abandoned the exercise. He later explained to
Sartre: 'I could never get a doctorate in the United States by criticizing
Camus.'[87] Young Americans were particularly prone to read Camus's
variety of existentialism as having religious connotations – *L'Étranger*
was published in England as *The Outsider* but published in America
with a title that sounded faintly biblical: *The Stranger*. The sales of this
novel peaked in the US in 1968 at 300,000 copies.[88]

Sartre did attract a revived interest in the United States around 68 but this was mainly because Black Power activists read his preface to Frantz Fanon's *The Wretched of the Earth* – a book that was itself the product of complicated transnational exchanges since Fanon, born in Martinique and educated in France, had written it while teaching Algerian militants in Tunisia. His thinking about race had been inspired in part by reading Chester Himes – a black American living in Paris who wrote hard-boiled detective stories set in New York.

As was stressed in the Introduction, this is a book about the Western industrialized democracies and it examines the long 68, which stretches from the early 1960s to some point in the 70s. However, it is a work with ragged edges. No account of 68 can ignore the late 1990s, when some former 68ers – Joschka Fischer, Bill Clinton, Jack Straw – held high office. In geographical terms, Western Europe and America cannot be entirely separated from the rest of the world. Even China occasionally impinged on the Western 68. Western Maoists may have had only the most abstract conception of what the Cultural Revolution really meant but British officials had to deal with its effects in Hong Kong and the New Territories.[89]

Finally, and perhaps most importantly, I do not believe that the study of 68 can be separated from what might be called 'mainstream political history'. Some 68ers dismissed all conventional politics and they often reduced these to cursory abstractions – 'fascism', 'imperialism', 'power'. Colin Crouch wrote that the attitude of his fellow students to authority, and particularly their propensity to assume that occupying a British university might be legitimate as a means of expressing discontent with American foreign policy, could be explained by the fact that '[for] the far left there is no such thing as individual "authorities". There is just one continuous, monolithic "authority".'[90]

But the divisions were never as sharply defined as some on both sides liked to pretend. The radicalism of the late 1960s often emerged out of reformism earlier in the decade and it sometimes blended back into more conventional kinds of politics – or labour organization – later in the 1970s. Far from interpreting this as a sign that 68ers sold out or that they were manipulated by the system, it seems to me that the long-term importance of 68 lies precisely in the ways that it interacted with mainstream politics.

2

The 68 Generation

Members of Students for a Democratic Society, Indiana, September 1963.

2

We are the people of this generation, bred in at least modest comfort, housed now in universities, looking uncomfortably to the world we inherit.
— Port Huron Statement by Students
for a Democratic Society, 1962

Generation: for years, I swore to myself never to pronounce this word . . . I do not like the idea of belonging to a coagulated block of disappointment and cronyism, which only begins to feel its identity with the massive betrayal of maturity.
— Guy Hocquenghem (*soixante-huitard*)
attacking his contemporaries in 1986[1]

I blame them [the mothers] for having all those dreadful children.
— Nancy Mitford during the student
riots in Paris, 12 May 1968[2]

'Generation' was a widely used term in the long 68. Jack Weinberg, a student demonstrator at Berkeley in 1964, shouted 'Don't trust anyone over thirty'. The fact that political rebellion should so often have erupted at a time when a large cohort of the population was around the age of twenty, and that it so often coincided with educational expansion and the growth of a 'youth culture', is significant. But what exactly it signifies is more complicated than it may appear at first glance. Some statements of generational identity came from people who had been born before the end, sometimes before the outbreak, of the Second World War. Tom Hayden, who drafted the Port Huron Statement (see chap. 4), had been born in 1939. Jack Weinberg had been born in 1940. His remark of 1964 was in fact an attack on the 'old left' rather than an attack on the older generation as a whole.

Sometimes the 'generation gap' of politics in the 1960s divided people who were quite close in age. Michael Harrington, the American socialist and social commentator, attended the conference that drafted the Port Huron Statement but quarrelled there with his younger comrades, particularly Hayden. Harrington later expressed contrition for his 'middle-age tantrum' and said that he interpreted criticism of him as 'an Oedipal assault on the father figure'. Harrington was thirty-four at the time of this dispute.[3] An encounter with student radicalism could give those in early middle age an obsessive consciousness of their own age. In 1967, soon after he had been a star turn at the London conference on the Dialectics of Liberation, the British psychiatrist R.D. Laing mused in his diary about his fortieth birthday. It reflected, he wrote: 'the transition from Icarus to Daedalus from Oedipus to Laius from *enfant terrible* to grand old man . . .'[4]

A significant minority of radicals in the late 1960s were not young at all. Maria Jolas was a leader of Americans based in Paris who opposed the Vietnam War. She translated into English the documents on the Paris protests of 1968 assembled by her friend Pierre Vidal-Naquet (born in 1930).[5] She had, however, been born – into a rich Kentucky family – in 1893. She had lived mainly in France since the 1920s and had at one time occupied the house at Colombey-les-Deux-Églises that later became famous as the country residence of de Gaulle.[6] Lady Dorothea Head, born in 1907, was the daughter of the Earl of Shaftesbury and the wife of a Tory politician. During the Vietnam War, she moved sharply to the left and once turned up at the Oxford Union to heckle her husband and son, who were speaking against an anti-American motion. Even among those who defined themselves as 'student leaders', which did not always mean that they were students, there was a considerable range of ages. Apart from Tom Hayden, the leaders of Students for a Democratic Society included Todd Gitlin (born in 1943), Carl Oglesby (1935) and Bernardine Dohrn (1942). Leaders of the SDS (such as Mike Spiegel or Mark Rudd), who had been born after the Second World War, were a minority, even in the late 1960s.

On the other hand, there were 68ers who were too young to be university students. The concentration of elite *lycées* in Paris, and the close links between such institutions and universities, meant that school children born in the early 1950s, such as Nicolas Baby of the Alliance Marxiste Révolutionnaire, became part of the student revolt and from 1967 formed *comités d'action lycéens*. In the United States, students at high schools were sometimes as radical as those at university – this was particularly true in the years after 1968. In 1970, Gael Graham protested against her country's invasion of Cambodia by tearing up the American flag. She could not burn it because she was twelve years old and her parents did not let her have matches. A Congressional enquiry discovered that 18 per cent of high schools had seen unrest in 1968; the following year the proportion had risen to 40 per cent.[7] In Italy, during the late 1960s and early 70s, there were 270 protests in high schools against 143 in universities. High school protests came later than university ones, which had peaked in the period from 1967 to 1969, and it seems to have been those radicalized at school rather than university who were most likely later to take up arms in terrorist groups.[8]

Some activists in 1968 expounded the theory that the young (by which they actually meant university students) should be a 'vanguard' providing the revolutionary leadership that the working classes were unable to provide for themselves, or that students were so numerous and, relative to their predecessors, so underprivileged that they had themselves become a kind of class. Many, however, saw youth as merely a stage in life rather than a class. Presented with a report on 'youth' in 1966, Charles de Gaulle responded:

> One must not treat the young as a separate category. One is young and then one ceases to be so. They will continue to be young for as long as good fortune allows it, but they do not constitute a separate category. They are French people at the start of their existence, it is nothing special.[9]

François Mitterrand put things more tersely when he told a group of student leaders in 1968: 'Being young doesn't last very long. You spend a lot more time being old.'[10]

Even relatively young people who participated in the protests of 1968 were sometimes hostile to the notion that generation might cut across ideology or class. This was true of many in France – where student activists saw themselves as part of a revolutionary tradition that stretched back through the Resistance and into the nineteenth century. They believed that generational interpretations trivialized their protest and emptied it of political content – Juliette Minces (a left-wing sociologist born in 1937) wrote shortly after the event: '[T]his revolt was . . . the sign of a serious political revolt and not, as some "thinkers" have tried to have us believe, a conflict of generations or the display of a new social class . . . of the young and of students.'[11]

In the United States, the black militants who surrounded Angela Davis were mainly young. Davis herself had been born in 1944. Jonathan Jackson, who tried to free his older brother from prison using a pistol that belonged to Davis, was seventeen when the police shot him in 1970. However, Davis talked about race and class rather than age. Indeed, she was acutely conscious of an intergenerational inheritance that tied her to the oppression of her elders, especially her grandmother – who had died when Angela was twelve and who had been born a few years after the emancipation of slaves in the American South.

Definitions of what constituted 'youth' were in flux during the late 1960s. In Britain in 1967, the Latey report advocated lowering the age of majority (i.e. the age at which people enjoyed all the rights of an adult) from twenty-one to eighteen; the report's recommendations were implemented in 1970. The minimum voting age was lowered from twenty-one to eighteen in West Germany in 1970, in the United States in 1971, in France in 1974 and in Italy in 1975. Social changes – such as the raising of the school-leaving age – moved the frontiers between childhood and adulthood.

The long 68 itself sometimes changed how people thought about their own age. Simply giving one's date of birth could be a political act. When Abbie Hoffman (born in 1936) was asked his age at his trial for inciting riot in Chicago in 1968, he gave an answer that said much about the American counter-culture. He claimed to have been born in 1960: 'spiritually, I am a child of the 60s'. When the German Thorwald Proll (born in 1941) was asked the same question at his trial for setting fire to a department store in 1968, he gave an answer that suggested the extent to which European 68ers remained rooted in older political traditions. He had, he said, been 'born in 1789', the year of the French Revolution.[12]

Women especially were conscious that their biological age no longer meant what it had meant to their parents. Sheila Rowbotham wrote of herself in 1968:

> I was nearly twenty-five, about to hit that old borderline which, only
> a few years earlier, had seemed to mean you were definitely grown up.
> But I wasn't feeling grown up at all. We had moved all the signposts
> anyway and nothing signified what it had done then.[13]

Luisa Passerini (born in 1941), referring mainly to Italy, asked: 'How many individuals, from the generations born between the end of the 1930s and the beginning of the 1950s, had a 1968?' She divided 68ers into those at university, those who had finished their studies and entered employment and those who were still at school. But added that 'biological age' was most 'determinative of affiliation' for those born after 1950 who 'experienced the university students' movement, but in their own schools'.[14]

Notions of age among Passerini's fellow students were different from those among the workers with whom they allied. By the age of twenty-six, an Italian worker would probably have spent twelve years in paid employment and have been married for several years. If a man, he would probably have done his military service; if a woman, she would have had children. As for Rowbotham, she encountered a different experience of age when she tried to organize office cleaners in the early 1970s. Her new comrades – women from the least privileged part of the working class – were mostly in their thirties or forties but 'looked older than their age'.[15] Even workers involved in the strikes of 68 were not all young. Records relating to men who sought hospital treatment after a confrontation between strikers and the riot police at the Peugeot factory in Sochaux reveal that only three, of twenty, were aged under twenty-five. Seven had been born in 1928 or before.[16]

Militancy itself could plunge some into what conservatives would have described as a prolonged adolescence – marked by failure to observe conventional rites of passage. A working-class man, born in 1940, dropped out of conventional society and took to the roads after failing the medical for his military service in the late 1950s. In early 1968, a psychologist told him that he must 'become an adult' and he sought full-time work, but the student riots then turned his life upside down again and he eventually enrolled at the new faculty at Vincennes, designed by *soixante-huitards* to take people without conventional qualifications: he prolonged his student days there until he was well into his thirties.[17]

Some historians break down the 68 generation into 'micro cohorts'. In Switzerland, 70 per cent of radical activists were under twenty-five in 1967. This number dropped to 62 per cent between 1968 and 1970, presumably because activists aged, but then increased to 75 per cent between 1971 and 1973, presumably because the upheavals of 1968 had radicalized new groups of young people, before declining to 54 per cent in 1974–6.[18]

In retrospect, some participants in 68 became increasingly likely to define themselves in generational terms. Sometimes they did so because their own sense of their lives was influenced by the way in which they were portrayed. The 'apolitical' quality of generation, or at least its lack of obvious links with the politics of the hard left, which had repelled some 68ers at the time, came to attract many of them later. People who had abandoned the specific political pro- grammes of their youth still associated themselves with what they came to regard as the general style of their contemporaries. Daniel Cohn-Bendit placed an increasing emphasis on his membership of the '68 generation' as a means of claiming consistency at a time when he had undertaken a political volte face by embracing electoral politics. In Germany, a sense of generation seemed to offer unity and mutual respect after the acrimonious fragmentation of radicalism that fol- lowed 1968. Klaus Hartung, a former student activist, began, in 1978, to talk of a '68 generation' in a deliberate bid to unify a part of the left.[19]

THE 'BABY BOOM' AND ITS ELDERS

Generational interpretations of 68 are closely associated with the notion of a post-war 'baby boom'. In North America and much of Western Europe, birth rates increased sharply after 1945 as servicemen returned home. In Germany and Italy things were different. Both these countries had experienced rises in the birth rate during the 1930s – partly because of government policies designed to promote population growth. The effects of Nazism and war created particularly complicated patterns of generational division in Germany (see chap. 6).

The post-war baby boom makes sense only if considered in the light of what went before. Those countries that experienced a boom – Britain, France and the USA – had also seen a sharp drop in birth rates in the aftermath of the economic depression during the 1930s. The French historian Jean-Marie Bercé, born in 1936, remarked that the baby boomers experienced 'a youth that was very alien to my generation'. Bercé believed that he and his contemporaries had been in awe of their elders partly because those elders outnumbered them so much.[20] Those born in the 1930s were still haunted by the memory of unemployment and deprivation that had overshadowed their early lives. They valued security and tolerated routines and regularity that those a few years younger than them would have regarded as drudgery. In 1950, sociologists interviewing a group of British men who had been born in 1932 were disconcerted to find that many of these eighteen-year-olds felt settled in their jobs and intended to remain in them for the rest of their lives.[21] None of this means that people born in the 1930s were hostile to 68 – many of them, young university teachers in particular, were sympathetic. But there was a reversal of the roles that one might expect the two to play. Those who were forty in 1968 were often followers rather than leaders, and the audacity of their juniors left them hesitating between horror and admiration.

Not every young radical in the 1960s defined themselves as in conflict with an older generation – some, on the contrary, believed that they belonged to a political tradition that was rooted in the past. Serge July had been born in 1942 but traced his experience of activism to the

Communist demonstration against de Gaulle's new constitution in 1958. He had attended the *lycée* Turgot but regarded his teachers as dispensers of subversion rather than political orthodoxy. He was particularly influenced by Pierre Halbwachs, who would himself be an important figure in the campaign to defend imprisoned political militants in the aftermath of 1968. Halbwachs had been born in 1916 and was already in his forties by the time he taught July. Furthermore, Pierre Halbwachs was the son of the historian Maurice Halbwachs (born in 1877) and the Halbwachs (father and son) had been deported during the occupation after protesting about the murder, by the collaborationist Milice, of Victor Basch – who was Maurice Halbwachs's father-in-law and Pierre's grandfather. Basch and Halbwachs espoused a radicalism that owed much to the Dreyfusard campaigns of the late nineteenth century.

The film director Romain Goupil was born in 1951 but even he did not see his rebellion as one that pitched him against the conformity of the 1950s. On the contrary, he believed that 'one understands nothing of 1968 if one does not see the mobilizations that preceded it, themselves nourished by an anti-colonial tradition'. He dated his own political awakening from the age of fourteen or fifteen and added that he felt himself an heir of earlier tradition: 'I thought in the categories of 1870' (i.e. the year of the Paris Commune). He distinguished the political avant-garde, to which he himself belonged, from the generation of baby boomers – who were moulded by 'pocket money, charter flights and rock music' and who 'felt stifled in their aspirations to sexual liberty'.[22]

After 1968, some argued that the baby boomer generation had grown up in circumstances that promoted self-indulgence and rebelliousness. The sociologist David Riesman, not usually an exponent of conservative views, said that radicals of the late 1960s had been 'the babies who were picked up' and added that, 'in consequence, they expect their demands to be met quickly'.[23] Spiro T. Agnew, who became vice president of the USA in 1969, was particularly exercised by the influence that he attributed to Dr Benjamin Spock (born 1903), whose *Child and Baby Care* (first published in 1946) had supposedly promoted lax discipline in the raising of children. But the incarnation of Spock that conservatives denounced was a product of 1968 rather than its cause. Spock became associated with the movement of opposition to the Vietnam War and ran for president in 1972 on a radical ticket. However, little of this radical influence is visible in his post-war views on childcare. Such views were mainly founded on common sense and 'common sense' tended to mean what mothers were already doing before the Second World War. An English professor attributed student protests of the late 1960s to the 'no-spanking gospel according to Dr Spock',[24] but Spock's work was not published in Britain until 1954. The first English students to be raised by Spock-reading parents would not have reached university until 1972.

As for continental Europe, a German student activist born in 1945 (herself the daughter of a doctor who had worked with the SS) later found that the female doctor who delivered her had worked at the Ravensbrück concentration camp.[25] Pierre Goldman was born on 22 June 1944 in a Lyons hospital that his mother, a Polish Jew fighting with the French Resistance, had entered under a false name. He later claimed that weapons were stashed in his cradle.[26] Whatever problems may have attended the early life of these people, it seems unlikely that permissive childcare was one of them.

SUBURBIA

In North America, the post-war baby boom went with new houses. In 1946, for the first time in history, most white people in the United States lived in homes that they owned. Large numbers of these houses were in the suburbs – the population of which increased from 36 to 74 million between 1950 and 1970.[27] Suburbanization was partly the product of easily available land and of technological change. Houses could be built quickly and cars made it easy to commute to work. Lobbying by road builders, and even the belief that a dispersed population would better survive an atomic attack, contributed to the growth of suburbs. Suburbanization was linked, as both cause and effect, with the rise of the nuclear family. Parents sought houses that would be designed around themselves and their children, and often removed themselves from more distant relations in doing so. Children grew up in areas where there were just two generations – their own and that of their parents.

Charles Webb's 1963 novella *The Graduate* – about a young man who drifts into an affair with a woman of his mother's age while contemplating, without much enthusiasm, entry into graduate school – epitomized the disillusion of the suburban young. The story acquired a new resonance when it was made into a film in 1967, by which time entry into graduate school had become a means to avoid service in Vietnam and the film's star, Dustin Hoffman, had begun to hang around on the fringes of the radical left.

Suburban childhoods fostered a generational consciousness that often went with a rejection of 'suburban values'. For some middle-class American radicals moving to the city, particularly moving to parts of cities, such as Haight-Ashbury in San Francisco, that were most associated with urban decay and racial mixing, might itself become a form of generational rebellion – though after 1968 increasing numbers of radical young Americans also sought escape from suburban conformity in rural communes.

In Europe, housing shortage, often caused by the physical damage of the war, was an important feature of many childhoods well into the 1950s. Suburbanization had been important in Britain before 1939 and some British radicals, like their American counterparts, defined themselves partly in opposition to suburbia. In continental Europe, the middle classes remained mainly urban. Indeed in France, the connotations of the word *'banlieue'* – the most literal translation of 'suburb' – were different. French cities, Paris especially, were surrounded by rings of factories and the working-class housing that went with them. The very poor had often concentrated in shanty towns (*bidonvilles*) on the outskirts of cities. It was reckoned that there were 48,000 such people around Paris in 1966. The best-known *bidonville* was at Nanterre, west of Paris. It had first been settled by rag pickers in the early part of the century, and Algerians (single working men at first) had arrived in the late 1940s. By the mid-1960s, there were 10,000 people on twenty-one hectares of waste ground (the North Africans lived in the west and Portuguese in the east).[28] Nanterre was also home to other completely different communities. There was a French-born working class that had returned a Communist mayor since 1935. There were also students at the new University of Paris X, which was built at Nanterre, who arrived in

1964, the earth piled up as the campus was constructed obscuring the shanty town for a while. Most of the students came from cities, especially from Paris itself, and they now discovered a 'suburb' that had nothing to do with well-tended lawns or washing cars on Sunday.

CONSCRIPTION

For men in most countries, the prospect of military service loomed over their late teenage years. Britain had abolished National Service by 1963. British youth culture of the 1960s sometimes seemed an explicitly post-military one. Some of the men who inspired elements of the British counter-culture – such as John Peel, the disc jockey, Kit Lambert, who managed The Who, or Robert Fraser, an art dealer known to his intimates as 'groovy Bob' – acquired their distaste for authority partly from having served in the armed forces during the last days of empire.

Conscription aroused most explicit political debate in the United States (see chap. 4), although most European countries, including Sweden, where many Americans seeking to avoid the draft took refuge, called up a larger proportion of their populations than did the United States. Military service could be an unpleasant experience – even though few European soldiers were required to do much fighting in the late 1960s. When French students were asked after 1962 about the things that worried them most, 16 per cent (13 per cent in Paris and 17 per cent in the provinces) answered 'military service'.[29] The avoidance of military service sometimes helped to define a certain kind of radicalism. The German student leader Rudi Dutschke had refused to serve in the army of East Germany, and thus excluded himself from university until he moved to the West. Daniel Cohn-Bendit's ambiguous national status (see chap. 5) sprang partly from an attempt to avoid the army – coming from a family that had been a victim of Nazism, he was excused service in Germany but would have been called up as a French citizen. Even if they could not avoid the army, students in continental Europe could often defer it – another of the reasons why the middle class and the working-class had different conceptions of when adulthood began. When Robert Linhart, a French Maoist intellectual born in 1944, sought to acquire a working-class identity so that he could get himself hired in a car factory in the autumn of 1968, he 'borrowed' the military career of a working-class comrade.[30] Linhart himself did not perform his military service until after he had finished working at the factory – by which time he was twenty- five. Unlike students, working-class men who participated in the strikes of 1968 in France had usually been through military service – unless they were immigrants who had sometimes left their native countries to avoid conscription.[31]

Serving conscript soldiers were the one group of young people who were almost completely absent from the protests of 1968 itself. In the Netherlands, a union of conscripts had been established in 1966, but elsewhere political organization of soldiers was forbidden. In France, a militant of the Jeunesse Communiste Révolutionnaire incited his comrades in the barracks at Mutzig to 'fraternize with the workers' and celebrate 'joy, love and creative work', but in general there were few disturbances in the French armed forces.[32] After the student demonstrations of 1968, the French authorities implied that they might rescind the educational deferments that had been granted to some students who had been active in the demonstrations and they did indeed make it more difficult to obtain deferments in 1970. Revolutionary movements were discomfited by military service, especially in France, where the left had traditionally defended the notion of a 'nation in arms'. The Trotskyist Ligue Communiste claimed that 'military service with real training in the use of modern arms is a fundamental demand of revolutionaries who, in this context, insist on its extension to all of young people'.[33] Not surprisingly, young men rarely shared this military enthusiasm. Students threatened: 'For every deferment cancelled a faculty occupied; for every ten deferments cancelled, a Ministry blown up.'[34]

Resistance to military authority, having been so limited in 1968 itself, grew in importance in the 1970s. In France, soldiers' committees were formed in some regiments and there were petitions about the conditions under which conscription was imposed. André Krivine, a leader of protest in 1968, stood for election in 1969 during his own military service. But political agitation among conscripts in France never presented a real challenge to the armed forces. Middle-class men who were conscripted relatively late in life after having been politically active at university generally found the experience an occasion for alarm rather than political opportunity. They encountered fellow conscripts who were younger, and from humbler backgrounds, than themselves – one Parisian recalled of his comrades: 'May 68 had not existed for the majority of them.'[35] They also met older regular soldiers, who regarded them with disdain or amusement. Jean-Daniel Bénard was posted to a commando unit where his seniors told him that they would teach him how to make a 'real Molotov cocktail'.[36] The most striking feature of the period after 1968, however, was the increasing absence of middle-class men from the armed forces. In France, the authorities made discreet efforts to ensure that many student radicals failed their army medical. More importantly, European states that had offered almost no grounds for political objection to military service before 1968 began to accept conscientious objection or to offer alternative forms of service for those who wanted to avoid wielding a gun.

'YOUTH CULTURE'

For the first two decades after the Second World War, 'youth' was often a word associated with obedience rather than rebellion. The Catholic Church was especially assiduous in its cultivation of the young. Sometimes, especially in Italy, people who had been members of Catholic youth organizations went on to left-wing politics but the initial intention of such bodies had been to promote the virtues of well-scrubbed conformity.

If Western politicians in the early 1960s had been asked for one word that they associated with youth, they would probably have said 'sport', and this association went with a wider belief that young people might cultivate the virtues of obedience to rules and teamwork. But this had begun to change in the later half of the decade. The money brought by television challenged the notions of amateurism that went with 'gentlemanly' conduct. The boxer Muhammad Ali and, in a more hesitant way, the tennis player Arthur Ashe brought race to the sports stadium.[37] In Britain, opponents of apartheid protested at pitches where teams from South Africa were playing rugby or cricket.

The Winter Olympics in Grenoble in early 1968 marked the last moment at which conservative politicians could admire the athletic feats of young men and women who stood up for the national anthem after having competed for no financial reward – the Gaullists were to deploy the French ski champion Marielle Goitschel as a speaker at their rallies in 1968 as they fought to regain control of France after the student riots.[38] Six months later, the Mexico Olympics took place in a different atmosphere. The Mexican government had savagely repressed protests over the costs of building the Olympic site; some of the athletes gave Black Power salutes as they stood on the victor's podium.

The student protests in Paris began with a conflict between two conceptions of 'youth' that related to sport. The minister of youth affairs and sports, François Missoffe, born in 1919 and formed by the austere world of the Vichy government's youth camps, suggested that the 22-year-old Daniel Cohn-Bendit take a plunge in the newly con-structed swimming pool at Nanterre University to solve the student 'sexual problems' of which he had complained. The student occupa-tion of Columbia University in New York began with an argument over the construction of a gym – students objected to the fact that it took no account of local interests in the part of Harlem in which it was to be located. For those who disliked the student protests of the late 1960s, old-style college athletes sometimes came to assume the role that the Cossacks must once have had in the fantasies of white Russian aristocrats. They relished describing how rugby or American football players had manhandled demonstrators – though some American football players (especially black men brought to white universities by athletics scholarships) had complicated relations with the politics of the period. Ben Davis (the brother of the activist Angela) played for the Cleveland Browns.

The most important novelty of youth culture in the late 1960s sprang from the changing role of popular music. The gulf between plebeian pop music and a student version of bourgeois high culture narrowed. An irate English professor wrote: ' "pop culture" as a studied affront to the standards and values of the middle aged has to be seen as a similar manifestation to student protest within the university context'.[39] The link between a broad youth culture and political, especially student, radicalism was closest in the United States. Many rock stars were college graduates and some from privileged backgrounds. Jim Morrison's father was an admiral. Grace Slick (of Jefferson Airplane) had been educated with one of Richard Nixon's daughters and was once invited to a White House party – before the Secret Service excluded her, she had planned to put hallucinogenic drugs in Nixon's drink. When the Chicago Seven were tried for conspiracy to riot during the Democratic Convention of 1968 (see chap. 4), one of the questions that defence lawyers asked as they tried to exclude unsympathetic jurors was: 'Have you heard of Jefferson Airplane?'

In Britain, in some respects the real capital of rock culture in the late 1960s, rock bands were, or at least affected to be, removed from the middle-class world of universities. Mick Jagger was a schoolteacher's son who rarely alluded to his brief attendance at the London School of Economics. The phrase to be cited in so many works on 68 – 'Talkin' 'bout my Generation' – was first sung by The Who in 1965. But they were followed mainly by 'mods' – working-class young men who prided themselves on their sharp dress sense and who often seemed the antithesis of both student radicalism and the American counter-culture. In 1969 The Who, having negotiated a large fee, appeared at the Woodstock festival. When Abbie Hoffman – of the Youth International Party – climbed on stage to make a political speech, Pete Townshend, The Who's guitarist and author of their songs, told Hoffman to 'fuck off my fucking stage'.

Brief collisions between popular music and politics in Britain gave a deceptive impression of the intimacy of relations between them. John Lennon granted an interview to Tariq Ali for publication in the radical newspaper *Red Mole* – though Lennon's own uncertainty about politics was revealed by the fact that he produced two different lyrics for a song that referred to Mao. Jean-Luc Godard, then a Maoist, filmed the Stones recording 'Sympathy for the Devil' in 1968 – though there is no evidence that the Stones shared his views and their own eventual move to France was a bid to escape the Inland Revenue rather than to engage with the Gauche Prolétarienne.[40] Mick Jagger's occasional flirtations with radical politics encouraged the Black Panthers to turn up, ask for support and make threats when it was not given, during the Stones' American tour of 1969. Tina Turner, who had grown up in a rougher neighbourhood than Jagger, offered the protection of her own gun-toting bodyguards.[41]

Political references in rock songs were rare – rarer than they had been in the folk music of the 1950s. Much of the music industry was comically apolitical. The *Melody Maker* reported the Warsaw Pact invasion of Czechoslovakia in August 1968 only to note that the European tour of the band Fluff had been disrupted.[42] Some songs – The Who's 'Won't Get Fooled Again' or the Rolling Stones' 'Street Fighting Man' – expressed disillusion with revolutionary projects. As for continental Europe, the hit of the summer of 1968 was 'Rain and Tears' by Demis Roussos – in France, it did not have much competition because workers from the record factory went on strike after they had finished pressing the disc.

Communists disliked rock music as a consumerist import from the United States – it was said to have been British Communists who organized the barracking of Bob Dylan when he signalled his conversion from folk to rock by brandishing an electric guitar at the Manchester Free Trade Hall in 1966. Sometimes those Western Marxists who broke with the orthodox Communism of Moscow became even more puritanical in their attitude to rock music and consumerist youth culture. When French Maoists, hoping to incite revolution after 1968, went to work in factories, their young colleagues laughed at their attempts to affect a working-class style that they seemed to have learned from watching Jean Gabin films, while 'the young guys in the factory already wore ear rings and long hair'. One Maoist was so staid that her workmates dubbed her 'Nana' – they were referring not to the Zola heroine but to Nana Mouskouri, the bespectacled Greek singer.[43]

A comparison between France and America sometimes reveals the gulf between style and substance in the politics of popular music. American records sounded revolutionary but rarely engaged with politics in an explicit way. Attempts by French singers to imitate the counter-culture of America were painful – as when Johnny Hallyday sang 'Jésus Christ est un hippie' in 1970. There was, on the other hand, a variety of French popular music that was rooted in a pre-rock tradition that sounded 'old-fashioned' even when the songs or the singers espoused radical politics. Dominique Grange – a member of the Maoist Gauche Prolétarienne who went underground for a time in the early 1970s – was such a singer.[44] The most influential anti-war song of the post-war years was 'Le Déserteur', originally written by Boris Vian in 1954 during the French war in Indochina, recorded by Léo Ferré during the French war in Algeria and then by Joan Baez during the American war in Vietnam.

Fashion and musical taste could divide young people as well as unite them and those who thought of themselves as leaders of youth were sometimes thrust into a kind of civil war that cut across the younger generation. In the US, motorcycle gangs – the Hells Angels especially – had featured in presentations of youth culture since the 1950s. Most such gangs, however, were right-wing, if they had any politics at all, and they were also violent. In December 1969, the Hells Angels were asked to provide 'security' at the Altamont rock festival. During the concert, as the Stones played 'Sympathy for the Devil', they stabbed a black youth.

English Hells Angels were less violent than their American counterparts but they were hardly flower children. Skinheads – working-class youths who combined a taste for black music with racist views and cropped hair – were the polar opposite of hippies.[45] A squat at Number 144 Piccadilly in London was founded by people, mainly former students, who sought to 'form a fused commune out of all the different elements around Piccadilly so we could organize effective resistance against the fuzz then begin to reclaim the area for our own scene'. Things did not work out as planned. Hells Angels and skinheads fought and a spokesman for the commune, a former student from Cambridge, plaintively pointed to his bruises and asked the police: 'Would I get beaten up like this if I was the leader?'[46]

POLITICS AND PARENTS

Student protest sometimes brought parents and children together rather than alienating them from each other. Édouard Balladur – a civil servant attached to the office of the French prime minister in 1968 – wrote a piece of autobiographical fiction in which he imagined a young man, François, who is a student at Nanterre. His father,

Ramel, 'imposes nothing and is thus complicit in nothing'. Ramel is used to the periodic well-ordered demonstrations of the organized left but has not felt much emotion about protest since the end of the Algerian War in 1962. Everything changes for Ramel and other bourgeois parents with the police attacks on students on the night of 12 May 1968: 'The fathers had no longer dared be fathers for fear of being ridiculous or indiscreet. Now they suddenly became fathers again and violently so . . . Nothing mattered except the defence of the threatened offspring.'[47]

Sometimes the anger of young radicals came partly from their resentment at conservative parents. This was true for children of former Nazis in West Germany (see chap. 6) and also of some parts of America. Jeff Shero Nightbyrd grew up in Texas, where his stepfather was a colonel in the Air Force reserve. For him, joining Students for a Democratic Society meant a breach with family – it was like 'joining a Christian sect' in ancient Rome.[48] However, such examples were rare. Even the politicians who conducted American policy during the Vietnam War were mainly Democrats and sometimes people who thought of themselves as liberals. When their children joined the anti-war movement, the anger on both sides was so intense that it could induce physical illness. But relations between fathers and children – sometimes mediated by mothers who themselves disapproved of the war – rarely broke down entirely. Stanley Resor was secretary of state for the army: his son and his friends slept at the family house when they came to anti-war demonstrations in Washington. When anti-war protesters picketed the holiday house of Robert McNamara, the secretary of state for defense, in 1966, his son Craig, then seventeen, went out to talk to them. He wanted to express his sympathy with their cause but he also hoped to 'soften the situation' for his father.[49]

In general, the parents of student radicals were often left-wing, or at least 'liberal', themselves. At the LSE, supporters of student protest were likely to have parents who voted for the political left – interestingly, given the Freudian emphasis that was often put on father/son conflict, there was a particularly marked correlation between the political opinions of mothers and those of protesters.[50] There was a similar pattern as regards parents of draft resisters in Boston. Among their fathers, 54 per cent were Democrats (35.7 per cent liberal Democrats); among their mothers, 83.8 per cent were Democrats (39.7 per cent liberal Democrats).[51] Sometimes mothers, influenced by the first stirring of women's liberation, were beginning to react against authority in ways that ran parallel to the rebellions of their children. In Switzerland, a daughter of orthodox Communist parents joined the Trotskyist Ligue Marxiste Révolutionnaire only to find that her mother had joined the even more radical Maoist Rupture group.[52]

In the febrile climate of 1968 – when social democracy was often presented as part of the extreme right – left-of-centre parents did not necessarily share the particular views of their children. However, parents supported their children's right to protest even when they disagreed with the way in which they exercised that right. In Britain, the opposition to the administration of art schools, the institutions at which the response to protest had been most heavy-handed, was frequently led by parents. Simply having parents who doubted established authority could put children on the way to radicalization. Henry Kissinger jibed that the students who denounced him so vociferously 'had been brought up by sceptics, relativists and psychiatrists'.[53]

Family relations could cut across political differences. Norberto Bobbio, a senior academic at the University of Turin, had to deal with student occupation. A democratic socialist who believed in the rule of law, he had little in common with the student protesters but he maintained good relations with his son, who was one of them, throughout the period. Pierre Mendès France was an established politician in his early sixties by 1968 but he was on good terms with his nephew – Tiennot Grumbach – who was a Maoist. Even Denis Healey – the British defence secretary whose hostility to student demonstrators was sometimes so vigorously expressed that the police cordons seemed designed to protect them rather than him – remained close to his seventeen-year-old son, who joined the protests in Paris in 1968.

In some ways, the key question was not whether members of the older generation shared the particular ideas of their children but whether they regarded the notions of progress and dissent with approval. Many middle-aged people from the centre left did. Indeed even Edward Heath – the leader of the British Conservative Party and the epitome of buttoned-up conformism – pointed out that he himself had demonstrated against fascism and for Republican Spain when he was a student.

The children of Communist parents had a special role in 68 – though this role was different in Europe and the USA. In America, such children inherited a leftish culture. However, 'red diaper babies' also sometimes viewed their parents with some condescension. Those raised in the comparatively tolerant atmosphere of the 1960s found it hard to understand the terror of McCarthyism and consequently often blamed those who had compromised or dissimulated when faced with investigation for 'un-American activities'.

In Europe, on the other hand, there was much institutional hostility between Communist parties and the student movement. Orthodox Communists disliked, or misunderstood, youth culture and the young radicals of 68 were usually hostile to those parties that were loyal to Moscow. But on a personal level, Communists and their children often regarded each other with a grudging respect. In 1968, when he was nineteen, Yves Cohen went to work, and promote Maoism, at the Peugeot factory. He later found that his father – a member of the mainstream Communist Party – had asked his comrades in the Communist trade union to go easy on Yves 'because he is sincere'.[54] For the children of European Communists, the beliefs of their parents meant the International Brigades or the anti-Nazi Resistance rather than shifty resorts to the Fifth Amendment. Besides, even apparently loyal Communists of the older generation were rarely unqualified believers in the orthodoxies they expounded. Such people had lived through the abrupt changes of position of the Soviet Union and their own national party. Middle-aged Communists remembered the Hitler/Stalin pact, the split and then reconciliation between Yugoslavia and the USSR, and the days when Mao had sat at Stalin's right hand.

Phil Cohen (born in 1949) remembered his Communist father's bookcase. Lenin was at the top and Marx and Stalin on the shelf below – apparently Stalin stayed in place even after Khrushchev's denunciation of 1956. Beneath this was Mao, whose work stayed in place even after the Sino-Soviet split. At the bottom was Trotsky. Cohen *père* denounced Trotsky but did not throw his books away. When Cohen *fils* joined the Trotskyist International Marxist Group – 'such a betrayal that it could not be talked about in polite company' – his parents did not disown him. Michael Rosen, another Trotskyist son of parents in the mainstream Communist Party, summed up the politics of his family thus:

> As far as arguments with parents, it was unity in action – I remained united with my parents in action. For instance, when I was arrested at Grosvenor Square [during a demonstration against the Vietnam War], who was there to get me out at 2 o'clock in the morning but my Dad . . . He may have thought all sorts of things about my politics, but I was doing the right thing.[55]

3
Universities

Malcolm X with members of the Oxford Union, 1964.

3

Their main enemy is the power structure of the United States.
They see the university as part of this power structure.
— Conservative student on the occupation
of Columbia University, 1968.[1]

Universities were the most obviously politicized sites of generational identity in the long 68. Some campuses – Berkeley in California, Nanterre in Paris, Essex in Britain or the Free University in Berlin – became bywords for political radicalism. The occupation of university buildings was common and became associated with wider protests that were not directly linked to university matters. 'Teach-ins' on matters of political significance, the Vietnam War in particular, were common. Some proposed the end of examinations or the abolition of the distinction between academics and students. In the United States, students demanded, and sometimes established for themselves, new courses on topics such as black studies. At Birmingham in England a 'Free University' offered courses on, among other things, 'workers' control, psychedelia and the theory and practice of counter-institutions'.[2] In London, an 'anti-university' offered for a time courses by thinkers such as the psychologist R.D. Laing.[3]

POST-WAR EXPANSION

More people in the West attended universities in the late 1960s than ever before. This made students an important political group and the alienation and/or overcrowding associated with rapid expansion contributed to wider discontent. American universities were already large by 1945 and expanded again in response to the GI bill, which subsidized college education for military veterans. The expansion of the 1960s took place on top of this. By 1970, there were around 8 million students in America and one in three of all those between the ages of eighteen and twenty-two were enrolled at college.

American university presidents – sometimes urged on by boards of regents who were recruited from local businessmen – began to talk of their institutions in terms of extravagant ambition. In 1963, Clark Kerr – the president of the University of California, which was already a huge network of campuses that took in both Berkeley and UCLA – spoke of the 'multiversity', which would combine many different academic functions. He added: 'What the railroads did for the second half of the last century and the automobile for the first half of this century may be done for the second half of this century by the knowledge industry.'

John Hannah, an expert in poultry science, became president of the University of Michigan in 1941, when it was still mainly an agricultural college. It expanded quickly after the war and the number of its faculty increased from 900 to 1,900 between 1950 and 1965. Hannah dreamed of creating the world's largest residential campus with a student population of 100,000 by 1970. He justified this expansion in terms that would soon seem sinister to many students. Universities, he said, should be 'as essential to the preservation of our country and our way of life as supersonic bombers, nuclear-powered submarines and intercontinental ballistic missiles'.

British universities took a smaller number of students and the expansion of the 1960s started from a low base: in 1969, a professor of philosophy at Birmingham complained that the number of students in his department had increased – from three to twenty-three.[4] The head of another philosophy department was said to have restricted admissions by insisting that all prospective undergraduates should be able to read the major works of philosophy in their original languages: Greek, Latin, French and German.[5]

The Robbins report, published in 1963, provided a formal structure for British university expansion and, indeed, the most thorough consideration of university expansion anywhere in the West. Robbins was an economist and he accumulated statistical information about birth rates, economic demand, cost and the educational sociology, to show that children from poor backgrounds were being denied an education from which they could benefit. His report was a good example of the technocratic approach to society against which some students would protest a few years later.

Robbins suggested an overall expansion of higher education that was to be achieved mainly by creating new universities – soon labelled 'plate glass' because of their modernist architecture. Elsewhere the construction of new universities was slower – though the total student population was often higher. The French built new universities – notably at Nanterre, which opened in 1964. In Italy, Trento was opened in 1962. In Germany, Bielefeld was founded in 1969, in time to deal with the relatively late post-war German baby boom.

The most important explicit or implicit model for much university expansion in the 1960s was the United States, or at least the best-known American universities. When Barry Supple, an English historian who had previously taught at Harvard and McGill in Montreal, took a job at Sussex in 1962, he organized a Thanksgiving dinner for those who had been drawn to the 'American-like campus'.[6] Admiration for American universities was relatively new. The English historian A.J.P. Taylor (born in 1906) never set foot in the United States; he could not see why anyone should be interested in a country with 'no food, no architecture and no history'. But the generation of academics who began their careers after the Second World War rarely thought like this. American universities had acquired the intellectual firepower that came with Jewish refugees fleeing Nazism. The United States was also a source of funds. Successful academics, such as Fernand Braudel in France and even the Communist Eric Hobsbawm in Britain, benefited from the grants of the Rockefeller Foundation.

Were post-war universities 'overcrowded'? In most Western countries, the funding for higher education was relatively generous. The British plate-glass universities were in fact often empty during their first few years. Essex's first vice chancellor had planned for up to 20,000 students – he asked the architect for 8,000 parking spaces. In practice the university's student population did not exceed 5,000 for many years. Having said this, students sometimes felt badly off. Those at old institutions in cities – which meant most universities in much of continental Europe until after 1968 – found that more people were crammed into the same libraries and lecture halls. The fact that fewer students lived at home meant that they were more dependent on the provision that universities made for their rooms and food. Some student protests in the late 1960s began with mundane complaints about the quality of menus in university refectories. Students were also exasperated by the absence of those employed to teach them. The grandest of professors often found that they had more interesting things to do than spend time in their own universities. In 1974, Bernard Donoughue became an adviser to Harold Wilson, a politician particularly disliked by student radicals. He wrote later:

> I was then a university teacher [at the LSE], which meant that even in mid-term time a great deal of spare time was available to anyone reasonably energetic . . . none of my academic colleagues (some of whom for various reasons in those easier days habitually followed a similar routine of only occasional professional attendance) was aware that I was working sixteen hours days at the centre of the general election.[7]

Raymond Aron, a professor at the Sorbonne, was giving a talk to bankers in New York as student protest, of which he disapproved, broke out in Paris in May 1968.

VARIETIES OF HIGHER EDUCATION

Student culture varied from country to country. In the United States, some universities were city-states – with their own radio stations, newspapers and, more sinisterly, their own police forces. Students, or those who had once been students, might hang around the large campuses for many years: Al Haber, who had been born in 1936 and became the first president of Students for a Democratic Society in 1960, enrolled as a student at the University of Michigan in 1954 and did not graduate with his first degree until 1965. In continental Europe, the openness of university admission policy blurred the boundaries of universities. Students frequently failed, or failed to sit, exams so they took longer to graduate, if they graduated at all. Some Europeans, such as Joschka Fischer in Frankfurt, lived on the fringes of universities – attending demonstrations, and occasionally lectures, without being formally registered as students. High rates of failure and dropout fostered discontent in the universities of continental Europe. They also created a cadre of militants who devoted at least as much time to activism as to their studies.

THE SOCIAL BACKGROUND OF STUDENT PROTEST

Two different theories were advanced in the aftermath of 68 to explain the relation between student protest and academic privilege. In Britain and America, those who studied the matter concluded that protest was most common at large, academically selective institutions that laid a heavy emphasis on research. The London School of Economics was such a place, as were the universities at Berkeley, Ann Arbor and Madison, Wisconsin. The number of student demonstrations at Harvard in every single semester of the 1960s exceeded the number of protests at Midland Lutheran College in Nebraska during the whole of the decade.[8] It also appeared that the most academically able students were the most likely to protest. A study of students who had been active during protests at Essex University in 1968 suggested that their degree results were better than average – a striking finding in view of the fact that protest was itself so time-consuming.[9]

Two French sociologists – Pierre Bourdieu and Raymond Boudon – advanced a different interpretation. They believed that student protesters were the academically undistinguished children of affluent families. Such people found that the expansion of university education reduced the economic value of their qualifications, and that devaluation was particularly marked for those who had studied sociology – the subject that was most associated with protest in 68.[10]

These interpretations may reflect real differences between France and the Anglo-Saxon countries. The fact that sociology was popular in French universities, which had no academic selection, reduced the value of sociology degrees, but the fact that it was popular in selective

British universities meant that only the well qualified were admitted to study it. Large research universities enjoyed special prestige in Britain and America, and those who studied student protest were often graduates of and/or teachers at such institutions. British academics at the LSE drew on American research to advance their arguments that student protest was linked to 'elite' universities – a good example of the Americanization of academic life.[11]

By contrast the *grandes écoles* – which were, in spite of their name, small – enjoyed special prestige in France (see chap. 5). Bourdieu and Boudon were both graduates of the very grand, and very small, École Normale Supérieure. The *grandes écoles*, unlike French universities, subjected their would-be students to savage entrance tests. Those who surveyed the education system from this Olympian height often assumed that the majority of French students were academically mediocre.

Both interpretations, however, have been challenged. With regard to British and American universities, it is hardly surprising that protest at prestigious institutions attracted more attention than it did at less well-known ones far from big cities. Many of those who wrote about student protest simply ignored institutions with which they were unfamiliar – in the United States, this meant that they rarely commented on the protests in the small colleges of the south. One sociologist asked drily of work by his colleagues: 'would their conclusions only apply to public institutions with at least a certain percentage of white students?'[12]

Radical movements did spring up in institutions that were far from privileged. This was true of the State University of New York at Buffalo, Michigan State and Kent State Ohio. In Britain, the sharpest conflicts – certainly the ones that provoked the most aggressive responses from the authorities – came not in universities but in colleges of art, especially at Hornsey in London and Guildford in Surrey. Here the conventions of academic freedom that regulated university life afforded no protection and college principals answered to the municipal politicians of the Local Education Authority rather than to a council of governors. The principal of Guildford, faced with protest, simply fired forty-two full and part-time members of staff.[13]

As for France, many recent scholars, particularly those who are *soixante-huitards* or the children of *soixante-huitards*, deny that the protesters of 68 were railing against their own social decline.[14] On the contrary, they argue, large numbers were drawn from comparatively humble backgrounds and had risen in the world through education. If such people endured unemployment or poverty, this was often a consequence, rather than a cause, of what they did in 68. One should also note that some prominent figures at the time rejected the idea that the upheavals of 68 could be explained by the social/educational decline of bourgeois young people. Charles de Gaulle's wife insisted that it was the excessively rapid ascension of parvenus who went to university without the cultural refinement that came from generations of genteel living that explained the agitation in French universities.[15] The British cabinet minister Richard Crossman advanced a similar explanation with regard to his country: 'We have vastly expanded the student population and brought into our university people who have not got a middle class or bookish background.'[16]

The truth is that the social basis of student protest cannot be reduced to a single cause. As protest expanded, it often spread to less prestigious institutions with less privileged students – this explains the growing importance of 'prairie radicals' from mid-Western universities in the United States (see chap. 4) and the growing importance of polytechnics rather than universities in the United Kingdom (see chap. 7). Even within each individual country, protest was often founded on heterogeneous coalitions of different classes and interests. Sometimes, the encounter of people from different backgrounds was partly what created upheaval in universities. In Britain, the son of a lorry driver, later to be convicted for his part in the bombings of the Angry Brigade, lived in college rooms close to those occupied by the heir to the throne. The emphasis on upward or downward mobility associated with 68 is also deceptive in that it ignores divisions that cut across simple questions of privilege and underprivilege. In America at least, it is true that many student radicals – particularly the most prominent ones and those who were present at the creation of protest movements – came from relatively privileged backgrounds, but their privilege was of a particular kind. Their parents were likely to work in those professions – law, medicine and university teaching itself – that placed a high value on educational qualification. It is also notable that their mothers were more likely to work than most middle-class women. As protest movements grew, they drew in more people from relatively humble backgrounds, but who often came from families who valued education.[17]

Interpretations that revolve around social mobility also assume a static society. In fact, most Western societies were changing fast in the late 1960s. These changes created a new kind of opportunities for graduates. The much maligned sociology degree frequently led to jobs in the education system, which was expanding fast. The upheaval generated by student protest itself fostered social change, which could bring a decline in economic prospects. Students who dropped out of university, neglected their studies or acquired criminal records limited their chances of obtaining certain kinds of employment but this was an outcome that they themselves often accepted or even desired. It was, however, possible for political turbulence to produce benefits. Working for the alternative press drew some former revolutionaries into journalism. One unexpected, long-term effect of the strikes of 1968 in France was that the students were assessed in less formal and less demanding ways. A substantial number of those born in the late 1940s seem to have found it easier to enter higher education and consequently to raise or maintain their social position. Economists estimated that there was a 'wage premium' of 2–3 per cent for those involved.[18]

NEW DISCIPLINES

European academics had often prized 'scholarship', which usually meant acquiring an ever more refined understanding of things that were already known. Scholarship went with a reverence for old texts, classical languages and the achievements of great men. A British Conservative MP believed that the 'hallmark of true scholarship is humility', and he attributed disturbances at Essex University partly to the fact that students took no pride in the 'achievements of the last 3,000 years'.[19]

Academics had not always been encouraged to publish their own work. In Britain, careers were built on brilliant exam results and many academics believed that their primary job was to prepare students for exams. The ferociously difficult *agrégation* examination was the first step into an academic career in France, and the most prestigious French institution of higher education – the École Normale Supérieure – existed to train young people for the *agrégation*. Louis Althusser was the most important Marxist theorist in France but he was employed as a *répétiteur*, or exam coach, at the École Normale.

'Scholarship' was now increasingly replaced by 'research', which implied expanding the frontiers of knowledge. It also implied a new professionalism of approach to academic life. Commenting on the relationship between social sciences and protest movements in the aftermath of 1968, two radical French sociologists drew attention to the 'all powerful' professional associations, the annual conferences that attracted 'two or three thousand' participants, and '*La règle de fer* publish or perish.'[20] The word 'research' was most used in the first instance by those who worked in the natural sciences. The United States government had sought to build up scientific research partly because of its fears that the Soviet Union might overtake it in this domain. European educational planners were also interested in science – partly because they supposed that it would foster economic growth. Robbins believed that university expansion should mean, in large measure, the expansion of science departments. The most flamboyantly novel of the new British universities – Essex – was initially intended to be a 'British MIT'.

In fact, university expansion went with what British official reports called a 'swing to the arts'. Fewer children studied science and mathematics at school. Perhaps affluence made them less concerned to equip themselves with skills that were obviously useful in the job market. In France, the proportion of students studying arts subjects rose sharply in the late 1960s. The national economic plan had suggested that one in three students should study sciences; by the academic year 1968–9, only one in five did so.[21]

Increasingly, though, even academics who were not physical scientists adopted the language of science. They emphasized objectivity and theoretical rigour. They placed research above scholarship. Their lives began to revolve around 'research institutes', 'laboratories' and the pursuit of large grants. In *Changing Places* (1975), David Lodge's novel about an academic exchange in 1969, the English Philip Swallow, who loves reading but has never finished his PhD and who sometimes contemplates publishing his exam questions because they are his most important contribution to the academic world, is the epitome of old-fashioned scholarship; the American Morris Zapp, who has published six books by the age of forty and who dreams of exhausting every possible theoretical approach to the novels of Jane Austen, which he personally finds a 'pain in the ass', is the epitome of new-style research.

New-style academics relished big collective research projects and the training of research students in graduate schools rather than the teaching of undergraduates. Computers generated excited discussion among scholars in the humanities – partly because they seemed to offer the chance of doing something that might look more like the natural sciences. In 1962, F.R. Leavis, a Cambridge literary scholar, had launched a bitter attack on C.P. Snow – the novelist and defender of scientific education – saying that his novels read as though they had been written 'by an electronic brain' (Leavis's deliberately archaic term for a computer). A few years later, some talked as though they really did think that computers might write books. The French historian Emmanuel Le Roy Ladurie pronounced in 1968 that the historian of the future would be 'a computer programmer or he would be nothing'.

Above all, the 1960s saw an expansion of the 'social sciences'. In 1968, for the first time the number of British students reading sociology exceeded those applying to read law or economics. They exceeded those applying for any other subject except medicine.[22] Sociology was a new discipline in Britain and was not taught at all in the oldest of British universities. It was better established in France, Germany and Italy but had traditionally been studied in these countries in an abstract way that involved broad speculations. What was new about sociology in the 1960s was the increase in empirical work that emphasized questionnaires, fieldwork and statistics. It also presented itself as a 'useful' discipline that could provide policy-makers with concrete advice based on objective and 'apolitical' information. Sociologists offered confident opinions on almost all topics, including by the end of the decade the explosion of student unrest in their own departments.

A large proportion of the most vociferous and dissatisfied students was drawn from the social science departments. At Berkeley in 1965, approval for the Free Speech Movement was highest (75 per cent) among students majoring in social sciences; it was lowest (42 per cent) among those majoring in business, engineering and architecture.[23] At the LSE, students of sociology and anthropology made up 17 per cent of all students but 34 per cent of those who expressed 'extreme support' for the student sit-in.[24]

Campus politics could pit disciplines against each other. If social scientists were the most radical, they often identified the physical sciences, and especially engineering, as centres of reaction. Sometimes this hostility was rooted in the specific links between research in universities and the military. Such links were particularly important in America. By 1968, American universities spent $3 billion on research, of which 70 per cent came from federal funds and over half of which related to defence.[25] No other Western country had the defence budget of the United States, but there were protests in Britain – especially at Essex University when it was visited by a speaker from Porton Down, a centre of research into chemical weapons. In Britain and America, science and engineering students were in general more politically conservative than the bulk of students and this was probably exacerbated by the fact that their studies were more structured and left little time for attending demonstrations. In Birmingham, the authorities discovered that they could confound radicalism by the simple expedient of cancelling lectures in engineering – thus releasing large numbers who could be relied on to vote against left-wing motions at the 'general assemblies' that activists had convoked.[26] In France, science was less likely to be identified with conservatism – perhaps because scientists themselves had been influenced by Sartrean notions of the engaged intellectual, perhaps because French technology was not deployed to promote American military power or perhaps simply because the working conditions of most French scientists were less good than those of their colleagues in Britain or America.

Sometimes the most savage conflicts seemed to take place within departments. Sociology students often reserved much of their venom for their own teachers. One pained – and liberal-minded – associate professor at the University of Chicago wrote: 'The sociological profession has been singled out for some of the most exquisitely vicious attacks ever launched by student protestors.'[27] He claimed that the leader of a student faction at his own university had expressed the desire to 'destroy the sociology department by pointing out that what the professors say is full of shit'.[28]

Sociology students argued that the discipline had been corrupted by its association with capitalism and state power. Private companies and governments used sociological research and this was linked to a turn of the discipline towards more specialized and empirical work. Social scientists advised those who framed American policy in Latin America and South East Asia. This could make them seem, as one French critic put it, like part of the 'military industrial academic complex',[29] though anthropologists who worked under American government auspices in Vietnam actually seem to have concluded quite quickly that support for the South Vietnamese regime was a mistake.

However, the links between sociology and power do not on their own explain student protest. Even the most self-regarding sociologist would presumably have admitted that, say, nuclear physics was more important to the Pentagon than sociological enquiry, but students of physics were less prone to protest than those of sociology. Besides which, political distaste for sociology sits oddly with the fact that increasing numbers of students were choosing to study it.

Perhaps the radicalism of students in the social sciences sprang partly from the very hope that had been invested in these disciplines and from their rapid expansion. Some radical students had themselves once been attracted to the technocratic vision of social science to a greater extent than they later cared to admit. Daniel Cohn-Bendit had initially wanted to train as an educational planner until he realized that he lacked the mathematical aptitude to conduct the necessary statistical analysis. Sociology students, who rarely had much experience of the discipline before they arrived at university, were often disappointed by the specialized studies they were required to undertake. University teachers of social science usually thought of themselves as having progressive political views. They believed that their discipline existed to question established opinions and institutions. Few of them were Marxists but many of them took Marx seriously at a time when few of their colleagues in other departments would have done so. However, social scientists sought primarily to make Western capitalist societies work better rather than to overthrow the existing order. The French sociologist Michel Crozier argued that France was a 'blocked society', which was paralysed by bureaucracy. For him the real division of industrial societies was between 'modernizers' and 'conservatives' rather than between left and right. A support for technocratic modernization made academic sociologists vulnerable as student radicals moved sharply to the left in the late 1960s. Professors, who had thought of themselves as critics of the established order, were now denounced by students who believed reform or 'modernization' implied complicity with power.

There were also more complicated reasons for disaffection in social science departments. These disciplines were most highly developed in America. A professor in the sociology department at Chicago remarked that his own subject was, along with jazz and modern dance, one of America's three distinctive contributions to world culture.[30] European social scientists were particularly influenced by their readings of American work and, for the most eminent among them, by their visits to the United States. In turn this aroused resentment among anti-American students. Radicals at Nanterre wrote bitterly: 'all current sociology in France is imported from the US, with a few years' delay. Everyone knows that the most esteemed sociologists are those who follow most attentively the American publications.'[31] The Nanterre students would have been even more outraged if they had known that one target of their attacks – Michel Crozier – had just attended a conference convoked by McGeorge Bundy, the former American National Security adviser, at the instigation of President Johnson, to plan the foundation of an East/West Institute, which would bring Western and Soviet specialists together to examine social problems.[32]

Young radicals did not just dislike the specific links that academics had with political or military power. They resented the whole tone of social science. They disliked its 'ideology of neutrality' and its belief that social 'problems' could be solved in ways that did not involve wholesale changes to society. The functionalism of the Harvard sociologist Talcott Parsons, who believed that 'mature' societies would work smoothly, was an object of particular scorn. Phil Cohen, who had repeatedly switched disciplines before dropping out of university, was an extreme example of academic disillusion. He planned to break into the LSE library so that he could glue the pages of works by

Talcott Parsons together – thereby illustrating the 'congealment of praxis'.[33]

Some liberal sociology professors understood that the very qualities that they most prized – objectivity and clarity – might partly account for the disquiet of their pupils. Michel Crozier had returned to France from Harvard in 1967 and taken a chair at Nanterre. He sought to introduce an American style into his teaching as well as American techniques into his research. After a lecture, one of his students complimented him on his clarity, which he contrasted with that of Alain Touraine, a younger sociologist who was to be more sympathetic to the student protests. The student said that Touraine was hard to understand and often seemed to contradict himself, but then suddenly hesitated and added: 'In the end, I like that better, it is stimulating.' Crozier was disconcerted but felt that he understood the student's remark. Students needed to be 'made to dream' and in France 'it was paradoxically through abstraction that one makes people dream, by escaping from reality'.[34]

POSTGRADUATES

The growth of graduate studies fostered radicalism in universities. It created a cadre of students who remained in place for long enough to establish political movements. The Teaching Assistants Association was formed at the University of Wisconsin in 1966 to represent graduate students who earned money teaching, and soon linked the material dissatisfactions of its members to wider questions relating to race and Vietnam. The lives of graduate students were not interrupted by the inconvenient obligation to sit exams. The leisurely pace of life was captured by the jibe in John Irving's novel *The World According to Garp* (published in 1978 and set mainly in the 1960s) that 'gradual school was where students gradually realize that they do not want to go to school anymore'. Graduate study expanded sharply in the 1960s. This was particularly notable in the United States – partly because of the institutionalization of research and partly because attending graduate school became a means to avoid being sent to Vietnam. The idea of graduate education, like most American educational innovations, spread to Britain and Europe. A lawyer at the trial of student activists – largely Americans undertaking postgraduate courses – who had stormed the administrative building at London University remarked briskly that 'doctorates are two a penny in the United States'.[35]

PROFESSORS AND THEIR ENEMIES

Who were students against? Sometimes there was a mood of bitter hostility to teachers who were seen as authoritarian or complicit in some wider power structure. Equally professors were sometimes hostile to student activists whom they saw as a threat to the qualities – order, tranquillity, reasoned debate – that they regarded as essential to university life. Though students often denounced their enemies as 'fascists', their bitterest critics were often Jewish professors – Alexander Gerschenkron, Raymond Aron, Theodor Adorno – who were old enough to have personal memories of Nazism.

However, the struggle in the universities was never a simple conflict of generations and never completely divided teachers from students. Some academics maintained good relations with their students in 68, or even presented themselves as neutral figures in a struggle between students and 'the university' – the rise of the professional academic administrator sometimes gave students and teachers a common enemy. During the occupation of Columbia University in 1968, students marked their political affiliations with various coloured armbands but members of the faculty wore white bands. Very few professors were either completely for or completely against the student protests and some took unexpected stands. The historians Rodney Hilton and John Saville, both ex-Communists in their fifties, acted as intermediaries between protesting students and the university authorities at Birmingham and Hull. René Rémond, a senior historian of relatively conservative views at Nanterre, later remarked that he was a *soixante-huitard* himself in a way because he welcomed the chance to reform his university.

Sometimes there was sympathy between student radicals and professors. The sinologist and historian of science Joseph Needham was master of one of the most conservative colleges in Cambridge but also belonged to Socialists in Higher Education, whose members sought 'a critical destabilization of the system'.[36] Antonio Negri – born in 1933 and a professor of sociology at Bologna – was a leader of the radical Marxist Lotta Continua. He was later prosecuted for having inspired terrorist acts by the Red Brigades, and the Italian authorities denounced him as the most prominent of the 'bad masters' – a term that implies that some Italian students listened to their professors too assiduously. Many academics led double lives that straddled the frontier between academic authority and student rebellion. Jonah Raskin spent some of his nights in 1968 participating in the student occupation of Columbia University but by day he commuted to Stony Brook University to teach his own classes. He was Dr Raskin to his students, Jonah to his colleagues and 'Jomo' to readers of his articles in the underground press.[37]

In any case, the expansion of higher education in the post-war period had blurred the boundaries between teachers and students. This was in part because university expansion brought an increase in the proportion of young university teachers. Even among academics of roughly the same age there were some sharp divisions, rooted partly in how fast they had risen up the academic ladder. Barry Supple (born in 1929) was pro-vice chancellor of Sussex University in 1968 and responsible for containing much of the student revolt. Stuart Hall, three years younger than Supple, was in a more junior position and widely regarded as the most important academic to support the British student protests. In the United States, the profession was divided into those who did and those who did not enjoy permanent tenure. In France, Germany and Italy, junior academics – often on temporary contracts – were expected to display ostentatious deference to the professors who controlled their careers. The number of these junior academics increased as universities expanded in the 1960s, and the increase was, of course, sharpest in those subjects, such as sociology, that grew fastest. 68 was sometimes as much a rebellion of assistants against professors as it was of students against their teachers.

Those who opposed student protest often presented it as a movement of savage philistinism – one that threatened scholarship itself as well as academic authority. The desacralization of the book was an important part of 68. Guido Viale, a charismatic figure among leftist students in Turin, remarked that books were 'as bad as professors'.[38] The belief that university libraries might be threatened by disorder obsessed some academics – David Landes at Harvard said that he would fire on students if they attacked the library.[39]

However, radical students often had a touching attachment to the written word. Members in a Danish commune admitted that books were the one form of private property that they found it hard to renounce.[40] During his years as university dropout, political activist and leader of a London squat, Phil Cohen often found solace in the reading room of the British Museum and he subtitled his memoirs *The Radical Bibliophile*. Seeking potential recruits to Students for a Democratic Society, George Brosi at Carleton College in Minnesota checked library records because he knew that readers of certain books were likely to have left-wing sympathies.[41] Access to libraries was itself sometimes a demand in 68. Students at Trento called for an 'American-style library . . . maximum development of the man/book relation – no intermediary – all the books on the wall and within hand reach'.[42]

Academics sometimes felt an odd sense of renewal in 68. Didier Anzieu at Nanterre wrote: 'My students sensed that I was preoccupied not so much with them as with the machine. They were bored of my boredom and I was bored of theirs. For the first time that year [during the uprising of May 1968] the University interested me again.'[43] Even Barry Supple, who defended order at Sussex University, admitted that he derived a frisson of excitement from the drama that he had lived through.

For all the lurid rhetoric, much of what students wanted in 68 could be accommodated by universities. Indeed student protests were often followed by an unexpected burst of consensus. At Nanterre student radicals joined commissions to discuss how teaching might be changed. Even the most dramatic innovations of 68 yielded quite conventional results. Edgar Faure, the wily centrist politician who became minister of education after the May events in France, helped create a new campus at Vincennes – housed in prefabricated buildings and opened in 1969. The new campus provided an intellectual home for radical thinkers – notably Michel Foucault – and took students who lacked conventional qualifications. As Faure probably anticipated, in the long term even Vincennes calmed down – partly because its relatively old, working-class students sometimes turned out to have rather conventional expectations of education.[44]

Some left universities during or after the protests of 68 – to take jobs in factories, become full-time militants or even go underground as urban guerrillas – but a surprisingly large number stayed in, or returned to, education. In 2006 Tom Hayden finally published the masters' dissertation which he had begun in the early 1960s.[45] Guido Viale, who had called for the destruction of books in 1968, also became a sociologist. A study of American radical activists from the 1960s found that thirty years later 17 per cent of the sample had become professors.[46] Dick Flacks – who had himself been a member of Students for a Democratic Society before becoming an academic sociologist who both sympathized with and studied the radicals of the late 1960s – summed things up: 'The Academy was one of the few institutional settings where former student activists could expect a degree of career and economic stability and yet feel relatively uncompromised.'[47]

4
The United States

Lyndon Johnson (who came to be hated by the radical left) with Robert Kennedy (who came to be admired by part of the left).

4

The United States played a special role in the long 68. The policies of its government – particularly in Indochina – were the target of hostility around the world but America also provided the model for much protest in the Western world. Timing was the key to some of this. The kinds of movements that were to become so common in the late 1960s had often originated in America in the early years of the decade – sometimes emerging out of the civil rights movement. However, in the late 1960s, and especially in 1968 itself, both radicals and defenders of the established order seemed to lose faith in the US.

Some Americans recalled 1968 in terms of physical sickness. Dean Rusk, the secretary of state, said that the whole year was a 'blur' and that he had lived on aspirin, scotch and cigarettes.[1] The journalist Joan Didion wrote: 'an attack of vertigo and nausea does not now seem to me an inappropriate response to the summer of 1968'.[2] The Democrat politician and social commentator Daniel Patrick Moynihan believed that his country had come close to 'nervous breakdown'.[3] Those in government felt squeezed between the military difficulties of the Vietnam War and the political difficulties (both at home and abroad) produced by opposition to the war. Lyndon Johnson – not usually noted for sympathetic treatment of his subordinates – worried that Robert McNamara, the secretary of defense, might kill himself.[4]

Those who opposed the government, however, rarely felt any better. In part this was because the year ended with the election of Richard Nixon – a president who attracted particular animosity from liberal-minded Americans and whose time in office was to be marked by further aggression in Indochina, though also by the eventual recognition that the United States would have to withdraw, and by the squalor of Watergate. Furthermore, some student activists believed that in 1968 the radicalism of the early 1960s had spiralled into violence, acrimonious internal division and a new obsession with ideological orthodoxies. James Miller, a member of Students for a Democratic Society (SDS), wrote that 'the movement collapsed at the end of the decade . . . leaving behind a fog of tear gas, drugs and pseudo-Marxist cant'.[5] One of Miller's comrades in the SDS admitted that some had come to regard the late 1960s as a 'chamber of horrors'.[6]

The disillusion that marked the end of the 1960s in the USA was partly linked to what some recalled as an age of innocence earlier in the decade when, so they came to believe, the 'New Left' had sought to escape the sectarian exclusiveness they associated with Marxism and when the non-violence and inter-racial alliance of the civil rights campaign had appeared to point the way to a new kind of politics. It seemed, ten years on, that this ideological innocence had been dissolved by the embrace of violence on the political left as well as by the rise of a counter-culture that was associated with the increasing distance between radical students and the mainstream left, especially the labour movement.

Most of all, the political divisions of the 1960s in the United States were, at least in the early part of the decade, a dispute about the meaning of America itself. Radicals frequently presented themselves as defenders of authentically national traditions rather than as innovators or exponents of foreign ideas. Tom Hayden – the best-known student leader in the United States – was later to remark that the radicalism of the 1960s was not simply about particular issues but rather constituted a general attempt at 'remaking America itself'– comparable to the Declaration of Independence or the Civil War.[7] The pessimistic mood of the late 1960s was partly produced by the optimism that had pervaded the early years of the decade and radical Americans who turned against their own country often denounced it with particular bitterness because they felt it had failed to live up to its elevated destiny.

ORIGINS

If many saw 1968 as an end in the United States, when was the beginning? The 'New Left' was not quite as new as some young Americans came to believe. By 1968, a foot soldier in a university occupation would describe Tom Hayden as 'the theoretical father of the whole New Left',[8] but, as Hayden himself knew, two older men had given the term currency in America. The first and most famous of these was the sociologist C. Wright Mills (1916–62), a professor at Columbia with a taste for leather jackets, motorbikes, women and playing the worldly older brother to earnest young men. Hayden, who wrote his graduate dissertation on Mills, believed that 'after Albert Camus and Bob Dylan, Mills ranked as the most pervasive influence in the first generation of SDS'.[9] Three of Mills's books exercised particular influence. *The New Men of Power: America's Labor Leaders* (1948) explained how trade unionists had becomes pillars of American consensual politics. *White Collar: The American Middle Classes* (1951) struck students because it seemed to describe the world of their fathers and the world into which they feared they might themselves be drawn. *The Power Elite* (1956) drew attention to the small group of men who directed US policy.

The second thinker to inspire student radicalism was Michael Harrington, born in 1928. Harrington had edited *The Catholic Worker* and helped transmit a certain kind of Catholic social thought from Europe, especially France, to America. He lost his own religious faith at the moment when the Church, at the Second Vatican Council, seemed to be drawing close to his social ideas – though he never lost the sense that religion was important to public life. Harrington became best known for his book *The Other America: Poverty in the United States* (1962), which explored the lives of those who lived on incomes of less than $3,000 per year. It made Harrington so famous that he was, to his own embarrassment, soon being offered $1,500 for a single lecture.[10]

Harrington and Mills did not always agree with each other or with every aspect of the emerging student movement. Harrington criticized some student leaders and Mills was probably protected from such acrimony only by his early death. Harrington, unlike Mills, was strongly anti-Communist. He was also close to organized labour, about which Mills was disdainful, and dubious about the virtues of Castro's Cuba, which Mills admired. What Harrington and Mills shared, and what gave them such influence, was an interest in the university campus as a potential site of radicalism and a personal charisma that commanded attention.

CIVIL RIGHTS

The American radicalism of the 1960s was partly rooted in the civil rights movement that had begun with an attempt to desegregate the southern states. The civil rights movement attracted national attention from the mid-1950s onwards, after a supreme court judgment that ordered the desegregation of schools and with the boycott of buses in Montgomery, Alabama in 1955–6, though its origins went back earlier. Civil rights activists were sometimes relatively old. Rosa Parks, who sparked the Montgomery bus boycott, had been born in 1913. The movement was entwined with Protestant Churches – especially after the Reverend Martin Luther King Jr (born in 1929) became its most visible leader.

In some respects, the civil rights movement was a conservative one. It had clearly defined aims. Its supporters were concerned with established institutions – schools, law courts, the electoral roll. It sought to ensure that the writ of the federal government ran throughout the country. There were, however, novelties in the movement. Its leaders espoused resistance to local authorities and in particular they experimented with non-violent resistance – an idea that some of them took from Mahatma Gandhi's campaign in India – though there was more violence in the early civil rights campaign than its leaders sometimes cared to admit.

White liberals had often assumed that the South was somewhere to be avoided or, if they had the misfortune to be born there, to be escaped from. For such people, racism was distasteful but politically unexciting. C. Wright Mills had left Texas in his twenties. He later wrote: 'I have never been interested in what is called the "Negro problem" . . . The truth is, I have never looked into it as a researcher. I have a feeling that if I did it would turn out to be a white problem.'[11] Harrington was more interested than Mills in questions of race and closer to the civil rights movement – though he was not an unqualified admirer of its 'amiable parliamentary chaos'.[12]

In the early 1960s, however, student activists came to feel that the 'negro question' was supremely interesting. In part, this interest sprang from the discovery of poverty and repression in their own country – a discovery that was as dramatic as the discovery of the third world by the European left at about the same time. Young people went south to join protests – most famously during the 'Freedom Summer' of 1964. White students saw, and to some extent endured, the treatment meted out to black people in the South. They were beaten by policemen, locked up and in a few cases murdered. Student radicals did not simply see race as a 'white problem' – to be solved by changing the behaviour of racists – or even as a political problem – to be solved with particular concessions. For some of them, the struggle was a noble thing in itself. Sandra Cason – a Texan student influenced by an unconventional Christianity – explained that she felt 'some pity for the segregationist'. For her, the civil rights campaign was not an ordinary political one – though she added, in terms that would have seemed strange to many a few years later, that it was emphatically not a revolution or, as she put it, a 'revolt'. She felt the campaign made 'all of us, Negro and white, realize the possibility of becoming less inhuman humans through commitment and action'. She said that she would have thrown herself into the campaign even if she had known that 'not a single lunch counter would open as a result of my action'.[13]

STUDENTS FOR A DEMOCRATIC SOCIETY

The Student Non-Violent Co-Ordinating Committee (SNCC) was founded in 1960 to provide support for the civil rights movement. It fuelled the militancy of other student political initiatives in the early 1960s. There were organizations in a wide variety of American colleges: Slate had been formed in 1957 at Berkeley; it was matched by Voice in Ann Arbor, Pol in Chicago, the Political Club at Swarthmore, the Progressive Student Alliance at Oberlin and Tocsin at Harvard.

A group of students from Michigan began to consider the virtues of a national federation. Particularly important were Tom Hayden and Alan Haber, Michigan's 'resident radical'. Hayden first looked to the existing National Student Association but he was disappointed by its wary attitude to direct action, and by his own failure to be elected as vice president. Haber persuaded him to invest his energy in Students for a Democratic Society, a body that had emerged in 1960 from the venerable but obscure Student League for Industrial Democracy.

Students for a Democratic Society was a loose federation dominated by a small number of students, at an even smaller number of institutions. It amalgamated existing bodies at different universities but did not exercise much control over them. Hayden reckoned that at first SDS amounted to 800 dues-paying members and a mailing list of about 2,000 names. Others estimated that in 1962 and 1963 the SDS was made up of nine chapters with only 400 members. Its leaders did not even know who was affiliated to their movement. When Todd Gitlin toured the country on behalf of the SDS in 1965 he discovered three chapters that he had not previously known about.[14] Simply having one's name on the books did not necessarily imply active membership: when the name of the 'leftist' who had assassinated Kennedy was announced, Hayden checked that Lee Harvey Oswald was not on the SDS mailing list.[15]

The most important initiative of the SDS came in 1962 when a few dozen young people gathered at Port Huron – a retreat belonging to the United Auto Workers Association with log cabins, forest trails, beaches and dining halls that gave it the feel of a summer camp for teenagers. The group at Port Huron was made up largely of friends recruited through personal contacts. Some of those present had family ties to an established left and they denounced talk of ideological exhaustion, but they were more animated by emotion than by the political argument that might have informed a similar gathering in Europe.

The meeting ended with the Port Huron Statement. This had been drafted mainly by Tom Hayden and it bore the marks of his self-confidence, moral fervour and sociological jargon. The statement expressed disquiet with the self-satisfied materialism of contemporary America and with the technocratic priorities that seemed to imply that the current generation had a 'program without vision'. The statement made much of the way in which the real differences in American politics cut across parties rather than dividing them, and in particular it underlined the role of the 'Dixiecrats' – i.e. those southern

Democrats who opposed civil rights for blacks. The statement also talked of a more radical 'participatory' politics that would bring 'people out of isolation and into community . . . a necessary, though not sufficient, means of finding meaning in personal life'.

The American New Left had peculiarly national characteristics. One of these was its distance from the labour movement. C. Wright Mills had urged the abandonment of the 'labor metaphysic', which assumed that only the organized working class could lead progressive causes. The trade unions in America did not have the explicit connections with left-wing political parties that marked their counterparts in Western Europe. Some of them had become ferociously anti-Communist after the Second World War. Furthermore, in the United States more than anywhere else, students were sufficiently numerous for it to be plausibly argued that they might constitute a force for progress on their own. Those at Port Huron regarded the labour movement as quiescent, which was all the more striking in view of the fact they were guests of a union, and that one of them, Sharon Jeffrey, was the daughter of a union leader.

The second characteristic of the American New Left was its relation to the Cold War. Anti-Communism had bitten more deeply into American internal politics than it did in France or Italy, where the Communist parties were well represented in parliament, or in Britain, where Communists were generally regarded as harmless eccentrics. In the United States during the 1950s, by contrast, expressing sympathy for Communism could ruin a career. Curiously, the legacy of McCarthyism left young radicals of the early 1960s in the US freer than their European contemporaries. Americans never had to take decisions about how they would place themselves in relation to a large Communist Party in their country. The Port Huron Statement took it for granted that no one would admire the Soviet regime but it suggested that peaceful relations with the Soviet Union were desirable. In this respect, the statement somewhat anticipated American diplomacy in the 1960s, and its authors had slightly ambiguous relations with John F. Kennedy, who seemed at that stage to alternate between being a cold warrior and a proponent of détente.

SDS excluded supporters of 'totalitarianism' until the mid-1960s but characteristically it took no concrete steps to enforce such exclusion.

Todd Gitlin (president of the SDS in 1963–4) was later to say that 'anti-anti-Communism was for the New Left what anti-Communism was for post-war liberals and social democrats: the crucible of a political identity'.[16] The failure of the SDS to denounce Communism underlay its first breach with its trade union sponsors.

THE COLD WAR AND THE NEW LEFT

In reality, the thinking of the American New Left probably owed more to the Cold War than its exponents realized. Anti-Communism inside America had often gone with the brutal exercise of state power and with the defence of business interests. Outside its own frontiers, though, the US government built alliances with non-Communist forces and often this meant adopting positions that were left-wing in terms of American domestic politics. Many of those whom the Americans supported in Europe were democratic socialists or even non-Soviet Marxists. Plenty of Europeans who would have been hauled before the House Un-American Activities Committee if they had been born in the US were beneficiaries of discreet American funding in the 1950s. Strom Thurmond – a senator of ferociously conservative views – grumbled that the CIA was 'building socialism behind the backs of the American people'.[17] The author that American student radicals most admired – Albert Camus – was the kind of left-wing non-Communist with whom American policy-makers often made common cause and, indeed, the young Henry Kissinger had tried to persuade Camus to write for a journal that he edited in the 1950s.[18]

Race was a particularly important issue in American foreign policy. Before the federal government had made the slightest effort to desegregate the South, it presented itself as an opponent of European colonialism and as the friend of non-European peoples. The face of American foreign policy was thus different from the face of internal politics in much of the country. The African American Ralph Bunche was a senior State Department official who won a Nobel peace prize for his role in negotiating between Israel and the Palestinians in 1950, at a time when he would not have been served in a coffee shop in Alabama. The American position was riven with hypocrisies. The

United States supported only the 'right' kind of decolonization – which meant that it was doubtful about anything that might lead to Communist regimes or exclude American business from newly independent countries. Defenders of American interests also often presented a deceptively benign picture of race relations in their own country. W.E.B. Du Bois, denied a passport in the 1950s because of his Communist sympathies, wrote that his fellow African Americans who wanted to travel abroad were obliged to 'say the sort of things which our State Department wishes the world to believe'.

However, support for the liberation of colonized peoples abroad, and Cold War competition, did have some influence on American internal policy towards race.[19] The granting of independence to states in sub-Saharan Africa in the late 1950s and early 60s created a new community of black diplomats and politicians with whom the United States sought to have good relations. One highway – Route 40 in Maryland – caused particular problems because foreign dignitaries driving between New York and Washington encountered segregation if they stopped for a meal. Mrs Leroy Merritt of the Bonnie Brae diner justified her refusal to serve a customer from Chad with the words: 'He looked like a run of the mill nigger. I couldn't tell he was an ambassador.'[20]

The fact that the United Nations was based in New York made it hard to separate American diplomacy from domestic politics. Dean Acheson, who had been secretary of state from 1949 to 1953, wrote in 1969 that it might have been better if UN headquarters had been built in Geneva or Copenhagen rather than among the 'conflicting races and nationalities' of Manhattan. Frank Graham, a former president of the University of North Carolina and briefly a senator, was attached to the United Nations by 1955. Graham wrote about civil rights as an instrument in American foreign policy. Desegregation mattered because of its 'strategic moral power in the world-wide struggle between democratic freedom and totalitarian tyranny'; implementing it would speak 'louder than the explosion of the hydrogen bomb'.[21]

Competition with the Soviet Union also stimulated the American government's interest in youth movements. Robert Kennedy, then attorney general, returning from a foreign tour during which he had been a target of student protest, urged that more attention be paid to cultivating young people abroad. It was after this that the government formed an Inter-Agency Committee on Youth Affairs in April 1962. Dean Rusk, the secretary of state, wrote in 1964: 'Young leaders have risen . . . We must broaden our horizon if we wish to gain the initiative against a resourceful and ruthless competitor in the Communist bloc and in the face of considerable disarray in our own ranks.'[22]

The National Student Association (NSA) had been funded by the CIA, as had the International Student Conference, which operated across the non-Communist world, partly so that liberal young Americans could counter Soviet propaganda at international youth meetings. This fact was to arouse much indignation when it was revealed in 1967 and probably contributed to the radicalization of the student movement. But the relationship between student leaders and the CIA was not as incongruous as it came to seem. There were those in the CIA who believed that supporting left-wing causes abroad – particularly with regard to race and decolonization – would serve American interests; in this respect, the agency was more liberal than the FBI, responsible for intelligence operations at home, which seems to have investigated the NSA at the very time in the early 1960s when it was being funded by the CIA.[23]

RELIGION

The final peculiarity of the American New Left lay in the role of religion. Statistical studies showed that there was generally an inverse relation between religious practice and political radicalism in America.[24] The typical American member of the New Left was less likely to practise a religion than his or her contemporaries. A disproportionate number of them – over half according to one study – were secularized Jews.[25] However, particular kinds of religious practice fostered political dissent. The absence of an established or majority Church sometimes underwrote this association. The frontiers between the Church and its enemies – so clear-cut in, say, France or Italy – were blurred in the USA, where there were numerous denominations and where it was possible to feel religious without accepting all the teachings of one religious authority. Religious belief blended with new currents of thought, such as existentialism.[26] Protestant chaplains in universities were often more radical than their colleagues who worked in parishes,[27] while Unitarians and Episcopalians were more likely to be sympathetic to the left than Methodists and Baptists. Quakers, whose belief was based on the rejection of much authority, played an important role in the anti-war movement and their taste for public statements of belief had sometimes made them appear more courageous opponents of McCarthyism than the American Communist Party. Quaker meetings could sometimes look like an anticipation of what the New Left called 'participatory democracy' – though the most famous person in America to have been brought up a Quaker was Richard Nixon.

By contrast, American Catholicism was an authoritarian religion, and the Catholic clergy in America – used to ministering to conservative immigrants from European countries, sometimes ones, such as Poland, that had fallen under Communist rule – were often fierce Cold Warriors. All the same, there were figures in the student movement who were either practising Catholics, such as Maria Varela, or who were in some way influenced by a Catholic upbringing. Vietnam radicalized a group of American Catholics who were increasingly prone to refer to the pope's Pacem in Terris encyclical of 1963 or to the older Catholic traditions that permitted distinctions between just and unjust wars. The priests Daniel and Philip Berrigan made dramatic protests against the war. Burning draft cards seems to have exercised a particular appeal to those who had been brought up on Catholic ceremonial – Tom Cornell, of the Catholic Peace Fellowship, once wrote to the authorities asking for a new draft card so that he could burn it again.[28] Parts of the American Catholic clergy moved so far to the left in the 1960s that student radicals who had reacted against their own Catholic upbringings in the early part of the decade were surprised to find themselves in alliance with priests and nuns by its end.

THE FREE SPEECH MOVEMENT

Berkeley would become the most notorious campus in America in the eyes of the American right (see below), but in the autumn of 1964

87

trouble at the university started over a comparatively trivial matter. The authorities attempted to prevent the setting out of political stalls around Telegraph Road. The resulting stand-off between police and demonstrators launched the Free Speech Movement on the campus. Students deployed the techniques that some of them had learned from the civil rights campaigns in the South. They sat down, climbed on top of a police car (having thoughtfully removed their shoes first) and sang protest songs.

The most prominent figure on the student side was Mario Savio, born in 1942, whose family were of Italian origin. In his youth he had felt a vocation for the priesthood. He had spent the summer of 1963 working in a Catholic anti-poverty programme in Mexico and had gone to Mississippi during the Freedom Summer of 1964. Savio was an intense and troubled person – it was characteristic of him that he spoke with a stammer in private conversations but became fluent when addressing a large audience, and characteristic too that he withdrew from the Free Speech Movement when he feared that he had become identified as its leader. He became famous for a speech delivered in December 1964:

> There's a time when the operation of the machine becomes so odious, makes you so sick at heart, that you can't take part! You can't even passively take part! And you've got to put your bodies upon the gears and upon the wheels . . . upon the levers, upon all the apparatus, and you've got to make it stop! And you've got to indicate to the people who run it, to the people who own it, that unless you're free, the machine will be prevented from working at all.

But this speech was unusual for Savio. In general, his tone was one of ostentatious restraint. He urged students to be 'responsible' in exercising the freedom that they claimed and, in an appropriation of tradition that was characteristic of American student activists in the early 1960s, he insisted that the campaign for free speech was 'conservative' in that it sought to restore the real purpose of a university: 'Our traditionalist view would liken the university to a classical Christian concept of men in the world but not of the world.'

The Free Speech Movement gained a partial victory when the faculty of Berkeley, shocked by arrests after a student sit-in and by the sight of Savio being dragged off stage when he tried to speak at a university meeting, voted to insist on freedom of speech on campus. But there were dangers in this success. It had brought Berkeley to the attention of the authorities and especially to that of the head of the FBI. J. Edgar Hoover wrote in 1966:

Agitators on other campuses take their lead from activities that occur at Berkeley. If imitational activity at Berkeley can be effectively curtailed, this could set off a chain reaction that will result in the curtailment of such activities on other campuses throughout the United States.

THE CULT OF THE GHETTO

Left-wing students, or those who had been students, looked beyond the campus. Involvement in civil rights campaigns had given them an interest in poverty, and the realization that poverty existed in America shook young people who had grown up in the suburbs of the 1950s. SDS established the Economic Research and Action Project (ERAP) in September 1963, which set up community projects in run-down areas of big cities. By 1965, the ERAP, or its affiliates, worked in Baltimore, Chicago, Philadelphia, Boston, Newark and a number of smaller towns. There was a revealing difference between the political evangelism of American students in the mid-1960s and that of their European (especially French) counterparts a few years later. The Europeans were mainly interested in the working class – which in turn meant factories and their largely male workforce (see chap. 9). The Americans, in contrast, concentrated on communities and the 'street' – they yielded to what Al Haber, who was older than most of his comrades in the SDS and more closely associated with the established labour movement, attacked as the 'cult of the ghetto'.[29] At first, this often meant trying to make contact with the unemployed (the SDS expected, wrongly as it turned out, that unemployment would increase in the mid-1960s) and with groups of alienated young people, often in street gangs. Sometimes, though, activists lobbied for improved public services – frequently concerning themselves with unglamorous matters such as potholed roads.

The radical student movement became a victim of its own success. The SDS grew rapidly. Its membership probably peaked in 1968 at about 100,000 – though statistics were never kept assiduously. The organization's formal leadership changed every year and leaders were increasingly selected from outside the small group of friends in the northeast who had first established it. In the mid-1960s, there were rebellions against the leaders of the SDS. Partly these were directed against the very idea of leadership. Partly they were rooted in social differences as the 'prairie power' of less prestigious universities in the west of the country was exerted against those from the most academically selective institutions.[30] Partly they were rooted in disagreements about strategy – particularly when some SDS leaders believed that they should redirect their interests back to the campus and away from community activism.

LYNDON JOHNSON

John F. Kennedy had been president since 1961. The New Left had mixed feelings about him. They disliked his intermittently aggressive anti-Communism, but his youth and the tone of his rhetoric sometimes seemed to mark a break with the complacency of the 1950s. When Kennedy was assassinated in November 1963, his vice president, Lyndon B. Johnson (LBJ), succeeded him. Johnson was a Texan born in 1908. By the late 1960s, he had become so hated by the left that it is hard to recapture the mood that marked the first two years of his presidency. He won the presidential election of 1964 partly by presenting himself as the antithesis of George Wallace, his Dixiecrat rival in his own party, and Barry Goldwater, the right-wing Republican candidate. In particular, Johnson contrasted his moderate stance in foreign policy with the more aggressive one of Goldwater – the most famous advertisement deployed by the Johnson campaign, which juxtaposed a three-year-old girl picking the petals of a daisy and the countdown to nuclear war, had a rather 68ish feel.

Johnson won by a large majority – the largest in modern times. His position was strengthened by Democratic victories in the Senate, the House of Representatives and many state legislatures. The country was prosperous, partly because of the tax cuts that Johnson implemented, and the divisions of the Cold War were less menacing than they had been even just a couple of years previously. *Newsweek* magazine wrote of Johnson in January 1965 that he stood 'at a pinnacle of power that no American had reached before' as leader of 'the mightiest nation in history at a time when that nation is prosperous, calm, and . . . generally sure of purpose'. Johnson, though, who knew that he had come to power 'naked with no presidential covering', never felt secure in his position. He was obsessively aware of comparison with his predecessor and always behaved, as his own vice president was to remark, like the second husband of a demanding wife: 'easily angered by real or imagined slights, trying constantly to erase any memories that might lead to negative comparisons'.[31]

Johnson's energy and ambition were directed for a time into promoting liberal causes. This meant, firstly, that he continued civil rights measures that had begun under Kennedy. He was painfully aware of the damage that supporting black rights would do to the position of his own party in the South, and sometimes, in private conversations with southern Democrats, he implied that legislation on the matter was an unwelcome bequest from his predecessor. Nonetheless, Johnson's public stance was often courageous. The Civil Rights Act – designed to prevent discrimination in areas including employment, suffrage and education – was passed in 1964 and a Voting Rights Act a year later, after Johnson commended it in a speech that included words from the civil rights anthem 'We shall overcome'.

Johnson, who, in conspicuous contrast to Kennedy, had grown up in relatively humble circumstances, also launched what he called a 'war on poverty'. This ran parallel with the community politics of the New Left. Some of the language in Johnson's 'Great Society Speech' of May 1964 had in fact been taken from the Port Huron Statement.[32] Legislation suggested that anti-poverty programmes should involve 'maximum feasible participation' by the poor themselves. Young activists realized that they could be 'insurgents' within government policy – guiding its implementation and using it to promote their own community projects. Tom Hayden wrote of the war on poverty: 'to us it seemed that our movements were again setting the agenda – as we had in civil rights – and the government was responding, giving us legitimacy and a sense of effectiveness'.[33]

In the mid-1960s, there was, therefore, a curious moment when it seemed that Johnson's government and the New Left might be working towards the same aims and might even be united by a wary and partial alliance. Robin Palmer, later to flirt with armed revolution, recalled that in 1964 he had stopped his car to get out and cheer when he heard Johnson's speech on civil rights.[34]

The moment of liberal promise did not last. Johnson had presented his anti-poverty programme in terms that were designed to reassure his own electoral base. He emphasized the benefits that it would bring to poor whites in areas such as the Appalachian hills and he suggested that it would foster economic independence. He also hinted in private conversations that the money might subsidize Tammany Hall politics.[35] However, as it turned out, beneficiaries were often black people in the cities. Furthermore, energetic community organizers realized that many people were not claiming payments to which they were entitled and their efforts, therefore, increased welfare spending. Radical involvement in community programmes evoked disquiet from the conservative Democrats whose support Johnson valued. Richard Daley wrote: 'Does the President know that he is putting money in the hands of subversives? To poor people who aren't part of the organization?'[36] Eventually Daley and Sam Yorty, mayor of Los Angeles, led a campaign against aspects of the anti-poverty programme for promoting 'class struggle'.[37]

Pressure to desegregate schools and housing alienated voters in the North who had supported the ending of more blatant discrimination in the South. Riots in cities – beginning with Watts in Los Angeles in 1965 – seemed to illustrate a new threat of racial violence. The violence in Watts partly occluded one of the last acts of extreme violence committed against civil rights campaigners in the South – the murder of Jon Daniels, an Episcopalian seminarian from New Hampshire who had gone to help with voter registration in Alabama. Johnson's Democratic Party was now losing votes. Northern Democratic leaders either resisted the policy of the federal government – as Daley did in Chicago – or lost to Republicans – as Pat Brown, the governor of California, did to Ronald Reagan in 1966. Most of all, though, American politics were changed by the Vietnam War.

VIETNAM

America was allied with the anti-Communist government that had been installed in South Vietnam, with its capital in Saigon, after the Geneva agreement of 1954, which ended the French presence in Indochina. The Saigon government was opposed by the Communist one ruling in the north of the country, with its capital in Hanoi. In 1964, Johnson had received the authorization of Congress to send troops to Vietnam and he began to do so in 1965. In the short term, this was not an unpopular measure (only two senators had voted against the authorization to send troops) and, importantly, support for the government's policy was at first more marked among the educated than the working class.

Leading members of the New Left, however, opposed the Vietnam War. Over time, this opposition grew and came to mobilize larger numbers of people. Vietnam destroyed all chance of left-wing support for Johnson and ensured that the American left in general was ever more alienated from its own government. In April 1965, the first big rally against the war in Vietnam brought 20,000 people to Washington; two years later, 200,000 demonstrated in New York and 250,000 in San Francisco.

The early demonstrations against Vietnam were restrained occasions. The American New Left was still relatively moderate and still reluctant to indulge in explicit ideological statements. A certain kind of patriotism, particularly one that claimed to represent a 'real America', had mattered to student radicals in the early 1960s. However, this was increasingly replaced by hostility to anything that might be used to justify militarism – demonstrators chanted 'Ho Chi Minh is going to win'. Some American radicals began to regard the history of their own country with a distaste that was probably matched only by their counterparts in West Germany. Young American radicals were increasingly likely to label their own country as 'fascist'.

The effects of the anti-patriotic turn by parts of the American left was magnified by the violence of the response that it evoked. The flag and the national anthem had significance in the USA that would have seemed extraordinary in Europe, where the left had its own anthems and often carried the red flag of Communism or the black flag of anarchy. In Britain in the late 1960s, Labour government ministers still sang lustily about the red flag that had 'shrouded oft our martyrs dead'. In the United States, by contrast, the Stars and Stripes was an important symbol – particularly among a white, working-class population that was often composed of people whose families had arrived in the US earlier in the century. Burning the American flag aroused fury.

Even as the anti-war movement radicalized, apparently aggressive rhetoric could conceal quite subtle positions. In 1965, Tom Hayden visited North Vietnam. This was a dramatic political gesture in itself and one that involved breaking American law. However, Hayden was not a Communist and his succession of brief stops – in Prague, Moscow and Peking – on his way to Hanoi did not encourage him to become one. He travelled with Staughton Lynd, a Quaker pacifist, and Herbert Aptheker, a Communist historian. Hayden's companions were a generation older than himself and they tried, without success, to see whether they could discern the basis of a negotiated peace. On a subsequent visit in 1967, Hayden helped secure the release of three American prisoners of war – an achievement that involved some discreet dealings with the State Department as well as the Vietnamese authorities.

Why then did Vietnam bring about such polarization in American politics? Part of the answer is that it came to suit some on both sides of the debate that it should do so. The political right gained from the most flamboyant gestures of the anti-war movement – conservatives almost certainly talked about flag burning more than radicals did. The right's chances of mobilizing an 'anti-anti-war movement' were better than their chances of mobilizing a pro-war one. Equally, some on the left relished the attention that they could attract with anti-patriotic street theatre.

Sometimes, the insistence of the authorities that opposition to the war must be a subversive act became a self-confirming prophecy. This was particularly true of resistance to the draft. An explicit statement of conscientious objection to the war was likely to be treated as an attempt to overthrow the American way of life. In 1968, two men from Louisiana turned up at a military recruitment centre and announced their refusal to serve. They were asked to look at a list of 300 'subversive' organizations and state whether they belonged to any of them. They refused to do so on the grounds that the request was a violation of their constitutional rights. The officer interviewing them then announced that they would be assumed to be members of all 300.[38]

THE VIETNAM GENERATION

The *Washington Post* described the Vietnam War as a 'generation-wide catastrophe' because so many young men risked being drafted. However, the weight of military obligations fell unevenly. Approximately 27 million men were eligible to be conscripted between 1964 and 1973. Only around 10 million of them served, and of these only a little over 2 million were drafted. The remainder joined as volunteers – though many may have done so because they thought they would be drafted anyway. In all, 2,600,000 went to Vietnam, one in ten of all those who reached military age during the war. France, with a population a quarter of America's, had sent around 1,750,000 men to fight in the Algerian War of 1954–62. In addition to this, the United States deployed a vast logistical back-up that included everything from the maintenance of their helicopters to the manufacture of ice cream for their mess halls – so the majority of American soldiers in Vietnam did not serve in combat units.

At first, young American men were called before draft boards to determine whether they should serve. In 1969 – in a bid to make the system fairer – a lottery was introduced to select the birth dates and initials of men who would be conscripted. Some escaped by good fortune or because they fell into some exempted category – such as only surviving sons. Large numbers of men took steps to reduce their chances of serving. Some claimed conscientious objection to the war. Others applied for educational or professional deferments in order to delay the draft and in the hope that they would reach the age of twenty-six (at which they were too old to be drafted) or that conscription would simply be abolished. Some went abroad – either to put themselves beyond the reach of the authorities or to continue their education in ways that were legal. Even those who submitted to the draft often took steps to ensure that they were not sent to combat units in Vietnam. In particular, many arranged to join the National Guard, whose members were rarely posted abroad. After graduating from Yale, George W. Bush was commissioned into the Texas National Guard as a pilot in May 1968.

Educated men understood the rules best and were most likely to be able to manipulate them – helped by good lawyers who drew attention to procedural irregularities in paperwork by the authorities. Educational deferment was itself the easiest way to avoid being drafted and, even in exile, educated men fared better than their less privileged contemporaries. The Canadian government granted 'immigration points' to men in accordance with their qualifications – so college graduates were most likely to obtain the right to stay in Canada legally and to earn their living. A man's chances of being drafted, going to Vietnam and serving in a combat unit were all inversely correlated with his social status. At first, the burden of combat fell heavily on blacks. At the beginning of the Vietnam War they made up a disproportionate number of combat soldiers – though, thereafter, the army tried to reduce the ethnic inequalities in service. Resistance to the draft was often presented in generational terms (sometimes by figures from the New Left who were disdainful of class-based analysis), but in fact conscription 'succeeded in drawing ever more sharply the lines of class in the United States'.[39] One conscript arrived at his camp in 1968 at the wrong time to begin training straight away and consequently spent his first day of service sorting documents relating to the local draft board. He rang his mother in distress because he had come to understand how easy it was for those with determination and the right contacts to avoid being drafted. He was later killed in Vietnam.[40]

Though Vietnam had the most dramatic effects on young men, it was not necessarily something that pitted them against their elders. There was a moment in 1966 when support for the war was higher among the young than the old. Even when Vietnam seemed to divide fathers and sons in a literal sense, those divisions were not always clear-cut. When James Farrell wrote to his parents to say that he intended to join an anti-Vietnam War march in Washington in 1969, his father, a veteran of the Second World War, replied in angry terms threatening to disown him. James sent a long reply in which he repeated his intention and explained his reasons. He was surprised to find the second letter among his father's possessions after his death. He concluded that his father had, in private, admired at least some aspect of his stand against Vietnam.[41]

Because there had been a good deal of social mobility through education in the 1960s, workers were likely to be older than the educated and the generational divide in a single family might also be a class divide that separated a blue-collar father from a graduate son. Workers often disliked the ostentatious anti-patriotism of much of the anti-war movement. However, their attitudes to the war were complicated. The fact that their sons were being sent to Vietnam in disproportionate numbers might make the working classes hostile to anti-war protest, but it did not make them approve of the war. In his history of campus activism, Kenneth Heineman recalls that his own blue-collar father, a veteran of the Second World War, loathed 'hippies and potheads', and voted for the right-wing George Wallace in the 1972 Michigan primary. But he opposed the Vietnam War and wanted his oldest son to go to Canada to avoid the draft – the son in question served in Vietnam before becoming a student anti-war activist. Heineman concludes thus. 'Our family hated Nixon, the Vietnam War and the peace movement.'[42]

Bruce Springsteen was born into a working-class family in 1949. A rock star with liberal politics, he belonged to the culture of the late 1960s but his songs were bittersweet evocations of blue-collar life. His relations with his own father – a truck driver who combined expressions of social conservatism with bursts of rebellion that prevented him from holding down a job – were awkward. His father taunted him that the army would make him cut his hair. But when Bruce Springsteen *fils* came home in 1969 to say that he had failed the army medical, his father said simply: 'That's good.'

One intergenerational argument occurred at a Passover meal involving three families – the Bluestones, the Reuthers and the Woodcocks – in 1967. Barry Bluestone, born in 1944, opened the event by reading from speeches by Martin Luther King and First World War poetry. Then Walter Reuther – born in 1907 and a leader of the United Automobile Workers Union – broke the family 'truce' by trying to defend his union's support for American policy in

Vietnam.[43] The argument was particularly poignant because some of the older members of the family had in fact tried to shift the policy of the union movement to the left on this issue. In private Walter Reuther wrote about the morality of the war: 'I wish God would give someone the wisdom to say with absolute certainty this is the right position.'[44]

POLICING THE AMERICAN 68

The style of American policing also helped radicalize the American left.[45] In much of Europe, police forces were discouraged from entering university premises. In the United States, universities had their own police forces and these sometimes took it upon themselves to spy on student organizations. They called for reinforcements from outside when they felt the need. Sometimes this meant local police forces but sometimes it meant the National Guard, soldiers whose lack of real military experience often made them trigger-happy. A French official – discussing the limited means at his own disposal when faced with the occupation of the Sorbonne in May 1968 – wistfully reported the view of an American that a similar disturbance at Berkeley would be put down with live ammunition.[46] The worst police violence on American campuses was usually seen at less prestigious institutions. In May 1967, Houston policemen fired 4,000 rounds while attempting to regain control of a mainly black campus at Texas State University.[47] They fired with such abandon that two of their own were wounded by ricochets. Violence by the police or National Guard often went with visceral contempt for protesters. After guardsmen had shot four unarmed students at Kent State in 1970, a father went to pick up his dead daughter's property. Her landlord informed him that 'everyone' in the area supported the National Guard and then asked for the outstanding rent money.[48] Division between policemen and protesters was associated with broader splits between parts of the working class and educated radicals. Policemen, often of Irish origin, were rooted in a culture that went with municipal machine politics, police unions, male camaraderie and an emphasis on working-class respectability that frequently entailed a strong racial element.

The FBI collected information so assiduously that it became a matter of pride for veterans of radical movements to summon up thousands of pages of reports on themselves, released under Freedom of Information requests, with which they enlivened their autobiographies. One historian was to write an academic article based on FBI surveillance of the various movements to which she had belonged.[49] The FBI did not simply watch protesters, as police and intelligence services did in all democratic countries. It infiltrated their movements and sometimes its agents promoted illegal acts – either to discredit activists or to provide the authorities with an excuse for repression. This meant that undercover agents could be pitted against each other. When the dean at Louisiana University was shouted down by a group of students, an undercover policeman in the crowd handed him a megaphone. But the leader of the shouting students was himself an FBI agent.[50] The FBI's infiltration of leftist groups produced some moments of high farce – partly because J. Edgar Hoover, the head of the bureau until his death in 1972, insisted that his men were tidy and clean-cut. Agents who wanted to blend in at demonstrations had to enter a kind of double clandestinity by cultivating an appearance that was against official rules: in California, one such unofficial squad referred to themselves as 'the beards'. Men under cover could find themselves in odd positions. An FBI man in Venice Beach in Los Angeles once watched Tom Hayden's car being vandalized. When he reported the matter, he was given to understand that the damage had in fact been done by another police agency.[51]

BLACK POWER

The changing political climate of America was also linked to race. The early civil rights movement had seen considerable violence inflicted on protesters by southern police, but the protesters themselves had made a virtue of 'non-violence' – sometimes, admittedly, a virtue that was preached more than it was practised. It was an optimistic movement – fuelled partly by the belief that a better, and more truly American, future lay ahead. Civil rights had underwritten a broad political alliance. This took in black and white. It cut across religion – mobilizing highly secularized people but also presenting its cause in religious language. Political liberals – and in the north many whose politics were fairly conservative – supported the aims of civil rights, even when they felt concerned about the tactics that civil rights campaigners sometimes deployed.

In the mid-1960s, things began to change. In part, this was because the early legal and political victories of civil rights opened up broader and more awkward questions about the disadvantages that might face African Americans. It was also because the focus of attention for some activists moved away from the South and towards the growing black populations of the northern cities – areas in which racial segregation, without being enforced by law, was sometimes as marked as it was in the South.

In any case, the black population of America had been moving north for some time. This was mainly a product of demand for industrial labour, especially during and after the Second World War, but it was exacerbated by the civil rights campaign itself. As black workers became more expensive and less deferential some white farmers substituted machinery for labour. The black population of Berkeley in California had stood at 3,395 (4 per cent of the population) in 1940; by 1960, it had reached 21,850 (20 per cent) and by 1970 was 27,421 (24 per cent).[52]

There was a change inside the organizations that had emerged from the civil rights campaign. In 1966, Stokely Carmichael, who had been born in Trinidad in 1941 and grown up in New York, became leader of the Student Non-Violent Co-Ordinating Committee. Carmichael, like many black activists, was influenced by Frantz Fanon, whose *The Wretched of the Earth* had been published in France in 1961 and translated into English in 1963. Fanon's work addressed questions of 'blackness' and anti-colonial struggle. He justified violence – or at least opposed non-violence – and some of the subtleties of his views on this were probably lost in translation. *The Wretched of the Earth* was a bleakly pessimistic book – written while Fanon was dying of leukaemia. Reading Fanon encouraged black militants to think of themselves as inhabitants of a colony making common cause with other parts of the Third World rather than as citizens of the United States seeking to exercise their rights in their

own country. The 1955 Afro-Asian Conference in Bandung, Indone-
sia, the creation of independent states in sub-Saharan Africa
(beginning in Ghana in 1957) and the Cuban Revolution of 1959 all
had an influence in America. Castro ostentatiously stayed at the
Hotel Theresa in Harlem when he came to New York. One journalist
was later to allege that the SNCC was 'Fidel Castro's arm in the
United States'.

In July 1966, Carmichael gave an impromptu speech after his
release from prison in Greenwood, Mississippi, where he had been
detained during a march. He claimed that black people had gained
little from the emphasis on integration and suggested that the civil
rights slogan 'Freedom Now' should be replaced by the call for 'Black
Power'. Soon after this the SNCC began to exclude white members.
One historian has written:

> Black Power is most remembered as the civil rights era's ruthless twin,
> an evil doppelganger that provoked a white backlash, engaged in
> thoughtless acts of violence and rampaging sexism and misogyny and
> was brought to an end by its own self destructive rage.[53]

In reality, things were more complicated. Black Power sprang partly
from disappointment with what had been achieved by King's Southern Christian Leadership Convention and disappointment with the
Democratic Party, particularly after its leaders refused to allow an
alternative delegation from Mississippi to replace the all-white one
that the state's established Democratic Party sent to the Atlantic City
Democratic National Convention of 1964. But the break with previous organizations was not absolute. Black Power drew in movements
and styles of activism that had been around in the 1950s and that had
often worked in parallel and in cooperation with the early civil rights
movement. Carmichael continued to work with Martin Luther King
and in 1967 helped persuade King to call for American withdrawal
from Vietnam. Carmichael denounced 'compromise-orientated political parties', but this did not mean a rejection of all electoral
politics – on the contrary, Black Power drew on the example of the
Lowndes County Freedom Organization, which had sought to circumvent the white Democratic establishment in Alabama by running
an independent slate of candidates.[54] Quite moderate politicians

deployed a radical language drawn from global struggles against imperialism and sometimes applied it to mundane issues of local politics – such as the financial problems caused by 'white flight' from inner cities. Donald McCullum of the National Association for the Advancement of Colored People in Oakland said that the suburbs 'are the ones that have enslaved us, we are their colonies'.[55]

Black Power activists were not as violent as their most widely quoted spokesmen suggested and the civil rights movement had not been as peaceful as some of its leaders claimed. In any case, when violence occurred, it often sprang not from incitement by leaders but from the despair of those faced with violence from the other side – this was what had provoked riots in Birmingham, Alabama in 1963 and it was to do so again on a larger scale after King's assassination in April 1968. The only reference to violence in Carmichael's speech of 1966 came when he urged black people to refrain from violence against each other.

At first, Carmichael opposed the exclusion of white people from the SNCC. In any case, far from being a terrifying monolith of political conformity, the SNCC was a ramshackle organization which had grown quickly – its staff had expanded from about two dozen to more than 150 in the aftermath of the Freedom Summer. It was often too poor to afford the modest salaries to which its organizers were theoretically entitled. Some white radicals supported Black Power and often expressed this with a touch of masochism. Greg Calvert, of the SDS, said in Princeton in February 1968: 'We owe the SNCC a deep debt of gratitude for having slapped us brutally in the face with the slogan of black power.'[56] Other white activists quietly left the SNCC of their own accord – either because they had come to think that black autonomy might be a good thing or because they did not want the movement to be damaged by public acrimony. At local level, white and black veterans of the SNCC sometimes remained on good terms. Even when they were separate, Black Power activists and white radicals continued in large measure to work in parallel – they were, in particular, both opposed to the Vietnam War.

In spite of all this, Black Power seemed a disturbing novelty to some whites who had supported civil rights. Casey Hayden wrote of her exclusion from the SNCC: 'to me the movement was everything:

home and family, food and work, love and a reason to live. When I was no longer welcome there, and then when it was no longer there at all, it was hard to go on.'[57] Black Power also often engendered fear or hostility among the white population of northern cities. The very ambiguity of the words 'Black Power' could evoke a sense of menace that underlined racial division. A survey in Detroit after large-scale riots in the summer of 1967 showed that most blacks interpreted 'Black Power' as a simple expression of support for a 'fair share for black people' or 'racial unity' – though a slight majority of black people seem to have actually disliked the phrase and almost a quarter said it meant 'nothing'. Whites were more hostile and almost 40 per cent believed that the phrase implied black power over whites.[58]

The most visible expression of Black Power came from the Black Panther Party (BPP). The name was first used by a black self-defence group in Alabama. But it was made famous in 1966 when Bobby Seale, born in Texas in 1936, and Huey Newton, born in Louisiana in 1942, founded the Black Panther Party for Self-Defense in Oakland, California. They incarnated the mood of relatively young men whose families had come from the South and who embraced a more aggressive style of politics than that traditionally practised by the northern black establishment. The Black Panthers offered to defend their communities against police harassment. They adopted a militaristic style of dress – black berets, gloves and leather jackets. They also carried guns. Almost the first thing that Newton and Seale did was to buy a pistol and an M1 rifle – Newton took the rifle because the terms of his parole forbade him from carrying a pistol. Guns came to define the Black Panthers in the eyes of many Americans – including, perhaps, their admirers. Newton was tried and imprisoned for shooting a police officer in 1967 – he was released in 1970.

Images of gun-toting Black Panthers were a gift to every magazine picture editor in the country but they were deceptive. Carrying guns was a piece of political theatre rather than a serious threat to the authority of the state – no one imagined that the Panthers would win a battle with the police. In Chicago in 1969, police raided an apartment in which Fred Hampton and other Black Panthers were staying. The Panthers fired two shots – one of which seems to have been the result of a post-mortem reflex action. The police fired almost a hundred rounds.

The people with most cause to fear violence from the BPP were other black activists as leaders sought to impose discipline and suppress rival groups. Angela Davis first started to carry a gun after a Black Panther, possibly an *agent provocateur*, held a pistol to her head.[59]

The attitude of the Black Panthers to firearms was in many respects a legalistic one. They were careful to observe the rules about how and when they could carry weapons. Just as the early civil rights campaign had insisted that black people should have the right to vote or to attend universities, the Black Panthers insisted that they should enjoy the same rights with regard to arms that were so valued by much of white America. The most dramatic incident staged by the Panthers – when they took their guns to the state legislature at Sacramento – was designed to exercise and defend a right rather than to make a threat.

The Black Panthers aroused huge interest. Hanif Kureishi, born in 1954 to a Pakistani father and an English mother and living in the London suburbs, tore down his Rolling Stones posters to replace them with pictures of Seale and Newton. Movements such as the Chinese Red Guards in San Francisco[60] or the Red Army Faction in West Germany modelled themselves on the Black Panthers, as did aboriginal activists in Australia. J. Edgar Hoover believed for a time that the Black Panthers were the most serious internal threat to his country.

For all the admiration and/or fear that they aroused, the Black Panthers never directly mobilized more than a few thousand people in the United States and many of these belonged more to a loose federation of different local associations than to a centralized organization.[61] When the BPP began to assert more centralized control, and to embark on a more institutionalized form of politics in the early 1970s, they withdrew to their original base in Oakland and effectively abandoned the claim to be a national party. The BPP was also undermined by internal feuding. At first, the BPP in Oakland existed alongside another one – 'a small cadre group . . . to develop theoretical analyses of the Black movement'[62] – based in Los Angeles. The two eventually reached a *modus vivendi* after having come close to violence against each other. In February 1971, Eldridge Cleaver, who had become the Black Panthers' 'minister of information' argued with Huey Newton during a television show – Cleaver participated by phone from Algeria where he had sought refuge from prosecution in the US. The two men expelled each other from the party and it was not until early 1972 that Newton and Seale regained control of the movement they had founded.

Their dramatic image sometimes concealed the relatively subtle positions that the Black Panthers took on some issues. They were exponents of racial autonomy but not racial separation. Their politics were designed for California rather than for the segregated South or, for that matter, for those northeastern cities in which black people might constitute the majority of inhabitants of large areas. They were interested in class as well as race. They built a cross-racial alliance and – to a greater extent than many white civil rights activists – they recognized the complexity of a population that included Hispanics, Asians and native Americans as well as blacks and whites. The BPP supported Cesar Chavez and the mainly Mexican United Farm Workers.[63]

Much of what the BPP did involved unspectacular local organization rather than armed insurrection. In January 1969, and working with an Irish Catholic priest, they provided free breakfasts in the hope that this would help black children to do better at school.[64] The BPP also sought to provide health care for racial minorities and to establish People's Free Medical Clinics.[65] Most importantly, the Black Panther Party was, as its name suggests, a political organization which, especially in the early 1970s, worked through the electoral system (see chap. 11).

VIOLENCE

Reactions to the Black Panthers, and to Black Power generally, became associated with a wider fear of violence in the late 1960s. Riots pitted the urban poor against the police. In the week that followed King's assassination in 1968, there were riots in 125 cities with 20,000 arrests and 2,600 fires that caused $100 million of damage. Buildings burned just a few blocks from the White House. Such riots did not usually have explicitly political roots. They also ran on a different clock from the student radical movement. In spite of the disturbances that followed the King assassination, urban riots in America seemed most dangerous in 1967 and declined thereafter, at the very moment when white leftists were becoming more attracted to violence. However, riots contributed to a general dramatization of American political conflicts. Conservatives often lumped rioters and political protesters together and a few radicals looked with interest to urban rioters as potential recruits to a revolutionary cause.

The simple availability of weapons was an important part of the American 68. A general alleged that the population of Chicago had more handguns than the US army.[66] Obsession with the right to bear arms was one of the ways in which certain kinds of radicals drew on a rhetoric that was similar to that of their enemies. Some black militant organizations were affiliated with the conservative National Rifle Association.[67] The Dodge Revolutionary Union Movement (a quasi-Marxist black nationalist organization at the Dodge main plant in Detroit, Michigan) offered an M.1 carbine as a prize in a fund-raising raffle.[68]

THE COUNTER-CULTURE

Alongside and sometimes intertwined with increasing political radicalism went a challenge to middle-class respectability. Men grew their hair longer and sported beards. In Berkeley, the 'Filthy Speech Movement' grew up in the wake of Savio's Free Speech Movement and insisted, much to Savio's distaste, that free speech must include the freedom to utter obscenities. Rock bands – Jefferson Airplane, the Grateful Dead, the Doors – came to be regarded as though they were the centre of religious cults rather than entertainers.

Drugs were nothing new for American young people. Marijuana was common in Texas and some of the earnest students from the Christian Faith and Life Community in Austin in the early 1960s had smoked pot, a habit that occasionally aroused disapproval among their more buttoned-up comrades from the north-east. What was new in the late 1960s was the use of LSD – pioneered by Timothy Leary – as a means to transform reality.

Sometimes it seemed that the counter-culture was a deliberate retreat from political radicalism. It offended potential allies – including Black Power militants – who were conservative on matters of personal behaviour. It sometimes revolved around a private world of meditation, hallucination and long stoned conversations about spaceships. The New Left had once sought to join the Washington government's 'war on poverty'. Now it sometimes seemed that hippies who stood begging on street corners had embraced poverty as a 'lifestyle'. The French sociologist Edgar Morin claimed that some of the hippies that he encountered in California in 1969 renounced shoes but kept their cars.[69]

REAGAN

The counter-culture, like Black Power, existed in a symbiotic relation with its most vociferous critics. One man in particular came to incarnate the 'counter-counter-culture'. Ronald Reagan was elected as governor of California in 1966 and again in 1970. A divorced film star who had never seen active service during the Second World War, though he rose to the rank of captain in a unit making propaganda films, Reagan was not an obvious representative of cultural conservatism and might have attracted some derision if he had risen to prominence in the 1950s. As it was, his campaign team quickly realized the advantages that could be derived from student unrest: 'Reagan escalated it into an issue and then it started showing up in the polls.' Reagan himself recalled: 'in the mountains, in the desert, the biggest cities of the state, the first question is "what are you going to do about Berkeley?" And each time the question itself would get the biggest applause.'[70]

When Reagan said 'Berkeley', though, he did not really mean the university. After his election, he contrived the dismissal of Clark Kerr, the liberal president of the university, but on the whole he interfered relatively little in the affairs of the most prestigious of the California state universities. The biggest confrontation between authority and students in California came at San Francisco State University, which had a less high academic profile and a less privileged student body. In fact, Berkeley suited Reagan as a symbol of a wider malaise that his supporters discerned in universities. He traded on the fact that Stokely Carmichael had visited Berkeley and invited students to burn their draft cards, and he claimed, in February 1969, that 'thirty-five negroes' had held a switchblade to the throat of a college dean.[71] The conduct of white students – relatively privileged young people – also exercised Reagan's electorate. He hinted darkly about drug use, sexual promiscuity and 'some indications of other happenings that cannot be mentioned', and in more amusing terms he commented on men who 'dress like Tarzan, walk like Jane and smell like Cheetah'.

ROBERT KENNEDY

The radicalization of left-wing politics in America was partly counteracted by preparation for the presidential election of 1968. There had been a Democrat in the White House since 1961. Vietnam had created an acrimonious division between most of those who thought of themselves as liberals, or especially radicals, and Lyndon Johnson. There was, though, a chance that a different candidate might transform politics. For a time, it seemed that Eugene McCarthy (a Democratic senator from Minnesota) might be such a candidate. He declared his intention to seek the nomination in late 1967, at a time when it was assumed that he stood no chance of winning. American reverses in Vietnam made his candidacy seem more plausible in 1968 and young activists joined his campaign during the New Hampshire primary. At one point, a barber was employed to get long-haired and bearded men 'clean for Gene'.

McCarthy's unexpected success partly provoked Johnson into declaring that he would not seek re-election. Johnson's withdrawal was especially important because Robert Kennedy, the younger brother of the assassinated president, had just announced that he would seek the Democratic nomination. Kennedy's relation with American radicalism was odd. Coming from a wealthy dynasty and having already served in his brother's administration as attorney general, he was hardly an outsider. He had supported an attempt to overthrow Castro and, as a representative of American power, he had provoked hostile student demonstrations when he visited Japan in 1962. As late as 1967, and in a book that was widely admired on the American left, the Frenchman Régis Debray had presented Robert

Kennedy as an arch exponent of American power.[72] Kennedy had called for a halt in US bombing of North Vietnam and the beginning of negotiations but he had done so relatively late. Even in 1968, he reproached McCarthy for suggesting that Communists should be taken into a coalition government in Vietnam. Lyndon Johnson feared that Robert Kennedy might outflank him on his right, and blame him for having squandered the hawkish legacy of the elder Kennedy.

However, Kennedy's image was to the left of his policies. At forty-two, he was seventeen years younger than Johnson and nine years younger than McCarthy. He looked even younger and his manner was sometimes that of a first-year philosophy student who is worried about the implications of Nietzsche for his religious faith. He had been shaken by his brother's assassination. It had stimulated him to think about questions of life, death and morality in ways that made him unusual among politicians – his commonplace book was full of quotations from Camus. The assassination had also given him some old-fashioned political advantages. It had meant that he had been out of power during the escalation of the Vietnam War – though nothing in his record suggested that he would have prevented that escalation. His visceral hostility to Johnson, which might have made him look petty in 1964, made him look like a statesman in 1968. He was imbued with the mystique that had been conferred on his family by his brother's early death.

Robert Kennedy made radical gestures. He was with Cesar Chavez when he broke the fast that he had undertaken in support of farm workers. His interlocutors believed that Kennedy was sincere, though they were continually disappointed by his reluctance to take clear stands – Hayden shrewdly compared him to Mendès France, whose silence in 1968 so exasperated his young admirers (see chap. 5).[73] Kennedy's hesitations, and his initial reluctance to take on Johnson, may have reflected real doubts that were rooted in his own emotional and intellectual crisis but they were also typical of a man with strong political instincts – one who understood the need to preserve his freedom of manoeuvre and to avoid alienating potential supporters.

The relation between Kennedy and American radicalism was mainly one way: the radicals cared about Kennedy more than he cared about them. Arthur Schlesinger Jr – the Harvard professor and one of the

Kennedy family's most important *consiglieri* – had himself been a Marxist in his youth. The leaders of Students for a Democratic Society brought him a copy of the Port Huron Statement when he was working in the White House[74] – though Schlesinger did not regard the episode as sufficiently important to be recorded in his diary. In 1967, Schlesinger met leaders of the Boston SDS – in a 'studiously dreary apartment' with a photograph of Che Guevara on the wall. Their 'murky abstractions' filled him with 'irritated nostalgia' though he still preferred their style to the 'ideological megalomania' of the 1930s.[75] His views about relations between Robert Kennedy, to whom he was close, and student radicalism were expressed in terms of flippant cynicism. He remarked that the Republican Nelson Rockefeller and RFK (i.e. Robert Kennedy) were the 'main hopes' and that without them 'the country risks a massive defection of the young to SDS . . . or LSD'.[76]

CHICAGO

In June 1968, Kennedy was shot dead in California by an unbalanced Palestinian who seems to have acted alone. The assassination turned Robert Kennedy into a martyr, in spite, or because, of the fact that no one could be sure what cause he had died serving. The political beatification of Kennedy as the incarnation of youthful idealism made surviving politicians seem drab. This mood was exacerbated by the Democratic Party Convention, which was held in Chicago from 26 to 29 August 1968. The competition to be the next Democrat presidential candidate now pitted McCarthy against George McGovern, who presented himself as Kennedy's replacement, and Hubert Humphrey. Humphrey was vice president and, though he had not even been a candidate in the primaries, was supported by a majority of delegates to the convention as well as by Johnson. If the Kennedy political machine had still been involved in the race, then Humphrey might have had a fight on his hands. As it was, Johnson found it relatively easy to manipulate the process. For many, the convention was all the more disappointing because it was the first to take place after the 'Dixiecrats' had lost their hold on the party in the South.

Anti-war protesters came to Chicago. At first the protest was coordinated by David Dellinger – a 53-year-old pacifist from a patrician background who had driven an ambulance during the Spanish Civil War and been imprisoned for resisting the draft in the Second World War. He was keen to prevent violence. He was joined by younger radicals, including Tom Hayden and Rennie Davis of the SDS. In addition to this, Jerry Rubin and Abbie Hoffman, who had founded the Yippies or Youth International Party at the end of the previous year, came to Chicago, as did Bobby Seale of the Black Panthers. Protesters gathered in a park about ten miles from the Hilton Hotel, in which the convention was taking place.

The organizers had promised hundreds of thousands would turn up. As it happened, only about 10,000 did so, but the atmosphere was now so febrile that the authorities behaved as though they were faced with an armed insurrection. Almost 12,000 policemen were on duty and they were supported by 5,000 members of the National Guard. Six thousand soldiers, including the elite 101st Airborne, were posted to the suburbs and it was said that around 1,000 undercover agents infiltrated the crowd.[77] The Yippies relished the chance to perform in front of such an audience and threatened, among other things, to put LSD in the Chicago water supply. At any other time, the authorities might have laughed this off, but the police placed extra guards on water-processing plants even after the Water and Sewer Department assured them that it would take five tons of the drug to have serious effects.[78] Writers – including Jean Genet, William Burroughs and Gore Vidal – gathered in Chicago like theatre critics preparing to review an opening night.

Chicago was already a divided city. The growth of industry during and after the Second World War had transformed its population. There were now more African Americans in Cook County than in the state of Mississippi – though there were also many whites from the South as well as a large population with Irish origins. The police force had been reformed since the 1950s, when the police commissioner had wealth that could not have derived from his modest salary, but it was still not noted for its liberalism or probity. There was no formal segregation in Chicago but there was much division and inequality and this had been exposed in riots – particularly those that followed the assassination of Martin Luther King – when the mayor, Richard Daley, had ordered the police to 'shoot to kill'.

In private, Daley was opposed to the Vietnam War. When Johnson asked him how to extract America from it, Daley tersely suggested that he recall how he had got into it and then retrace his steps. But the mayor's opposition to Vietnam, and for that matter his later expression of regret about the behaviour of the police in 1968, were private. In public, Daley – a 66-year-old Irish Catholic who sounded tough on law and order and conservative on social issues – was tailor-made for the demonology of protesters. Daley himself was pathetically anxious for the convention to provide a showcase for his beloved city and consequently keen to deter demonstrations. He failed. The studied moderation of early protests against Vietnam had vanished.

Many on the streets of Chicago revelled in their estrangement from the political mainstream – notably when they staged a ceremony to elect a pig as a presidential candidate. The pig was seized by the authorities and handed over to the Chicago Humane Society, a lucky escape for an animal in a city that had until recently built its prosperity largely on slaughterhouses. Eventually, the city gave authorization for the protesters to hold a rally in Grant Park. But by this time the police were tired and angry – one official saw some of them weighting their gloves with lead shot. When a young man tried to pull down the American flag, the officers advanced and launched what a report referred to as a 'police riot'. One woman later recalled: 'It was like the Bastille stormed us.' A few demonstrators subsequently managed to get through to the Hilton Hotel, in which the convention was based, and the police sprayed tear gas with such abandon that Hubert Humphrey could smell it in his room on the twentieth floor.

Daley had wanted to keep the convention separate from the demonstrations. Heavy-handed security men were hostile to anyone, even accredited delegates, who looked as though they might not be favourable to Humphrey. Dan Rather, the anchor man for CBS, was manhandled by security guards as he was broadcasting. Delegates found it hard to ignore what was happening outside. Abraham Ribicoff, a 58-year-old senator, nominated George McGovern with the words 'with George McGovern as President of the United States we wouldn't have to have Gestapo tactics on the streets of Chicago'. The words that Daley shouted in response were drowned out in the noise, but some claimed that they were: 'Fuck you, Jew son of a bitch.'

Humphrey's final nomination took place at the very moment when broadcast companies began to get tapes of street violence that had happened forty minutes previously. Some cut away from the nomination to show film of this. The convention broke up in chaos with some delegates singing 'We shall overcome' while the band played on stage in an attempt to drown them out. Both sides lost. Johnson and Daley had thwarted what seemed to be the wishes of most Democrats, but the police violence had turned many liberals against the Democratic establishment and the demonstrations themselves turned much of Middle America against any kind of Democrat. No one could have regarded the denouement of the convention as a triumph for Humphrey.

Eight people – including Dellinger, Hayden, Hoffman, Rubin, Davis and Seale – were prosecuted for riot after the Chicago convention. Seale managed to secure a separate trial and was eventually sentenced for contempt of court. The judge and prosecutor adopted some extraordinary expedients: at one point, Seale was made to sit in court after having been bound and gagged. In the end, five defendants were sentenced to jail terms. The convictions were overturned on appeal and further convictions for contempt of court did not attract a prison sentence. Hoffman and Rubin regarded the trial as a useful piece of political theatre. For the others, it was an exhausting and depressing waste of time.

Tom Hayden later drew bitter comparisons between the violence that he endured at police hands in 1968 and that which he had suffered earlier in the decade during the civil rights campaign. Civil rights had pitched protesters against state authorities and the local branches of the Democratic Party but the protesters felt that they were to some extent supported by the federal government. Now violence came from the police in a major city of the north and was supported by someone who was close to the White House.

Hayden also knew that neither he nor anyone else was really in control of the movement in whose name he sometimes spoke. He felt that there was a new mood on the left, which he found unsympathetic. It was more ideological and less humane. Students for a Democratic Society was now divided between two factions – both of which would have been regarded as extreme in 1962. One was associated with the Progressive Labor Party (PLP), a breakaway from the American Communist Party, which had infiltrated the SDS after the latter had abandoned its ban – never, in any case, very strictly enforced – on Communist members. The PLP was made up of puritanical Maoists who disdained the counter-culture and sought to incite revolution among the American working class – though their only real working-class contacts were to be found in a small segment of the New York garment industry (see chap. 9). On the other side was the Revolutionary Youth Movement (RYM), which emphasized international struggle and which admired the Black Panthers. The RYM in turn divided into two factions, the most extreme of which became the Weathermen and began to advocate armed action. At its Chicago conference in June 1969, the SDS broke up acrimoniously into two different bodies. Both claimed the name. The Revolutionary Youth Movement kept the files and membership lists although a greater number of delegates at the conference had supported the PLP. By this time some members of the SDS had come to regard the gyrations of their own organization with disdain, and at its last convention one group suggested that a garbage can be elected as its leader.

Those who were part of the American 68 were often aware of a paradox. On the one hand, radicals in the US had substantial achievements to their credit. They played a part in changing the place of race in America, they turned much of the population, especially among the young and educated, against the Vietnam War. They had established organizations in the most unpromising of territories – including the University of Georgia, where students had at the beginning of the 1960s campaigned *against* racial integration.[79] They had helped to destroy the presidency of Lyndon Johnson. On the other hand, 68 in America, more than almost anywhere else in the world, was regarded as a 'failure'. One historian wrote:

> The protests in the United States never came anywhere as near to bringing about fundamental political transformation as did protests in countries like France and Czechoslovakia, where major segments of society beyond the academy mobilized. Even together, the anti-war

student and civil rights Black Power and developing Mexican American movements remained too small, marginal and diffuse to threaten the basic social order.[80]

In part, the sense of failure was rooted in one word: Nixon. Richard Nixon won the presidential election in December 1968. Political defeat was not in itself unusual for 68ers – the French faced the Gaullist victory in the legislative elections of June 1968 and the Czechs faced the Warsaw Pact invasion of August. Nixon's victory, however, had a particularly sharp edge for his enemies. It was they who had damaged his predecessor and his campaign was based to a large extent on mobilizing against radicalism. Nixon had been greeted by a crowd of 400,000 people at a rally that he staged in Chicago immediately after the Democratic Convention of 1968. Curiously, Nixon's own policies were in some ways constrained by the protests of 68. It was partly the anti-Vietnam protest movement that persuaded him that the United States needed to withdraw from Vietnam.[81] One result of 68 in the USA was that a movement that had, at least in its early stages, expounded 'idealism' and 'authenticity' ended by forcing a settlement on men who were driven by tough-minded realism.

The architect of Nixon's foreign policy – Henry Kissinger – seemed the antithesis of 68. Kissinger's own youth had been one of discipline and hard work. He had come to America as a German-Jewish refugee, worked his way through college and served in the American army – the institution that did most to mould him. He was a clever, witty and ostentatiously cynical man who combined an admiration for the USA as a force for good in the world with a breezy lack of interest in American culture or society. He admired the European statesmen of the nineteenth century, whose definition of national interest had owed little to electoral considerations, and he regarded Charles de Gaulle as the last survivor of this breed. Kissinger despised student agitators though, unlike his French friend Raymond Aron, he never took them seriously enough to view them as a threat to the established order.

In part, the sense of failure associated with 68 in the United States went with with a long-term shift in American domestic politics. The fact that 68ers constituted a minority was, again, not in itself that unusual – the same would have been true in most European countries. What was unusual was the fact that reaction against 68 was an important part of a realignment that brought large parts of the white working class to move from supporting the Democrats to the Republicans. The greatest beneficiary of this was not Nixon but the one man who had most self-consciously defined his political position in opposition to 'Berkeley': Ronald Reagan.

The fact that the student left had mobilized in America before it mobilized in most of Europe meant that some felt the later 1960s had not lived up to the promise of the earlier part of the decade. The relatively non-ideological nature of the New Left in the early 1960s also contributed to this disappointment. Unlike their European counterparts, many American student radicals did not enjoy the emotional detachment entailed by Marxism and some of them interpreted the increasing emphasis on explicit ideology in their own movement as an ominous sign. The acrimonious splits (on political grounds) in Students for a Democratic Society and (on political/racial grounds) in the Student Non-Violent Co-Ordinating Committee left many feeling that they had been evicted from their own political homes. Most of all, the New Left in America shared one important quality with many of its enemies. Both sides believed that America was special. This exceptionalism was, as the decade wore on, increasingly turned upside down. From having believed that the United States had a unique potential for good, parts of the American left came to believe that 'Amerika' was uniquely bad. 68 itself became part of this exceptionalism – something that was understood not as a political disappointment but as, in the word that historians of America often use, an 'apocalypse'.

5
France

Though this appears at first glance to be a photograph of student protest, it looks, on closer examination, as though these young people are attending the pro-Gaullist demonstration of 30 May 1968.

The Short 68: The May Events in France

Wednesday 1 May	March in Paris by left-wing parties and Communist trade unions
Thursday 2 May	Georges Pompidou leaves for Iran
Friday 3 May	Meeting at the Sorbonne which is evacuated by police. Courses there suspended
Saturday 4 May	Trials of those arrested in agitation
Sunday 5 May	Some of those arrested given prison sentences
Monday 6 May	Students from Nanterre appear before disciplinary council. First barricades erected in Paris
Tuesday 7 May	Student demonstration crosses to right bank of Seine but does not attack any institution of government
Wednesday 8 May	Anniversary of end of Second World War in Europe. Demonstrations in west of France
Thursday 9 May	Rector of the Sorbonne announces that courses will start again but the offer is withdrawn after student threats to occupy the Sorbonne again
Friday 10 May	Barricades built in Latin Quarter in evening
Saturday 11 May	Barricades attacked by police in small hours of the morning. Pompidou returns to France and makes broadcast announcing reopening of the Sorbonne
Sunday 12 May	Minister of education, who had opposed reopening of the Sorbonne, offers resignation to prime minister. It is refused
Monday 13 May	Tenth anniversary of de Gaulle's return to power. One-day general strike and large demonstration. Students reoccupy the Sorbonne
Tuesday 14 May	De Gaulle leaves for Romania. Pompidou speaks in National Assembly
Wednesday 15 May	Unofficial strike and occupation of Renault factory at Cléon. Students occupy Odéon theatre in Paris
Thursday 16 May	Unofficial strike of Renault workers at Flins
Friday 17 May	Strike of Renault workers at Boulogne-Billancourt. The main trade unions begin to put themselves at head of strikes

Saturday 18 May	De Gaulle returns from Romania
Sunday 19 May	De Gaulle orders evacuation of Odéon theatre – order is not carried out
Monday 20 May	Occupation of schools by *comités d'action lycéens*
Tuesday 21 May	Censure debate in National Assembly
Wednesday 22 May	Those loyal to de Gaulle announce existence of Comités de Défense de la République
Thursday 23 May	Meeting between Mitterrand and Mendès France
Friday 24 May	Demonstration by students at Gare de Lyon. Mendès France visits students. Television broadcast by de Gaulle. A policeman killed in Lyons
Saturday 25 May	Beginning of negotiations between unions, employers and government in rue de Grenelle
Sunday 26 May	Minister of education suggests to prime minister that there should be a negotiation with all those involved in universities. Nothing happens
Monday 27 May	Agreement at Grenelle, which is almost immediately renounced by unions after angry response of workers at Boulogne-Billancourt. Meeting at Charléty stadium, attended by Mendès France, who does not speak
Tuesday 28 May	Mitterrand gives press conference and announces that he will be a candidate if de Gaulle resigns. Resignation of minister of education accepted
Wednesday 29 May	De Gaulle flies secretly to French garrison in Baden-Baden
Thursday 30 May	De Gaulle returns to Paris and makes radio broadcast. National Assembly dissolved and elections called. Large demonstration in Champs-Élysées in favour of de Gaulle
Friday 31 May	Ministerial reshuffle
June	Gradual end of strikes and student occupations. Large Gaullist victory in two rounds of legislative elections on 23 and 30 of month

5

Mon Dieu, mon Dieu, la vie est là. Simple et tranquille.
> – Charles de Gaulle, quoting Verlaine,
> New Year's message, 1968

*The student revolt that started at Nanterre on 22 March 1968 ...
ended with the most serious political crisis that France has
known since 1871, if not 1848 ... It was brought not by a few
dark points in a calm sky but by a devastating cyclone that no
meteorologist foresaw.*
> – Dominique Julia (historian born in 1940), June 1968[1]

In the first few months of 1968, French politicians congratulated
themselves on their light escape from the student rebellion seen elsewhere. In March, there was trouble at the Nanterre campus outside
Paris, which was shut for a time. Even then, however, the president,
Charles de Gaulle, found it hard to take student agitation seriously.
When one of his ministers suggested surveillance, phone tapping and
house searches as a means to 'paralyse [and] frighten' ... subversive
movements, he was incredulous: 'Those kids? Those jokers?'[2] At the
beginning of May protest spread to central Paris and soon turned the
Latin Quarter into a battleground between students and the riot
police. There was also agitation in much of the rest of the country.
Most importantly, a general strike, which surprised the leaders of
French trade unions as much as everyone else, paralysed industry. It
looked likely that de Gaulle, who had ruled France for ten years,

would fall. For a couple of weeks, the country seemed to hover on the edge of some kind of revolution – though no one really knew what kind. The leaders of the Communist Party, which had been talking about revolution for fifty years, were mystified by, and usually hostile to, the student protest. All sorts of groups were touched by the apocalyptic mood. Children walked out of school, professional footballers went on strike, the jury at the Cannes film festival resigned in sympathy with the students.

The end of this turbulence was as surprising as its beginning. De Gaulle suddenly seemed to regain his grip. There was a large demonstration in his favour on 30 May. Then the crushing Gaullist victory in the legislative elections of June 1968 marked a return to order that disconcerted the general himself. The following year, however, de Gaulle's proposal for decentralization was defeated in a referendum and he resigned. Within a year he was dead. Alfred Fabre-Luce – one of the figures from the Pétainist right who had relished the upheavals of 1968 because they relished almost anything that might damage de Gaulle – reflected bitterly that sudden death was the general's last great *coup de théâtre*. He compared it to the ritual suicide of the Japanese novelist Mishima.

Looking back, some saw the French 1968 as an event that came close to observing the classical unities of Greek tragedy. It happened in one place – Paris, and especially a few streets of the Latin Quarter. Indeed an important part of the action happened on stage because the students occupied the Théâtre de la France. It also happened over a short period of time. The sociologist Michel Crozier was later to write: 'it is one of the peculiarities of the French case that rarely has a social and cultural event that was profoundly spontaneous been so tightly framed in time'.[3]

Some, however, argue the French 68 should not be confined to one place and time. They have pointed to a longer cycle of protest (particularly one that involved workers rather than students) and to a geographical span that took in the provinces as well as Paris. The debate about these two interpretations has political implications. Generally, those who regard the protests of 1968 with favour have looked to the long term. Those who opposed 1968 emphasized its ephemeral nature. They see it, in Raymond Aron's words, as a 'pyschodrama' without real social roots or long-term consequences.[4]

One might argue that this debate relates to a wider division in French intellectual life. In the second half of the 1960s, the work of Michel Foucault emphasized 'structures' and was sometimes associated with a kind of political quiescence – though Foucault remarked that the bourgeoisie would be in trouble if his work was their 'only rampart'.[5] Foucault would later be associated with the radicalisms of the 1970s and denounced by Luc Ferry and Alain Renaut as representative of *la pensée 68*,[6] but he played little part in the events of May 1968. Indeed, 1968 was marked by an emphasis on the event and the individual rather than the 'structure' and by a renewed importance for the philosopher who had seemed to be displaced by Foucault just a few years earlier – Jean-Paul Sartre. Students chalked on walls a phrase that was often wrongly attributed to the literary theorist Roland Barthes: 'Structures do not take to the streets.'

The long 68 (*les années 68*) of structures and the short one (*mai 68*) of events cannot be completely separated. There were long-term movements that began in the 1960s and carried on into the following decade. But there was also a briefer and more spectacular eruption around May 1968 – the effects of which were mainly, though not exclusively, felt in Paris rather than the provinces. The long and short versions of the French 68 were linked, but there are also some respects in which May 1968 can be seen as a parenthesis – or a play within a play. For this reason, May 1968 in France deserves special attention and some of that attention should be focused on individuals rather than structures.

COHN-BENDIT

One man, above all, became associated with the student protests in Paris. Daniel Cohn-Bendit was a 23-year-old with striking red hair, ostensibly studying sociology at the new faculty of Paris University at

Nanterre. His parents were German Jews who had taken refuge in France and he remained, as his many enemies pointed out, a German national. Largely indifferent to the theoretical debates that preoccupied some of his contemporaries, Cohn-Bendit was mostly interested in action, or at least movement. He was frenetically energetic and, for all his charm, a bully who could make life miserable for his victims. He had a taste for theatrical gestures – such as getting his comrades at Nanterre to disrupt lectures by repeatedly opening and shutting umbrellas. The mass meeting, which conferred importance on anyone with the nerve to speak out, provided him with a natural platform. He was to become a ubiquitous figure in the protest movement.

Michel Crozier came upon a crowd of students at Nanterre surrounding Cohn-Bendit who had just returned from the Latin Quarter. It was clear from his extravagant gestures and from the laughter of those around him that Cohn-Bendit was imitating someone and it dawned on Crozier that Cohn-Bendit was in fact parodying Cohn-Bendit. Even Crozier could not help himself from laughing at the performance.[7] At one point in May 1968, the minister of education was speaking on the telephone with Daniel Roche, the rector of the Sorbonne, who was negotiating with students but who had sworn that he would not talk to Cohn-Bendit. The rector insisted, apparently in good faith, that Cohn-Bendit was not part of the student delegation. 'Well,' asked the minister wearily, 'is the man sitting opposite you a red head with a round face?' It turned out that he was.[8]

Cohn-Bendit first attracted widespread attention in January 1968 when François Missoffe, the minister of youth, came to Nanterre to open a swimming pool. Cohn-Bendit asked him a question about the failure of a recent report to address students' sexual needs and remarked that his policies were 'Hitlerian'. Students without French nationality were not supposed to be politically active and the minister of education was keen to use this episode as an excuse to deport Cohn-Bendit. His efforts were confounded by Missoffe, who laughed off the incident, and who was rewarded for his good grace by being consigned to history as a footnote in biographies of Cohn-Bendit.

THE STUDENT MOVEMENT

On 21 March 1968, students protesting about American policy in Vietnam attacked the American Express office in Paris and some were arrested. The following day, university buildings at Nanterre were occupied in protest at these detentions. From this emerged the 22 March movement, which was formed quickly in response to events. There was no accompanying ideological programme and it drew in people from a variety of political groupuscules as well as those who had no previous political affiliation. The dean of Nanterre, Pierre Grappin, sought to discipline members of the movement. The tone of dispute became ugly. Grappin had been a member of the Resistance during the war and after his arrest had saved himself from near certain death by jumping from a train that was taking him to Germany. Not surprisingly, he did not take kindly to being called a 'fascist'.

At first student agitation involved relatively small numbers. Trying to force his way into one of the lecture halls at Nanterre, the historian René Rémond realized that 200 students behind him (those who wanted to hear his lecture) were more numerous (though, as it turned out, less determined) than the rebels who had occupied the hall and who wished to prevent him from teaching.[9] Protest was not controlled by any single body. The Union Nationale des Étudiants de France (UNEF) had been important during the Algerian War but its membership had declined since that time and the withdrawal of government subsidies (initially a sanction for its political action during the Algerian War but rendered definitive in 1965) threw it into financial crisis. Other groups, less formal and less encumbered by procedure, sought to circumvent the UNEF. The Mouvement d'Action Universitaire had been founded in early 1968. Like the 22 March movement at Nanterre, it was not based around a single programme or ideology.

On 2 May, the dean of Nanterre, believing it impossible to maintain order in his faculty, closed it. This meant that the centre of protest shifted to the Sorbonne in the Latin Quarter in central Paris. On 3 May, the Sorbonne was also closed. Police forcibly cleared it of demonstrators and took some away to have their identity checked.

Enraged by what they assumed to be the arrest of their comrades, students attacked the police for most of the evening. A few days later, a policeman told a court:

> I saw for the first time in my life the police obliged to withdraw when faced by demonstrators who bombarded them with paving stones. There were some ringleaders, perhaps around forty. But I think that, as a whole, the demonstrators acted spontaneously for the pleasure of destruction.[10]

Those who had been taken from the Sorbonne on 3 May were quickly released – though others who had been arrested during the subsequent disturbance were rushed before judges on 4 and 5 May. In addition to this, Daniel Cohn-Bendit and some of his comrades from Nanterre were summoned to appear before the disciplinary council of Paris University on 6 May. A large crowd gathered to support them and fighting between demonstrators and police, perhaps the worst of the whole month, went on for much of the night.

After this, there were a few days of relative calm. Demonstrators managed, much to the government's alarm, to cross the Pont de la Concorde and get to the right bank of the Seine on 7 May but they did not attack the Élysée Palace (the presidential residence) or any other centre of government power. Discreet negotiations between the students and the authorities began but broke down over the question of whether a few arrested demonstrators could be released. Then, on 10 May, protesters built barricades on a scale that exceeded anything seen before. These were works of performance art rather than military engineering. De Gaulle's son-in-law, an officer, said with grim relish that none of them would resist assault by an armoured bulldozer.[11] Barricades evoked the revolutions of 1830 and 1848 or at least what students had read of revolution in novels. The most impressive barricade was erected (perhaps intentionally) by the street named after Royer-Collard, a nineteenth-century royalist.[12]

The government took the public challenge to authority implied by the barricades seriously. They were dismantled on the night of 10–11 May – the police moved in after the last metro had run in the hopes that all but the most committed militants would have gone home. Demonstrations now became larger. When his aide, Jacques Foccart, relayed police reports to de Gaulle, he always chose the lowest of the estimates for the number of people who had marched. In truth, he had little idea of the real numbers and suspected that the much higher newspaper estimates might be more accurate.[13] It was hard to distinguish demonstrators from bystanders and in any case the two categories sometimes blurred into each other. Some Parisians were drawn to the marches by curiosity or by nostalgia for their own radical youth. The Gaullist deputy and Resistance veteran Robert-André Vivien joined a demonstration on 21 May – ostensibly because he wished to be in a position to rescue his left-wing parliamentary colleagues if the need should arise.[14]

In the small world of the Paris *grande bourgeoisie*, there were odd links between the two sides of the barricades. André Malraux, the minister of culture, lunched with the writer José Bergamín, whom he had first met during the Spanish Civil War. Afterwards Malraux offered to give his friend a lift in the ministerial car and Bergamín asked to be taken to the occupied Sorbonne. Malraux, who was heading for the National Assembly, said: 'You are going towards the irrational and I am going to the unreal.'[15]

Even those who lived in central Paris did not always know what was going on in the crowded streets below their windows. Broadcasters acquired a new importance. They sometimes provided the only way in which people could tell what was happening a few hundred metres away. In the mid-1960s, the French national radio and television company (ORTF) had been a force for cohesion. Families gathered round television sets and the whole country watched more or less the same programmes – particularly when de Gaulle himself spoke. In 1968, everything changed. Transistor radios, which could be carried everywhere, mattered more than televisions and the most important radio stations were often private ones based outside France. The authorities eventually blocked the short-wave channels used by radio cars to prevent direct reporting on riots, but journalists just phoned in their reports – sometimes knocking on doors and begging the use of a telephone from sympathetic local residents.

THE POLICE

The police were not good at distinguishing between demonstrators and those who just happened to be on the street at the wrong time, and their attacks on both groups led many Parisians to side with the students. Hundreds of demonstrators were arrested. Their detention was usually brief, but in the confusion their own comrades often knew nothing of their release and sinister rumours spread. On 13 May, a journalist was told, wrongly, that a dozen demonstrators were dead.[16]

To the relief of the authorities, no demonstrator was killed in May 1968, though two left-wing militants were killed later in the summer. A policeman died in Lyons on 24 May, when demonstrators sought to break through police lines with a truck. The forces of order were more restrained than they sometimes appeared. The Compagnies Républicaines de Sécurité (CRS) – riot squad – looked terrifying with their shields and gas masks, but men who were trained and equipped to deal with civil disorder did not run out of control. Leaders of the CRS union got in touch with the protesters (they were keen to distinguish themselves from the non-unionized *gardes républicaines*) and insisted that they wished to avoid casualties.[17]

The prefect of the Paris police since 1967, Maurice Grimaud, was a liberal-minded man who wanted to avoid violence as much as possible. This, and even a certain melancholy sympathy for the students, did not, however, mean that he wanted to see authority overturned. He compared himself to an angler who pays out the line in order to let the fish exhaust itself.[18] He allowed officials to negotiate with student leaders about the routes that demonstrations should follow. Alain Geismar, one of the most prominent leaders of the protest, recalled that he was in 'constant contact' with Grimaud.[19] Grimaud's instructions to the police under his command were explicit – in particular, he forbade the beating of demonstrators after their arrest. He distanced himself from his predecessor Maurice Papon, who had incited his men to 'react quickly and firmly'[20] and who had presided over the suppression of demonstrations during the Algerian War, when Algerians had been killed in police custody. Minister of the Interior Fouchet recognized that students needed to be handled more gently than North Africans, 'for whom the Paris population did not have excessive affection'.[21]

DE GAULLE AND HIS ENTOURAGE

Tall and physically awkward, Charles de Gaulle was easy to caricature. Crude drawings of him appeared on posters in May 1968 as though the head of state had become a cartoon character – though the most intelligent student leaders came to recognize that there was a complicated personality behind the stereotypical depictions. De Gaulle had been born into a Catholic, royalist family in 1890, become an army officer, fought in the First World War (in which he was wounded and captured) and, rebelling against the government of his own country, flown to London to call on the French to fight on after their defeat of 1940. Having resigned as head of the French government in 1946, de Gaulle endured years of political exile before being recalled to power in May 1958 when it seemed that the Fourth Republic was unable to hold on to French Algeria. A new constitution (that of the Fifth Republic) created a stronger executive, reinforced by the introduction of direct election of the president in 1962. However, as it became obvious that he proposed to withdraw France from Algeria, which he did in 1962, de Gaulle became the target of savage political attack by the right, numerous assassination attempts and, in 1961, an attempted military coup.

Historians of 1968 have often commented on the extent to which the left had been influenced by the Algerian War. Less commonly noted has been the mark that Algeria left on Gaullists. Christian Fouchet, the minister of the interior, had been high commissioner in Algeria during the last six months of French presence as desperate settlers resorted to bombings and assassinations in their fury at what they saw as betrayal by Paris. Jacques Foccart, the secretary of the Élysée, had organized the 'anti-terrorist commandos' that had attacked the pro-Algérie Française secret army in the early 1960s, and done so employing techniques that were barely more legal than those of their adversaries.[22] Born in 1913, Foccart was everything that student radicals despised. His personality seemed to suit the steel corset that he had worn since being injured in a parachute accident. Not surprisingly, men such as this found it hard to believe that the students at Nanterre would prove more dangerous than the legionnaires and paratroopers with whom they had joined battle after the Algerian War: 'We had complete confidence in the solidity of the state that the general had rebuilt. The idea that a few students could shake something that three-quarters of the army and most of the political class had failed to do . . . was absurd.'[23]

This myth built around de Gaulle by his admirers can make the real man harder to understand. Jean-Jacques Becker, a historian who came to admire de Gaulle, remarked, when recalling 1968, that the general was 'greater dead than when alive'.[24] The inspired audacity of de Gaulle's earlier years seemed to have disappeared by the late 1960s. He was given to vulgar tirades about the shortcomings of the modern world that made him seem like what he was – an elderly, retired army officer. Even his insults sounded dated and the British ambassador primly referred to the 'antique vulgarity' of the word *chienlit*,* with which de Gaulle dismissed student protest.[25] In March 1968, the journalist Pierre Viansson-Ponté had written an article in which he claimed that France was 'bored' and that the general – condemned to spend his life radiating 'official bonhomie' while inaugurating 'exhibitions of chrysanthemums' – was even more afflicted by this mood than most of his compatriots.

De Gaulle's position was incongruous because he had some things in common with the protesters of 1968. Like them, he regarded the consumer society with disdain. He had opposed Israel during the 1967 war. He had opened diplomatic relations with China in 1964. He had withdrawn France from NATO's joint command structures in 1966 and, most importantly, he had opposed American intervention in Vietnam.

Some *soixante-huitards* later became among the most enthusiastic propagators of the myth of de Gaulle. The historian Maurice Agulhon, who wished to overthrow the 'Gaullist regime' in 1968,[26] wrote a sympathetic book about the general's mythology.[27] Other figures from 1968 became obsessed by de Gaulle's asceticism and refusal to compromise

---

* *Chienlit* is a version of *chie-en-lit* – 'shit in the bed'.

in 1940. They were especially prone to contrast de Gaulle's virtues with what they came to consider to be the vices of François Mitterrand, who was president from 1981 to 1995. This retrospective admiration for de Gaulle was expressed by the one-time Maoist Serge July and above all by the former Trotskyist Régis Debray.[28]

In 1968 itself, however, the left did not so much attack de Gaulle as ignore him. Sometimes it looked as if the students were simply indifferent to him as an individual because they were preoccupied by more abstract matters – imperialism, capitalism. Some of them seemed to distinguish between the heroic de Gaulle of 1940 and the old man of 1968. One, Alain Geismar, wrote: 'As paradoxical as it may seem, I felt great admiration for general de Gaulle. Above all he epitomized in my eyes the Resistance.' But with regard to 1968 itself, Geismar recalled de Gaulle 'aroused our derision more than our hostility' and that he seemed 'out of the game, stuck in total incomprehension'.[29]

The paradoxes of de Gaulle's reputation were illustrated by two films released in the aftermath of 1968. The first of these was Jean-Pierre Melville's *L'Armée des Ombres*, which was made in early 1969, after the end of the student protests but before de Gaulle's resignation. Melville had himself fought in the Resistance – it was while doing so that he first adopted his American-sounding *nom de guerre* – and was fifty-two in 1969. His film was melancholy and pessimistic. It began with a revealing quotation: 'Bad memories you are welcome . . . you are my distant youth.' The Resistance that it portrayed was largely one of the middle-aged and middle class; the central character was a bespectacled engineer in his forties. The film showed a Resistance that was loyal to de Gaulle and, indeed, featured a brief scene in which the hero, having got to London, meets the general. *L'Armée des Ombres* was a modest commercial success but derided by critics who saw it as crude propaganda. The film magazine *Cahiers du Cinéma* described it sarcastically as the 'first and greatest example of Gaullist film art'.[30]

More successful in critical terms was Marcel Ophüls's documentary *Le Chagrin et la Pitié*, which was made in 1969 but not released in cinemas until 1971. It had been intended for broadcast but was not shown on French television until 1981. Ophüls, unlike Melville, was sympathetic to the *soixante-huitards*, and his scriptwriters – André

Harris and Alain de Sédouy – were both dismissed from the French national broadcaster in 1968 because of their leftist views. *Le Chagrin et la Pitié* describes Resistance, collaboration and Pétainism, but its most conspicuous feature is an absence: Charles de Gaulle is hardly mentioned. Many of the interviewees are notable anti-Gaullists. Some – such as Pierre Mendès France or Emmanuel d'Astier de La Vigerie – were drawn from the non-Communist left. Some – such as Georges Bidault, who had defended French Algeria, or Christian de la Mazière, who had fought on the Eastern Front for the Germans – were from the right. It sometimes seemed that the driving force of the film came from a desire to pull French history out from under the crushing weight of de Gaulle.

THE LEFT

Gaullism was not the only political force to have drawn support from its apparent role as keeper of the Resistance flame. After the invasion of the Soviet Union in 1941, the Parti Communiste Français (PCF) had thrown itself into the Resistance, and at Moscow's bidding had accepted de Gaulle's leading role. This did not, however, mean that Resistance veterans led the party after the war. The Resistance legacy was the property of the party and not of any individual member of it. More than its counterparts in other Western countries, the PCF was a workers' party. Its organization intertwined with the unions that belonged to the Confédération Générale du Travail (CGT). Intellectuals and artists were important, but they were ornaments rather than leaders and by the 1960s many intellectuals had left the party. They disliked its authoritarianism and its slavish obedience to the Soviet Union.

The Parti Socialiste Unifié (PSU), founded in 1960, was intended to be more democratic than the PCF but more radical than the venerable Section Française de l'Internationale Ouvrière (SFIO), which was a conventional social democratic party. The PSU drew in ex-Communists and some left-wing Christians. Above all, the PSU stood for opposition to the brutality that French forces had exhibited during the Algerian War. The new party was often quicker on its feet than more established ones. Between 1968 and 1972, it swung so far to the left that it appeared for a time to be a revolutionary movement. However, with 16,000 members and four deputies in parliament, the PSU was larger than any of the leftist groupuscules that came to prominence in 1968.

From 1967 to 1974, the PSU's general secretary was Michel Rocard, who had been born in 1930 into a Protestant family and proceeded via the elite École Nationale d'Administration (ENA) into the civil service before devoting himself to politics. Rocard marched at the head of demonstrations but prided himself on having avoided violence and his private views were more measured than his public statements suggested. He took time off from agitation in May 1968 to meet Jacques Chirac, a Gaullist minister and his old classmate from ENA. It is revealing that he seems to have felt most at ease with another young-ish man who combined a distinguished career with unconventional political views: the English diplomat Crispin Tickell.[31]

The PSU had an important following in universities and among the young. Two prominent *soixante-huitards* were associated with the party. Jacques Sauvageot, born in 1943, was effectively head of the Union Nationale des Étudiants de France and a member of the PSU. Alain Geismar, born 1939, a university teacher and head of the Syndi-cat National de l'Enseignement Supérieur, had left the PSU in 1966, though it said much about the atmosphere of 1968 that the latter had better relations with Rocard during that year.

The Trotskyist Jeunesse Communiste Révolutionnaire was founded in 1966 by a group of Communist students at the Sorbonne who had refused their party's instruction to support François Mitterrand in the 1965 presidential campaign. Among its leaders were Alain Krivine (born in 1941) and Daniel Bensaïd (born in 1946). Others left the Com-munist Party to join the Maoist Union des Jeunesses Communistes Marxistes-Léninistes (UJCML). Mao had broken with the Soviet Union because of Khruschev's destalinization, and Maoism could be an indirect way of remaining loyal to Stalin, but not all French Maoists thought of themselves in this way and in any case few French people were in a position to follow the upheavals of the Cultural Revolution. The UJCML was separate from the Parti Communiste Marxiste-Léniniste de France, which was loyal to the Chinese government. The very power of the French Communist Party meant that a section of the French left defined itself against it in a way that would have been inconceivable in Britain or the United States. The word *'gauchiste'* first used as a term of abuse by the PCF came to be adopted by some student radicals.

De Gaulle's entourage found themselves in an odd position. They often presented the Communist Party as the gravest threat of 1968. Some, such as Foccart, assumed that Communism was a permanent threat and that every manoeuvre of the party was designed to bring it closer to power. Others recognized that the party was itself alarmed by the events of 1968 and that under these circumstances it might even be a defender of order. The minister of the interior remarked wistfully that it had once been possible to strike a deal with the Communist Party but it was now outflanked on its left by 'organized and brutal but incomprehensible movements'.[32] De Gaulle himself seems to have felt, especially at the time of his flight from Paris in late May (of which more below), that there was a real threat of a Communist takeover. He may have been influenced by those more subtle analysts who argued that the vacuum created by the weakness of other parties might encourage or force the Communists to take power in a way that they had not anticipated. The party's own leaders were conscious that they were not in complete control. In a private conversation after a meeting of the party's Central Committee, one of them said:

> He simply did not know what would happen. The Communist Party and the Communist trade union confederation were categorically against any form of insurrection but they were not in full control of their rank and file. There might, for example, be a general strike and in that case the army might be sent in to maintain essential services . . . This could lead to a dangerous confrontation. Likewise future demonstrations might get out of hand. If serious violence took place, he failed to see how the regime could continue. The government could hardly count on the loyalty of police and soldiers if 9 millions strikers were against them.[33]

The hostility between *gauchiste* students and the established Communist Party was evident at Nanterre because the university was in a Communist municipality. The Communist mayor told the dean of

Nanterre that he had nothing to do with the agitation.[34] The Communist deputy Pierre Juquin was relatively young – he had been born in 1930 – intellectually distinguished and politically liberal. He would be excluded from the Communist Party in the 1980s and eventually make common cause with former Trotskyists and supporters of the PSU. Nonetheless, he was treated with derision when he attempted to address students at Nanterre on 25 April 1968. Georges Marchais, a member of the PCF Central Committee, born in 1920, was the incarnation of Communist orthodoxy. On 3 May, he wrote in the party newspaper *L'Humanité*:

These pseudo revolutionaries who claim to give the working class movement lessons . . . must be unmasked vigorously because, objectively, they serve the interests of the Gaullist power and the big capitalist monopolies . . . The theses and activities of these revolutionaries might make one laugh. All the more so because they are, in general, the children of the upper class who will soon turn down their revolutionary flame to go and run daddy's business.

FRENCH HIGHER EDUCATION

The politics of French students intertwined with concerns about their conditions of study and prospects of getting jobs and also about the byzantine complexity of French higher education. The rapid expansion of universities in the 1960s meant that many were overcrowded, particularly because anyone who passed the *baccalauréat* (high-school leaving certificate) was entitled to attend university. The effects of this were felt with special force at Nanterre because it was a new campus of ugly concrete buildings – some still unfinished – and because it was removed from the cafés, cinemas and bookshops that provided the charm of student life in the Latin Quarter. Rapid expansion may also have meant that some students came to feel that their qualifications were less valuable (see chap. 3).

If students resented the increase in numbers, they also often resented the measures that might have addressed this problem and in particular attempts to introduce selective admission to universities.

Not all of French higher education, however, took place in universities. *Grandes écoles* were designed to prepare students for particular careers. Particularly important were the École Polytechnique, which trained engineers and which was still in theory a military school, the École Normale Supérieure (ENS), which prepared students for teaching in French *lycées*, and the Institut d'Études Politiques.

The *grandes écoles* had ruthlessly difficult entrance examinations. Elite *lycées*, mainly in Paris, ran two-year *classes préparatoires* that followed the *baccalauréat*: the *khâgnes* – designed to train students in humanities for the ENS – and the *taupes* – designed to train scientists for the Polytechnique – which had a language and mythology of their own. Much of their work overlapped with that undertaken in universities, which partly explains why *lycéens* played such an active part in the protests of 1968.

Selective admission meant that many of the material problems that weighed on university students were irrelevant to those at the *grandes écoles*. Their highly trained graduates had little difficulty in gaining employment. Indeed, at some institutions students were employees of the state from the moment of their arrival. Many in the *grandes écoles* regarded 68 with benign amusement. At the École Polytechnique, students continued to attend their lectures even when they had spent the night on the barricades and their clothes smelled of tear gas.[35]

The École Normale Supérieure, particularly its most venerable and selective branch in the rue d'Ulm, had a special role in 1968. On the one hand, its students were supremely privileged. Even those of them who studied philosophy or literature could usually obtain lucrative employment in administration, business or politics if they wanted it. On the other hand, the ENS was a traditional centre of the political left, which by the late 1960s often meant Maoism or Trotskyism.

It is hard to overstate the importance that the ENS assumed in the eyes of those who wrote about 1968. The autobiographical novels of the one-time Maoist Olivier Rolin are saturated with references to it. A single incident in 1960 – when de Gaulle had visited the ENS and a star student had refused to shake his hand – aroused particular interest. Régis Debray, a *normalien* who was under sentence of death in a Bolivian prison in 1968, wrote that this episode was 'as sublime as a barricade of the second of December [i.e. during the coup d'état of 1851]'.[36] Alain Peyrefitte, minister of education in 1968, and inevitably a *normalien*, went to great lengths to track down the man who had refused to shake de Gaulle's hand. He believed that the encounter illustrated how a small determined group of agitators could change history and hence explained much about 1968.[37]

In fact, the Maoists and Trotskyists of the ENS played only a small direct part in the events of 1968 itself – as opposed to its aftermath. Many of them disdained student politics as 'bourgeois'. Some had already become *établis*, that is they had taken jobs in factories in order to become political missionaries (see chap. 9). Nicole Linhart was married to Robert Linhart – one of the most important Maoists from the ENS – and had herself begun work in a factory. In early May, her Maoist comrades refused to believe her when she said that her colleagues at the factory were turning up at work with bandaged heads because they had spent the night fighting alongside the students.[38] Only when workers launched a general strike on 13 May were the *établis* free to join them on the barricades.

POMPIDOU

The most important *normalien* in France was not, however, a Maoist or a Trotskyist but the Gaullist Prime Minister Georges Pompidou. His appointment in 1962 had been a surprise and de Gaulle himself seems to have originally intended to make him education minister. Pompidou admired de Gaulle, had served him loyally since the liberation and owed his position to the general's patronage, but the two men were very different. Their respective characters were exemplified by an encounter in the 1950s when de Gaulle showed Pompidou a first draft of his memoirs. Pompidou remarked that the general had not fully explained how he had been transformed in 1940 from soldier to saviour of his country. When, he asked, did de Gaulle feel 'touched by grace'? De Gaulle replied that he had always felt it. Pompidou once remarked that the casual intimacy of those who had been with de Gaulle since 1940 reminded him of the way elderly nuns might evoke Christ. Pompidou, who had grown up on the anti-clerical left, admired such faith without sharing it.

While de Gaulle was an aristocratic army officer from the north of France, Pompidou was descended from Auvergnat peasants and grew up in the south. Both men's fathers were teachers but Pompidou's had risen from humble origins and belonged to that large group of French teachers who regarded themselves as missionaries of the republic; de Gaulle's father, a royalist who taught in a Catholic school, took pretty much the opposite view. Pompidou became a *lycée* teacher and an eminent scholar of classical literature and then spent fifteen lucrative years working for the Rothschild Bank. If de Gaulle's most striking characteristic was rigidity, Pompidou's was a serpentine subtlety.

During his early life, Pompidou had been a socialist like his father. He had participated in anti-fascist demonstrations during the 1930s and, as he liked to recall in 1968, sometimes given clenched fist salutes. Though his views on economics had moved to the right after 1945, Pompidou was liberal on cultural matters. He was more at home in the 1960s than de Gaulle or in some ways than the student protesters. He was a bon viveur who enjoyed good food and who chain smoked; de Gaulle, in a characteristic act of will, had broken this habit in his early fifties. Pompidou admired the films of Jean-Luc Godard – an admiration that the Maoist Godard did not reciprocate.[39]

Pompidou had been relatively unscathed by the savage ideological divisions of twentieth-century France. He had not accepted office until after the end of the Algerian War. His behaviour during the Occupation had been honourable but he had not been an active Resistance fighter. He remarked, with characteristic self-deprecation, that he 'did not have the fibre of a hero'. Curiously, this was an advantage in 1968. Unlike those of his contemporaries whose Resistance careers had been more dramatic, he never felt the bitter sense that his own youthful idealism had been appropriated or betrayed.

Pompidou had another advantage in May 1968. He was on a state visit to Iran and Afghanistan from 2 to 11 of the month. Before he left, he had advised his colleagues to be 'firm'. However, he had not been directly involved in any of their subsequent discussions. While they agonized about the possibility of imminent revolution, he wandered around ancient ruins and relished the intricate courtesy of oriental negotiations. On one of the most dramatic days of the Paris events, 10 May, he was in northern Afghanistan – one of the few places in the world where there were no televisions to relay news from France and no journalists to ask difficult questions. He did not even find out what had happened at home until he returned to Kabul. On the following day, his *chef de cabinet* warned him that the 'worst was possible and even probable'. On the long plane journey back from Afghanistan, Pompidou decided on a strategy. In Paris, he convoked his aides – one of whom described him as being 'provocatively calm'.[40] He told them: 'I am not implicated in what has just happened . . . I am free, in the end the only one to be so, and I can, without the government seeming to break with its policy, adopt a different attitude to yours.'[41]

Pompidou's most important decision was to reopen the Sorbonne. He knew that this would mean its immediate occupation by student radicals but there was method in his moderation. He believed that there was only a 'one in a hundred' chance that his actions would appease the students. He wished, 'like a general', to withdraw to a more defensible position. Pompidou believed that it was neither possible nor desirable to repress the students with force, especially when public opinion was on their side. Ceding the Sorbonne, on the other hand, prevented a demonstration from turning into a riot and gave the student radicals licence to behave in a way that was bound to turn opinion against them. In any case, Pompidou was more worried by the prospect that the Communists might exploit the agitation to provoke revolution than he was by the student agitation in itself.[42]

Pompidou's behaviour in 1968 marked a shift in his relations with de Gaulle. When he proposed reopening the Sorbonne, one of his colleagues asked him whether he was not frightened of de Gaulle's response. Pompidou replied: 'The general no longer exists . . . he is nothing now.'[43] When de Gaulle was told of Pompidou's plans, he replied simply: 'If you win . . . France wins with you. If you lose, too bad for you.'

In the short term, it seemed that Pompidou had lost. Monday 13 May marked the tenth anniversary of de Gaulle's return to power. Left-wing politicians joined demonstrations under the slogan 'ten years is enough' and the trade unions called a one-day strike to mark their sympathy with the students, or at least their opposition to the repression of the students. The demonstration of 13 May passed without much trouble – indeed, it seemed for a moment that conventional political argument had returned. But the protesters now took over much of the Latin Quarter and seized the Odéon theatre on 15 May. Left-wing Gaullists – some of whom had been with the general for longer than Pompidou – attacked the government in parliament.

STRIKES

Large-scale strikes now broke out among workers, beginning at Sud-Aviation, near Nantes, on 14 May. These were different from the twenty-four-hour strike of 13 May, which had been called by the unions and more or less under their control. The strikes that took hold in the second half of May did not always look to be under anyone's control. Simply finding out how many workers were on strike was hard because the statistical services of the ministry of social affairs broke down.[44] The best estimates suggested that something between 5 and 10 million people had joined the strikes. Debate was not simply about their scale, though, but about their nature, and this mattered because some in 1968 hoped that there was a new kind of working class – one that might ally more easily with middle-class protesters and that might break with the discipline of the Communist-dominated CGT. Some pointed to a change in industrial relations that had begun before 1968. There were more white-collar workers and/or highly skilled technicians. Such people were less likely to join the CGT and less likely to accept union leadership of any kind during negotiations with their employees. There was also a different kind of 'new working class'. This was made up of the least privileged workers: often those – the young, immigrants and women – who had not fitted neatly into the structures of the established trade unions. This refusal to accept leadership could, however, make workers more, rather than less, radical. Not trusting to disciplined organization, they might take direct action by seizing their workplace or refusing to allow employers to leave their offices.

The idea of workers organizing themselves was disconcerting to the established political parties. The Communists felt uncomfortable with a challenge to the CGT. Even the leaders of the PSU, the most radical of the parties with representation in parliament, had mixed feelings. Michel Rocard had followed the new style of protest with interest – his lover, the sociologist Michèle Legendre, had studied labour unrest at the Berliet company. But in private discussions Rocard expressed doubts about the idea that workers should run their own factories (see chap. 9) and admitted: 'even his organisation was being propelled from below, above all in those factories where workers seemed to be taking over permanent control'.[45]

Some workers went on strike without presenting demands, which suggested a protest against the whole industrial order rather than just rates of pay. Occupation of workplaces by workers was common. Police reports suggest that at least twenty-three factories, with 80,000 employees, had been occupied by 17 May.[46] Sometimes the greatest threat to the established order was not the violence of strikers but their self-conscious restraint. In Lyons, postal workers occupying their depot were reminded to sign a register. When they finally evacuated the building, they took care to tidy it up and then handed back the keys to the management in a carefully staged ceremony.[47] If workers could control their strikes, they sometimes implied, they could equally well control their work. A trade unionist in the Basses Alpes wrote that workers occupied his own factory in such a peaceful and thoughtful manner that they realized they would be able to run it without the management.[48]

Employees of the aluminium factory at Saint-Jean-de-Maurienne did not stop work but, to the annoyance of the CGT, ran their own enterprise for several weeks. Some talked of 'strikes' in which workers might provide services for free rather than withdrawing them. There was a shift in balance between the trade unions in 1968. The Communist-controlled CGT lost some of its power – though it remained by far the biggest of the confederations. Force Ouvrière (FO) – associated with democratic socialism and sponsored in its early days by the Americans as a means of weakening Communism – gained importance, especially in the shipyards of Nantes, where it had become a refuge for Trotskyists or anarchists who had been excluded from the CGT. The Confédération Générale des Cadres, representing some managers, was surprisingly radical. The Confédération Française Démocratique du Travail (CFDT) was particularly important. The CFDT had emerged out of Christian trade unions and, though it was no longer explicitly religious, it preserved a sense that workers might have interests that could not simply be expressed in material terms. The CFDT put things thus: 'We need to substitute democratic structures based on self-management for the industrial and administrative monarchy.'[49]

Excited observers probably overstated the novelty of the strikes in May 1968 and one should note that some battered union militants were sympathetic to 1968 precisely because it seemed to them to recall previous strikes, particularly those of the late 1940s.[50] Experiments in self-management were rare and were not attempted in the largest plants. Most strikers seem to have been male,[51] and only a small proportion of strike leaders were young[52] – though it may be that the proportion of both women and the young involved was higher than it would have been in previous strikes. Immigrant workers were an important part of the workforce and were usually less privileged than their French-born colleagues. Some immigrant workers became involved in strikes, but they were vulnerable: the CFDT reported that 183 immigrant workers of thirty-seven nationalities were deported between 24 May and 20 June. Spaniards and Portuguese, groups that were to be quite active in the labour movements of the 1970s, often stayed out of trouble by the simple expedient of going back to their country of origin during the strikes of 1968[53] – at least one special train was run for this purpose.[54]

Some believed that the strikes were opportunistic – that workers had taken advantage of the upheaval to secure simple material benefits. The British ambassador wrote: 'The aims of the workers are less far-reaching than those of the students; a commentator has said that while the students want to cut down the tree of society, the workers simply want to enjoy more of its fruits.'[55] The truth is probably that no one, including the strikers themselves, knew exactly what was going on in the chaos of 1968. The strikes were on such a scale that they acquired a momentum of their own. In Nantes, a central strike committee set up in the town hall and effectively ran the town for a few days in late May – though it appears to have done so as much because of the pragmatic need to keep things going when all other authority had broken down as because its members sought to seize control in any revolutionary sense. Many people were prevented from getting to work by the fact that there was no means of transport or no power in their factories. Teachers had often undertaken symbolic strikes of one hour or one day, but in May 1968 the whole education system stopped working and teachers went on being paid regardless of whether they considered themselves to be on strike or not.[56] Furthermore, the tone of labour dispute in 1968 was quite often set not by the large numbers of people who stopped work but by the relatively few who were most active in workplace occupations.

In some respects, May 1968 separated workers and students rather than bringing them together. Before and after this, students frequently joined worker protests. In May, however, the focus of protest on central Paris sometimes drew students away from factories. On 15 May a director of Renault described the workers' occupation of the factory at Cléon as the 'Nanterre of the workers',[57] but the university at Nanterre was closed by then, and in the industrial suburb that bordered on Nanterre students were said to have been in contact with workers involved in only nine of eighty-eight strikes.[58] The most important workplace to be occupied in central Paris was the Odéon theatre and this was anything but a workers' occupation since the technical staff of the theatre resented the presence of students and, indeed, came to blows with them.[59]

The unions, especially the CGT, were often keen to prevent too much interaction between students and workers – though workers, especially the young, sometimes sought out student protests. Outside Paris, fraternization between workers and students was easier – partly because the national leaders of the CGT exercised less power and partly because student radicalism in the provinces was less flamboyant. In Brest a student leader commented that the movement was 'more concrete and realistic' than in Paris and that there had not even been graffiti on the walls.[60] Workers as well as students occupied the Théâtre de la Cité de Villeurbanne in Lyons.

Some workers took advantage of the strikes in their own factories to indulge in political tourism – visiting the centres of student protest in Paris. These trips sometimes heightened their sense that students were alien beings – though not necessarily ones that they regarded with hostility. Georges Valero, an autodidact postman married to a teacher, was himself an ex-Communist who would eventually pass through a variety of *gauchiste* parties. All the same, he regarded the students he met at the Odéon theatre as 'delirious'. One of them talked about 'draining the canals of Venice to find treasure'.[61] Jean Caliot, a 37-year-old CFDT delegate from the Dassault factory in the Basque Country, visited students at the Sorbonne, but said 'we did not feel that we lived in the same world'.[62] Sometimes, though, the very incongruity of student culture influenced workers in ways that took a long time to be felt. Bernard Rauch was a semi-skilled factory worker from Troyes. He travelled to Paris on an outing organized by the *comité d'entreprise* in 1968 and, though he had no 'heroic memories' of the time, he recalled, years after the event, a single sentence that he had seen written on a wall: 'Looking in her eyes, he made a child in her soul.'[63]

THE GEOGRAPHY OF 1968 IN FRANCE

Protest spread to unexpected corners of provincial France – partly because workers or students returned to their native villages as factories and universities closed, and brought their radical language with them.[64] Some companies had devolved part of their production to factories in Brittany and the west because strikes had been rare in these Catholic and conservative areas. But, as it turned out, the installation of large factories may have speeded up a change of political complexion that was already happening in the west. Catholicism remained important. Many of those who were active in politics or trade unions had been raised in Catholic youth organizations. But in the 1960s the influence of French Catholicism became more diffuse – less identified with the imposition of clerical authority or with the political right.[65] Brittany was the only region in which the CFDT, an explicitly Christian trade union confederation until its secularization in 1964, had more members than the Communist CGT. The PSU, which had attracted an important group of left-wing Christians, was also strong in Brittany. In fact, protest movements in the west had begun before May 1968. Now, a large rally – 'L'Ouest veut vivre' – had been planned for 8 May 1968. Stimulated by events in Paris, this attracted thousands of people. The minister of the interior complained that he had been obliged to send so many riot police to the west of France: 'one cannot simultaneously hold the streets of Paris and the artichokes of Brittany'.[66] Though prefects in the south noted that the riot police from their own relatively quiet areas were being sent to both Paris and Brittany.[67]

Even in the west, protest was uneven. There were strikes in Nantes but not in nearby Deux-Sèvres. Elsewhere differences were even more marked. Strikes were more common in the north than in the east, which, unlike Brittany, remained true to its socially conservative traditions. In Dijon, a municipal by-election held in May 1968 took place in much the same way that it would at any other time.[68] In the Basque Country there was a difference between inland areas, which were rural and little touched by industry, and the more developed coastal regions. There were strikes in the latter, but relations between employers and workers were very different from those in Paris. One industrialist summoned union leaders from his factory, which was on strike, to negotiations at Vichy, where he was taking the waters.[69] In Provence, the village of Cadenet was less touched by 1968 than the neighbouring commune of Lourmarin, where intellectuals from Marseilles and Paris had houses. Almost all the policemen were removed from around Cadenet and sent to Gardanne, where miners were on strike. The main effect of 1968 on Cadenet was that a clothing boutique called Les Sans-Culottes, which had opened in the rue Danton, did a roaring trade because of the new fashion for red shirts.[70]

Generally speaking, May 1968 had a paradoxical effect on relations between Paris and the provinces. There was protest outside the capital; indeed, 1968 saw the birth of new kinds of regionalist protest – identified now with the left when traditionally such 'anti-Jacobin' movements had been seen on the right. However, in the short term, May 1968 increased the focus on Paris. The Paris region contained the most important concentration of large factories in France. The number of students in Paris was higher than in any other part of the country and the most dramatic episodes of May 1968 were not merely concentrated in Paris but in that small part of the city around the Sorbonne. At the height of the protests, there were 3,000 people crammed into the Théâtre de la France.[71] This was three times the number who joined a demonstration by *lycéens* in Pau and was, indeed, greater than the number of all those who took their *baccalauréat* examination in the Basque Country that year.[72]

GRENELLE

Relations between government, employers and unions never entirely broke down. Jacques Chirac, the young secretary of state for employment, maintained discreet contacts with the CGT, which was itself worried about the uncontrolled nature of the strikes. Using the pseudonym Walter, he telephoned Henri Krasucki, a CGT official, almost every day. Krasucki was fighting on all fronts – working to ensure the continued publication of Communist newspapers and worrying about his sons who were on the barricades.

From 25 to 27 May, leaders of the unions and the main employers' association met under government aegis at the ministry of social affairs in the boulevard Grenelle. With unexpected ease, employers agreed among other things that there should be a rise in the minimum wage of 35 per cent and greater recognition for union representatives at work. The CGT were keen to get a quick agreement because they feared that the CFDT were deliberately dragging out negotiations in the hope that workers would radicalize further. As it turned out, the so-called Accords de Grenelle was never signed. CGT leaders presented it to workers at the large Renault plant at Boulogne-Billancourt and were booed. Hastily they pointed out that they had not called the strikes and had no authority to end them. The head of the French employers' association (the Conseil National du Patronat Français) remained optimistic that the agreements could be applied in spite of the opposition of 'some big and important factories'. He was keen to 'keep the economic, social and political problems on separate levels'. He thought that the employers could count on the support of 'trade union leaders [who] were disturbed at their loss of control over their own rank and file and anxious to re-establish it'. He anticipated that things would be easiest where the CGT was strongest and that 'the CFDT was the only union group which seemed to be flirting with the idea of linking social demands, e.g. those for university reforms, with questions of pay and working conditions, which were their direct concern'.[73]

FIN DE RÉGIME?

De Gaulle was absent from Paris on an official visit to Romania from 14 to 18 May and things had not improved by the time of his return. He broadcast on 24 May, remarking vaguely on the need for reform, but also evoking the threat of civil war. He announced that there would be a referendum in which the French people would be asked to mandate the state – 'and especially its head' – to undertake reform. The speech went down badly. De Gaulle seemed complacent and out of touch – his interest focused on the universities, at a time when millions of workers had gone on strike, and in the circumstances nothing was more calculated to sound archaic than his references to modernization. A well-connected British official watched the speech and noted: 'He looked his age and sounded weary and at one point nearly forgot his lines. At the end he returned to something like the old form. But a good deal of the fire was lacking.'[74]

For a few days in late May, it seemed possible that de Gaulle would be overthrown. Some Gaullists, including Jacques Chirac's *chef de cabinet*, sought to open discreet negotiations with the left because they assumed that the government could not last.[75] The journalists of ORTF, the state broadcaster, went on strike. Some seem to have done so because they sympathized with the students; others because they were Gaullists who nevertheless hoped to avoid saying anything that might tie them to a dying regime.[76]

MENDÈS FRANCE

If de Gaulle went, who would replace him? One possibility was Pierre Mendès France. Mendès was sixty-one years old. He had been a member of parliament before the Second World War. Escaping from a Vichy prison, he had joined the Free French air force. He enjoyed a curious cult status among French people of a certain age – those born in the early 1930s, who had grown up during the occupation but been too young to join the Resistance.[77] This meant in effect that he was a man in late middle age, admired by those of his compatriots in early middle age who were sympathetic to the student demonstrations without being part of them. His admirers recalled his anti-colonialism and especially his decision, during his short period as prime minister, to withdraw France from Indochina in 1954.

Mendès had opposed de Gaulle's return to power in 1958, and had remarked, in terms that were to haunt him in 1968, that power which had been seized in the street would one day be overthrown in the street, but his personal relations with de Gaulle were good. François Mauriac, who admired both men, wrote that they had much in common.

> A conjunction between PMF and De Gaulle would be best for the nation. Its impossibility is written in the very nature of PMF, in that inflexibility that is his greatness ... all the same ... De Gaulle and Mendès ... both have an idea of France which is, deep down, the same.[78]

Both men had often refused to take the easy way out. They both commanded high degrees of loyalty and admiration. On 29 May 1968, at a moment when it seemed that all might be lost for de Gaulle, his wife remarked bitterly that Mendès was now *'leur grand homme'*.[79]

Mendès had joined the PSU and, in 1967, having held no elected office for ten years, he became one of the party's four deputies in parliament. He represented the town of Grenoble and it seemed to sum up his own particular appeal. The city was a centre of industries based on new technologies, which sometimes appeared to promise the end of the working class on which more established left-wing parties had been based. It was a Catholic area and – though he was a secularized Jew who had once been a freemason – Mendès's high moral tone attracted a certain kind of left-wing Catholic. Even the clean, alpine air seemed to evoke the political integrity that many associated with Mendès.

Mendès liked the young (or at least the idea of youth) and, as one of his associates remarked, he liked it more as his own youth became more distant. His notion of youth was, however, a particular one. For him, 'young people' meant partly the earnest political enthusiasts who had supported him in the 1950s. It also meant young workers – whom he assumed to be interested in largely economic issues, particularly full employment. He talked to his juniors with courtesy – a quality that they did not always reciprocate in 1968 – but he visibly belonged to a different world.

Did Mendès understand 1968? He wanted de Gaulle removed from power and he wanted a constitution in which the executive would exercise less power. He was not, however, a Marxist and the more theatrical radicalisms of 1968 were alien to him. Michel Rocard, the leader of the PSU, regarded him as 'too parliamentary by half'.[80] Under these circumstances, it was not clear by what means Mendès anticipated de Gaulle's removal and he became, as one of his exasperated admirers put it, a 'mute orator'. Though other people talked about Mendès more in 1968 than they had at any point since he had been prime minister in 1954, his own public statements were less numerous than they had been in 1967,[81] and he did not even return to Paris from Grenoble until the second week of May.[82]

Mendès asked Françoise Seligmann (a former *résistante* and journalist who was ten years younger than himself) to put him in touch with students.[83] He marched in the demonstration of 13 May – though he was not at the front and some did not even realize that he was present. His own curious status was summed up by the fact that he could pass through police lines – partly because the officers recognized him as a former prime minister but partly just because he was an obviously respectable man accompanied by a few friends. Demonstrators with black or red flags kept their distance from him – sometimes ostentatiously so. Cohn-Bendit, summing up the leaders of the major left-wing parties on 15 May, remarked that Mendès was the 'least devalued of your stars'.[84] Mendès attracted a heterogeneous group of supporters in May 1968. The ex Pétainist Alfred Fabre-Luce put him forward as an alternative to de Gaulle while loyal Gaullists, such as the journalist Michel Droit, recognized that Mendès might be the least bad alternative if de Gaulle were to be forced from power.[85]

On 27 May, Mendès attended a meeting of the non-Communist left at the Charléty stadium. The location marked a tacit compromise between the government, which wanted to take demonstrations off the streets, and some of the leaders of the left, who were keen to avoid violent repression. Michel Rocard had hired the stadium with difficulty and had been obliged to pay a large insurance premium. Mendès seems to have been unsure about whether to speak right up to the moment that he arrived at the stadium. In the end, he did not do so. His silence may have owed something to the fact that he had talked to Raymond Aron, a fierce opponent of the students, a few hours previously.[86] Rocard later said that the meeting was a 'burial' that marked the end of the movement.[87]

Mendès kept his moral purity in 1968 but he had disappointed his own supporters. In the legislative elections of that summer, he had, with a characteristic mixture of scruple and awkwardness, resigned his membership of the PSU but not told anyone in order not to damage the party's electoral chances. He lost his seat in Grenoble to the Gaullist Jean-Marcel Jeanneney. His opponents put up posters that captured Mendès's own uncomfortable relations with power. They recalled that he was *'un homme libre'* and invited voters to *'Rendez-lui* [Mendès] *sa liberté.'* They added, in words that would have cut Mendès deeply: *'Soyez sérieux. Votez ... Jeanneney.'*

MITTERRAND

The other established politician of the democratic left to play an important role in 1968 was François Mitterrand. Born in 1916, he was younger than Mendès, but his relations with the young were worse. It was characteristic of Mitterrand that he admired his favourite mistress (who was twenty-five in 1968) partly because her brisk common sense and Catholic piety contrasted with the 'superficial esotericism of the hippy revolution'.[88] If Mendès stood for purity, Mitterrand stood for compromise. During the occupation Mitterrand had served both the Vichy government and the Resistance. Doing so involved more risk to his life than if he had simply joined the Free French in London – but people who had grown up after 1945 rarely sympathized with the nuances of his position. Mitterrand had first held ministerial office before he was thirty years old. For almost fifteen years, his professional life revolved around the deals with which Fourth Republic coalitions were held together – it was a sign of how far he had become associated with the old order that the PSU refused his application to join. Mitterrand, leading an alliance of left-wing parties, had challenged de Gaulle for the presidency in 1965, but his stance had done him little good. He recalled: 'The very fact . . . of having confronted de Gaulle in the presidential election . . . had paradoxically . . . identified me with the dignitaries of the regime against which I had never stopped fighting . . . Those who wanted a future without de Gaulle also wanted a future without me.'[89]

Mitterrand did not condemn the student demonstrations and said that he was proud his own sons took part in them. He met Alain Geismar, the leader of the university teachers, who, of all the protest leaders in 1968, was the one most willing to countenance a deal with conventional politicians. But Mitterrand's style was too far removed from that of the student protest. He was a formal, subtle man and in cultural terms a conservative. He believed that his supporters, especially in the provinces, would not understand if he associated himself with the barricades. His strategy revolved around building a coalition of Communists and what remained of the old SFIO – both groups despised by most of the protesters.

If Mendès said too little in 1968, Mitterrand said too much. He challenged the government in parliament, almost coming to blows with Gaullist deputies, but his objection to the constitution of the Fifth Republic seemed dated. Many of his speeches in May 1968 were given to audiences of middle-aged notables in the provinces rather than in Paris. At a meeting in Vichy, of all places, he spoke of the Vietnam War in between two performances by sentimental singers.[90] On the evening of 23 May, Mitterrand met Mendès. Someone suggested that they go to the boulevard St Michel to express their support for the students. Mendès dismissed the suggestion, but the following evening he did make a brief and widely reported expedition to see the student demonstrations. Mitterrand feared being eclipsed and decided to make a move of his own. On 28 May, he gave a press conference in Paris at which he called for a provisional government to be formed under Mendès and announced that he himself would be a candidate for the presidency in any forthcoming election. The statement was a mistake and, indeed, Gaullists seem to have ensured that it was broadcast repeatedly because they knew that his apparent hunger for power would damage Mitterrand.

THE GENERAL VANISHES

The dramas of the French left were suddenly overshadowed in late May 1968 because de Gaulle disappeared. He delayed a cabinet meeting and told his ministers that he was planning to spend the weekend at his country house but the helicopter never arrived. For a few hours, his own ministers and aides did not know where he was. In fact, he had flown with his wife and other members of the family to Baden-Baden in Germany, where there was a French garrison.

Did de Gaulle himself know what he intended to do in the next few days? He compared his own mood to that which had followed the failure of the Free French expedition to Dakar in 1940,[91] a time when he had, according to some accounts, considered suicide. Charles de Gaulle's son – Philippe – was one of the few people who could dare to suggest retirement to the general's face and he was struck by the furious response when he did so. He recalled that his father suddenly looked 'like a wild boar about to charge' – a metaphor that implied energy and anger rather than calculation or effectiveness.[92]

Philippe de Gaulle, a naval officer, suggested that, if Paris became too dangerous, his father might find refuge with the fleet at Brest. De Gaulle had been reluctant to go *chez les marins* but suggested in return that his son, who was nursing a stomach complaint, might take the waters at Baden-Baden. The hoteliers of the modest French spa town of Contrex, the epitome of the prudent provincial middle classes, had made it clear that they would not welcome the upheavals that might go with having a member of the president's family as a guest. Eventually de Gaulle *père* had decided to take the whole family to Baden-Baden. Perhaps this was simply because he wanted to reach a safe refuge. Perhaps he wanted to see for himself whether the French army, part of which was posted to Germany, could be trusted to restore order in France.

The commander in Baden-Baden, General Jacques Massu, recalled he was dozing in the garden with a copy of *Le Figaro Littéraire** when he was told that de Gaulle was about to arrive. Massu and his

---

* Massu's memory must have been at fault, the *Figaro Littéraire* had not been published since mid-May.

family were hung over on the day of the general's arrival because they had spent the previous evening entertaining a group of visiting Red Army officers. Massu remembered a Soviet marshal insisting that the French government should 'crush' the students and accompanying this statement with such vigorous gestures that Massu did not need to listen to the subsequent translation.[93]

Massu had fought with the Free French and was in his gruff way fiercely loyal. When, during an inspection, de Gaulle asked him, 'Alors, Massu toujours con?', Massu replied, 'Toujours con et toujours gaulliste.' Massu had incited rebellious Algerian settlers to call for de Gaulle's return to power in 1958. Later he was reprimanded for expressing his doubts about the general's Algerian policy. However, he did not join the attempted putsch of officers who opposed withdrawal from Algeria – though he called for clemency towards those who had done so, which earned him another rebuke from de Gaulle. He was in a good position to gauge how far soldiers still resented the loss of Algeria and how this might affect the loyalty of the army.

On arrival, de Gaulle was downhearted. He fished in his bag for his glasses, which he hated wearing but without which he was almost blind, and declared 'tout est foutu'. In spite of this, de Gaulle returned to France within hours – though he seems not to have been entirely sure even then how things would turn out. He told his son and grandchildren (some of whom were the same age as the student protesters) to stay in Germany. Madame de Gaulle insisted that her jewellery should be left there for safekeeping.

No one in France was sure how things would turn out either. A week earlier, the British ambassador had written: 'prefects and politicians alike ruled out the use of the army'.[94] The British defence attaché had heard 'from the army authorities that no-one wants to call on the army to use force and that they themselves would not be happy to order in young troops against students or workers'.[95] Politicians sensed danger in military intervention. The conscripts who made up the bulk of the army might have refused to fire on civilians but some of de Gaulle's ministers were more worried by what the toughest professional soldiers would do. Pierre Messmer, the minister of the army, had said in early May that the legionnaires and paratroopers 'would not hesitate to shoot and then the worst could happen'.[96]

At the end of the month, however, the tone of reports changed. Bloodshed now seemed possible. Officers were pawing the ground. The British Army of the Rhine noticed that French units in Germany had been sent back to France.[97] Troops had been discreetly posted around Paris 'and could intervene quickly'.[98] The British defence attaché now thought that officers were being sent back from the staff college to their units – perhaps to be ready for action or perhaps to clear the college itself for use as a barracks.

It is probably wrong to look too hard for calculation in de Gaulle's flight and return. He was often guided by intuition rather than logic. In the previous few weeks, his entourage had felt that his intuition was no longer reliable, but in the last few days of May the general seems to have become himself again. He had removed himself from the febrile atmosphere of the Élysée Palace. Perhaps flying over provincial France reminded him of the flight to London in 1940 or perhaps it simply reminded him that the provinces, in the east especially, were quieter than Paris.

During the last week of May, de Gaulle had often seemed absent even while he was installed at the Élysée. On 28 May, the British ambassador had written that Pompidou was the only figure with authority and that 'the general is up in the clouds pursuing his idea of a dialogue (or rather a monologue) between himself and the people'.[99] He reported on a lunch of leading bankers and industrialists. He was struck by the fact that 'There was astonishingly little mention of General de Gaulle.'[100] The ambassador thought it possible that de Gaulle would be forced to go abroad – not to flee revolution but simply because his presence might become an embarrassment. Switzerland or Italy were the most likely countries to which de Gaulle might retire: 'I cannot see him returning to Britain if he has any choice in the matter.'[101] On the morning of 29 May, the embassy reported that 'the French government now looks in a state of disintegration'.[102]

COUNTER-REVOLUTION

Curiously, a few hours of physical absence made de Gaulle more present. For the first time since the beginning of May, he was the centre of attention. On his return, he made another speech. This time, he talked on the radio rather than on television. This was a good move. On television, de Gaulle was unattractive: an elderly lady from Alsace, an admirer of the general and a friend of his family, told him that she could tell from his expression during his television broadcast of 24 May that 'you are cross with us'.[103] The disembodied voice on the radio had no age. It evoked the broadcast of 18 June 1940, which had first called on the French to resist the Germans. Alain Peyrefitte wrote:

> For all of that day, we had nothing of the general except a voice . . . he was going to speak only on the radio, as he had done in London in the crackling night broadcasts. He had rediscovered the confidence to try to reverse the situation with, as his only weapon, words: a naked voice.[104]

De Gaulle also gained from changes in France. The conservative bourgeoisie, cowed or silent for much of May, began to show itself again. Some right-wingers had initially seen the student protests in a benign light. There had once been right-wing riots and demonstrations in the Latin Quarter and some aspects of the new left that was visible in 1968 – its distaste for Jacobin centralism and consumerism – appealed to an old right. The historian Philippe Ariès heard students echoing the views of 'our reactionary youth'. He was struck in particular by the 'rejection of politics, the return to our world of collective and repressed depths'.[105] There was fighting between right-wing groups and student radicals in 1968 but there were also times when the two sides regarded each other with grudging respect. A member of a *comité d'action lycéen* recalled a meeting addressed by Georges Sauge – a Catholic from the pro-Algérie Française right. The young left-winger compared Sauge's 'sincere' attitude favourably to that of the 'more static' Communist Party and to the 'retrogressive power of Gaullism'. He added: 'For them [i.e. Sauge's variety of the right] the consumer society is something to be rejected.' Sauge told his audience 'to do their utmost for the revolution because existing society is abominable in the eyes of Christ'.[106]

Most of all, parts of the extreme right in 1968 were driven by loathing for de Gaulle. For some, this loathing stretched back to the liberation and the purge of Pétainists. For others, it was rooted in resentment at the loss of Algeria – a resentment that was felt keenly by the million European settlers who had come to France from Algeria, soldiers and sections of the political right, including some former Gaullists. Some of these people remained fiercely anti-Gaullist, others decided that de Gaulle might be the lesser evil. The key figure in this realignment was Jean-Louis Tixier-Vignancour. Tixier had been a right-wing deputy in 1940 and a supporter of the Vichy government. At the end of the Algerian War, he had acted as a defence lawyer for those who rebelled against de Gaulle – including some who were sentenced to death – and he had represented the anti-Gaullist right in the 1965 presidential election.

Tixier, however, decided that Communism was the main enemy in 1968 and that de Gaulle should be backed. There were also discreet negotiations with the former supporters of Algérie Française. De Gaulle himself made no promises – though he cannot have been under any illusion that Massu wanted an amnesty for soldiers convicted of rebellion in the early 1960s and his government did give such an amnesty in the summer of 1968. Other Gaullists had had more explicit conversations with veterans of the Algérie Française campaign – sometimes the very men against whom they had once fought.[107]

Throughout May, some Gaullists had worked quietly to build, or revive, organizations that might defend the Fifth Republic. Jacques Baumel, a deputy for the Seine, had brought together leaders of various groups – particularly those of *anciens combattants*. Pierre Lefranc revived the Association Nationale pour le Soutien de l'Action du Général de Gaulle and the Service d'Action Civique, which dated from 1958 and 1960 respectively.[108] These organizations created the Comités de Défense de la République (CDR). For the next two weeks, these could do little – not even protect the headquarters of the Gaullist youth movement. However, the CDRs were reckoned to have signed up 14,000 people in Paris and 7,000 in the provinces, which made them considerably larger than any of the left-wing groupuscules that they opposed. The tone of these movements was progressive, though some of the men most closely associated with them, notably Charles Pasqua, came from the right wing of Gaullism and, indeed, often from parts of the right that had flirted with violence.

Around 27 May, some Gaullists began to talk of organizing a demonstration in favour of de Gaulle – it was intended first for 31 and then 30 May. The apparent failure of the Grenelle Accords had spurred them to action. Pierre-Charles Krieg, deputy for Paris, also began to talk of a demonstration after the offices of his newspaper, *La Nation*, were burned down on the night of 28–29 May. As was often the case with Gaullism, activists seem to have worked on their own but to have had discreet contacts with, and encouragement from, some figures in de Gaulle's own entourage. The general himself appears not to have known about these manoeuvres – he prided himself on being above sordid deals and organizational details. However, his flight to Germany and return to France helped to dramatize a demonstration that was being planned anyway. Jacques Foccart prevailed on the general to bring forward his speech of 30 May from 8 p.m. to 4.30 – so that it would precede and encourage the demonstration.

The Gaullists marched from the place de la Concorde to the place de l'Étoile. This was the home territory of the Parisian bourgeoisie – away from the Latin Quarter, occupied by the students, and from those areas in eastern Paris, around the place de la Bastille, where the left usually marched. The organizers were nervous. The police anticipated that there would be 20 or 30,000 participants – which would hardly have filled the place de la Concorde. As it turned out there were many more. The organizers claimed a million; the real figure was probably between 300,000 and half a million. As with all demonstrations in May 1968, no one could be sure of numbers but it seems likely that this was the biggest one of the year.[109] Left-wingers advanced dark conspiracy theories – rather as the right had done earlier in the month. They alleged that the demonstrators had marched in circles to make their numbers appear greater.[110]

The government's supporters no longer had to put forward particular proposals: they simply had to be against 'disorder'. There were no speeches at the demonstration and relatively few slogans. The organizers intervened mainly to prevent things from happening – in particular to prevent attacks on opponents and to prevent the demonstration from continuing after its formal end – rather than to incite action. The marchers claimed to represent a 'silent' France and silence – or at least the absence of specific declarations – suited their purposes well. There were glimpses of awkward divisions within the crowd as when, for example, some of them shouted 'Cohn-Bendit to Dachau'. Generally, though, the demonstration was an uncontroversial one – revolving around the tricolour flag, the 'Marseillaise' and the Tomb of the Unknown Soldier.

In some ways, 30 May 1968 was a glorious moment for de Gaulle – one when he had rallied his supporters with a speech that seemed to evoke his illustrious past. There was also, though, a sense in which de Gaulle was confounded by his own victory. He had been most successful at moments – as in 1940 or at the end of the Algerian War – when he had defied expectations of what a conservative might do. He had often managed to inspire enthusiasm among parts of the left and to communicate a sense of adventure and drama around his projects. The demonstration of 30 May, however, was overwhelmingly bourgeois. It seemed now as though de Gaulle represented order and stability rather than risk and adventure.

It was not immediately clear that order and stability would win. A headmaster of a provincial *lycée* who wrote an article on 'the school revolt' took care to give it a precise date, 3 June, and added: 'in a fortnight it may seem to have been overtaken by events'.[111] The close of the academic year brought some relief to the authorities. Employers and the state applied the Grenelle Accords – even though they had not been signed by the unions – and most strikers returned to work in June. Most importantly, the government called legislative elections for the end of June. The fact that elections were held at all was a defeat for many of the protesters, who insisted that 'real democracy' involved the public displays of demonstrations and general assemblies. In any case, the *gauchiste* parties who had been so active in 1968 had almost no electoral support, if they fought elections at all. Consequently, legislative elections pitched the Gaullists directly against the conventional left, particularly the Communists, who could now be blamed for events in May 1968 that they had in fact done little to foment.

De Gaulle secured a large majority and seems to have felt uncomfortable with the sense that he was now the leader of a conventional conservative group. He remarked: 'here is a PSF chamber [i.e. a parliament dominated by the Parti Social Français, a right-wing league of the 1930s] with which I will make a PSU policy'. De Gaulle's main initiative – calling a referendum that might impose, among other things, a devolution of greater power to the regions – did, in fact, provoke debate in the PSU precisely because it seemed close to their own ideas.[112] Pompidou was dismissed as prime minister on 12 July and replaced by Maurice Couve de Murville. René Capitant, a left wing Gaullist who had expressed some sympathy with the protesters of May, was made a minister. But de Gaulle's proposals were defeated in the referendum and he resigned. He supported Pompidou as his replacement, which seemed to suggest that de Gaulle himself understood that the attempt to revive a certain kind of 'historic Gaullism' had failed.

AFTERMATH

De Gaulle's was not the only important departure. Daniel Cohn-Bendit was expelled from France and, though he occasionally crept back across the border, he spent most of the next ten years in Germany. The left-wing groups that had been most active in 1968 were largely banned. The main Maoist party broke up acrimoniously after arguments about whether its leaders had failed to understand the significance of the May protests.

None of this means that the events of 1968 had no consequences in France. Many of the radical movements that arose in the 1970s drew inspiration from 1968 or can be seen as part of long-term movements that had themselves given birth to 1968. However, the spectacular quality of May 1968 in France set it apart from what went before or after. There were those who assumed in its immediate aftermath that it was a 'dress rehearsal' that would in due course be followed by a 'real revolution'. It soon became clear, though, that the 'rehearsal' had been the one and only performance of a play that would never be staged again. Before and after, there were strikes in particular companies, but the great general strike of 1968 was not repeated and strike levels were not particularly high during the eighteen months after May 1968 (see Table 1). Peace returned in other domains: the Cannes film festival had broken down in well-publicized chaos in May 1968 but the following year directors and producers were back in evening dress.

Table 1

Working Days Lost in Strikes in France, in Thousands, 1968–70

	1968	1969	1970
January	105.2	22.8	96.7
February	65	76.4	227.2
March	86.8	752	190.6
April	73.3	76.2	275.1
May		48.5	117.5
June		78.9	250
July	12.7	35.4	42.5
August	3	14.1	10.7
September	8.9	304.4	99.9
October	18.6	327	222.4
November	23.3	423	119.2
December	26	64.9	130.3

Source: *Annuaire Statistique de la France*. (No statistics available for May and June 1968, though the figures must have run into millions.)

The differences between May 1968 and what followed were partly ones of scale, but quantitative differences were so extreme that they became qualitative. The spectacular effervescence of 1968 – the sense that everything might be changed and that change might, indeed, produce a world that was beyond any realistic projection – could not be reproduced. Radicalism after 1968 was more specific. The playful and utopian quality of 1968 disappeared. Militants felt that revolution was a serious matter that required organization and detail. Perhaps it was precisely because they took it seriously that some were to recoil when they understood what the implications of violence might be.

In some respects, 1968 produced reform rather than revolution. This was true in universities where many, even at Nanterre, assumed that the aim should be to produce a less hierarchical, formal and archaic style of teaching but not to abolish notions of academic authority entirely.[113] In France as elsewhere, the established left that had been so denounced in 1968 was often its long-term beneficiary. In 1968 Mitterrand had seemed to incarnate everything that protesters most despised, and it was Mitterrand who appeared to have lost most in the immediate aftermath of 1968. But, in the 1970s, he rebuilt his political career partly by drawing on currents that came out of 1968, most notably from the PSU. French commentators who talk of *les années 68* usually end their story with the election of Mitterrand to the presidency in May 1981. Thirteen years earlier, Cohn-Bendit remarked dismissively that Mitterrand might be 'useful'; as it turned out it was Mitterrand who used 1968.

6
West Germany

Demonstration in Berlin after the attempted assassination of Rudi Dutschke.

6

The alienation of one generation from the other has been particularly marked in West Germany where the elder generation is more discredited than perhaps in any other country. Most over 40 are more or less tarnished by their association with Nazism, whose ugly history is increasingly well known to German youth. Those in their thirties are still likely to be dismissed as mere hedonists, wallowers in the 'economic miracle'. Germany's recent history, which is probably more thoroughly known than is the case in other countries, serves as a lesson in what to reject. Aside from the resistance conspirators against Hitler, there are almost no heroes.

CIA report into 'Restless Youth', 1970[1]

'ZERO HOUR': THE GERMAN POST-WAR

If 68 was partly a reaction against the institutions and assumptions of the post-war years, then this reaction had a special edge in Germany because there was no other country in which 1945 marked a more dramatic caesura. Six years of war and twelve years of Nazi rule produced a devastation beyond anything seen in France and Italy or, *a fortiori*, in Britain and the US. Millions of Germans (civilians as well as soldiers) were dead. Hundreds of thousands of prisoners of war were in Soviet camps; the last did not return until 1956. Many

cities were bombed flat. Soviet occupation had terrifying consequences for much of the civilian population, especially women.

Germany surrendered 'unconditionally', which meant that its government ceased to exist and all power was handed to the victorious
Allies. At first, some thought that Germany would be ruled as a 'colony' for twenty years. The British labelled the moment of surrender
(midnight on 8 May) 'zero hour'. This brisk military term came to
have a wider resonance. It implied a whole national history that was
to be restarted. For a time the British, French, Americans and the
Soviet Union had a free hand in how they were to mould the country
and each was given a zone of occupation, though it soon became clear
that the first three, who merged their zones in 1949 and created a new
state, the Federal Republic of Germany, had very different plans from
the Russians, whose zone became the German Democratic Republic
(GDR). The Soviet Union installed what was effectively a Communist
government (the ruling Socialist Unity Party was in name an alliance
of parties) in their zone with the aid of German Communists who had
escaped from Hitler. The Western powers, especially Britain and the
United States, sought to 'denazify' the areas that they controlled and
also to create new institutions that would break with the pre-1933
German past.

The reconstruction of West Germany had three curious results.
First, the Allies, the British especially, had created a country that was
moulded in the image of what they would have liked their own country to have been, particularly with regard to trade unions and
industrial relations. The British ruling class came to regard Germany
as a model of political consensus and economic efficiency. Only occasionally did they glimpse dark memories beneath the urbane surface
of West Germany. At a London dinner party in 1974, the conversation turned to the guests' memories of their weddings. The German
ambassador, Karl-Günther von Hase, recounted his. He had been an
officer on the Eastern Front in February 1945 and his unit had been
forbidden to retreat. He was allowed to marry his fiancée in a ceremony that was conducted over the radio. After this, his position was
overrun and his new wife did not know whether he was alive or dead
for two years. He returned from a Soviet camp in 1950.[2]

The second feature of the remaking of Germany was that the Allies – the British and Americans in particular – thought of themselves as a force for progress in post-war Germany, especially as they increasingly defined their policy in opposition to what the Russians were doing in the east of the country. One result of this was that they imbued some German institutions with the very qualities – consensus, technocracy and 'political maturity' – against which part of the student left was to react in 68. Indeed, some of the people who were to confront student protesters in Britain and America had worked to recast Germany in 1945. Henry Kissinger, who had left Germany as a fifteen-year-old Jewish refugee in 1938, returned as a sergeant, responsible for denazification, in the US army. Noel Annan, who, as a British university principal would write a report on student unrest in 1972, was, as a 26-year-old colonel in the British army, charged with advising German politicians who were decades his senior.[3]

It is notable that the epicentre of German student radicalism in the late 1960s was not some ancient university of student duelling fraternities and magisterial professors. Rather it was the Free University of Berlin, which had been established by the Allies to provide an alternative to the Humboldt University, now in the Soviet zone. The Free University had been designed to allow for more student participation and to escape the rigid hierarchies traditionally associated with German higher education. Its structure was devised in large measure by the liberal English educationalist, and later headmaster of Eton, Robert Birley. During the student troubles of 1967, an English diplomat wrote: 'The allies, or rather the Americans and ourselves, have a special relationship with the Free University in that the basic idea of such a university was thought up by the British (specifically Dr Birley) and has subsequently been heavily backed by American money.[4]

The third feature of post-war Germany was that the destruction of the Third Reich did not mean that all individuals or institutions associated with Nazism lost power nor that all references to Nazism disappeared. On the contrary, they were ubiquitous on the radical left in the late 1960s though so much so that they appeared to have become an all-encompassing means of attacking the post-war political system rather than a reference to specific Nazi crimes.

GENERATIONS IN POST-WAR GERMANY

The generational foundations of post-war German politics were particularly complicated. The manner of the war's ending cast a demographic shadow. Whereas France, Britain and America all experienced post-war 'baby booms', the German birth rate, which, partly because of Nazi population policies, had been relatively high in the 1930s, was low in the years after 1945 and did not begin to pick up again until the 1950s. The cohort of Germans who reached the age of twenty in 1968 was small. The post-war division of Germany also had an influence on the generational structure of the West. Until the Berlin Wall was built in 1961, movement between East and West Germany was relatively easy. Over 3 million people moved from the Communist-ruled East to the West; the young and the educated were over-represented in this group. East Germany, which invested heavily in education, was the unwilling source of graduates and students flowing into West Germany. In political terms, these new arrivals provided some of the most prominent leaders of protest in 1968.

Nazism and war meant that small differences in age could be associated with very different kinds of experience. The real Nazi generation – those who had supported Hitler in 1933 or exercised influence in the Third Reich – had usually been born in the nineteenth century. Younger than them were those who had been of fighting age in the Second World War. In 1957, the sociologist Helmut Schelsky (himself born in 1912 and a bitter opponent of student radicals after 1968) christened his contemporaries the 'Sceptical Generation'.[5] He believed that they were marked by distaste for the extremism of their elders – some of them would also dislike this quality when it appeared among their juniors in the late 1960s. The Social Democrat politician Helmut Schmidt (born in 1918) was a good example of the sceptical generation and summed up his attitude to student protest with the remark 'people who have visions should see a doctor'.

Younger than the sceptical generation were those sometimes labelled the 'flak generation'. Members of this group were too young to serve as ordinary soldiers but old enough to operate anti-aircraft guns during the last desperate defence of the Reich in 1945. The philosopher Jürgen Habermas (born in 1929) was a member of this generation. More politically radical than Schmidt, he was nonetheless disturbed by the irrationalism and intolerance that he associated with student protest in 1968.

Younger than the flak generation were those who had been children during the Second World War – too young to fight even in its final stages and too young (so long as they were not Jewish) to be directly touched by Nazi repression. For them the Second World War had sometimes gone with an incongruous freedom. Far from having been oppressed by paternal authority, many had grown up when their fathers were away at the front, sometimes not to return. Andreas Baader, who was to found the Red Army Faction terrorist group, was born in 1943 and grew up 'in a community of grieving women'.[6] The childhoods of these young people were often marked by the destruction of family homes and flight from the Red Army. Theirs was a world in which an American GI with chocolate to give away might be more powerful than any schoolteacher or policeman. For those who had been children during the war, the restoration of conventional authority that came with the establishment of the Federal Republic of Germany in 1949 might seem unwelcome – especially if this political change coincided with the return of a bitter, broken father from a Soviet prisoner-of-war camp.

The particularly German pattern of relations between the generations was also influenced by the fact that, even by the standards of continental Europe, German students, male students in particular, took a long time to complete their studies.[7] The Chancellor of West Germany noted at the beginning of 1968 that, whereas 80 per cent of American students were under twenty-one, 70 per cent of German students were aged between twenty-three and thirty, that is the majority of them had been born before 1945. An unkind journalist added that: 'At the age when Alexander conquered the world, Napoleon won his battles, Einstein and Planck made their first great discoveries, the majority of German students are still sitting in their classrooms.'[8] The eternal student free to pursue intellectual and political projects for years was an important feature of German universities.

THE ECONOMIC MIRACLE

In 1945 Germany did not even have its own currency – in practice much trade in 1945 was conducted in cigarettes. Part of the population was starving. The Allies, who had considered turning Germany into a purely agricultural country, eventually allowed Germans to rebuild their industry, and they did so in spectacular fashion. By the mid-1960s, the West German economy was the most successful in Europe. Its GDP exceeded that of France or Britain. Prosperity was a feature of all Western countries in the 1950s and 60s and radical protesters often disliked the complacency that they associated with this development. In Germany affluence had a special dimension. The speed of economic growth underwrote a generational divide that revolved partly around how and whether people remembered the immediate post-war years. Those who had endured the worst hardships of wartime often welcomed the comfortable society of the 1960s and this accounted in particular for the relative political quiescence of the working class that sometimes exasperated the student left in 68. Furthermore, Germany was, as Helmut Schmidt was to put it, an economic colossus and a political pygmy. This created a disconcerting sense that the country's whole identity was rooted in production statistics. It was easy to make this prosperity seem obscene when its beneficiaries were men who had exercised power in the Third Reich.

POLITICAL PARTIES, STUDENTS AND THE 'EXTRAPARLIAMENTARY OPPOSITION'

German politics revolved around three parties. The Christian Democrat CDU/CSU (the CSU being the Christian Democrat Party in Bavaria) was dominated by Konrad Adenauer, born in 1876, who insisted that he was too old to have political ambitions and who was still doing so in 1963 when he was finally forced out of the party leadership. The Liberal Party was relatively small but important because of its role as a pivot in many coalitions. The Socialist SPD was the third of the big parties. It was partly because of the power exercised by these major parties that the West German radical left often defined itself in opposition to parliamentary politics and that the phrase 'extraparliamentary opposition' was often used as a synonym for the radical left. Students made up a large part of the radical left but German students were not always left-wing. In the late 1950s, a survey suggested that only 9 per cent of students were 'authentic democrats', 16 per cent were 'authoritarians' and the remainder were simply 'conformists'.[9] Most German students were drawn from relatively prosperous backgrounds (more so than their French counterparts); they were also largely male – partly because bourgeois families concentrated their resources on the educations of sons rather than daughters.[10] Both male and female students were conservative in their views about the family. A particularly male pattern of conservatism was reflected in the popularity of traditional student fraternities (survivals from the days of Bismarck), which took in 40 per cent of all men in German universities in the early 1960s.[11]

The student organization that attracted most attention was the Sozialistischer Deutscher Studentenbund (SDS), which started out as the student wing of the SPD. In the late 1950s, however, the SPD and SDS diverged. The SPD was moving towards the right. At the Bad Godesberg conference in 1959, the party stated that it would seek to reform capitalism rather than abolish it. This helped pave the way for the 'Grand Coalition' of Socialists and Christian Democrats that formed a government in 1966. Around the same time, the SDS moved to the left at its Mannheim convention of October 1958. Increasingly the SDS began to associate with the New Left that it discerned in France and Britain and a little later in the United States. However, the policies of the New Left (particularly nuclear disarmament and dialogue with the Soviet Union) were more controversial in a country with Red Army units posted on its own frontiers than they were in Britain or America.

The foundation of the American Students for a Democratic Society also had an influence on the German student movement. Though the German SDS had no formal link with the American movement which shared its initials, the two groups recognized that they had certain things in common. A member of the German movement, Michael

Vester, born in 1939, who happened to be studying in America, attended the Port Huron convention of 1962. He exercised a considerable influence on the statement that was drafted there – partly because his energy and seriousness extracted 'comatose assent' from American radicals who were less hardened to long political meetings.[12]

In February 1960 the SPD established a new student organization designed to be properly under the control of the party leadership, and in November 1961 the SPD forbade its members from also belonging to the SDS. Even after its break with the SPD, the German SDS was by its later standards remarkably conventional. Its members accepted their expulsion from the party. They did not stage sit-ins at party headquarters, as they almost certainly would have done a few years later. Many members of the SDS at this stage continued to look to the working class and the trade unions for future action. Michael Vester had disagreed with his American comrades at Port Huron who had seen the working class as a spent force. For the next three years, the German SDS devoted much of its energy to reflecting on Marxist theory and considering the changes that might be coming over the working class. They were influenced by the work of C. Wright Mills, whose *The Power Elite* was published in German in 1962, and by the Frenchman André Gorz's thinking about a 'new working class' of technicians, which might make university students increasingly important.

What changed the German SDS, however, were deeds rather than abstract reflection. The activist group Subversive Aktion, founded in the early 1960s, presented itself as an incarnation of 'situationalism', which used theatrical forms of intervention to expose the 'spectacle' of consumerist capitalist society. Dieter Kunzelmann, who had been born in 1939 and spent some months studying in Paris in the late 1950s, became its leading figure in Munich. In Berlin in 1963, Rudi Dutschke (of whom more below) and Bernd Rabehl joined Subversive Aktion. The group staged flamboyant protests – using stink bombs and throwing tomatoes – against the visits of foreign leaders. Their notion of direct action was different from the more earnest teach-ins and sit-ins that marked the American student movement at that time. Subversive Aktion infiltrated the SDS. It blamed the established leaders of the SDS for being too respectable, too bureaucratic and too tied to the labour movement, which was itself a pillar of West

German society. The leader of the SDS, Helmut Schauer, tried to expel the Subversive Aktion faction but found, somewhat to everyone's surprise, that he was unable to do so and that members of his own organization were becoming increasingly interested in direct action.

RUDI DUTSCHKE

One person above all became associated with student radicalism in West Germany. Rudi Dutschke – a small, intense man whose rapid speaking style was said to derive partly from his early ambition to be a sports commentator – had been born in Brandenburg in 1940. His father did not return from a Soviet prisoner-of-war camp until the boy was seven. He spent his early years in East Germany but moved to the West, partly because his studies in the East were blocked on account of his refusal to perform military service. Like many student radicals, Dutschke had grown up as a devout Lutheran but, unlike many, his adult life was lived within a fairly conventional Christian framework. He married an American theology student, Gretchen, and had children with her – one of them predictably named Che.

Dutschke presents an interesting contrast with the other great star of student rebellion in Western Europe: Daniel Cohn-Bendit. Both men had an extraordinary self-confidence and a capacity to enthuse crowds. But Cohn-Bendit's cheerful self-mockery was different from Dutschke's intensity. Cohn-Bendit also had a strong sense of the concrete. He was largely indifferent to political theory and most of his interventions were designed, even in the extraordinary climate of May 1968, to achieve specific goals. Dutschke did consider theory important, and his departure from the GDR seems to have gone with an increased determination to grapple with the canon of Marxist writing.

Dutschke did not always feel comfortable as a charismatic leader, a role that raised particular problems for any thoughtful German. In addition to this, his oratory sometimes worked spells that he did not fully control. His friend Bernd Rabehl commented that one of Dutschke's speeches was like a performance by a jazz musician who did not entirely know where his brilliant improvisation might take him. Often his style was separate from the substance of what he said. It was revealing that those who lived under Communist rule sometimes admired Dutschke. This was most obviously true of East Germany, but also of Hungary and Czechoslovakia. His associates in these countries sensed his moral seriousness and were grateful for the fact that he did not equivocate in his opposition to Communist repression, but they also regarded much of what he actually said as absurd. One recalled: 'There was immediately something akin to love between us, a very great closeness ... The love lasted but the problem with Dutschke was that he only talked nonsense, leftist, stupid 68er nonsense.'[13]

Dutschke's personal manner could produce strange effects. His public and private personas seemed very different from each other. Michael Baumann, a working-class young man who was himself eventually to take up arms in a terrorist group, remarked: 'His [Dutschke's] speeches were so abstract that no one understood them ... but when you just talked to him he was totally cool.'[14] Those who got to know the private Dutschke often commented on his gentleness and lack of pretention; they were struck by the fact that his care for children and respect for women seemed at odds with the aggressively masculine culture of much of the student left.

Violence was a particular problem. In 1977, Dutschke condemned the terrorism of some his contemporaries and he never advocated action against people, as opposed to property. But the very intensity of his manner could seem like an incitement to violence regardless of the words he used. Furthermore, in the late 1960s his statements sometimes seemed to entail a degree of ambiguity. In 1968, he drew a Jesuitical distinction between violence in places such as Iran – where 'fascism' might be associated with a single individual and where assassination might therefore be useful – and violence in West Germany, where authoritarianism was more systematic and thus an attack on any single politician would not change anything.[15] The tragicomic quality of Dutschke's odd mix of pacifist intentions and fiery rhetoric was revealed when Alain Krivine found a revolver in the glove compartment of Dutschke's car – buried under political tracts and banana skins. Dutschke's comrades had insisted that he carried the weapon for protection, though he would never have been able to use it.[16]

EMERGENCY LAW

Three partly related movements marked German student radicalism in the second half of the 1960s. One of these was opposition to the Emergency Law that had been proposed by the coalition of Social Democrats and Christian Democrats in 1966. The Emergency Law would grant the executive greater powers in moments of crisis. It was designed partly to ensure that Germany enjoyed full sovereignty so that the Allies would not assume powers themselves in the event of invasion. There was nothing particularly shocking about such legislation, especially after the SPD redrafted it to restrict its use against civil unrest. Britain invoked a state of emergency six times between 1966 and 1974. However, the idea of an Emergency Law brought back awkward memories of such legislation under the Weimar Republic. The prospect of an Emergency Law also alarmed the German trade unions, who feared that it might be used against the right to strike. For this reason, it provided a rare opportunity for unity between student radicals and the organized working class – something that the more conventional leaders of the SDS were keen to exploit.

THE THIRD WORLD

The second important movement sprang from an interest in the Third World. German radicals became engaged by Latin America, Asia and Africa partly because of their contact with non-European students, who had been brought to German universities by academic exchange programmes. Furthermore, third worldism offered a means to circumvent the East/West division that was so apparent in Germany. Guerrilla wars outside Europe seemed to be a motor for revolution at a time when the working class in affluent countries, and especially in Germany, had reconciled itself to living with capitalism.

The sympathy for such causes blurred into increasing interest in the protests of African Americans, in particular a fascination with the Black Panthers. Reference to the third world and/or non-white minorities was always an oddly abstract matter in Germany which, unlike the United States, did not have an established non-white population. References to empire were also rather abstract. Some German left-wingers had been involved in the campaign against the French presence in Algeria between 1954 and 1962 and they frequently denounced the 'imperialism' of the United States. However, like the British (see chap. 7), German left-wingers rarely referred to their own country's imperial history – though students at Hamburg University did pull down a statue of the colonial administrator Hermann von Wissmann, which they covered in red paint and fruit yoghurt from the student cafeteria.[17]

In practical terms, the third worldism of German students was expressed in protest around particular events. The showing in Berlin in 1966 of a film, *Africa Addio*, with a racist portrayal of the Congo, provoked demonstrations. The movie was particularly offensive to German radicals because it depicted Siegfried ('Kongo') Müller – a former Wehrmacht soldier who had become a mercenary – executing a prisoner.[18]

The Vietnam War had special resonance in West Germany. Germany and Vietnam were both divided countries in which an American-supported sector faced another that was under Communist rule. The Americans were not above drawing this fact to the attention of the Germans, but the comparison went only so far. West Germany was democratic in a way that South Vietnam was not and the strategic importance of Germany was infinitely greater than that of Vietnam. German conservatives were keen for the Americans to show resolution in Vietnam but also keen that doing so should not distract them from the main theatre of the Cold War – which they believed to be in Europe. Adenauer said, in private and after he had ceased to be Chancellor, that he regarded US intervention in Vietnam as a 'disaster' which risked America getting 'sucked deeper into the morass in South East Asia' when 'Europe was the decisive area'.[19] There was no serious prospect that German troops would go to Vietnam – West Germany had been allowed to rearm only when it joined NATO in 1955 and West German soldiers did not serve outside their country's frontiers. Still, West Germany was more vulnerable to American pressure than most other European countries. Large numbers of American soldiers were stationed on its territory and in return it was obliged to buy American military equipment for its own forces. It was also persuaded to send non-military aid – notably a hospital ship – to South Vietnam.

American attitudes to West Germany were double-edged. It presented Germany as one of its strongest allies and West Berlin as an outpost of freedom – hence Kennedy's famous 'Ich bin ein Berliner' speech of 1963 and Khrushchev's more earthy remark that West Berlin was 'the testicles of the West' – but the US was also conscious of Germany's dependence. For all his fine words, Kennedy subordinated the interests of Germany to his wider relations with the Soviet Union, and his successor, Lyndon Johnson, summed up his view of how he should deal with the Germans thus: 'You keep patting them on the head and then every once in a while you kick them in the balls.'[20]

The heavy American presence in West Germany also provided opportunities for protest against US policy in Vietnam – this was especially true of West Berlin. The city had been used as a showcase for Western values, which also meant that it became a stage for the kind of political theatre to which the student left was increasingly disposed. West Berlin was governed under special rules. The Communist Party was tolerated there even when, from 1956 to 1968, it was illegal in the rest of West Germany. Radical leftists were drawn to West Berlin by the fact that housing was cheap and also that residents of the city were exempt from military service. One observer estimated that a quarter of the most active student militants in West Germany lived in Berlin. Götz Aly (a student at the Free University from November 1968) later said that the conservative states of southern Germany should pay compensation to Berlin for having 'shunted their potential rebels' to the city.[21]

In February 1966, anti-Vietnam War demonstration brought 2,000 people to Berlin. This was the first of a number of protests in the city that culminated in early 1968 with a march that drew radical leaders from across Europe to Berlin and that turned the city into the capital of European protest until the beginning of the May events in Paris.

It was, however, a demonstration about another part of the non-European world that produced the single most dramatic moment for the extraparliamentary left. In June 1967, the Shah of Iran visited West Berlin, and German and Iranian students organized protests against the presence of this authoritarian ruler in the city. During one of these, on 2 June, a student protester, Benno Ohnesorg, was shot dead by a policeman, Karl-Heinz Kurras. The death, and the fact that Kurras was subsequently acquitted of any crime, outraged many. Some traced the radicalization of the student movement that was to lead to the terrorism of the 1970s back to this moment and one terrorist group adopted the name '2 June group'. Ohnesorg himself was not a particularly radical figure. He was a married man with a pregnant wife; he was a member of a Protestant student association and had never previously attended a demonstration.

THE LEGACY OF NAZISM

References to the crimes of the Third Reich gave generational conflict a particularly sharp edge in Germany. Sometimes such references became stock terms of abuse that both sides threw at each other. In Frankfurt in November 1967, the rector accused student demonstrators who disrupted a lecture of being concerned 'not with the exercise of democratic rights but with the use of fascistic terorism'; they replied that his remarks expressed 'contempt for the victims of Auschwitz'.[22] Gudrun Ensslin, who was born in 1940 and would join the Red Army Faction in the 1970s, was widely believed to have justified violent action after the death of Benno Ohnesorg by saying: 'You cannot talk to the generation who made Auschwitz.' In fact, it is not clear that Ensslin ever used these words,[23] but the frequency with which they are cited perhaps illustrates the way in which Nazism came to seep into every aspect of radical politics in West Germany. Ensslin's own family epitomizes the complexity of relations between individuals and the Nazi past. Her father was a Protestant pastor who had led a life of unheroic passivity under Nazism – though he followed his daughter's political career with sympathy. Ensslin's lover, Bernward Vesper, was the son of a writer who had been prominent under Nazism. Ensslin and Vesper sometimes funded their radical activities by selling editions of Vesper *père*'s work.

Some leaders of the German radical left in 1968 were indeed the children of Nazis. Rainer Langhans (born in 1940) was the son of a party member and was himself educated for a time at a military school, immersed in an institution that had not entirely purged itself of the Nazi past. However, most German 68ers, like most student radicals in the West, came from families with relatively left-wing views. One activist, interviewed thirty years after the events, remarked that their opposition was expressed with regard to 'abstract' rather than biological parents.[24]

For some 68ers, the most troubling aspect of their own family history was its ambiguity rather than the clear sense that left-wing children were pitted against Nazi parents. Many 68ers were related to people who had complicated relations with Nazism. Ulrike Meinhof, the radical journalist and later founder of the Red Army Faction, was born in 1934. Her father had been a Nazi but he died when she was young and her mother also died, in 1949. Thereafter, she was raised by her mother's friend Renate Riemeck. Riemeck was a Christian peace activist after the war who concealed the fact that she had once been a member of the Nazi party. Karl-Dietrich Wolff (born in 1943) quarrelled with his father, who had been a judge under Nazism. Only after his father was killed in an accident did he steel himself to read the letters of his parents, at which point he realized that his mother had been the more committed Nazi.[25]

The militants of 68 lived in a world of clear moral choice and often found the messy world of compromise and survival that had marked their parents' lives hard to accept. Joschka Fischer, born in 1948, was later to remark that he learned to divide Germans into 'victims and heroes'.[26] In the 1960s, a succession of revelations made this image harder to sustain. Adolf Eichmann, an architect of the extermination of the Jews, was kidnapped in 1960 and subsequently tried by the Israelis. From 1963 to 1965, the Germans tried a number of Auschwitz guards. Revelations did not necessarily produce a more nuanced view of the moral divisions of Germany. On the contrary, young people often simply added the category of 'criminals' to those of victims and heroes. Sometimes, in their bid to fit their own families into simple moral categories, 68ers dreamed up an imaginary ancestry for themselves. Maren Sell was the daughter of parents who had tried 'not with a huge amount of courage' to avoid involvement in Nazism, but she remembered fantasizing that her mother might have been a resister and she recalled that she and many of her contemporaries liked to think that they had Jewish origins.[27]

Relations with the Nazi past were complicated by the very radicalization of the German student left. In 1958, the SDS had organized an exhibition on 'Unredeemed Nazi Justice', about Nazis who remained active in the judiciary. Other students simply displayed the doctoral dissertations that their own professors had published during the Third Reich, dissertations that often sought to justify aspects of Nazi policy.[28] In 1966, a new and dramatic occasion for protest was presented when Kurt Kiesinger, who had worked for Joseph Goebbels's propaganda department and who was now a CDU politician, was appointed as Chancellor in the Grand Coalition government that brought together the Christian Democrats and the SPD. There were protests against Kiesinger – the most dramatic of which by Beate Klarsfeld, who publicly slapped the Chancellor. But Klarsfeld was not a student radical. She was a housewife in Paris, where she had moved and married a French Jewish survivor of the occupation. Klarsfeld was grateful for the support of some of the German left, notably Dutschke, but she felt that the SDS was generally so interested in Nazism as an abstract entity, one that in practice encompassed much of the post-war state, that it had ceased to be interested in individual Nazis and their specific crimes:

> They could not understand, because, wanting to install a revolution straight away, they found it normal that an ex Nazi should be carried by German capitalism to the head of the Federal Republic. It was in the logic of a situation that they wanted to fight as a whole.[29]

THE GERMAN DEMOCRATIC REPUBLIC

Where was East Germany in the West German 68? In one sense, it overshadowed all politics. The West German state was founded on the assertion that Germany was a single country that ought to be reunified. Radical students often denounced anti-Communism, sometimes suggesting that it played the same role that had once been played by anti-Semitism. They also often defined themselves in opposition to official government policy by suggesting that the *de facto* frontiers between East and West should be respected – though Dutschke supported reunification, arguing that a unified Berlin might show the way to a new kind of politics that would escape from divisions of East and West. Some 68ers joined the Communist Party when it was re-formed in 1968 – though others joined a kaleidoscope of Communist parties owing allegiance to a variety of states other than those of the Warsaw Pact – China, Albania, North Korea. Generally, though, the German radical left did not support the East German regime and was discomfited when the black American activist Angela Davis, much admired in West German radical circles, was received favourably in East Berlin.

The GDR itself was keen to make mischief for its Western rival. It provided information for those investigating the Nazi past of Western officials and helped Beate Klarsfeld – though there were plenty of former Nazis who played some role in the GDR. When the funeral cortège of Benno Ohnesorg drove down an East German *autobahn*, citizens were encouraged to show sympathy, but the West German authorities believed that the ruling party in the East was in fact worried about the possibility of unrest in its own universities: 'All this showed that the East German authorities were not quite sure how to treat this phenomenon.'[30] One assumes that those in the East German authorities who knew that the policeman who had shot Ohnesorg was an East German spy must have been particularly unsure. There were people, probably just a few hundred, in East Germany, especially East Berlin, whose activities seemed to run parallel with 68ers in the West. But, in general, the East German 68 was one in which the political left – often reluctant to break with Communism entirely – was separate from the counter-culture of rock music and rebellion. Kongo Müller – the German mercenary who was so reviled by the West German left was brought to the attention of East German young people by their own government's propaganda, but some of them responded by treating him as a hero, whose name they sometimes bracketed with that of the Rolling Stones.[31]

THE CRISIS OF THE
EXTRAPARLIAMENTARY LEFT

Some saw 1968 as a year of crisis for the German radical left. In April of that year, a young housepainter, inspired – many leftists believed – by articles in the right-wing Springer newspapers, shot Dutschke. He survived, but was badly injured and died eleven years later without having fully recovered. He spent years out of Germany and never again played the same role in public life – although characteristically he wrote to his would-be assassin urging him to take up arms on behalf of his own class rather than against the student left. The assassination attempt sometimes looked as though it had itself become part of the political theatre associated with Dutschke. It provoked demonstrations as far away as New York and concentrated attention on Dutschke as a radical icon. But it also removed him from the centre of the political stage at precisely the moment when part of the German student movement was turning towards the most extreme radicalism. It is hard to know what role Dutschke would have played if he had remained in good health. Would he have joined some of his former colleagues in support of violence? Or would he, like Cohn-Bendit, have turned to a more conventional form of politics?

Parliament finally passed the Emergency Law on 30 May 1968, the same day that Gaullists demonstrated in favour of order in Paris. The trade unions found the revised version of the law tolerable and the single cause that had seemed most likely to unite students and workers disappeared. By 1970, the CIA believed that 'The frenetic activity of previous years, particularly 1967 and 1968, has subsided' and given way to a 'landscape of smoking but presently inactive volcanoes'. Its analysts explained the change thus:

> In retrospect, the Dutschke affair may have been both the high point and the start of a downward slide for the radical student movement. As violence mounted and extremism became rampant, sympathy and support from moderate elements ebbed. Issues became scarcer, and without the magnetic Dutschke – robbed of his demagogic talent and fighting zeal by a head wound – the remaining far leftists began to

vent their aggressions increasingly on each other and less on society as a whole. Liberal opinion has been outraged by bombings and by such incidents as a May 1970 shoot-out in which a radical charged with arson was helped to escape from prison.[32]

The SDS became increasingly radical as was illustrated in November 1968 by the student occupation of the Institute for Social Research at Frankfurt. This was the centre of the 'Frankfurt School' of Marxism, which had been established largely by Jewish intellectuals forced into exile by Nazism. The bitterness of ensuing debate was captured in correspondence between two members of the school – Theodor Adorno, who was director of the institute, and Herbert Marcuse, who remained sympathetic to the German students, perhaps, at least in part, because he was living several thousand miles away from them in California. In 1970, the SDS was disbanded. By this time, some of its former members had turned to violence and were on the road that would take them to murder in the 1970s (see chap. 10).

The German 68 is often examined through the prism of the Nazi past and/or that of the terrorist future. Often the two are related because reference to Nazism was couched in such general terms that it seemed to justify almost any kind of violence and because opponents of the radical left drew attention to the ways in which its approach paralleled that of fascism.

There is a more general point that one could make about the 68 in Germany. Some sections of the radical left denounced their opponents in such sweeping terms that they treated the whole political spectrum, including the democratic left, with equal contempt. Helmut Schelsky summed matters up thus:

There is hardly any revolutionary movement which has given itself less intellectual trouble ... to define its enemy. It proceeds largely by defamatory and polemical concepts. The 'authorities' in all institutions are designated as the 'establishment' or the 'rulers' regardless of how democratically or legitimately they have come to their leading positions and regardless also of which political and social tasks and beliefs they acknowledge and represent. The polemical and strategic intentions of this type of analysis permit it to be applied equally to conservative politicians like Kiesinger, Barzel and Strauss and to social democrats like Schiller, Leber and Helmut Schmidt.[33]

There was an element of truth in Schelsky's view. The propensity to consider indistinguishable all political opponents of the radical left, at least for a time, a form of radical opposition in Germany that had little parallel elsewhere. But the emphasis on extreme division can be deceptive. The article in which Schelsky denounced student radicals for lumping all their enemies together contained an interesting paradox because Schelsky also lumped all 68ers together and included, for example, those who were members of the SPD.

The truth is that the German 68 contained multiple levels of political engagement. Substantial numbers of students supported the established parties against which the 'extraparliamentary opposition' defined itself. Indeed 50 per cent of students, as opposed to 37 per cent of the general population, had supported the Emergency Law when it was first mooted in 1966. It is true that 30 per cent of German students sympathized with the aims of the SDS, but this sympathy often amounted just to a desire for university reform.[34] Later developments, particularly the killing of Benno Ohnesorg, provoked student protest but this did not necessarily imply extreme radicalization – the Christian Democrat student body protested about the killing.

The number of the most committed radicals was relatively small. Membership of the German SDS probably peaked at 2,000; membership of the American group that shared its initials peaked at 100,000. There were probably just 20,000 active student militants in the whole of West Germany. The number of those involved in the most flamboyant groups was far smaller. Kommune Number 1, which staged dramatic protests and was eventually expelled from the SDS in 1967, was made up primarily of the inhabitants of a single Berlin apartment. Often, as one historian has put it, the history of student radicalism in Germany 'was less a history of SDS per se than of a series of interventions on SDS by a small group of individuals'.[35] Even more than in other countries, there was a symbiotic relation between the most extreme radicals in West Germany and the mainstream media. Much of what the former did provided stories for the latter, which in turn gave an exaggerated sense of the importance of extreme radicalism.

Large numbers of German students – particularly in the south – were relatively little touched by radicalism. The most extreme figures in West Berlin turned against the liberal institutions – notably the Free University – that had been created by the victorious Allies after 1945. However, some students were actually moving towards the democratic left, and often away from the implicit conservatism of traditional student fraternities. It is revealing that British officials in Berlin and Bonn took a benign view of student protesters, many of whom they believed to be relatively moderate: 'It would seem that, in the context of recent German history, we should be encouraged by signs that a politically aware, left-inclined university generation may be emerging, which is prepared to rebel against the social and political patterns of its parents.'[36]

The German 68 was unusual in one revealing respect. Elsewhere, the protest movements of the late 1960s coincided with and sometimes helped to produce right-wing electoral victories – those of Heath, Nixon and the Gaullists. Germany, though, moved to the left in 1969. The Grand Coalition of the SPD and Christian Democrats was replaced by a coalition of the Liberals and SPD under Willy Brandt. Brandt was hardly a 68er – on 13 May 1968, as the French trade unions launched a general strike in support of the students, he had been in Burgundy being inducted into the Confrérie des Chevaliers du Taste-vin. He was, nevertheless, quite sympathetic to aspects of the student movement – partly because his son, Peter, was active in it.

Brandt, born in 1912, had gone into exile under Nazism and, indeed, fought against the Third Reich as a member of the Norwegian Resistance. He had been mayor of West Berlin in the first half of the 1960s and had been willing to talk to student protesters there. The CIA suggested 'the image of a lenient father [Brandt] with radical sons of his own is more appealing than that of former Chancellor Kiesinger, the aloof patriarch, inclined to condemn youthful excesses'.[37] Brandt recognized that there was not always a sharp division between protesters and those they attacked. He feared that protesters might repeat the mistake of those Marxists who had helped bring down the Weimar Republic through their own radicalism – though he also admitted that he had been one of those radicals. He saw the SPD as a party that was always influenced by dialogue with intellectuals and added that student protest left a legacy, even when its most dramatic manifestations had passed: '[It] introduced our societies to a process of manifold change which penetrated the most varied domains and even left its mark on conservative schools of thought.'[38]

The government that Brandt headed was the most left-wing one since the Weimar Republic. Democratic politics in Germany did not collapse. Some prominent 68ers eventually decided in the 1980s that such politics provided the best way to change their country and they invested their hopes mainly in the Green Party. Even before this, large numbers of Germans supported the SPD and the youth wing of this party was in fact one of the great beneficiaries of 68. The influx of radicals into the youth wing of the SPD was sometimes awkward for the main party, especially after Karsten Voigt became its leader and took it to the left. Generally, though, Brandt's associates considered that it was easier to have radicalism contained in their own party than attacking it from outside. The youth wing of the SPD had 250,000 members – a number that dwarfed any other group on the radical left.[39]

In 1967, after the shooting of Benno Ohnesorg, Rudi Dutschke made a speech in which, with a characteristic mix of striking phrase and ambiguous meaning, he referred to the 'Long March through the institutions'. He was almost certainly not suggesting that the German left should compromise with the established institutions of the Federal Republic and yet, looking back on 68, it is hard not to argue that it was precisely what large numbers of German student radicals were to do in the next few decades.[40]

7
Britain

Karl Dietrich Wolff (on the left), Tariq Ali (centre) and Daniel Cohn-Bendit at Karl Marx's tomb in Highgate Cemetery in mid-June 1968.

7

Unrest among university students in the United Kingdom has so far been on an altogether smaller scale than in many other countries ... Where there have been disturbances, the great majority of students have taken no part in them and in a number of cases student majorities have turned out to vote that 'sit-ins' and other similar activities should be terminated.
– Memorandum by vice chancellors and university principals, 21 January 1969[1]

David Lodge's comic novel *Changing Places* (1975) concerns an academic exchange in the late 1960s between a lecturer at Rummidge, an industrial city in England modelled on Birmingham, and a professor at Euphoric State, an American university modelled on Berkeley. The mere notion that the atmosphere in California might be compared with that in the English Midlands evoked amusement. A law professor at Birmingham, seeking to explain student protest there to an American audience, wrote: 'for a staid provincial and heavily scientific University to suffer such upheaval was surprising'.[2] Events in Britain sometimes seemed like a pale imitation of disturbance elsewhere. Indeed protest at Birmingham University was in some ways an imitation of an imitation. Dick Atkinson, a temporary lecturer in sociology, brought with him a radical argot that he had learned as a postgraduate student at the London School of Economics an institution that had in turn been radicalized by the presence of visiting American students.

Satire was an important part of 68 everywhere but in Britain it was woven into radical movements in revealing ways. *Private Eye* maga-zine, which had emerged from student publications in the early 1960s, was admired by many 68ers.[3] Some of them wrote for it – Germaine Greer contributed a gardening column under the name Rose Blight. Gerald Scarfe's cartoon of Harold Wilson licking Lyndon Johnson's arse, which first appeared in the magazine, was carried like a battle standard in demonstrations against the Vietnam War. But in spite, or because, of its links with young radicals, *Private Eye* never took the protests of 68 seriously. Indeed, it mocked the earnest attempts of more established publications to understand student protest and printed a glossary to help its readers translate such analysis. When the correspondent of *The Times* wrote about a 'feeling of being manipulated by uncontrolled concentrations of power', he meant 'boredom'. 'A new approach to the organization of human societies' meant: 'A lot of mad frogs charging around as per usual.'[4]

There is a comic tone even in the memoirs of some leaders of the Brit-ish radical left. They describe their own apparent failure with a masochistic relish and present Britain as a model of philistine insularity. Their counterparts elsewhere took national traditions seriously – either because they respected them, as in France, or denounced them, as in West Germany, or moved from respect to denunciation, as in the United States. Only in Britain did activists regard their own national traditions as simply ridiculous and assume that being 'radical' and being British were mutually exclusive. One remembered that his attraction to the 'cultural and intellectual milieu of Paris' (about which he knew rela-tively little) was fuelled by 'growing disdain for Anglo-Saxon attitudes as exemplified by the public school [St Paul's] I attended and had come to hate'. His attitudes to the Bloomsbury Group were double-edged because they were 'at once open to foreign influence (good) and quintes-sentially English (bad)'.[5]

Historians too have tended to present protest in Britain in 68 as trivial or to see Britain as an intrinsically conservative country. One writes:

> But politically, what impressed me most about Britain around the end
> of the 1960s were not the politics of the student revolt (a fairly tame
> affair) or even of the protest movement against American action in

Vietnam (however impressive). It was rather the unapologetic racism of the Smithfield meat porters marching in 1967 [sic] in support of Enoch Powell, [and] the gerrymandered Protestant state of Northern Ireland.[6]

Much is made of incidents such as that when, in October 1968, at the end of a rally against the Vietnam War, demonstrators linked arms with policemen and sang 'Auld Lang Syne'.

There is an element of justice in such portrayals. The student radicalism of the late 1960s was less spectacular in mainland Britain than in the United States or continental Europe – the working-class rebellions of the 1970s and events in Northern Ireland were a different matter. However, an emphasis on the political quiescence of Britain in the late 1960s and early 70s can be deceptive. First, observations were often based on a narrow comparison with France at the most dramatic moment of student protest in 1968. The intelligentsia in Britain (which was not quite the same thing as the British intelligentsia) were much impressed by events in Paris in May 1968 and judged their own country as dull when set beside it. Maurice Kirk, a sociology lecturer at Leeds, recalled 'a girl walking up Woodhouse Lane carrying the red and black banner of the Sorbonne anarchists, because the Leeds students were very taken up with the troubles on the street in Paris in May 1968'.[7] Sheila Rowbotham sensed that 'history might have been happening across the channel'.[8] Angelo Quattrocchi filed a breathless report to an Italian newspaper: 'at this moment I am standing by a window on the left-bank, the revolutionaries claw at the cobblestones, their eyes bright, their hands bloody'. He was, in fact, in Fulham and looking out at the number 31 bus.[9]

Second, presenting Britain as an island of conservatism ignores the number of foreign radicals who gathered in London and who often sought refuge there from repression in other Western countries. Rudi Dutschke came to Britain after being shot in Berlin. Daniel Cohn-Bendit visited London for a brief period after being expelled from France – the fact that he was there on 18 June, the anniversary of de Gaulle's 'call to honour' of 1940, evoked a flurry of concern from those who thought that Cohn-Bendit might broadcast his own call for 'resistance' in France.[10] Americans seeking to evade the draft frequently settled in London,[11] as did intellectuals from Pakistan, Jamaica and especially Australia. London, like Amsterdam, mattered to 68 because it was a place where radical ideas were brewed up, even if they were applied elsewhere. The meeting on 'Dialectics of Liberation' at the London Roundhouse in 1967 – addressed by Stokely Carmichael and Herbert Marcuse among others – was particularly influential. Third, and finally, treating Britain as a 'naturally' conservative country distracts attention from the ways in which protest was managed and contained and the extent to which this management was undertaken by even the most apparently archaic institutions.

ANCIEN RÉGIME

The archaism that radicals mocked did much to structure the ways in which the authorities responded to protest. Britain was an *ancien régime* with an hereditary monarch, an established Church and an unelected upper house of parliament that was composed in large measure of those who had been born into the aristocracy. This produced some piquant episodes. In early 1967, an anti-war movement planned a demonstration at which Kathleen Farr would impersonate the Queen and hand out medals to Australian soldiers surrounded by protesters pretending to be dead. The demonstration was intended to draw attention to the fact that the Queen was head of state in Australia as well as Britain and that Australia had sent soldiers to fight in Vietnam. The authorities were not worried about the attack on militarism in a Commonwealth country but rather by the fact that impersonating the monarch was a criminal offence – one rooted in the activities of medieval 'pretenders' to the throne. The demonstrators sought to avoid misunderstanding by insisting that they were portraying 'Queen Kathleen' and the Director of Public Prosecutions concluded that a criminal charge would 'not be in the public interest'.[12]

Nowhere was the *ancien régime* more deeply embedded than in universities. This often made it hard to know where real power lay. In continental Europe, students knew that each university was run by a rector, who answered to the minister of education. In Britain, by contrast, defining the university authorities, or even defining the state that ostensibly stood behind them, could be awkward. In 1967, reform at Oxford University was discussed by the Privy Council – the group that formally existed to advise the Queen.[13] Some academic positions were chosen directly by the monarch – in practice, by the prime minister's appointment secretary after having taken appropriate 'soundings'. One of these appointments – R.A. Butler, the master of Trinity College, Cambridge – was a former Conservative home secretary. Another was General Sir John Hackett, a former paratrooper, the British equivalent of Jacques Massu, who became principal of King's College London in 1968. Perhaps because they were not directly subordinate to a government minister, both Butler and Hackett proved to be sympathetic to some student demands, or at least skilful in appearing to make concessions. Hackett, wearing his homburg hat and regimental tie, was famously to lead a student demonstration in 1972.

Even after the expansion that followed the Robbins Report of 1963 (see chap. 3), students in Britain made up a smaller part of the population than their counterparts in Western Europe or the United States. Furthermore, university expansion had sometimes increased the gulf between students and the rest of the population. The redbrick universities with their origins in the nineteenth century had been built in industrial cities. The new universities were built near small towns, sometimes – another touch of the *ancien régime* – cathedral cities. Students lived in specially built accommodation on campus, and this meant that most went home to their parents at the end of each term. A sociologist at Sussex summed up the political effects of this: 'The one redeeming feature of all the unrest is that revolutions always go on holiday.'[14]

British university students received relatively generous state grants and money created a common interest between students and the universities they attended. Academics often united with their pupils against the government when discussing grants. The demonstration of London students that was joined by General Sir John Hackett concerned grants. The academics who wrote to *The Times* to complain about attempts to increase fees for overseas students in 1967 included Max Beloff, Isaiah Berlin and Hugh Trevor-Roper – men who were in other respects strongly opposed to the student demands of the late 1960s.

Political radicalism in Britain tended to engage a narrow age range.

Those under eighteen were rarely touched. Radicals who tried to mobilize schoolchildren in Britain had less success than their counterparts in the United States and continental Europe. The Schools Action Union (established by Trotskyists in 1969 and later under the influence of Maoists) did not manage to bring more than 800 children to demonstrations.[15] The idea that there might be rebellion in privileged boarding schools, of the kind portrayed in Lindsay Anderson's 1968 film *if . . .* aroused excitement, and one radical claimed that the headmaster of Rugby expelled fifteen boys to 'prevent extremes of modernity'.[16] The truth was that such agitation was so rare that the head of the civil service was moved to intervene personally when a single boy at his own old school, Westminster, joined the National Union of School Students and the International Marxist Group.[17]

Partly because they received generous grants and partly because academic entry requirements were set relatively high, British university students tended to finish their courses, which were quite short, on time. Most of them spent three years, usually from the age of eighteen to that of twenty-one, at university. They arrived from school and, given the buoyant labour market of the late 1960s, most of them went straight into full-time work after university. Even the institution of 'sabbatical officers' for student unions in the 1960s underwrote the idea that being a student, and even being a student organizer, was a distinct and finite phase of life. The result of this was partly, as two academics wrote: 'The scope for "perpetual" or "professional" students as a "continuity staff" for students organizations is, therefore, highly restricted.'[18] John Saville, a historian from the old left (he had been a Communist) who watched the student occupations at the University of Hull with exasperated sympathy, knew that the university authorities would win if they simply succeeded in holding out until the end of the academic year, at which point many radicals would leave.[19]

British universities were small by comparison with, say, Berkeley or the University of Michigan. They were less able to support an independent political culture. British universities were also less centralized than universities in continental Europe, especially France. Indeed, a parliamentary inquiry pointed out that British students were often asking for more centralization at a time when French students were demanding less.[20] Oxford and Cambridge were composed of constituent colleges – each one more or less governed by its own fellows. London did not provide the same national focus for student activism that was provided by Rome, West Berlin and Paris. London University itself was divided into different colleges, which sometimes seemed to inhabit different worlds. The London School of Economics was one of the most important centres of student radicalism in the late 1960s. It was a few hundred yards from King's College, which contained, at least until the early 1970s, one of the most conservative student bodies in Britain. While the revolutionaries at the LSE talked about the overthrow of capitalism, students at King's plotted japes that involved the college mascot – Reggie the Lion.

The British National Union of Students (NUS) was also a force against radical action in universities for most of the 1960s. It had been founded by a student from King's College London in the 1920s and traditionally sought to avoid political involvement. In 1965, the NUS refused to join the International Student Conference. This was not because they knew about the CIA subsidy for it,[21] but because they regarded its condemnation of 'imperialism, colonialism, neo-colonialism, militarism and totalitarianism' as being worthy goals but ones at odds with the NUS's own apoliticism. Even in 1968, the NUS, to the annoyance of some radical students, sought to negotiate with vice chancellors. Its lack of enthusiasm for explicit and radical political engagement was reinforced by the fact that its leaders were often members of the Labour Party and expected that they might seek long-term careers in that party, which was, in the context of the late 1960s, a pillar of the established order.

There were changes in the NUS itself during the late 1960s. The Radical Student Alliance (RSA) was founded in late 1966 and held a conference early in the following year, which attracted 400 students from 108 institutions. Its founding group included six presidents of student unions and two representatives each from the Liberal, Labour and Communist parties – one RSA leader claimed that members of the Conservative Party had been invited to join but declined.[22] Most seem to have seen the RSA as a means of working within the NUS rather than as an alternative to it (though Essex University did leave the NUS for a time),[23] but even with these limited ambitions the RSA did not enjoy much short-term success in making the main student body more overtly political.

In 1969, Jack Straw, with the support of those who had been members of the RSA, displaced Trevor Fisk as president of the NUS. His opponents presented this as marking a sharp move to the left. In fact, as president of the students' union at Leeds in 1968, Straw had condemned attacks on a visiting Conservative MP. His concern during the subsequent sit-in had been mainly to ensure that the union itself should retain control of events and not be outflanked by more militant forms of protest. Straw adopted the accents of radicalism when it suited him. He had remarked in 1968 that student protest sprang partly from 'the increasing disillusionment with traditional party politics caused by the growth of consensus politics'.[24] He claimed in 1969 that he was 'not a very active member of the Labour Party' – it was a sign of the times that anyone who wanted to enjoy the support of the left should distance themselves from the party. Shrewd observers, however, were sceptical. One wrote that Fisk and Straw were both 'establishment figures, smooth and experienced student politicians'. He compared the relations between them to those between the two Labour ministers Anthony Crosland and Barbara Castle.[25] Straw did indeed become a close associate of Castle's and eventually a Labour minister himself.

Some changes in the 1960s, and even more in the early 70s, partly counteracted the quiescence of British students. Graduate students were more politically active than undergraduates and their number increased sharply during this period. An important group of American graduate students came to Britain – sometimes motivated by a desire to escape the draft. Their presence was particularly important at the LSE, where they made up a tenth of students in 1968.[26] A few temporary lecturers transmitted radical ideas from one university to the next – they were sometimes helped on their way by the desire of vice chancellors to dispense with the services of those whom they regarded as troublemakers. This was true of Dick Atkinson (mentioned above), who moved from being a postgraduate student at the LSE to being a temporary lecturer at Birmingham and then at Manchester.

PARTY POLITICS AND THE NEW LEFT

How did students interact with the more general politics of the British left in the 1960s? The British party system was simpler than those in most of Europe. There were two main parties – Conservative and Labour. There were a few Liberal MPs, remnants of what had been a great party before the First World War, but there was after 1950 not a single MP who represented any party to the left of Labour. The British Communist Party was small and many of its members, particularly intellectuals, had resigned in protest at the Soviet invasion of Hungary in 1956. Curiously, left-wing intellectuals sometimes appeared to exercise more influence after they had left the party than they had done inside it – so much so that one of Enoch Powell's paranoid correspondents 'began to wonder if these mass resignations could not be part of a plot'.[27]

Two small publications sprang out of disillusion with the Communist Party in the early 1950s – both of them based partly in universities. *The New Reasoner* was founded by academics in northern England, notably the historians John Saville and Edward (E.P.) Thompson, most of whom were old enough to have fought in the Second World War. At about the same time, a group of younger people (born in the 1930s) in Oxford founded the *Universities and Left Review*. In 1960, the two publications merged to form the *New Left Review*. Its presiding spirits were, however, quickly divided. Those associated with *The New Reasoner* began to refer to themselves with some bitterness as the 'old New Left'. The most important figures of the *New Left Review* were Stuart Hall, a Jamaican-born academic who was interested in what came to be known as 'cultural studies', and Perry Anderson, whose significance derived partly from his immense intellectual self-confidence and partly from the fact that he was rich enough to subsidize a loss-making publication. Anderson was interested in high theory and wrote about British national traditions with disdain. Thompson regarded himself as the defender of a more empirical approach and believed that there was special value in a certain kind of English political culture.

In 1960, the cause that most mobilized the British left was support for unilateral nuclear disarmament (i.e. the belief that Britain should abandon nuclear weapons regardless of what other countries did), and in that year supporters of unilateralism prevailed in the Labour Party itself, but that victory was quickly reversed. In spite of this, the radical left did not entirely turn its back on Labour. In 1965, Perry Anderson co-edited a collection of essays that included contributions by Lord Balogh, an economist and Labour peer, and Richard Crossman,[28] an eccentric Labour cabinet minister who by the end of the decade would compare the atmosphere produced by student protest to the 'early days of the Weimar Republic'.[29] Membership of the National Association of Labour Student Organizations grew from 1,500 in 1956 to around 6,000 in the mid-1960s.[30]

What changed the mood on the left was partly the victory of the Labour Party in the 1964 general election and then, more decisively, in 1966. A couple of American student radicals, studying and agitating at the London School of Economics, likened the Labour victory to Lyndon Johnson's 'peace candidacy' or Kurt Kiesinger's Grand Coalition. Just as these had 'shattered the illusions of American and German youth about the efficacy of change through parliamentary methods, so Harold Wilson's ascendancy to the throne had the same effect on young British leftists'.[31] Labour's victory ended thirteen years of Conservative rule, which had finished with the premierships of Harold Macmillan, who was a caricature of an English aristocrat, and Alec Douglas-Home, who was the real thing.

Harold Wilson, the new Labour prime minister, was, at forty-eight, the youngest prime minister since the early nineteenth century. He came from a relatively humble background and had risen partly through the force of his considerable intelligence. He had been seen for most of his political career as being on the left of the Labour Party, but his manner was calculated to annoy the radical left. He seemed to celebrate an amoral pragmatism – once remarking that 'a week is a long time in politics'. Dean Rusk warned Lyndon Johnson, a man who set the bar high when judging cynicism, that Wilson was 'not a man of strong political convictions' and that 'somehow he does not inspire trust in many people'.[32]

Wilson denounced 'restrictive practices', which was widely taken to be an attack on trade union power. When seamen went on strike in 1966, Wilson declared a State of Emergency – using legislation that had been designed for the agitations that followed the Bolshevik Revolution of 1917. In some ways, however, the awkward relations between the Wilson government and the New Left sprang from similarities rather than differences. Both were fascinated by novelty and both were also partly influenced by a sense that the left might have to move beyond a dependence on the working class. Both were interested in education, especially in universities. Wilson's ministers would later enact such cultural reforms as the abolition of the power of the Lord Chamberlain (another institution of the British *ancien régime*) to censor theatrical productions.

Some in Labour saw themselves as part of an international movement. Often, this meant looking to continental Europe – joining the European Common Market was an important ambition for some of them. It also meant admiration for America. The wartime alliance and in particular relations with Roosevelt had given the British left a sense that America was associated with 'progressive' politics and that the US was a more 'open' society than Britain. Shirley Williams, a Labour politician who had been evacuated to Minnesota as a child during the Second World War, wrote that she discovered there 'a classless society, whose members all shared the same accent and the same values'.[33] The lure of the United States was reflected in the dates on which British Labour politicians first visited it. Denis Healey went in 1949, Hugh Gaitskell in 1950, Roy Jenkins in 1953 and Anthony Crosland in 1954. By contrast, Margaret Thatcher did not cross the Atlantic until 1967. Some in the Labour Party were influenced by the works of American writers, especially Daniel Bell, whose *The End of Ideology* (1960) described many features of a 'post-ideological age', and the economist John Kenneth Galbraith, whose *Affluent Society* (1958) suggested that economic problems would in future revolve around distribution rather than production.

Of course, Labour ministers who admired the United States knew only about certain aspects of it. They knew the east coast and California better than the area in between. They mixed with a transatlantic elite – often made up of people, such as Arthur Schlesinger Jnr, who had been partially educated in Britain. Events of the 1960s showed them a different and less consensual America. Some of them were caught up in the American 68 and it is notable that even Labour moderates often placed themselves on that part of the US spectrum where liberalism intersected with radicalism. In the summer of 1968, Shirley Williams attended the Democratic National Convention in Chicago, where she was charged with conveying messages between the Connecticut delegation and Eugene McCarthy and where she ended up running from Mayor Daley's policemen as she attempted to visit the protesters on the shore of Lake Michigan.[34] Williams's colleague Roy Jenkins, Chancellor of the Exchequer in 1968 and an exponent of an economic orthodoxy that the radical left disliked, happened to be in America at the time of Martin Luther King's assassination. With his friend Robert Kennedy, he attended the funeral – an incongruous figure sweating in a pin-stripe suit as the crowds marched through Atlanta.[35]

Tony Benn was a long way to the left of Williams and Jenkins by the late 1960s, and he had curious relations with the British student left. He recognized that his membership of the Labour government discredited him in the eyes of radicals. After appearing on a television discussion programme he wrote: 'The students attacked me because I was the representative of the Labour government and a Minister and all the rest.'[36] Privately, however, Benn was sympathetic to those who denounced him and sometimes slipped discreetly to the other side of the barricades. In June 1968 he turned up incognito to the 'Free University' in Bristol – 'I . . . put on my specs and took off my jacket and suddenly no one took any notice of me.' Sessions on black power and Vietnam made him think that he had 'done no serious thinking about politics'.[37]

No one better incarnated the paradoxical relations between the New Left and the Labour Party than Anthony Crosland. Crosland's *The Future of Socialism* (1956), with its insistence that the Labour Party could live with a modernized, technocratic capitalism, gave him 'almost diabolical status' among the New Left.[38] In the mid-1960s, Crosland promoted 'comprehensive' rather than academically selective schools, but at the same time introduced a 'binary' system into higher education with the creation of polytechnics, which were designed to teach practical subjects and which commanded less prestige than universities. Opposition to the 'binary divide' became an important issue in the student politics of the late 1960s. Yet there was also a sense in which Crosland's disdain for 'British philistinism and dreariness' and his embrace of equality as an aim of social (if not economic) policy ran parallel to many of the ambitions of the New Left. A historian who had expounded radical student politics in 1968 was to ask in 1986 whether Crosland had not in fact anticipated the future better than the New Left of the early 1960s.[39]

The disenchantment of young radicals with the Labour Party in the late 1960s had curious effects. The proportion of students in some institutions willing to identify themselves as Labour supporters dropped to almost microscopically low levels. Of 490 students beginning their studies at Essex in 1968, 88 per cent answered questions about their politics. Of these, just 1 per cent described themselves as 'left Labour' and a further 1 per cent described themselves as 'centre Labour' – a few years previously these two positions would have encompassed almost all students who thought of themselves as progressive. The number of students who described themselves as 'Powellites' (i.e. those who identified with the figure most hated by the student left in 1968) was exactly the same as those who identified themselves as 'Labour'. On the other hand, 26 per cent of the sample regarded themselves as 'non-party moderate left' and 5 per cent as non-party extreme left – this label included the 4 per cent who described themselves as 'anarchist' and the 1 per cent who were 'Communist'. Conservatives and Liberals each made up 13 per cent. Revealingly, the self-identification of most students was different from their voting intentions and 20 per cent of the intake at Essex did in fact intend to vote Labour – the figure for the Conservative Party was 15 per cent and that for the Liberals 18 per cent; 25 per cent of students had decided to abstain and others were uncertain or planned to vote for 'other groups'.[40]

The Labour Party retained a special status as the only left-wing party that stood any chance of forming a government, which may explain both the fact that even those who did not describe themselves as 'Labour' still planned to vote for it and also the fury with which radicals often regarded the party leadership. Some on the British left flirted with 'entryism' – the strategy of joining the Labour Party in order to transform it from within – though this strategy was less discussed in 1968 than it had been five years earlier, perhaps because more direct forms of political action seemed feasible.

In a curious way, the Labour Party overshadowed radical politics in the late 1960s precisely because opposition to it, or at least to its leaders, became so important. Colin Crouch – who considered himself on the left of the Labour Party before his bruising encounter with the more extreme views of his fellow students at the LSE – wrote:

> If a revolutionary student in Britain is asked to say why he protests, why he uses direct action, why he is continually seeking new demonstrations and confrontations, he is likely to answer in terms that have very little to do with the university as such. He will tell how the working class in Britain has been betrayed by the hierarchy of the Labour Party.[41]

A leader of the Federation of Conservative Students described the effect of all this thus:

> It is important to realise that in student politics today, the traditional Party labels are not entirely relevant. Simplifying matters, the divisions are between Moderates (Tory and Labour supporters) and Extremists (Revolutionary Socialists). The distinction . . . lies in the desire of the former to improve the present system, and the determination of the latter to sweep it away.[42]

As these remarks suggest, the Conservative Party itself retained a considerable presence in universities. The Federation of Conservative Students claimed that its membership in 1968 (11,000) exceeded that of all other student political groups combined.

Conservative students were not hostile to all university reform. They supported student grants and the right of students to protest without risk of reprisal. In addition to this, Conservatives had two great advantages: first, their party was not in power in the late 1960s and was not, therefore, an immediate target for hostility; secondly, being relatively unconcerned with the questions of principle that exercised much of the left, their leaders sometimes enjoyed a wide margin for manoeuvre. Peter Watherston became leader of the Students' Union of the LSE, succeeding Colin Crouch. Watherston's first action was to support a student occupation of buildings – though he seems to have anticipated, wrongly as it turned out, that this would provide a distraction that might draw the sting of radicalism at the LSE.

Among the established parties, the greatest beneficiary of 1960s radicalism was the Liberal Party. The fact that it had not exercised any serious power since the 1920s was an advantage for those who disliked the compromises of government. The Young Liberals became almost a separate political party – somewhat resembling the French Parti Socialiste Unifié (see chap. 5) – and were regarded with disquiet by the party's national leadership. The very sense that the Young Liberals were separate from the conventional politics of the mainstream left made them open to ideas, notably workers' control, that would not have fitted into the conventional politics of the labour movement.

To the left of all these parties was a range of groups that proclaimed themselves to be revolutionary. The Revolutionary Socialist Students' Federation (RSSF) was founded in November 1968. Unlike the National Union of Students or even the Radical Student Alliance, it presented itself as a primarily political movement rather than a means of representing student interests. It was committed, among other things, to 'the revolutionary overthrow of capitalism and imperialism and its replacement by workers' power'. However, just a few months later, a Conservative student noted that 'even members of the RSSF are worried about what they call an extremist fringe which is tacking itself on them – anarchists and such like. They are the people causing the violence and not the stabler members of the RSSF.'[43] The RSSF, in fact, seems to have peaked soon after its foundation, when it had 1,100 members and contacts in a hundred institutions. By the end of 1969, it had only 200 members and the following year it ceased to exist.[44]

The groupuscules of the extreme left in Britain were even smaller than their equivalents in continental Europe. Tariq Ali, having made his name campaigning against the Vietnam War, wanted to join a political party in 1968. He decided on the International Marxist Group – a Trotskyist organization. He recalled that his new comrades numbered about fifty and that, as such movements were prone to do, this one was on the verge of splitting.[45]

The British Trotskyist groups were often bitterly hostile to each other. The Socialist Labour League (SLL) and the International Socialists (IS) were divided partly by style – the former was more austere and disciplined – and partly by the debate of inexhaustible interest in such circles as to whether the Soviet Union was an example of a 'degenerated workers' state' or 'state capitalism'. They also had different attitudes to the working class. The SLL believed that no political action was possible without it. On 26 May 1968, the Socialist Labour League marched on the French embassy. The IS joined the demonstration – ostensibly in solidarity with the French, though the police believed that they were actually motivated by jealousy of the SLL. The police attended mainly to keep the rival factions of Trotskyism apart rather than to protect the embassy. They prosecuted one demonstrator who had apparently addressed the crowd with the words: 'all those in favour of tearing up paving stones and pulling down trees show hands'.[46]

NORTHERN IRELAND

Northern Ireland (Ulster) had a particular status in the British 68. Elsewhere in Britain, and for that matter in most of the industrialized democracies, protest was frequently directed against the consequences of post-war modernization or affluence. In Northern Ireland, by contrast, the left was often animated by a painful sense that modernization had passed the province by. Bernadette Devlin, a student activist elected as an independent member of the Westminster parliament at the age of twenty-one in 1969, wrote:

> Should an anthropologist or a sociologist be looking for a bizarre society to study, I would suggest he comes to Ulster ... one of Europe's oddest countries. Here, in the middle of the twentieth century, with modern technology transforming everybody's lives, you have a medieval mentality which is being dragged painfully into the eighteenth century by some forward looking people.[47]

Northern Ireland had been created with the partition of Ireland in 1920. A majority of the Northern Irish population were Protestants and almost all of these were Unionists – that is to say that they supported union with the rest of the United Kingdom. Catholics made up the rest of the population and most of them were 'republicans' or 'nationalists' who wanted Northern Ireland to become part of a single independent Irish state. The province had its own parliament and government (meeting at Stormont Castle), which controlled most of domestic policy, though Northern Irish voters also returned MPs to the British parliament in Westminster.

In elections to the Stormont parliament, and to that at Westminster, people in Northern Ireland voted on the same terms as those on the mainland. Municipal elections, by contrast, were weighted in favour of Protestants – electoral boundaries secured their interests, as did the fact that votes were granted to 'the householder and his wife', which disadvantaged those numerous Catholic households that contained more than one adult. The result of this was that even predominantly Catholic cities, such as Londonderry, had Unionist councils. Catholics were also disadvantaged by the provision of public housing. Northern Ireland was poorer than mainland Britain; over 7 per cent of its working population was unemployed and Catholics figured disproportionately among these.[48]

The Northern Ireland Civil Rights Association had been formed in early 1967. It sought equal rights for Catholics, with particular reference to votes, housing and jobs. It did not espouse the kind of illegality that had often marked the civil rights campaign in the American South. One of its more radical members compared it to the National Council for Civil Liberties in England.

Students at Queen's University Belfast – one of the few places where Catholics and Protestants mixed on equal terms – provided much support for the civil rights campaign. In November 1968, People's Democracy was founded at Queen's and at first concentrated on issues of suffrage and housing. In theory, these were matters that could be addressed without overthrowing the political order – though, in practice, some supporters of People's Democracy seem to have backed such proposals because they assumed that even modest reform would break the Unionist Party.

People's Democracy attracted much attention from the radical left elsewhere and is often regarded as the Northern Irish face of 68. One of its founders, Eamonn McCann, had previously lived in London and attended the 1967 conference on dialectics. He remarked that events in Northern Ireland were linked to 'the black struggle in the US, the workers' fight in France, the resistance of the Vietnamese, the uprising against Stalinism in Czechoslovakia'.[49] One of his comrades said in 1969 that People's Democracy had been 'considerably influenced by the Sorbonne Assembly and the concepts of libertarianism as well as socialism'.[50] The new movement operated through a general assembly and tried to avoid having conventional leaders – though, in practice, the need to fit in with the law imposed some aspects of a conventional structure on it. People's Democracy also quickly went beyond the relatively limited demands of the early civil rights movement. Its manifesto of February 1969 called for government-financed home building, workers' control of state-owned factories, the religious integration of education and the break-up of large landed estates.

Not everyone in People's Democracy shared the same outlook. Bernadette Devlin, who became the movement's most prominent representative, had been brought up in the traditions of Irish nationalism. She was, at least at first, rather dismissive of the kind of radicalism seen in Europe or mainland Britain and more prone to compare her struggle with that of black people in the American South. The division and uncertainty in People's Democracy was made all the more evident because events in Northern Ireland happened so fast. The province moved from a peaceful civil rights campaign to armed conflict in just three years – and young activists were caught up in events that were beyond their control.

Two issues were particularly awkward for People's Democracy. The first of these was class. In some ways, the relative economic backwardness of Northern Ireland meant that class was particularly visible there, and those who thought of themselves as Marxists were keen to emphasize class as something that might cut across religious and ethnic divisions. Furthermore, Protestants, who held most unionized, industrial jobs, were 'the decisive part of the urban proletariat',[51] and some in People's Democracy were particularly keen to gain their support. However, the violent divisions of Northern Ireland after 1968 revolved around religion rather than class. Some leaders of People's Democracy became exasperated by 'pope-heads' and by the sense that 'the cry "get the Protestants" is still very much on the lips of the Catholic working class'.[52] The leaders of Unionism became more populist and plebeian, and in 1974 the Protestant working class was to exercise its 'decisive' power in ways that the Marxists of 1968 had not anticipated (see chap. 9).

The second issue was revolution. Many student radicals in 68 talked of revolution, but in Northern Ireland such rhetoric intersected with popular traditions that dated back at least to the Easter Rising of 1916. This meant: "The idea of revolution is not at all alien to the Irish working class as it is to the English."[53] More quickly than their counterparts in the rest of Europe or the United States, leaders of People's Democracy were faced with questions about the precise mechanics of revolution and particularly whether they supported armed action. Their position was especially awkward because for a time they enjoyed considerable electoral success. Seven of their members were elected to the Stormont parliament at around the same time that Devlin was elected to the Westminster parliament. They often treated these successes rather disdainfully – implying that old-fashioned electoral politics was only a means to an end. But they also believed that progress would come from some sort of political process rather than armed revolution. Bernadette Devlin wrote:

> Ten years ago the IRA was the stronger campaigning explosively to 'free the Six Counties' from English over-lordship and planned to work for socialism when the link with Britain had been cut. Today the political side has the upper hand, and tries to preach a peaceful, political path to reunification through socialism.[54]

The 'political side' did not keep the upper hand for long. The Provisional IRA, a break away group from the old Official IRA, was formed in December 1969 with the initial intention of protecting Catholic areas from attack by Protestants and the police. 'Protection' went with the exercise of power. Devlin was to say: 'Armed defence took away from the people themselves the responsibility for their own defence and put it in the hands of somebody . . . who was supposed to be looking after them.'[55] The increasing importance of armed struggle drew attention to the fact that revolutionary traditions could also in a curious way be conservative traditions. In 1968, supporters of the IRA, Provisional or Official, looked to their own past more than they looked to an international movement. In July 1969, Harold Wilson's government allowed the bodies of two IRA men executed in England in 1940 to be brought back to the Republic of Ireland for burial. At the funeral, Jimmy Steele, an IRA veteran who had first been arrested in 1923, made a speech in which he complained: 'one is now expected to be more conversant with the teachings of Chairman Mao than those of our dead patriots'. His words were greeted with applause.[56]

More generally, the international, especially European, associations of the Northern Irish 68 can be overstated. For one thing the institutional links between the Northern Irish civil rights movement and left-wing organizations in continental Europe were relatively weak. The movement's most important interlocutors were to be found in other English-speaking countries – mainland Britain, Australia, the United States and the Irish Republic. It is true that twelve organizations in the main countries of continental Western Europe had some relations with the Northern Irish civil rights campaign, but the number of such organizations in the United States was thirty-five, the number in the Republic of Ireland was fifty-three and the number in mainland Britain eighty-two. As for practical support, continental Europe counted for almost nothing. The Northern Ireland Civil Rights Association got 42.1 per cent of its funding from the United States and no measurable amount from continental Europe.[57] The relation between the civil rights campaign and the Republic of Ireland was particularly important because the Republic was an island of cultural conservatism and this put civil rights campaigners in an awkward position when, for example, they campaigned against the censorship of books. More generally, the whole island of Ireland was influenced by Catholicism, and often a pre-Vatican II variety of Catholicism at that. Identification with working-class Catholicism could sometimes push civil rights campaigners into an unwilling association with conservative morality. Protestant women taunted female civil rights marchers with the chant 'ask the Pope to let you have the pill'.[58]

Above all, relations between the civil rights campaign in Northern Ireland and the wider radicalisms of 68 were complicated by America. Civil rights campaigners regarded their natural allies as being blacks and Hispanics but Irish Americans often combined support for Irish nationalism with distaste for the civil rights campaign and for the protests of 68 in their own country. The National Association for Irish Justice tried to mobilize support in America for both civil rights in Ireland and wider forms of liberation but this brought it into violent conflict with older and more conservative bodies, such as the American Congress for Irish Freedom and the Ancient Order of Hibernians.[59] The Irish Americans were, indeed, a key part of the white working class that was turning to the political right by the late 1960s. Mayor Richard Daley of Chicago, the man who crushed demonstrations against the war in Vietnam (see chap. 4), was a quintessential Irish American politician. Bernadette Devlin ran up against Irish Americans during a fundraising tour when she claimed she was greeted by a crowd shouting: 'Brits out of Belfast; niggers out of Boston.'

RACE AND EMPIRE

What of race in the 68 of mainland Britain? Sometimes the radical left was mobilized by distaste for white minority rule in southern Africa. South Africa had instituted the explicit segregation of apartheid in 1948. Rhodesia, the government of which also wanted to maintain white minority rule, issued a Unilateral Declaration of Independence on 11 November 1965. Rhodesia had particular resonance in British politics. Ian Smith, the country's prime minister, claimed that Winston Churchill would have felt more at home there than in the Britain of the late 1960s. British Conservatives often sought to defend the white population of Rhodesia. Sometimes, this defence overlapped with a more general assault on the culture of the 1960s – Mary Whitehouse, a Christian housewife who campaigned against 'permissive morality' on television, also complained about unfavourable references to Ian Smith.[60]

The radical left mobilized against the governments of South Africa and Rhodesia, encouraged by (mainly white) dissidents from Southern Africa who had sought refuge in Britain. The appointment of a director (i.e. principal) who had previously worked in Rhodesia was an important *casus belli* for the protest movement at the LSE. The left also campaigned against racial discrimination in Britain and against the 1968 Commonwealth Immigrants Act, which restricted non-white immigration. In the main, however, protest was directed at a small group of Conservative politicians to the right of their own party leadership, who called for further restrictions of immigration or the repatriation of immigrants. Duncan Sandys was such a figure, as was Patrick Wall, whose attempt to give a talk at Leeds University provoked much agitation.

Above all, the ire of left-wing students was aroused by one man: Enoch Powell. Powell was an eccentric figure in Edward Heath's shadow cabinet, in which he was defence spokesman. On 20 April 1968, he made a speech in Birmingham, on the dangers of non-white immigration. Quoting Virgil, he talked of the Tiber 'foaming with blood'. The speech made Powell an object of hatred on the left. Demonstrations against him became so frequent and vociferous that he was in effect excluded from every university in the country.

Everything about Powell – the staring eyes, the rasping voice, the classical references, the odd combination of a Midlands accent with the officerly bearing of a man who had held the rank of brigadier in 1945 – seemed calculated to enrage student radicals, but there were some respects in which Powell, like de Gaulle, whom he much admired, was himself a rebel against the very things that the radicals of 1968 disliked. Powell often expressed himself in terms that could equally well have come from the mouth of a student radical – the word 'technocrat' was a particular sign of disdain for Powell. He was anti-American and expressed dark suspicions that the British might send troops to fight in Vietnam.[61]

Powell couched his appeal as one that could be directly addressed to 'the people' and that was designed to circumvent 'the establishment'. The 1968 speech met with an enthusiastic response from sections of the white working class. Within a month, Powell had received 43,000 letters and 700 telegrams – overwhelmingly in his support and apparently largely from working-class women. Working-class men expressed their backing in more direct ways. A thousand dockers marched to Westminster in support of Powell on 23 April. Workers at St Katharine Docks declared a one-day strike and workers at some enterprises in the West Midlands also walked out, as did porters at Smithfield meat market.[62] Immigration officers at Heath-row wrote a letter in support of Powell – for which the Home Office disciplined them.

Working-class support for a right-wing politician was in itself shocking to the radical left – especially in view of Powell's espousal of free market economics and his opposition to trade unions – and the Powellite movement was all the more disconcerting because it some-times took 68ish forms. It circumvented established trade union structures and was, indeed, opposed by the most important trade union leaders. In Wolverhampton, a branch official of the Transport and General Workers' Union presented a petition in favour of Powell, much to the annoyance of his own national leaders. At Smithfield market, 'Big Dan' Harmston was a figure from the knuckle-duster right – he supported the fascist Oswald Mosley's Union Party – but he himself was struck by the spontaneous quality of the reaction of his own colleagues to Powell's speech:

> [I]f that day I'd said, 'Pick up your cleavers and knives and decapitate Heath and Wilson', they'd have done it. They really would, but they wouldn't have done it next week. It was just that mood of the moment – like the storming of the Bastille I suppose.[63]

Decolonization had been less violent and contentious for the British than for the French. A substantial group of radicals came from coun-tries that had once been part of the Empire. This was true of the South Africans and of the Australians grouped around Oz magazine, as well as of Tariq Ali, whose grandfather had been prime minister of the Punjab. But explicit references to the British imperial past played surprisingly little role in the politics of 68.

Imperial amnesia sprang partly from the way in which Britain's own history was occluded by an obsession with the evils of American power. The effects of this could be incongruous. The most alarming atrocity of the British wars of decolonization was exposed partly as a result of Vietnam. Referring to the My Lai massacre of 1968, George Brown, a right-wing Labour minister, remarked that the British should not leap to condemn America without recognizing that their own hands might not be entirely clean. This led to discussion of the killing by British soldiers of unarmed Chinese villagers at Batang

Kali in Malaya in 1948.[64] But this matter evoked little interest in the radical left. Calls for investigation came from Denis Healey (the defence secretary and a target of student hostility) and the *People* (a newspaper known for its antipathy to the 'counter-culture').[65] The investigation into Batang Kali was stopped by the new Conservative government in 1970.

VIETNAM

The largest demonstrations of the British 68 concerned Vietnam. Harold Wilson had resisted pressure from Lyndon Johnson to send troops, even just a symbolic number of them, to Vietnam. Denis Healey thought: 'the case against America's involvement was . . . compelling, and the unsuitability of America's strategy . . . obvious'.[66] But Britain was America's most self-consciously loyal ally and no British minister could publicly denounce American policy. In the febrile atmosphere of the late 1960s, failure to denounce was often taken to be complicity. Wilson's exasperated insistence that he was in fact working to secure peace in Vietnam, or his suggestion that demonstrators might care to protest outside the embassy of Mao's China – which was, unlike Britain, sending arms to Vietnam – counted for little. Indeed, in some respects the fact that Britain was not fighting made protest easier. British anti-war campaigners, unlike their American counterparts, did not have to grapple with the complicated detail of what they wanted their country to do. Peter Sedgwick, a rare example of a radical who dissented from left-wing orthodoxy on this point, noted with asperity that 'Victory for the Vietcong' had come to seem an almost uncontroversial slogan in London.[67]

Protest over Vietnam seemed to provide the chance to build a movement on the left that would circumvent the Labour Party. Tariq Ali said in April 1968 that the Vietnam Solidarity Campaign aimed eventually 'to form an external opposition to the Government along the lines proposed by German students' and that the young people it attracted were frustrated by 'party conventional politics and by a rubber stamp parliament'.[68] Vietnam protests were deceptive, though.

The largest of them mobilized tens of thousands of people. This was an impressive number for a single demonstration, but it was tiny compared to the 13 million who had voted Labour in the 1966 general election and not much larger than the number who had voted personally for Harold Wilson in his own constituency. Furthermore, the organizations behind the Vietnam protests were small and often bitterly divided. One journalist wrote that many had only two or three members and that 'Only a microbiologist could properly keep track of the continually dividing and multiplying Left-wing groups which are now claiming their share in the Vietnam demonstration of October 27.'[69]

MANAGING 1968

Though the radical left often hated the Wilson government, on the whole ministers were restrained and flexible in their attitude to the radical left. They were often willing to debate with those who attacked them and even to concede that some of the specific demands of the students (especially with regard to university discipline) might be justified. Particularly striking was the attitude of Home Secretary James Callaghan. Callaghan seemed to stand for everything that 1968 was against. He was an intelligent but proudly unintellectual man who had risen up through the trade union movement without attending university. A patriot and a royalist, he was a parliamentary representative of the Police Federation and was widely known to be hostile to drug taking and sexual permissiveness. He was responsible for the 1968 Commonwealth Immigrants Bill that had restricted non-white immigration. This background appears to have had a curious effect. Perhaps the fact that he had not attended university made him less exercised about the assault on academic institutions than those of his colleagues who had themselves been dons. Perhaps, too, his reputation for the defence of 'freedom under the law' (a phrase that he preferred to the Tory slogan 'law and order') meant that he did not fear being outflanked on his right.

Callaghan teased both radicals and reactionaries with his refusal to embrace the apocalyptic rhetoric of 1968. He was amused when the Conservative Quintin Hogg came to see him 'in a state of great agitation' to ask that a Guards regiment be held ready to deal with the demonstrations of 1968. He refused to ban an anti-Vietnam War march of 1968. During one rally, he even walked out of the control room in Whitehall to say a cheery hello to the waiting demonstrators who were being held behind police lines.[70] Callaghan often seems to have regarded the language of both demonstrators and those who feared the collapse of order with benign amusement. In June 1968, there were questions in parliament about why Daniel Cohn-Bendit – the French student leader – had been admitted to the country. Callaghan replied that he saw no reason to depart from the tradition of admitting foreigners so long as they did not break the law and added that the visit might do Cohn-Bendit good: 'I even thought of teaching him the words of the Internationale, as he does not seem to be too sure of them. When he expressed a desire to see Buckingham Palace I could think of nothing better for his education.'[71]

The impact of student protest in Britain was limited by the fragmented structure of universities, the relative affluence of British students and the fact that university study, to a greater extent than in many other countries, tended to be sharply demarcated from the rest of young people's lives. British students were divided from the working class geographically – because so many universities, especially those built in the 1960s, were located away from industrial cities. They were also divided from the working class politically because trade unions were almost invariably affiliated to the Labour Party. Indeed Callaghan, who, as home secretary, did so much to contain student protest, was close to the unions. The most widely reported example of spontaneous working-class rebellion of 1968 was one in response to Powell that took place on the right rather than the left.

However, this does not mean that Britain is insignificant in the long 68. This is partly, as has been suggested, because agitators from other countries so often passed through Britain at some stage. It is also because the British 68 happened late. The student movement became more political in the early 1970s, especially after the National Union of Students lifted its ban on political activity in 1972. The greatest agitation in a British university was seen not in 1968 but 1972, at

Essex. In addition to this, a feature of the Labour government's modernization in the 1960s was to create polytechnics. These institutions were less privileged than universities, they tended to be located in cities and, against the government's original intentions, polytechnic students were particularly prone to study those disciplines, especially sociology, that were most closely associated with political dissent. Not surprisingly, therefore, polytechnics, especially the Polytechnic of North London, became centres of radical protest.[72]

More generally, radical political parties expanded in the 1970s. Membership of the International Marxist Group, which had been so small in 1968, peaked at between 4,000 and 5,000 in 1974.[73] The radicalization of Britain in the 1970s extended beyond the campus and beyond the intellectual middle classes. It was seen in strikes on the British mainland (see chap. 9) and in political violence in Northern Ireland (see chap. 10). In this sense, the important point about the British events of 1968 itself was not so much that they were small in scale as that they came to seem overshadowed by the dramas of the following years.

8

The Revolution within the Revolution: Sexual Liberation and the Family

Children of the Revolution. Rudi Dutschke and baby.

8

The protests of 68 spilled from the political into the personal sphere and made many doubt whether the two could be distinguished. They called into question thinking about everything from the celibacy of Catholic priests to whether women could wear trousers on American campuses – the FBI took time out from spying on anti-Vietnam War demonstrations to report that women had broken rules at the University of New Orleans by wearing slacks on 1 April 1968.[1] Authorities often associated new kinds of sexual morality with political rebellion. The French ministry of the interior counted the number of women emerging from male dormitories at Nanterre, the epicentre of student radicalism: 132 on a February morning in 1968.[2] Radicals also frequently saw sex and revolution as intertwined. A member of the Revolutionary Socialist Students' Federation at Cambridge, where only three out of over twenty colleges accepted women students, said: 'what happened in France happened because some guys felt that they didn't like being told when they could and when they couldn't have a fuck'.[3] For some women, such talk illustrated the crude machismo of political radicalism in the long 68. For them, the 'liberation' movements of the 1970s were reactions *against* such attitudes. They cited a leader of Students for a Democratic Society who was said to have told his male comrades in 1967 that they should cement their relations with working-class men by 'balling a chick together',[4] or the answer that the Black Power leader Stokely Carmichael was said to have given, when asked what the position of women would be in the revolution: 'prone'.

Violent protest sometimes seemed to push women to the margins.

Jo Freeman recalled being told in 1968 that a Chicago newspaper, where she sought to get a job, could not allow more than a small number of women to work on its city desk because they would be unable to cover riots.[5] Tom Hayden described an incident in Chicago, where he had gone to protest at the Democratic Convention of 1968, that seemed to epitomize a dichotomy between violent men and passive, sexually available women: 'Drowsily, I saw a naked woman, who had risen earlier. "Maybe she'll come back to bed", I was thinking, when she said quietly: "There's a man outside with a gun."'[6]

But such dichotomies did not explain everything. Women often did experience the political movements of 68 as a liberation, even if it was a liberation that in retrospect felt incomplete. Women were less numerous than men among the most visible participants in radical movements but they were often more numerous than they would have been in other political groups. Sometimes, indeed, women's role in the radicalism of the 1960s contrasted with their participation in more conventional forms of politics that had declined in that decade – the number of women in the Italian parliament sunk to its nadir in 1968. Furthermore, the reaction against the machismo of 68 did not come just from women. Men rethought their own behaviour. Such rethinking was most explicit in the gay liberation movement, but even heterosexual men who had once associated sexual conquest with political liberation often changed their views in the 1970s, and in a curious way the very fact that they were so explicit about their sexual assumptions opened those assumptions to challenge. Finally, 68 was not just about relations between men and women. Sometimes it appeared to open the possibility that the very idea of the couple or the family might be overthrown. Some remembered the most shocking slogan of the Italian 68 was: 'I want to be an orphan.' In short, those who sought to challenge conventional views of sexual relations and the family often took some of their language and style from other sorts of liberation movement but were neither simply a part of those movements nor a response to them. They might best be described, in terms that Régis Debray devised in another context, as a 'revolution within the revolution'.

WOMEN AND THE STUDENT REBELLION

The paradoxes of women's emancipation were especially visible in universities. On the one hand, their presence in such institutions expanded quickly in the 1960s – though in the US, where women had made up almost half the student population in the 1920s, expansion happened after a sharp post-war decline. The subjects that expanded fastest, humanities and social sciences, were also those that attracted the largest number of women, and the institutions created in the 1960s were almost always co-educational from the start. But what were women going to university for? Were they being educated to work and, if so, could they expect the same professional opportunities as men? In the 1920s, education had sometimes seemed an alternative to marriage – particularly in those countries that had suffered high male casualties in the First World War. In the 1960s, however, universities came to seem, as Germaine Greer, a lecturer at Warwick University from 1968 to 1972, put it, 'shops where [women] could take out a degree while waiting to get married'.[7] For many women, graduation was followed by a few years of relatively menial office work, to support their husband through further study or the early stages of his professional life, and then by the birth of children.

The very expansion of women's education drew attention to the ways in which their lot differed from that of men. The citadels of privilege remained largely male. In the mid-1960s, only 5 per cent of all American universities excluded women, but this included most of the Ivy League institutions. The first women to be admitted to Yale (first as postgraduates and then, from 1969, as undergraduates) found a student social life that still revolved around all-male fraternities and dining clubs.[8] Linda Tinkham drew attention to the asymmetric provision of higher education for men and women in Britain. She pointed out that (at the beginning of the 1960s) only 593 women, against 4,002 men, had been admitted to Oxford and Cambridge. On the other hand, students at colleges of education, established to train teachers, were predominantly women. The staff/student ratio was lower than at universities, and the teaching was less interesting. Tinkham's reflections were published in a volume on student power and the book says as much about the distribution of power on the radical left as it does about that in higher education. Of the twelve essays in the collection, eleven were by men. Tinkham's contribution focused on the particular college that she had attended. The male authors came mainly from grander universities and wrote wide-ranging pieces with breezy self-confidence. Robin Blackburn (an Oxford graduate) entitled his essay 'A brief guide to bourgeois ideology'; Perry Anderson (Eton and Oxford) tackled 'Components of the national culture'.[9]

Oddly, genteel convention had sometimes guaranteed women a degree of influence, albeit limited, that was swept away by student radicalism in the late 1960s. When student organization had revolved around committees, conferences and formal votes, women had often been patronized but they had also had at least some means to make their voices heard – if only because it was usually a woman who wrote up the minutes recording decisions. Student unions at British and American universities had often reserved positions for some women. King's College London seemed to epitomize the new world of sexual radicalism in 1973: the year in which it abolished the post of 'Lady Vice President' and established a 'GaySoc'.[10]

At the height of student protests, 'general assemblies' – tumultuous occasions at which women sometimes felt that they were shouted down – often replaced formal meetings. A Trotskyist woman in Switzerland later said: 'It was years before I dared to speak in front of a general assembly. So we [women] were just there to make coffee and run off tracts.'[11] Even women who had some formal position in the student movement were often circumvented by men. In 1967, Dominique Bazire, who led a society of geography students at the Sorbonne, was surprised to see her name appended to a letter supporting the Arab position in the Six-Day War, published in *Le Monde*. A male comrade had written it and signed on her behalf without consulting her.[12] When Noel Annan wrote his report on 'troubles' at the University of Essex in 1972, he suggested that

> The President [of the students' union] Miss Davis was, so I understand,
> not well at the time and it seems that the militants never bothered to

consult her and were determined to act independently of the Union Executive. She and the Executive were at that time politically inexperienced: the truth is that she could not deliver what she had promised.[13]

Annan attributed the disturbances to 'a small number of wild men who belonged to no political group but by their force of personality at times took the lead'. Annan was courteous and liberal, but his report betrayed the casual assumption that the major figures in any university (on either side of the barricades) would be male. He commended Essex for having attracted 'some exceptionally brilliant men' to its staff and described the sociologist Michael Mann as an 'eloquent and attractive spokesman'.[14] The president of the National Union of Students similarly looks to have assumed that women would be confused and passive spectators in protests dominated by men. He said of the disturbances at the LSE in 1967: 'it was those few professional publicists who were ever ready to take over from the sleepy girl who did not know what she was protesting about and to shout down the microphone that this was a fight to the bitter end'.[15]

The fact that women played less of a role than men in radical movements, especially during the most dramatic events of the late 1960s, does not mean that the spirit of 68 was simply 'anti-feminist'. Women may have been a minority but they were a more significant minority than they were in mainstream politics. In Turin, women made up about a third of all those arrested after the student occupations of 1968 – though they usually constituted less than a fifth of the politically active population.[16] In Switzerland women were reckoned to make up only 16 or 17 per cent of candidates for the Conseil National but the proportion active in radical movements was at least twice this.[17] The proportion of women in the student organization of the French Parti Socialiste Unifié increased from one in five in the early 1960s to one in four by 1968 and then almost one in three by late the following year.[18] The rise of radical feminism that came after 1968 may have been in part, to use a phrase dear to sociologists of the period, 'a revolution of rising expectations'.

Sex, emotion and politics often intertwined in complicated ways during the student protests. Occupations of university buildings meant that young people were crammed into small spaces without external supervision. Women could find such occasions intimidating: some remembered being abused or incited to strip. But Laura Derossi – one of the few women to be prominent in the student occupations at Turin – insisted that a sense of liberation went with forced intimacy. Students who might usually have apologized if they accidentally brushed someone's leg were piled on top of each other, sometimes sitting on each other's laps. They often embraced but Derossi recalled nothing 'annoying' or any attempts to 'be the big stud': 'it was like that type of attitude had suddenly been abolished'.[19] The fact that women had usually led more constrained lives than men meant that 'emancipation' might simply involve doing things that men took for granted – staying out all night during university occupations, swearing in public or stubbing out their cigarettes on the floor. Women could find the novelty of such experiences to be intensely emotional, and men, convinced that their own approach was based on a more concrete kind of political engagement, sometimes implied that this emotional response was 'irrational'. Colin Crouch recalled a student reunion a year after the 'troubles' at the London School of Economics at which a 'girl' made a speech: 'her main point was to say that the only "real" and "valid" experiences she had had at the LSE had been the sit-in'.[20]

SECOND WAVE FEMINISM

What would later be called 'second wave feminism' can be traced back to the early 1960s. It was marked by a broad interest in the social and cultural oppression of women that distinguished it from the feminism of the 'first wave' that had in large measure been concerned with issues of suffrage. In the United States, Betty Friedan's *The Feminine Mystique* (1963) argued that women were crushed by the emphasis that society placed on marriage and 'homemaking'. Friedan helped form the National Organization for Women (NOW) in 1966.

Friedan's book was about the white, middle-class America of the suburbs, but white women who joined the Civil Rights Campaign in the South were acutely conscious of the sharp edge that racial differences gave to relations between the sexes. Even in the late 1960s, and even in the North, an FBI informer could write that a female student radical was a 'negro lover' because 'she always smiles very openly when a black man walks by.'[21] The emphasis on equality that went with the civil rights campaign fed into feminism. Relations between the campaigns for sexual and racial equality could, however, be complicated. Some white women seem to have found some consolation in the women's movement after their own eviction (along with white men) from the leadership of the Student Non-Violent Co-Ordinating Committee (see chap. 4).

West European feminists had their own history – partly because the Cold War and economic prosperity, which loomed so large in Friedan's analysis, had different consequences in Europe. French feminists of the early 1960s had grown up with a particularly complicated set of influences. Some of them had been members of the Communist Party and been exposed to its odd mix of egalitarianism, particularly in matters of work, and puritanical morality – the party disapproved of abortion and preached the virtues of childbirth without painkillers (the 'Lamaze method'). Many had read Simone de Beauvoir's *Le Deuxième Sexe* (1949) – a work whose French original was more radical than the first English-language translation.[22]

REFORM AND THE STATE

Radicals in the long 68 often presented the state as an agent of sexual repression. French feminists talked about the morality of '*tante* Yvonne' – meaning the Catholic conservatism of Charles de Gaulle's wife. In Italy and West Germany, the post-war state was associated with a conception of the 'family' that owed much to the Catholic Church, as expressed by powerful Christian Democrat parties. The state was not, however, always an agent of repression. Post-war legislation was rarely designed to return to some previous moral order, and even those who strove most assiduously to protect the conventional family sometimes did so with reforms that made life easier for those who did not fit into it. In the USA, the Civil Rights Act of 1964 had explicitly referred to 'sex' as one of the grounds on which discrimination was to be prohibited in employment – though some believed that southern legislators had inserted references to women in the hope of thwarting the intentions of those who had framed the amendment with regard to race. In Britain, it was under the Wilson government of 1966–70, the one that was so despised by the radical left (see chap. 7), that legislation laid the way for the 'permissive society'.

In France, Prime Minister Georges Pompidou – a fierce defender of property and capitalism – was ostentatiously relaxed about the sexual behaviour of the young. He believed that the French should become 'like the Scandinavians'.[23] Charles de Gaulle, brought up in the stern atmosphere of northern French Catholicism by a mother who regretted that God had not devised a more dignified way for humans to procreate, did not share Pompidou's liberalism. Nonetheless, de Gaulle's government legalized contraception in France in 1967. De Gaulle himself believed that choices in this matter should be 'rational'. His own wife (the '*tante* Yvonne' who attracted such ridicule) had no further children after giving birth at the age of twenty-eight to Anne, a daughter with Down's syndrome.

WOMEN'S LIBERATION

In the aftermath of 1968, many feminists became more radical. Some, in fact, did not much care for the word 'feminist', which seemed to belong to a bourgeois era when women had campaigned for jobs and votes and a 'room of one's own'. They felt that women's status would change through their own mobilization rather than as the result of concessions from the state and they disliked the distinction between private and public that underlay much thinking about sexual morality in the early 1960s. For them, the term 'women's liberation' evoked something that might parallel movements of American blacks or third world liberation struggles. A Mouvement de Libération des Femmes was founded in France in 1970 by Antoinette Fouque – who later, to the outrage of some, copyrighted the name.

Feminist movements had sometimes sought to integrate the sexes and men had joined feminist organizations – because they sympathized or because they regarded such organizations as useful parts of a broader revolutionary coalition. From about 1970, however, some women began to establish autonomous organizations. In France, the organization Féminin Masculin Avenir, founded in 1967, was changed into the more radical and exclusively female Féminisme Marxisme Action.

Women's liberation implied something that was at once more radical and less sharply defined than conventional politics. Women sought to raise their own consciousness as well as challenge the society around them. If there was one issue that united the women's liberation movement, it was abortion, which had been legalized by an act of parliament in Britain in 1967 and was to be legalized in the United States by a judgment of the Supreme Court (Roe v. Wade) in 1973. In France and Germany, in a manner that was characteristic of women's liberation, women based their campaign for legalization on their own experience. In France in 1971, 343 women signed a petition claiming that they personally had had an abortion; 374 women signed a similar petition in Germany.

Even more than with other radical movements of the period, there was a symbiotic relation between women's liberation and its enemies. Women sometimes used terms – 'Virago', 'Witch' or the 'Society for Cutting up Men' – that mocked the abuse to which they were subjected. Equally pictures of young women and references to sex made good copy for newspaper articles. Women protesting against the Miss America contest in Atlantic City in 1968 planned to burn symbols of female oppression, including bras. They never did so because the municipal authorities forbade them from lighting fires, but Lindsy van Gelder – a sympathetic New York journalist – reported their plan and this single article aroused years of weary jokes from television comedians – 'I shudder to think that this will be my epitaph,' said van Gelder. Conservatives found it convenient to pit themselves against sexual radicalism. Margaret Thatcher was discomfited by the word 'feminism', partly, perhaps, because it was hard for her to deny that she was in some sense a feminist, but she frequently expressed her disdain for 'women's lib'.

The attention given to women's liberation around 1968 distracted from important advances made by 'old-fashioned' feminists – sometimes those who were associated with the political movements that radicals most disliked. In France, Simone Veil, a survivor of Auschwitz and health minister in the centre-right government of Valéry Giscard d'Estaing, legalized abortion in 1975. Françoise Parturier was a feminist Gaullist who, in 1968, sent her 'open letter to men' to the president with a dry inscription 'to general de Gaulle, the misogynist who gave women the vote'.[24] In Britain, Barbara Castle attracted abuse from the radical left (sometimes expressed in crudely sexual terms) for her attempts to curb the powers of trade unions, but it was she who passed the legislation requiring equal pay for men and women. Castle's colleague Shirley Williams, who also sometimes came up against the radical left when she was minister of universities, was the daughter of a first-wave feminist (Vera Brittain). As a minister at the Home Office, she had once, in a rather *soixante-huitard* experiment, arranged to spend a night in a women's prison – telling the other inmates that she had been caught 'on the game'.[25]

SEXUAL REVOLUTION?

Alongside explicit calls for sexual liberation went social changes. The contraceptive pill, first prescribed in 1960, was seen to have inaugurated a sexual revolution – though unmarried European women did not always find it easy to get during the 1960s. Anne Wiazemsky, a nineteen-year-old student at Nanterre and the lover of Jean-Luc Godard, sought to obtain a prescription for the pill in 1967. Being a minor, she had to take her mother to a consultation with a gynaecologist – 'well off and self-satisfied' – who acceded to the request only after telling her mother: 'This girl should be more chaste and you should be more authoratitive.'[26] In truth, it is hard to know whether the young of the late 1960s were more or less sexually active than their predecessors. Sheila Rowbotham, a member of the British women's liberation movement, recalled teaching working-class girls who disliked conversations about sex on the grounds that '[t]here's them that does and them that talks about it'.[27]

The notion of 'sexual liberation' raises questions about who was being liberated from what. Consider the singer France Gall, born in

1947. She expressed cheerful and patriotic opinions and in 1966 urged her contemporaries to participate in the collection of information for the report conducted under the aegis of the Gaullist minister for youth, François Missoffe. It was this report that would be so derided by Daniel Cohn-Bendit because of its alleged inattention to 'sexual problems' (see chap. 5).[28] A few months later, Gall recorded a song written by Serge Gainsbourg – 'Les Sucettes' – that revolved around a double entendre that would have been obvious to most people even before they saw the accompanying film of the singer sucking an improbably large lollipop. Apparently, Gall herself did not understand the significance of the song and never forgave Gainsbourg for having exploited her.

Some political groups seem deliberately to have cultivated sexual promiscuity as a means of breaking down personal loyalties that might interfere with political commitment. Mark Rudd claimed that he and fourteen comrades from the Weather Underground once had sex with each other on the floor of a van travelling from Detroit to Chicago.[29] On a more mundane level, questions about whether men and women could share accommodation on university campuses attracted much attention and this was especially so when the campus in question was seen as a centre of political radicalism. Mixed halls were more controversial at Essex than at Edinburgh, where student political agitation was less marked.[30]

Whether or not 68 went with a real change in sexual behaviour it certainly meant that sexual behaviour often acquired a particular kind of significance. An example of this was provided by the case of Gabrielle Russier in Marseilles. Born in 1937, she was a teacher of literature in a *lycée*, but having passed the ferociously difficult *agrégation* exam in 1967 she seemed likely to move to university teaching. Half American, thin and with cropped hair, she resembled the actress Jean Seberg – who had a similarly unfortunate fate. For most of her life, she had not held particularly marked political views, but she was conscious of the ways in which she failed to fit into conventional society. In a letter to her estranged husband she referred to herself as 'an androgynous hippy'. She enjoyed good relations with the pupils at the co-educational school where she taught. One of these was Christian Rossi, whose beard and self-confidence made him seem older than his sixteen years. Russier and Rossi began an affair, and eventually the boy's parents complained. Russier was prosecuted for 'corruption of a minor' and, in the summer of 1969, she killed herself.

The political rebellion of 1968 did not cause the affair but it did, as one of Russier's friends later wrote, act as an 'accelerator', which encouraged the lovers to display their affection more openly. It seems likely, however, that Rossi, a member of the Trotskyist Jeunesse Communiste Révolutionnaire, or even his parents, members of the orthodox Communist Party and sympathetic to its liberal wing, attributed more political importance to the affair than did Russier. After her death, Russier became the subject of films and songs and also a political hero for the Maoists of the Gauche Prolétarienne. One of their posters read:

> Since May [1968], the power that the bourgeoisie has in the schools through the authority of the teacher is more and more shaken. In these conditions, it [could not] allow a teacher, one of the agents of its authority, to pass into the enemy camp, that of the students in revolt . . . be ready to follow her path and to struggle against all the decadent and authoritarian relations between students and teachers.[31]

Russier's friends thought that she would no more have understood the agitation that followed her death than she understood the vituperation that preceded it. The one politician who seemed concerned with her personal tragedy was Georges Pompidou.

WOMEN WORKERS

Writing about women in 1968 often focused on quite a small group of people – usually educated and middle class. The first 'women's liberation' conference at Ruskin College Oxford attracted an audience of 500. In 1970, French feminists laid a wreath dedicated to the 'unknown woman' by the Tomb of the Unknown Soldier at the Arc de Triomphe. One of those involved was amused by later accounts that talked of a thousand participants. She recalled that she had actually been one of just nine women present.[32]

Alongside these well-reported expressions of explicit liberation, there were larger mobilizations of women who were drawn from less privileged groups. In Britain, the strike of 1968 that attracted most attention in retrospect (though not at the time) was that of female machinists at the Ford works in Dagenham who struck for equal pay. In France, the years leading up to 1968 were marked by increasing disturbance among groups of workers who had not usually been well organized, especially women. The general strike of May–June 1968 seemed to mark a return to the fore of male workers in large factories, but then in the 1970s women became more important in labour protest. This was particularly true during the most famous French strike of the decade – that at the watch factory Lip in Besançon. Most workers there were women – though the strike was led by a man, Charles Piaget, whose wife, Anne, became increasingly exasperated at the way in which she was left with responsibility for the couple's children.

Trade unions were overwhelmingly led by middle-aged men. In Britain women activists found it hard to interest the Transport and General Workers' Union in the struggle of night cleaners (female and often of non-British origin) for better pay and conditions. Union leaders often talked of women in condescending terms. The leaders of a strike at a factory in Lille in 1968 announced: 'very young girls are taken under the responsibility of the delegates'.[33] Trade unions themselves, however, were not as static or homogeneous as they sometimes seemed. Before the 1960s, feminists and the labour movement had worked together. Betty Friedan, later strongly identified with middle-class American feminism in the 1960s, had written for trade union papers.[34]

American unions had sometimes seemed to break with feminism – partly because the Cold War made them wary of those aspects of their own traditions that seemed close to Communism and partly because they felt uncomfortable with the more flamboyant radicalisms of the late 1960s. Female members of the American United Automobile Workers (UAW) almost withdrew from the National Organization for Women (NOW) in the late 1960s. But in the 1970s unions changed their position. The UAW itself now supported equal rights and its female members became active in NOW once again. Younger trade union leaders sometimes saw expressions of support for feminism as a means to distance themselves from their older colleagues – Arthur Scargill, who was eventually to become head of the British miners' union, was close to the feminist academic Peggy Kahn. In any case, the membership of trade unions was changing by the early 1970s as larger numbers of white-collar workers, many of whom were women, joined them.

MEN AND SEXUAL IDENTITY

If 68 gave some women a new consciousness of their sexual identity, what happened to men? Some separated the personal and the political. Male memoirs rarely have the confessional tone of much women's writing on the period. Michel Rocard (the secretary general of the Parti Socialiste Unifié) left his wife to set up house with the sociologist Michèle Legendre on 15 May 1968, in the middle of the student riots, but he mentioned this event in his retrospective recollections only to draw attention to the fact that his party – which had decided to match his salary to that paid to a worker at Renault – agreed to foot the bill for his alimony payments.[35]

Left-wing politics could go with a casual and violent misogyny. In 1968, graffiti invited Paris students to 'rape your alma mater' or told them that the university is 'an old whore'. When Margaret Thatcher, then secretary of state for education, visited Lanchester Polytechnic in 1971, students shouted: 'Fascist pig; get her knickers off'.[36] There was also hostility to feminism in parts of the Black Power movement. Some, including some women, simply argued that 'racist police murders of Black people' were more serious than 'the sexist verbal abuse of white women by their husbands'.[37] Some went further. They believed that racism had 'emasculated' black men and that restoring their dignity required a reassertion of masculine roles. Eldridge Cleaver, who became the 'minister of information' for the Black Panthers, was an extreme example of such attitudes. A former pimp who attracted notoriety with *Soul on Ice* (1968), a memoir he wrote in prison, claimed to have believed that 'rape was an insurrectionary act'.[38] Cleaver repented in jail but, even after his conversion to revolutionary politics, he was often bitterly hostile to feminists and homosexuals. On these matters he was at odds with his former comrade Huey Newton.

Sometimes, though, relations between male left-wing politics and feminism were more complicated than they looked at first glance. C. Wright Mills – the sociologist so admired by the founders of Students for a Democratic Society – was almost a parody of American masculinity. He made much of his motorcycles and the fact that he had built his house with his own hands. His political language could come across as aggressively male: 'Let the old women complain wisely about the end of ideology. We are beginning to move again.'[39] In autobiographical essays that purported to be an exchange with a Soviet friend, Mills distinguished between 'a very public letter' and the private matter of 'my women and all of that'.[40] But there was a paradox in Mills's writing. The denial that relations with women were 'public' was itself a public statement and Mills's own masculine swagger implied a self-consciousness about his sexual identity. He was in fact one of the first Americans to write about de Beauvoir's *Second Sex* and to recognize that the book might have implications for men as well as women: 'perhaps in sharing Mlle de Beauvoir's passions for liberty we would forgo masculinity and femininity to achieve it'.[41]

There were also younger men whose apparent machismo went with a willingness to criticize their own conduct towards women. When they came to write their autobiographical accounts of the late 1960s, both Tom Hayden and Daniel Cohn-Bendit interviewed their former lovers – women who had become active feminists. For a few men, the feminist 'separatism' of the 1970s could be as painful as the black separatism of the 1960s had been for those involved in the early civil rights movement. Jeff Shero Nightbyrd from Texas recalled that attacks by women whom he had considered to be comrades brought him close to a nervous breakdown and induced suicide attempts among his friends.[42] Many women felt angry about the way in which they were treated by male comrades in radical groups in 68: one described the culture of male activists in the Italian student movement as a form of 'terrorism',[43] but some remembered a more complicated pattern of relations between the sexes. A female *soixante-huitard* in Paris recalled a change in the behaviour of the men she knew after 1968. This was partly a matter of specific campaigns, for example in favour of nursery schools, but it was also a question of style. She recalled the discovery that being a man did not mean being a *'mec'* – a slang word meaning 'bloke' or 'guy' – and that it did not imply the ostentatious masculinity that she later associated with the conservative politician Jacques Chirac.[44] One of her former comrades had rethought his sexual identity in a particularly dramatic way and in the 1980s had decided to live as a woman.

Sometimes, left-wing groups in the 1970s seemed more troubled by the nature of their sexist language than by the use of violence. The Weathermen changed their name to the Weather Underground. The most notorious moment of friction between the male left and feminists in Italy came in 1975 when some men from Lotta Continua assaulted women at a rally in favour of abortion rights, after having turned up uninvited to provide 'security'. But the leadership of Lotta Continua did not condone their members' action and, indeed, the episode contributed to the dissolution of the group.

VIETNAM

Opposition to the Vietnam War interacted with thinking about sexual identities. Some American women who opposed the war made much of their status as mothers. The organization Another Mother for Peace was formed in 1967 and printed a thousand Mother's Day cards to be sent to members of Congress. Not all feminists felt comfortable with this. Betty Friedan said: 'I don't think the fact that milk once flowed in my breasts is the reason I am against the war.' A group of anti-war feminists staged a ceremony to bury 'traditional motherhood' at Arlington National Cemetery.[45]

Draft resistance could encourage men to think about their own masculinity because war was so often presented as quintessentially male. However, plenty of men who resisted the draft did so in ways that did not challenge conventional sexual identities. Draft resisters sported bumper stickers that read 'Girls say "yes" to guys who say "no"', a slogan that was, to the distaste of some feminists, adopted by the folk singer Joan Baez. A student newspaper in Tennessee in 1966 suggested that women should limit their own academic performances to ensure that men were ranked higher and thus more likely to obtain academic draft deferments.[46]

Pro-war New York construction workers carried placards saying 'Don't worry – they don't draft faggots'. It was true that homosexuals were not drafted and that the last question on the form presented to candidates for conscription was 'Are you or have you ever been a homosexual?' This had a curious effect on sexual politics in America. Men faced, perhaps for the first time in their life, a direct question about their sexuality. Answering 'yes' would exclude them from certain civilian jobs but it might also get them out of military service. Some heterosexual men affected 'homosexual manners' in a bid to escape service. A Berkeley guide for draft resisters suggested that men should watch the 'Frisco North Beach crowd' to acquire an appropriately homosexual style and also that they should ask their girlfriends for advice on how to 'move your body like chicks do'.[47] In 1966, some homosexual organizations (keen to emphasize the respectability of their members) campaigned in favour of drafting homosexual men. However, homosexual organizations became more radical a few years later and were increasingly likely to associate attacks on the Vietnam War with an assault on conventional sexual morality. Keith St Clare of the radical Vanguard movement in San Francisco suggested that people should 'Fuck for Peace'.

GAY LIBERATION

Male homosexuals discussed their sexual identity more than most men around 1968. The festive mood of protests opened up possibilities for sexual adventure. One Turin student recalled that he had his first homosexual experience during the university occupation of 1968 – though he did not begin to define himself as a homosexual until ten years later.[48] Sometimes, homosexuality took a more explicitly political turn. Until the late 1960s, movements for homosexual rights were usually discreet groups of middle-class men. They emphasized the respectability of their members.[49] In the US, the Mattachine Society was founded in the late 1940s, the name alluding to masked festivals in Renaissance France. In France, Arcadie, the name derived from the Greek literature, was founded in 1954.[50] These movements defined themselves as 'homophile' rather than 'homosexual' – a distinction that puts one in mind of Jean Mauriac's remark that his father, the novelist François, was *'Homo, certainement, sexuel j'en doute'*. In California, one group was said to have lost half its members as soon as it put the word 'homosexual' in its title.[51]

There was no simple relation between homosexual causes and the political left. The most prominent homosexual in France before 1968 was probably Roger Peyrefitte, an unrepentant Pétainist – it was he who had suggested the name Arcadie. His novels on *'amitiés particulières'* had aroused such scandal that an ambitious young civil servant who shared his name had changed it to avoid confusion – *Alain* Peyrefitte (as he had now become) was a Gaullist minister by 1968. Communist leaders discouraged open displays of what they regarded as a 'bourgeois vice' – though ordinary party members often seem to have regarded the moralism of their leaders with some distaste.

Movements for homosexual rights became more ostentatiously militant in the aftermath of 1968. Male homosexuals, like feminists, frequently adopted a language of 'liberation'. The British Gay Liberation Front was formed in 1970. There were important differences between new movements. Was the aim simply sexual freedom? Did homosexuality imply a radical critique of sexual conformity? In France, Guy Chevalier established a Comité d'Action Pédérastique Révolutionnaire in the spring of 1968 but this group was short-lived. Guy Hocquenghem exercised a more lasting influence. He claimed to have thrown the first *pavé* in the rue Gay Lussac. Four years later, at the age of twenty-five, he wrote a famous open letter in which he spoke on behalf of 'three million perverts'.

Not everyone shared Hocquenghem's insistence on the links between homosexuality and politics. Some saw the gay communities of the 1970s as an escape from politics, or at least an escape from the particular kinds of politics that had been born in the late 1960s. One talked of 'casting aside all the political clothes that people normally wore and getting in touch with aspects of their sexuality that were normally denied by their politics'.[52] The flight from politics was especially marked in the United States, which had been, for most of the post-war period, more repressive than many countries in Western

Europe. Generations of American gay men and lesbians had taken refuge in Paris or London. However, perhaps precisely because the transition was so quick, the United States, or at least New York and San Francisco, rapidly became the centre of a new male homosexual subculture, which sometimes seemed all absorbing. Tom Hayden recalled how Carl Wittman had been reborn as a gay rights' activist in San Francisco after having been an activist in Students for a Democratic Society, and eventually died with AIDS.[53]

Attitudes to the AIDS epidemic of the 1980s differed in revealing ways among 68ers in France and America. Americans often regarded death from AIDS as the end of a certain kind of 68, which had come to be conceived as a largely personal journey. French writers remained focused on the public and political significance of 68, which they partly distinguished from their personal lives. Two of them, Hocquenghem and Daniel Bensaïd, wrote their political autobiographies without directly alluding to the fact that they were dying of AIDS.[54]

FAMILIES

Conservatives often talked of 68 as a rebellion by children against parents but many 68ers became parents themselves – sometimes at the very moment when they were most politically active. When Virginie Linhart wrote about French Maoists of her parents' generation, she discovered that her mother had gone into labour during a political meeting in 1966. Sue LeGrand gave birth – using the Lamaze method – while she and the baby's father, Mark Rudd, were living under false names on account of their activities with the Weather Underground. Sometimes 68 was welcomed precisely because it appeared to offer a release from the claustrophobia that could afflict women looking after children, but some also looked back with regret, especially when activism or imprisonment had separated them from their children for a time. Ulrike Meinhof was a particularly extreme example of the pain that came from trying to combine political action with motherhood. She had separated from the father of her children to devote herself to politics. At one time, Meinhof seems seriously to have considered having them brought up in a Palestinian orphanage.

She stopped answering letters from her daughters shortly before she committed suicide in prison.

Some people talked of 'liberation' for children. This could mean attempts to organize school children politically, but it could also mean sex. Guy Hocquenghem recalled how he had been seduced at the age of fifteen by René Schérer, his philosophy teacher at the *lycée* Lakanal. The men remained friends and appear to have had benign memories of the liaison. Other relations – most famously that of Gabrielle Russier, recounted above – attracted the attention of the law. Sometimes the sexuality of very young children was discussed. Daniel Cohn-Bendit described – in words that he came to regret – the sexual experimentation of his charges when he worked in a Frankfurt Kindergarten in the 1970s. In Britain in 1970, *Oz* magazine was prosecuted when it produced a 'school kids' issue' that featured, among other things, Rupert the Bear sporting an erection.

Many parents sought to bring their children up in ways that subverted or circumvented existing institutions. The first of these was school. At the hippy commune established in California by Don McCoy, an eccentric and rich property developer, Garnet Brennan, dismissed as a headmistress after she admitted to having smoked marijuana for eighteen years, ran a 'Not School'.[55] The English educationalist A.S. Neill had published *Summerhill: A Radical Approach to Education* in 1962, a book that celebrated a school that eschewed conventional discipline. This work acquired a new international importance after 1968. It sold 2 million copies in the USA and the French translation (first published in 1970) sold half a million. Debate over education had a sharp edge in France because traditional schools were so authoritarian. Some *soixante-huitards* sought to educate their children outside conventional schools entirely; others, often graduates of the most demanding *grandes écoles*, continued to value academic rigour even when they had rebelled against almost every other feature of bourgeois society.

The second institution to be challenged was the family. 68ers experimented with communal living. Some communes were seen primarily as a means to promote political action – this was the case of Kommune no. 1 in West Berlin. Others, by contrast, were retreats from, or at least alternatives to, political action and a means by which

68ers, especially in America, turned away from collective action towards more personal concerns. The Villa Road Commune in Brixton in London was said to be divided between 'politicos' and 'primal screamers'.[56]

Communes expanded quickly after 1968. In Denmark, by the late 1960s, communes encompassed 100,000 people, out of a total population of 5 million.[57] In the United States, which already had a tradition of religiously inspired communities, there were 2 million people living in communes in the early 1970s. These were largely rural institutions. They marked a shift in direction away from the radical politics of the 1960s, which had been largely focused on cities. Communes often revolved around farming or craft production, activities that were time-consuming and that also raised questions about commerce and property.

Communes were not necessarily 'liberating' places. Living in them involved hard work and long hours of tedious collective discussion – the latter sometimes dominated by assertive men. Susan Stern first read Betty Friedan's *Feminine Mystique* in 1968 and recognized the world being described – even though Friedan had been talking about the oppression of women in middle-class suburbia and Stern was living in a hippy commune.[58] There was much prurient discussion of sex in communes but it is not actually clear that experimentation in this domain was any more adventurous than it would have been among the suburban couples of the 1960s whose lives were described in the novels of John Updike. In any case, communal living tended to attract more men than women, which skewed the terms of sexual exchange. At a commune in Virginia it was reported that 'Bill had envisaged a group-marriage community where members would rotate sleeping partners. As Kathleen was the only female member at the time, she was the crucial factor in this experiment. But she did not want to sleep with anyone but George.'[59]

The Vicolo Cassini community in the small town of Macerata in central Italy revolved around an artist's studio rented by one of its members: it bore an odd relation to the Catholic, conservative morality of the town. There were more men than women in the group; interviewed decades later, the men recalled road trips and visits to other towns, whereas women recalled the internal life of the studio.

Most members of the community, especially the women, did not live there but remained with their families and spent a few hours at a time in the studio. A historian conducting interviews found it hard to pin the former members of the community down on the extent to which they had practised 'free love' – perhaps whatever 'liberation' they had once achieved did not incline them to talk about such matters with someone who was the same age as their children.[60]

A few communes discouraged the birth of children as likely to distract from political action,[61] but most were seen partly as places to raise children and adults experimented with ways in which to ensure that children were raised collectively rather than being the sole responsibility of their parents. At the Kana Commune near Copenhagen, one adult was nominated as 'house pixie' to look after all children – though this arrangement acquired a less idealistic hue when members of the commune returned to university and decided that childcare should become a full-time job given to one person and subsidized by the Danish social security system.[62] Some saw collective living as a mean to 'abolish the family' and this aroused excited comment, but generally it was families that subverted communes rather than the other way round. The battered veterans of a commune in rural Michigan came to believe that it would have survived if it had allowed individual families to live in their own cabins.[63]

One of the most dramatic rebellions of 68, at least so far as its participants were concerned, brought a move towards 'traditional' families rather than a rebellion against them. Some Catholics had anticipated that in the aftermath of Vatican II priests would be allowed to marry. When this did not happen, a few took matters into their own hands and married anyway. One group of Frenchmen ordained after 68 defined itself in 1976 as open to priests 'whatever their situation', which meant, *en clair,* that it included those who had married and that the association brought together men who were still priests in the conventional sense with those who had in the eyes of the Church broken their vows.[64] Debates over celibacy in the Church could produce a curious kind of inverted 68. Those who had rebelled most dramatically were often not beautiful and sexually experienced young people but middle-aged former priests – frequently looking awkward in secular clothes and earnestly trying to embrace married life. Some communities underwent a kind of counter-revolution as their members decided that sexual relations would interfere with their social role. The community of Bose was founded in 1965 in Piedmont. It brought together men and women and Catholics and Protestants but eventually its members abandoned their street clothes and started to wear habits in the style of the Benedictines. At Easter 1973, members of the community took vows of celibacy.[65]

THE CHILDREN OF THE REVOLUTION

How did the children of 68ers look back on it all? Some remembered they had been given comparatively little attention by parents who were absorbed in political action. Children whose hippy parents went back to the land were mocked by their classmates at the village school because they smelt of goat. Given the emphasis that 68ers put on spontaneity and authenticity, it is interesting to note that their children sometimes recalled the curious abstraction with which they appeared to have managed family life. One pupil at a French alternative school founded by *soixante-huitards* had to refer to her mother by her name rather than saying '*maman*'. She felt, she said, like a 'theoretical child'.[66]

Some children of 68ers became bitter but most were tolerant – indeed, more tolerant of their parents than their parents had been of their grandparents. Sometimes there was a curious circularity. The parents of 68ers had frequently been relatively moderate left-wingers who tolerated the revolutionary adventures of their children; the children of 68ers frequently returned to democratic socialism. Jean-Louis Péninou gravitated from factory activism in the 1960s and 70s to being an editor of *Libération*. His son, born in March 1968, grew up to become a municipal politician and member of the Parti Socialiste – he was undaunted by the fact that his parents had named him 'Mao'. The economist Thomas Piketty was born of *soixante-huitard* parents and brought up on a farm in the south of France – though his wealthy grandfather ensured that the conventional aspects of his education were not entirely neglected. Piketty became famous for work on economics that blended a very *unsoixante-huitard* concern with statistics with calls for reforms that might be enacted within the capitalist system.

Tom Hayden tells a poignant story of life in the Red Family Commune that he helped found in Berkeley in the late 1960s. He lived there with Anne Weills Scheer and became close to her son, Christopher, whom he took to the Blue Fairyland nursery, where men were encouraged to 'get in touch with the nurturing side of themselves'. One day Hayden returned from giving a speech on the east coast to be confronted by his lover and her comrades. Influenced by a mixture of radical feminism and left-wing politics (Hayden claimed that they had come to admire Kim Il Sung of North Korea), they had decided to expel him for being 'an oppressive male chauvinist'. He was not allowed to see Christopher for years and found this separation painful. In 1984, a young man tapped him on the shoulder. It was Christopher. The boy had grown up to be a student at the University of California and had taken a vacation job as a uniformed guard at the National Democratic Convention – an interesting thought for Hayden, who had been tried for incitement to riot during the convention sixteen years earlier.[67]

9
Workers

Alfa Romeo workers in 1972.

9

[T]he conflict as it is today is only possible because May 1968 happened.

– Charles Piaget, leader of worker occupation at the Lip factory in Besançon, 1973[1]

Students and workers sometimes allied in 68. The former often supported strikes by the latter and, in France and Italy at least, workers joined student demonstrations. Both drew on similar techniques – direct action, occupation of buildings – and both were sometimes in rebellion against the organizations that claimed to represent them – left-wing parties and trade unions – as well as against employers or the political right. The long 68 did not, though, bring complete unity between workers and students. Strikes were often most important in countries that had seen relatively limited rebellion by students, or even where important parts of the working class were hostile to aspects of student radicalism.

The workers' 68 was different from the student one because large numbers of workers belonged to trade unions. In the short term, it sometimes seemed that the agitations of the late 60s would circumvent these unions: that workers would organize themselves outside existing structures, that non-unionized workers (women, immigrants and migrants from the countryside) would become more powerful and that strikers would no longer be satisfied with the concessions on pay that unions had traditionally sought. Union leaders, however, proved adept at dealing with discontent in their ranks. The unions were changed by 68, but their power, if anything, increased, and they often used that power to focus on the concrete demands that the most radical protests of 68 had sometimes seemed to disparage. Anyone looking back from the end of the 1970s would probably have concluded that workers were the great beneficiaries of 68, in material terms at least.

INTERNATIONAL VARIATION

The French general strike of 1968 aroused interest among left-wingers throughout the democratic world. A member of the British International Socialists, Tom Fawthrop, recalled its effect thus:

> In France ... you had this magnificent solidarity which cut across class lines, in the sense that most students are at least middle-class ... In many countries ... like Britain the notion of any kind of unity between workers and students is largely an illusion. But ... it's the Holy Grail of Trotskyism.[2]

Fawthrop was painfully aware of the limits of unity between British workers and the middle class left because some of his classmates at the University of Hull were former workers whose education had been sponsored by the trade unions and who were tepid in their support for the occupation of university buildings that Fawthrop led in 1968.[3]

The labour movement was more confined by national frontiers than the student one. Few workers were in a position to go to Paris in May 1968, as Fawthrop had done. Trade union leaders had formal links with organizations in other countries but those links, especially those of the Communist unions with the Eastern Bloc, did not always dispose them to radicalism in the long 68. The internationalization of the economy, particularly associated with the growth of the European Economic Community (EEC), was an important feature of the late 1960s and 70s. The dramatic events of 1968 often obscured one of the most significant long-term changes of that year: the abolition of many internal tariffs in the EEC. In subsequent years, trade unions mobilized a nationalistic rebellion against the EEC. The French

CGT, in particular, blamed Germany for the decline of the steel industry in Lorraine.[4]

In cultural terms too, national frontiers mattered to the working class. Television stations, which often reinforced a strong sense of national identity, dominated popular culture. Even pop music was locally produced: a Maoist student who went to work in a factory found that her colleagues preferred Mireille Mathieu to 'rock anglais'.[5] There were substantial immigrant groups in many industrialized countries but they were usually drawn from non-industrialized countries with weak traditions of labour organization, which was one of the things that made them attractive to employers. Migrants from the Italian south constituted the one exception to this rule: they took up employment in West German factories and then sometimes returned to work in the north of their own country in the late 1960s.

In France itself, the strikes of 1968 were an exceptional event, as statistics show. Very few French workers went on strike in the second half of 1968 and for the two years after that. Even when strikes increased in the 1970s, they never came close to those of May 1968. It is impossible to say exactly how many workers were on strike that month because the official statistical services themselves broke down. If we take the most conservative estimate and assume that there were 5 million on strike on, say, 27 May, this would mean that the number of working days lost in those twenty-four hours was greater than the number lost *in any year* between 1964 and 1974. If we assume that 7 million were on strike for at least a week in May, then the number of days lost in strikes in that week was greater than the number of days lost *in every year* from 1964 to 1974 combined.

Statistics also reflect national variation. The numbers of workers on strike in 1968 in West Germany, Sweden and Switzerland were so small that the International Labour Organization did not even bother to record them. Rates in Germany, Scandinavia, Switzerland and the Netherlands increased slightly in the 1970s, but still remained low by international standards.[6] Some defenders of order explained the relative tranquillity of these countries by suggesting that there was an inverse relation between upheaval and the strength of trade unions. In the aftermath of the May events in France, Raymond Aron wrote:

Table 2
Working Days Lost in Strikes, in Thousands, in France, 1964–1974

1964	2497
1965	980
1966	2524
1967	4204
1968	–
1969	2224
1970	1782
1971	4529
1972	3755
1973	3914
1974	3377

Source: *Annuaire Statistique de la France*. (There are no overall figures for 1968 – though figures for all months except May and June can be found in chap. 5.[7])

in developed industrial societies the fundamental conservative force is the trade union movement . . . in the United States, in Scandinavia and the Federal German Republic. The trade unions make demands but they are not revolutionary . . . Unlike the gilded youth of the 16th arrondissement, they are in favour of a consumer society.[8]

The secretary of the Gaullist party remarked after the strikes of 1968: 'The workers' unions are not sufficiently well-organized in France, and . . . they did not resist subversive action . . . having often been overtaken by the demands of activists who benefited from the weakness of the union environment.'[9] In the 1970s, European governments invested much hope in 'corporatism' or the notion that labour disputes could be avoided with structures that would knit unions and employers into formal agreements. Until the Thatcherite victories over labour in the 1980s, their model was often Germany, where 'concerted action' drew unions and employer organizations into

Table 3
Days Lost in Strikes per Thousand Employees, 1964–1974, in Selected Western Countries

	1964	1965	1966	1967	1968	1969	1970	1971	1972	1973	1974
Belgium	250	40	320	90	230	100	830	720	190	520	340
Canada	560	730	1570	1200	1670	2550	2190	800	1420	1660	2590
Denmark	30	400	30	20	20	80	170	30	40	440	330
Finland	80	20	150	410	250	200	270	3300	520	2470	460
FRG	–	–	–	30	–	20	10	340	–	40	60
Eire	1620	1720	1420	520	910	2170	490	670	600	420	1260
Italy	1270	540	1710	580	930	4160	1730	1060	1670	2480	1800
Netherlands	20	30	10	–	10	10	140	50	70	330	–
Norway	–	–	–	10	10	–	70	10	–	10	490
Sweden	10	–	110	–	–	30	40	240	10	10	30
Switzerland	–	–	–	–	–	–	–	10	–	–	–
UK	170	220	170	220	370	520	740	1190	2160	570	1270
USA	850	860	880	1430	1590	1390	2210	1600	860	750	1480
France	280	100	240	430	X	200	180	440	300	330	250

Source: Department of Employment Gazette (reporting figures from International Labour Organization). Dashes indicate that there was not a significant number of recorded strikes. In France the strikes of May and June 1968 were not recorded because the statistical services broke down.

economic planning. However, strong unions did not in themselves guarantee tranquillity in industry. British unions were well established and powerful; the industrial population was more unionized than that of even West Germany and all major unions were, unlike their counterparts in France or Italy, affiliated with a democratic socialist party that, in the context of 68, stood on the right of the political spectrum. In spite of this, the number of days lost per thousand workers through strikes in the United Kingdom was higher than that in France in every single year between 1969 and 1974, and more than three times higher for the period as a whole.

FORMS OF PROTEST

In some ways the most notable feature of the period after 1968 was not so much the scale of strikes as their nature. In France, strikes spread to new kinds of workplace – affecting small enterprises and areas in which industrialization was comparatively recent. Workers were more likely to accompany strikes with other forms of challenge to the authority of their employers. In France and Italy the offices of managers were ransacked and managers themselves were occasionally held hostage. Italian workers undertook 'cortei interni' or marches across the factory itself during unofficial strikes. Often these were accompanied by charivari or mockery of power, in which, for example, foremen were made to hold red flags.[10] Factory occupations, even when small in number, attracted huge attention. A radical priest preaching on Christmas Eve 1972 inside the Superbox factory in Brianza in Italy, occupied by its workers, said that if Christ were to be reborn it would be in an occupied factory.[11] Workers drew on new techniques – such as the hunger strike – to draw attention to their grievances. In July 1975, one trade unionist estimated that 180 factories in France were on strike and that forty-two of these involved worker occupations. Most of these strikes affected only one company at a time and were unlikely to bring down capitalism but they influenced the mood of the country – a visiting group of militants from the Algerian Front de Libération Nationale went home with the false impression that France must be on the verge of revolution.[12] Alongside these more or less explicit protests went a variety of forms of insubordination. Workers abused foremen, refused to obey orders and simply walked out of their work – the latter was encouraged by a climate where it was relatively easy to obtain a new job.

The single most discussed strike in France was that at the Lip watch factory in Besançon in 1973. It was provoked by the sale of a traditional family-owned company to a Swiss enterprise and by the threat of sackings. The strike revealed a new attitude to authority. The workers occupied their factory, but they also began to sell stock and to operate the factory under their own direction. The number of strikers at Lip was tiny by the standards of the general strike of 1968 but it attracted much attention. On 29 September 1973, 100,000 people marched through the streets of Besançon in support of the strike and there was brief talk of putting forward the strike leader as a candidate for the Parti Socialiste Unifié (PSU) in the presidential election of 1974. The strike raised awkward questions for the left, even the *soixante-huitard* left. For one thing, this was a relatively small enterprise in a provincial town – a long way from the bastions of working-class strength, in which Marxists had invested such hope. The leader of the strike – Charles Piaget – was a Catholic and influenced by a distinctively Christian tradition of trade unionism. Some middle-class activists went to Lip, but the strike suggested that workers were capable of organizing their own action without the help of intellectuals. Most of those who travelled to other factories were Maoists who sought to incite revolution in the workplace. Those at Lip included a Dominican priest and the philosopher Dominique Bondu, who stressed that his aim was to help workers to become intellectuals rather than to turn himself into a worker – a number of workers from the factory did indeed go to the new university established after 1968 at Vincennes.[13] Jean Raguenès, the Dominican who went to become a worker at Lip, wrote at the time that the 'rules of the road are well established and dreaming of a different set of rules is difficult'.[14] How far his fellow workers ever did dream of an alternative is hard to say. Most seem to have thought of their own strategy as one of simple survival rather than as a new departure in worker management.[15] Judged in these terms, the strike failed because the factory eventually closed.

All the same, the strike put *autogestion*, or self-management, at the centre of debate. It was important in the early 1970s to the newly formed Parti Socialiste. Pierre Rosanvallon, at that point the house intellectual of the Confédération Française Démocratique du Travail (CFDT), published a book in 1976 entitled *L'Âge de l'Autogestion*. However, as Rosanvallon later admitted, vagueness was one attractive quality of *autogestion*. The word could be applied to almost any context in which people could be seen as taking control of their own lives.[16] It provided those who sought to renew socialism with a means of distinguishing themselves from both capitalism and the *étatisme* of the old left. Not everyone who used the word believed in it. Michel Rocard's Parti Socialiste Unifié was the party most publicly identified with *autogestion*, but at the height of the strikes of 1968, he conceded in private that 'autogestion had been forced on the PSU by its militants in the factories. He thought the idea was impractical and feared for its consequences on the French economy if it spread further.'[17]

There were also experiments in worker management in Britain. Ken Coates, a Trotskyist and former miner, founded the Institute for Workers' Control in 1968. Workers at Upper Clyde Shipbuilders restarted work under their own aegis after their employer sought to close the yard in 1971.[18] Partly inspired by this example, there were over a hundred workers' occupations over the next three years. Tony Benn, appointed secretary of state for industry after the Labour Party's victory in the 1974 election, took an interest in these experiments, and for a time the government subsidized a workers' cooperative at Meriden Motorcycles. Worker control of private sector companies was always bound to be difficult – partly because efforts to establish such control were usually made as a response to job cuts or attempts at closure. Workers were almost invariably trying to run their factories at times of declining demand. Outsiders saw brave experiments but the workers involved were often actually making desperate efforts to preserve their former lives. The more austere Marxists argued that as long as capitalism existed, workers' control was bound to end in either bankruptcy or the creation of enterprises that ran on capitalist lines.[19]

MISSIONARIES TO THE
WORKING CLASS

Some middle-class activists in Western Europe and even the United States tried to infiltrate the working class after 1968. They joined picket lines or handed out leaflets at factory gates. A group of students from the London School of Economics moved from occupying their own institution to supporting the strike by building workers at the Barbican. Some went further and took manual jobs. Trotskyist and Maoist groups sponsored large-scale entry into factories. Maoists were particularly keen to undertake an experiment that they believed to be modelled on the Chinese Cultural Revolution. Steve Jefferys went from the LSE to the Chrysler plant in Glasgow, where he became a shop steward for the Amalgamated Union of Engineering Workers. In the United States, a few movements, such as the Philadelphia Workers' Organizing Committee[20] or the Maoist Progressive Labor Party,[21] sought to promote middle class entry into industrial labour around 68. In Germany, the writer Peter Schneider worked in a factory. Some radicals worked at the Opel factory in Bochum for several years and even managed to get representatives elected to the factory council in 1972.[22] Generally, though, attempts to infiltrate the working class in Britain, Germany and the US had little success. All these countries had a well-established working-class culture into which intellectuals found it hard to fit. There was a painful earnestness about American Maoists who tried to ingratiate themselves with their workmates by talking about baseball and beer.[23] Generally, if the radical left made contact with the working class in these countries, it did so by turning away from the workplace and launching itself into campaigns that involved, say, teaching German to migrant Turkish women, organizing crèches or providing leisure activities for disaffected teenagers.

The most significant migration of left-wingers to factories was seen in France. As early as 1967, some Maoists became *établis*, that is to say, established themselves as workers. In this area as in many others, May 1968 itself actually marked a break rather than a continuation because the Maoist leaders did not approve of the student agitation and were disconcerted when some workers supported it. Most *établis* withdrew from factories and the most important movement that had sponsored their activities – the Union des Jeunesses Communistes Marxistes-Léninistes (UJCML) – broke up in disarray (see chap. 5).

After the general strike of May–June 1968, the number of *établis* increased again. The total of those entering factories peaked in 1971 and 2–3,000 people were involved in all.[24] Getting factory work was rendered relatively easy by the fact that the French economy was booming and that employers were often keen to make up the production they had lost during the strikes. Marie-Josée Revillon d'Apreval was amused to discover that even her obviously aristocratic name did not prevent her from being hired in Roubaix.[25] The largest group to promote entry into the factories was the Maoist Gauche Prolétarienne, formed after the break-up of the UJCML in 1968.

Activists were fascinated by large, famous factories with a reputation for working-class militancy and some of them applied themselves to getting hired by Renault at Boulogne-Billancourt or Peugeot at Sochaux with the same obsessive ambition that they had once brought to the entrance examination of the École Normale Supérieure. Some got jobs in smaller enterprises or with interim agencies in order to construct the appropriate kind of curriculum vitae before applying to the most celebrated factories. The aim of the *établis* shifted. They had initially sought to promote radicalism within the CGT, but after 1968 they began to establish new bodies designed to circumvent existing unions. *Établis* invested most hope in those of their colleagues who were marginalized within the working class – women, immigrants and semi-skilled workers on production lines.

At the time the *établis* were emphatic that their action should be separated from the self-indulgence that they associated with middle-class *soixante-huitards*. In retrospect, though, many of them came to feel that their fascination with the working classes was emotional as much as political, and that it often had a tragicomic dimension. Working in a factory could provide a means of atoning for a privileged background. There was a touch of self-mortification in the way that some approached the factory and a few recalled their experiences in religious terms. Marnix Dressen had been training as a Protestant pastor before he was converted to Maoism and went to work in a factory. One activist wrote that left-wingers went to the Renault factory at Flins 'as others go to Lourdes to be present at the miracles'; another compared the *établis* to St Bernard and the monks of Clairvaux.[26] Such evocations were themselves deliberately blasphemous acts for those who had been brought up on a Marxist catechism. The *établis* endured great personal sacrifice. They interrupted their education (a particularly dramatic break for those who were so young that they had not yet finished school) and they abandoned careers. Some were disowned and/or disinherited by their families. One came to believe that he had driven his father to suicide.[27]

For all their sacrifices, middle-class people who went to work in factories could usually find a way back. Most of them left the factories – especially after the dissolution of the Gauche Prolétarienne in 1973. Getting sacked for a political offence often provided a quick and, from their point of view, honourable escape from industrial work. Some were imprisoned – a brutal experience but also one that sometimes satiated the desire of young idealists for sacrifice and even provided them with opportunities. Yves Cohen, who went on to become a historian, completed the first part of his university degree while serving a prison sentence. The educational and professional costs of *établissement* were often high but, at least for the luckiest of *établis*, these costs were sometimes partly offset by the rigid hierarchy of the French education system – a *normalien* remained a *normalien* even if he or she had disappeared from the academic world for several years. By the late 1980s, almost half of former *établis* were in 'upper management' positions, the liberal professions or university teaching. By this stage most of the former *établis* had reached a social position that was higher than that of their fathers.[28]

Things could be more awkward for those *établis* who themselves originated in the working class and who consequently lacked the contacts that might have helped extract them from the factory. One of the first Maoists to take a working-class job, in November 1967, was the son of a worker who had become a science student in Paris. He never returned to study and his intellectual capacities were diminished by a suicide attempt in 1977. His former comrades barely dared evoke his militant past at his funeral in 2012.[29]

The highest price was often paid by those workers who engaged most closely with the *établis*. For young people who disliked the harsh disciplines of industrial work, the arrival of charismatic and highly educated radicals (a few years older than themselves) could be an exciting experience. Such workers sometimes felt betrayed when their new comrades disappeared from the factory or, worse, renounced their original political views. Guy Paillot grew up determined to avoid working in the Peugeot factory that loomed over his home town of Sochaux. However, his encounter with Maoist *établis* took him into political actions which got him sacked from the job at the post office that had seemed an escape route from the factory floor. He sought employment in factories to promote the revolutionary cause but, when his comrades moved on, he sank into twenty years of drug abuse and intermittent spells in prison. In the 1980s, he met one of his former associates who had once urged him not be ashamed of his working-class manners. Now the same man told him to remove his shoes before coming into his apartment.[30]

TRADE UNIONS

Unions were attacked by middle-class militants in the long 68, and they sometimes seemed to lose control of their own members. The strikes of 1968 in France and 1969 in Italy were not initiated by trade union leaders. Shop stewards, union officials in individual work-places, seem to have called the shots at least for a time – though governments sometimes feared that workers' agitation was controlled by no one at all. In 1969, Barbara Castle, secretary of state for employment in the Labour government, told her cabinet colleagues that a strike at the British Leyland motor company arose from 'a mood of near-anarchy on the shop floor'.[31]

Union leaders, often proved good at working with and channelling worker agitation, even agitation that was initially directed against the unions themselves. In Britain, unofficial strikes, such as that of London dustmen in 1969, were declared official after they had begun. Similarly, German trade union leaders managed to claim credit for pay increases after strikes in the Ruhr and Saar in 1968, which had in fact been unofficial.[32] British trade union leaders, knowing that too much formal regulation might bring them into conflict with their most radical members, simply refused to register their unions under the legislation with which the Heath government of 1970 to 1974 sought to control strikes. Subsequent agitation against this legislation occasionally brought unions into alliance with parts of the radical left. In Germany, the unions and the student movement had worked together in opposition to the Emergency Law that was eventually passed in 1968 (see chap. 6). After this, growing student radicalism alienated many trade unions, which tended to represent the interests of skilled, male, German-born workers. Union leaders disciplined some of the most radical figures in the factories, including three shop stewards at the Daimler-Benz factory, significantly one of them was an Italian, who stood against the official candidates of the IG Metall union in elections to the factory council in 1972.[33]

In France and Italy, unions seemed threatened by unofficial action from below in 1968 and 1969. Leaders of the French Confédération Générale du Travail were denounced by their own members for having negotiated with the government at Grenelle in May 1968 (see chap. 5). But they quickly reversed their position and refused to sign the Grenelle accords; it is a measure of their success in riding the tiger of worker agitation that many employers came to believe that the GGT had been leading the strikes all along.[34] The CFDT, which had emerged from Christian unions, was well suited to the climate produced by 1968, when questions of dignity and autonomy sometimes appeared more important than pay (see chap. 5). However, the CGT survived unexpectedly well. Henri Krasucki – who had risen through the metal workers' union, held secret talks with the Gaullists in May 1968 and helped negotiate at Grenelle – was a characteristic CGT leader of the 1970s. He was radical in his willingness to support strikes and, indeed, his own union had stayed out longer than most in 1968. But he was pragmatic when it came to the aims of strikes. He focused on material demands that might realistically be achieved. He discouraged those who talked of fighting 'to the end'.[35]

In Italy, the strikes of the late 1960s were initially directed by improvised groups that existed alongside, sometimes, at first, in opposition to, established trade unions.[36] By 1972, there were 4,291 such 'factory councils' in the metallurgy industry representing over a million workers. The Italian trade unions, however, sought to make common cause with the factory councils rather than opposing them and eventually the main unions declared that the councils were their agents on the shop floor. The Communist trade union confederation (the CGIL) obtained a greater degree of autonomy from the Communist Party than the CGT was able to achieve in France – in part because the Italian party itself was more flexible in response to the agitations of 1968 than its French counterpart. The Christian Democrat Federation (the CISL) was never as independent as the CFDT in France, but it did partly emancipate itself from the control of the Christian Democratic Party and its metalworker section played an important role in the strikes of the 'hot autumn' of 1969 – sometimes outflanking the Communists.

The success of trade unions in dealing with the effect of the long 68 was reflected in their membership figures. Trade union membership in Britain stood at just over 10 million in 1968; it had risen to 12 million by 1975. The membership of German trade unions rose from 6.5 million in 1966 to 7.4 million ten years later. Membership of the CGT in France went from 1.4 million in 1967 to reach a peak of 2.3 million in the 1970s. Membership of the CFDT, starting from a lower base, increased from 454,000 to 529,000 and then again to something between 750,000 and 827,000. The combined membership of the two main Italian trade union confederations grew from just over 4 million in 1968 to 5.4 million in 1972 and to about 6.7 million in 1975.

Trade unions were changed by the aftermath of 1968. Veterans of the student movement, even those who had disapproved of trade unions, often became members and leaders of unions once they started work themselves. This was true of the *soixante-huitards* in France who went to work for the public sector: particularly in teaching. It was true too of the United States, where many former student activists became union organizers or lawyers specializing in labour cases.[37] In France, the *établis* had a particularly curious relation with trade unions. After 1968, they were hostile to the unions, especially the CGT, and sought to encourage direct action that would circumvent them, but those *établis* who stayed in factories often found that, as their initial ideological certainties declined and as they sought practical means to improve the lot of their comrades, they did become union activists. One of them realized that all the elected representatives of the CFDT in his factory were actually middle-class radicals like himself.[38]

The working class itself changed as the number of white-collar workers increased in the 1960s and 70s. The most powerful, and sometimes left-wing, trade unions were often ones that contained few members who worked with their hands. In Britain, the Association of Scientific Technical and Managerial Staffs was founded in 1969, through the merger of existing unions. Its leader was Clive Jenkins, a 68ish figure who had contacts with radical movements in the US and who had visited North Vietnam. He turned the union into a powerful force on the left – even though he suspected that a large proportion of its members voted Conservative. Teaching and social work, both professions that tended to attract student radicals, grew after 1968. The educated classes were increasingly likely to be members of unions and their unions were increasingly likely to strike. The British National Union of Teachers held its first national strike and affiliated to the Trade Union Congress in 1969.

DIFFERENT KINDS OF WORKING CLASS

The struggle over who would represent workers went with a shifting sense of what the working class might actually be. Here there was a curious paradox. Even though white-collar work was becoming more common, the rhetoric of 68 sometimes redefined the working class in ways that made greater allowance for peasants or factory workers recently drawn from the countryside. Maoists – inspired by what they understood of the Chinese Cultural Revolution – made much of rural populations. In Norway, they sought to mobilize the inhabitants of the arctic periphery.[39] In France, some *établis* went to work on farms: Gérard Miller, later to be a fashionable Parisian psychoanalyst, spent some time tending pigs in the Sarthe. Parts of the French peasantry were sympathetic to the idea that they might be defined in Marxist terms. Bernard Lambert, a Breton farmer and organizer who had begun his career in Catholic activism and Christian Democracy before moving to the left, published *Les Paysans dans la Lutte des Classes* in 1970. Radical farmers began referring to themselves as 'peasant workers'. Sheep farmers on the Larzac plateau in the Massif Central demonstrated against plans to extend an army base that encroached on their land. Larzac, like Lip, attacted attention across the country and its peasants, unlike the workers of Lip, were largely successful. Protesters from across France came to Larzac and the local inhabitants took their demonstrations to the towns – on one occasion putting their sheep to graze on the Champ de Mars in Paris.

Not only did peasants become increasingly likely to think of themselves as working class, growing numbers had actually sought employment in factories. In France and Italy, rapid post-war industrialization had drawn many from the countryside into the factories. In France, this process had sometimes been accelerated by industrialists who built factories in the rural west because they hoped to find a more quiescent workforce (see chap. 5). In Italy, factories in the north recruited workers from the south – 100,000 arrived every year from 1967 until 1974. The population of Turin increased by 700,000 between 1955 and 1970 and it drew in so many migrants from the south that some labelled it the 'third southern city', after Palermo and Naples.

Relations between established workers and those who were new to factory life, especially if they were migrants from other areas or other countries, were not always easy. Radicals from the student left, especially Lotta Continua in Italy, invested much hope in migrant workers who might draw on rural traditions that would provide an alternative to the more institutionalized protests of the established working class. In practice, however, it was often skilled and unionized workers who started strikes in Italy. Migrant workers sometimes joined in later on, and occasionally seemed to draw on the culture of rural *jacquerie* – hence the use of rabbit heads (to imply cowardice on the part of workers who broke strikes), donkeys and manure in worker protests. But the radicalism of migrants from the Italian countryside was more complicated than it first appeared. They came from different areas and did not even necessarily understand each other's dialects. There were also differences that related to when they had come to industrial work. The most recent arrivals, those who had come during the surge of hiring that began in 1967, were sometimes militant. This might have been because of their relative youth, or because they were conscious of the power that the tight labour market conferred on them. It might also have been because by this stage factories preferred to recruit men from southern cities (or those who had experience in German factories), rather than peasants, and consequently the 'primitive rebels' were more educated and experienced than their accents might suggest.

By contrast, those southerners who had been in northern cities longer were less keen to strike. The difference was especially marked at the large Fiat works in Turin. Those who had arrived from 1955 to 1965 knew that employment at Fiat, which was relatively well paid and secure, was a privilege that had once been reserved largely for northern Italians who already had family connections with the firm. For these southerners, working at Fiat was often the culmination of a career that began with less desirable work in smaller factories and they were reluctant to compromise their new privileges by going on strike. In the hot autumn of labour protest in 1969, some of these older southerners rebelled against rebellion. They jumped over factory walls and even used tunnels, which dated from the Second World War and were unknown to some younger workers, to get past picket lines into the factory.[40]

'New' working classes – either a relatively privileged one made up of technical and white-collar workers or an underprivileged one made up of women, immigrants and migrants from the countryside – attracted much attention in the aftermath of 1968. However, the most successful strikes of the 1970s (or at least those that produced the most dramatic results) involved workers from a traditional working class in the country where industrialization had happened earliest: Britain. These strikes were those of the National Union of Mineworkers (NUM) in 1972 and then again in 1974, the latter bringing down the Conservative government of Edward Heath. Miners belonged to the 'old' working class. They did hard physical labour. Because the industry was in decline, most of them were relatively old (their average age was forty-four in 1972)[41] and most of them had worked in the pits since they left school at fourteen or fifteen. Most of them, indeed, were the sons of miners and some lived in communities almost exclusively composed of miners.

One official of the NUM was linked to the middle-class left that had emerged from 68. Arthur Scargill, born in 1938, had returned to higher education in adult life. He had broken with the Communist Party partly because he disliked its discipline. He was impatient with formal regulations, including those of his own union, and often put his faith in various forms of direct action. In 1968, he supported demonstrations against the Vietnam War, and in 1975 gave an interview to the *New Left Review* which would be read assiduously by Tory ministers for many years. Scargill was an important but unusual figure. More common was the view expressed by a Kent miner: 'since the 1972 strike and the foundation of Canterbury university [i.e the University of Kent], the left-wing sects have made an appearance and collected a handful of often-transient adherents. There is widespread distrust of intellectuals.'[42]

The new Marxist organizations that emerged from the late 1960s had little influence in the pits. Trotskyists took a considerable interest in miners during the 1970s, but at the end of the decade the British security services believed that they had made almost no progress. They reckoned that among a quarter of a million miners in 1980 there were fifteen members of the Militant Tendency, nine members of the Socialist Workers Party and five members of the International Marxist Group.[43] To put these figures in context, there were fewer Trotskyists in the most important of British trade unions than there were among the staff at North London Polytechnic, and the number of miners who were actively involved in Trotskyism was smaller than the number involved in pigeon breeding or dog racing – the security services investigated those interests too. The one group of left-wing intellectuals who exercised some influence over the miners was the one least associated with the radicalism of the late 1960s: the Communist Party. It was a Communist sociologist (Vic Allen of Leeds University) who formed the Miners' Left Club that recruited some local miners' leaders in the early 1970s. The Communist Party counted about 1,000 miners among its members – a small proportion of the total but one that included some significant figures on the national executive of the union.

Joe Gormley, a member of the national executive of the British National Union of Mineworkers who became its leader in 1971, was hardly a 68er. Born in 1917, he was a fiercely patriotic monarchist and a conservative in cultural terms. He wrote in his memoirs that he wanted a world in which 'every miner would have a Jaguar at the front of his house to take him to work and every miner's wife would have a Mini round the side to take her to the shops'.[44] The middle-class left did not know what to make of Gormley. The Marxist historian E.P. Thompson remarked that there must be more to Gormley than met the eye: 'a startled wombat caught in the headlights of a motorway'.[45] There was in fact a good deal more. Gormley was the supreme example of a trade unionist who knew how to make use of 68 without being part of it. He drew on the support of middle-class radicals, particularly in universities, and also on the kind of direct action that went with 68 – the latter was seen particularly in 1972, when Arthur Scargill mobilized pickets from the miners and their allies to close the Saltley Coke depot. Gormley was skilled at per-suading Conservative governments that they should give him concessions in order to strengthen his hand against 'extremists' in his own union.

RACE

The working classes of the industrialized countries were divided by race and religion, as well as by the kind of work they did. West Germany and Switzerland owed their low strike level partly to the simple fact that a large proportion of the workforce was made up of tempor-ary migrants – who could easily be sent home if a decline in production made their services unnecessary or if they proved insufficiently docile. If immigrants did rebel, it was hard for left-wingers to mobilize native workers on their behalf. At the Ford works in Cologne, there were 24,000 workers, of whom most were 'guest workers', about half of them Turks. In the summer of 1973, 500 returned late from their summer holidays (travelling from provincial Anatolia to Western Germany overland might take a week) and were sacked. The Maoist Artbeitskampf tried, and failed, to launch a strike over the issue.[46]

In France the complexity of relations between race and class was illustrated by thinking about North Africa. A large number of workers had served as soldiers during the Algerian War of 1954 to 1962. Of twenty men involved in a violent conflict with the police at one factory in 1968, seven belonged to the age group called up during the Algerian War.[47] Such men sometimes referred to their experiences as ways of explaining their rebellions during and after 1968. They often likened the discipline of the factory to that of the army and drew attention to the fact that some managers were former officers. Some believed that veterans of the Organisation de l'Armée Secrète (the illegal organization that had fought to defend French Algeria) were recruited as security guards by private companies in the early 1970s.[48] Being opposed to the legacy of French Algeria did not necessarily mean that workers were favourable to Algerians, or to North Africans more generally. On the contrary, they sometimes regarded the hiring of such workers as a strategy to undermine union power and attributed it to the legacy of French Algeria. In some factories they thought that the Algerian workers were *harkis* (Muslim auxiliaries who had fought for the French army). French workers also believed – perhaps with some justification – that foreign workers, Moroccans especially, were under special surveillance. The Association des Travailleurs et Commerçants Marocains de France (ATCM) was established in 1973 to 'prevent bad influences that might give birth to divisions'. At Chausson – which made parts for the car industry – the exclusion of the ATCM from the factory was among the demands of strikers in 1975.[49]

Race and class were tied up in particularly awkward ways in Brittany. Here French-born workers were themselves often relatively recent entrants to the factories and they were particularly conscious of the arrival of non-French-born workers after 1968. Although Bretons sometimes talked of their own opposition to the authority of Paris in terms of 'decolonization', Breton workers were incensed by the notion that they might be treated in the same way as *bougnoules* (a derogatory word for Algerian).[50]

In Britain, race had seemed likely to separate white workers from the student left after Enoch Powell's 'rivers of blood' speech in 1968 (see chap. 7), though the most vociferous support for Powell looks to have come from a relatively small group of workers. More significant were the effects of ethnic division in Northern Ireland. Here, the most secure industrial jobs were largely reserved for Protestants, but the division between the two religions was so sharp that Catholics did not become instruments of industrial radicalism in the way that marginalized workers in continental Europe often did. On the contrary, Catholic protests took place on the street rather than in the workplace. There was an important political strike in Northern Ireland in 1974. The Ulster Workers' Council mobilized strikers in ways that involved civil disobedience and sometimes near revolutionary insurrection as well as strikes, and they used the power of a small number of key workers – electricians in particular – to bring much of industry to a halt. The strike forced a change in government policy and haunted British governments well into the next decade. In some ways it was the most successful political strike in post-war Europe. However, this was a strike led by Protestants and one designed to defend the status quo – by thwarting the London government's projects to impose power sharing on Protestants and Catholics.

THE UNITED STATES

Divisions in the American labour movement were sharper than those in Europe and were often rooted in race and Vietnam. The strikes that attracted most support from middle-class radicals were those that involved black or Mexican workers, often presented as continuations of the civil rights struggle. Cesar Chavez had led the mainly Mexican farmworkers of California and sought to form broader alliances that took in everyone from Robert Kennedy to the Black Panthers. In Brighton, Colorado, workers at the Kitayama Brothers horticultural company, mainly women of Mexican origin, went on strike in 1968 to fight for better conditions – their action was supported by members of the Boulder branch of Students for Democratic Society.[51] Unionized workers in northern industrial cities, by contrast, enjoyed relatively high wages and reasonable job security. The labour movement itself was sometimes divided. The Chicago Federation of Labor and Industrial Union Council was close to the political machine with which Mayor Daley ran the city; the United Packing-house Workers of America was more left-wing.

Martin Luther King Jr said in 1965 that 'the missing ingredient in the civil rights' struggle as a whole has been the power of the labor movement'. King wanted to get the backing of those unions who might be powerful allies but also to help those workers who were least privileged and often not yet organized to defend their own inter-ests. He was assassinated in Memphis while visiting the city to show solidarity with the strike by sanitation workers there. Race became particularly important to the American labour movement because the Democratic Party had historically been founded on an alliance of northern unionized workers with white southerners. Civil rights called that alliance into question. When George Wallace, who had been Democratic governor of Alabama, ran for the presidency as an independent in 1968, he directed his appeal partly at workers from the north whose relatively privileged position might be threatened by the increasing prosperity of African Americans. Strikes by primarily black workers – such as the sanitation workers of Memphis or of St Petersburg in Florida – received little support from the white working class.[52]

In addition to this, the American trade unions had often been founded on strong anti-Communism – partly because they were keen to distance themselves from any Marxist element in their own his-tory. Most trade unions supported the Vietnam War and many individual workers expressed a fierce patriotism, which sometimes went with the fact that they themselves were drawn from ethnic groups that had arrived recently in America and invested particular hopes in it. The most notorious expression of this patriotism came with the 'hard hat riot' of 8 May 1970, when New York construction workers attacked a rally in protest at the shooting of students at Kent State University, who had themselves been protesting against the US invasion of Cambodia. This did not mean that all workers were happy with American policy in Indochina – many of them, especially those with sons in the army, were not (see chap. 4). But it did mean that workers often felt hostile to the more flamboyant expressions of opposition to the war and this in turn created a spiral of mutual con-tempt between the unions and the student left. One Berkeley radical had written in 1967: 'The next time some $3.90 an hour AFL [American Federation of Labor] type workers go on strike for a 50 cents raise, I'll remember the day they chanted "Burn Hanoi not our flag", and, so help me, I'll cross their fucking picket line.'[53]

Beneath its patriotic rhetoric, in reality the American labour movement was divided in the years after 1968. Walter Reuther of the United Automobile Workers had worked in the Soviet Union as a young man, which may have been why he could not afford to say anything that might sound like an expression of sympathy for Communism in later life. He supported civil rights and had strong private doubts about the Vietnam War. However, his freedom of manoeuvre was more limited than that enjoyed by his European counterparts, and in any case he was killed in a plane crash in 1970. In contrast George Meany, head of the American Federation of Labor (AFL), was strongly anti-Communist and in favour of the Vietnam War. He was largely responsible for the fact that the AFL did not back the Democrat George McGovern's campaign in the 1972 presidential election – the first time in many years that it had not supported the Democratic candidate.

After 1968, Nixon and his associates sought to construct a new electoral base for the Republican Party – one in which blue-collar workers would be mobilized to counteract middle-class liberals. Meany was invited to golf, dinner and then, along with several thousand union families, to a performance of the 1812 Overture at the White House in 1970. Nixon courted conservative unions – those representing teamsters, federal employees, construction workers and policemen. The Nixon White House also seems to have made a deliberate effort to split automobile workers from their 'socialist' leaders.[54] Peter Brennan of the New York construction workers, who had resisted government attempts to impose the admittance of more black workers into his industry and who was held by some to have been responsible for the 'hard hat riot', became Nixon's secretary of labor.

There was, however, a paradox about the American labour movement in the early 1970s. Certain sections were strongly opposed to the middle-class left and this opposition seems to have played a part in reconfiguring the electorate in ways that would take some unionized workers into support for first Nixon and eventually Reagan.

This move to the right in terms of what the labour movement said, though, sometimes coincided with radicalism in terms of what it did. Between 1967 and 1974, the average number of workers on strike increased sharply; in 1970, there were thirty-four strikes involving at least 10,000 workers each.[55] In the year 1968 itself, the number of strikes, per thousand workers, was higher in the United States than in any other industrialized country except France (where numbers reflected the exceptional events of May) and Canada, whose labour movement was in any case intertwined with that of the United States. From 1970 to 1975, the proportion of American workers on strike was invariably higher than that in France and most West European countries. Italian strike rates were higher than those of the US from 1972 – though they had been lower during the supposedly radical years that preceded this. British rates only exceeded US rates in 1972, the year of the miners' strike.

Some strikes were undertaken with illiberal aims – thus, for example, New York teachers walked out in 1968 against the increasing power exercised by elected school boards that sought to advance the interests of African American children.[56] Similarly Detroit policemen had become increasingly organized to protect their material interests in the 1960s (transforming their professional association into a real union), and in the 1970s this protection of interest came increasingly to entail resistance to affirmative action that might favour black recruits.[57] Sometimes conservatives bought off strikes – Mayor Richard Daley kept the public sector workers of Chicago quiet by the simple expedient of paying higher wages than other cities.

Sometimes a strike by workers who purported to be conservative might threaten the very social order that they claimed to revere. Construction workers were the lynchpin of Nixon's blue-collar conservatism. The workforce industry was almost all male, often aggressively masculine and hostile to 'sissy' liberalism.[58] Control of apprenticeships had given unions great power over entry into the profession, which they had often used to exclude black candidates from any but the most menial positions.[59] Construction workers were behind both the 'hard hat riot' and the march of 20 May 1970 when 100,000 demonstrators, this time with the official support of the Building and Construction Trades Council of Greater New York, had expressed support for the war, and held up signs saying 'God Bless the Establishment'. Yet American construction workers actually posed one of the biggest problems for private companies in the world's leading capitalist power. In October 1970, *Fortune* Magazine suggested that the demands of construction workers were 'the most important obstacle in the way of subduing inflation'.[60]

10
Violence

Wanted by FBI

The persons shown here have been active members of the revolutionary Weatherman organization, an outgrowth of the Students for a Democratic Society (SDS).

Federal warrants have been issued concerning these individuals, charging them with a variety of Federal violations, including one or more of the following: interstate flight to avoid prosecution, Antiriot Laws, conspiracy, destruction of government property and National Firearms Act

These individuals should be considered dangerous because of their known advocacy and use of explosives, reported acquisition of firearms and incendiary devices, and known propensity for violence

It should be noted that individuals being sought may have altered their appearances. Where available, dual photographs have been included to depict such changes in appearances.

If you have information concerning these persons please contact your local FBI Office.

William Charles Ayers
W/M, Dob 12/26/44,
5'10", 170, br hair,
br eyes. I O 4366

Lawrence David Barber
W/M, Dob 2/25/50,
5'8", 140, br hair,
br eyes.

Judith Emily Bissell
W/F, Dob 3/6/44,
5'0", 110, br hair,
gr eyes. I.O. 4401

Silas Trim Bissell
W/M, Dob 4/27/42
5'11", 135, br hair,
gr eyes. I.O. 4401

Kathie Boudin
W/F, Dob 5/19/43,
5'4", 128, br hair, blue eyes.
I.O 4367

Peter Wales Clapp
W/M, Dob 10/14/46,
6', 150, br hair,
gr eyes.

Bernardine Rae Dohrn
W/F, Dob 1/12/42
5'5", 125, dk br hair,
br eyes. I O 4364

Wanted poster for members of the Weather Underground. The FBI, even more than police agencies in other countries, helped define the long 68.

10

Hans Joachim Klein, a working-class German, first became involved in politics during the anti-Vietnam War demonstrations of the late 1960s and then joined a terrorist group that, under the direction of the Venezuelan 'Carlos' and acting in the supposed interests of the Palestinians, attacked an OPEC meeting in Vienna in 1975. The assault killed three people. Klein was seriously wounded although he, the other guerrillas and their hostages were then flown to Algeria and released. Klein went into hiding in France but was arrested in 1998 and tried in 2001. His trial attracted attention partly because in the early 1970s he had been a friend of Daniel Cohn-Bendit and Joschka Fischer. Fischer, now foreign minister of Germany, and Cohn-Bendit, now a member of the European parliament, were character witnesses at Klein's trial – the latter had stayed in contact with Klein and helped persuade him to give himself up.

This episode revealed two sharply differing aspects of the long 68 – one marked by extreme and increasing violence, the other by a more peaceful, even playful, approach in the short term and by the embrace of democratic politics in the long term. There was a German dimension to all this. West Germany was the country in which terrorism took its most extreme form. This was not measured in terms of numbers killed; in that, Italy and Northern Ireland were worse. Rather what made Germany special was the sense that a small minority were at war with the whole population – the writer Heinrich Böll talked of 'six against sixty million' – and the unrepentant savagery of those involved. Andreas Baader, the most notorious of German terrorists, was a particularly vindictive character. Journalists made much of the fact that the names of German terrorists included Böse (evil) and

Teufel (devil). On the other hand, the German 68 also gave birth to the Green Party, which was characterized by distaste for violence and an embrace of democratic politics; both Fischer and Cohn-Bendit became members of the Green Party.

The distinction between a 'good' and a 'bad' 68 was not clear-cut. There were hippies who put flowers in the rifles of soldiers and there were ruthless assassins, but there were many gradations in between. Cohn-Bendit had never shared the fascination of many of his contemporaries with armed revolution. But he had encouraged his supporters in Paris to prevent lectures with physical force, occupy buildings or defend barricades and he recognized that it was easy to slide from the rhetoric of 1968 to the shootings of the 1970s: 'power, in theoretical terms, sprang from the barrel of a gun but how did some take us at our words and go on'.[1] As for Fischer, he had been involved in street fighting in Frankfurt. A photograph published in the magazine *Stern* showed him and other demonstrators attacking a policeman in 1973. The photo had been dug up by Bettina Röhl, a 38-year-old woman who had special reasons to feel bitter about the violence of the German left because she was the daughter of urban guerrilla Ulrike Meinhof.

THE TURN TO VIOLENCE

Generally, politics became more violent in the aftermath of 1968. A 27-year-old law student said that the Algerian War of 1954 to 1962 had radicalized him but that 'the brawl [of 1968] revealed me to myself'.[2] *Le Monde* initiated a rubric devoted to 'agitation' after May 1968. In the first few months of 1970, it recorded, among other things, an attack on a police station in Nantes, the emptying of a rubbish bin over the philosopher Paul Ricoeur at Nanterre, and the burning of offices at the coal mine at Hénin-Liétard.

Some radicals began to use violence in a more calculated and systematic way. The Weathermen (later the Weather Underground) sprang from the break-up of Students for a Democratic Society in the United States. They staged the 'Days of Rage' in Chicago in October 1969. Protesters damaged buildings and cars and attacked the police.

In 1970, the Weather Underground issued a 'declaration of war' against the government; it turned to clandestine organization and armed action. In Germany, Andreas Baader, Gudrun Ensslin, Horst Mahler and Ulrike Meinhof founded the Red Army Faction (or Baader-Meinhof group) in 1970. In Italy, Renato Curcio and Margherita Cagol established the Red Brigades in the same year. In mainland Britain, a succession of violent attacks on property in 1970 and 1971 were attributed to the Angry Brigade.[3] In Northern Ireland, the Provisional Irish Republican Army (so-called to distinguish it from the Official IRA that had existed since the 1920s) was founded in December 1969 following Protestant attacks on civil rights campaigners and after the British army had been sent to the province to keep the two sides apart (see chap. 7).

Alongside these organizations were less well-known ones – usually smaller and less disciplined – with which they sometimes allied. In the US, they included the Melville group, named after the *nom de guerre* of its founder Sam Melville. In Germany, they included the 2 June group. In Northern Ireland, the Irish National Liberation Army existed alongside the Provisional IRA and violent 'loyalist' organizations fought to defend what they perceived as Protestant interests. In Italy, it was reckoned that there were several dozen left-wing organizations and 484 pseudonyms were used by those claiming responsibility for attacks – though the bloodiest of these, on Bologna railway station in 1980, turned out to have been carried out by the extreme right.

The number killed by German terrorists in the 1970s probably amounted to fifty-seven, including those killed at the OPEC office in Vienna and on board a hijacked German aircraft that was eventually stormed at Entebbe airport. In Italy, the ministry of the interior dated the first terrorist acts to 1969 (before the formation of the Red Brigades) and estimated that 398 attacks in that year caused nineteen deaths. The total number of incidents peaked at 2,513 in 1979 – though the number of deaths in that year was a comparatively modest twenty-four and overshadowed by 125 deaths (largely attributable to the Bologna bombing) of 1980. In all in Italy, there were 14,591 attacks causing 419 deaths between 1969 and 1987.[4] The provisional IRA was reckoned to have killed 1,823 people between 1969 and

1997 and to have accounted for about half of all the violent deaths of the North Ireland Troubles.

THE FRONTIERS BETWEEN POLITICS AND VIOLENCE

Members of terrorist organizations often came to feel a sense – both liberating and oppressive – that they had cut themselves off from their former life. Ulrike Meinhof said that winter was her favourite season because the darkness made it harder to identify her. There was, however, no clearly marked frontier that people crossed as they moved from political militancy into what came to be seen in retrospect as 'terrorism'. Political categories were not as clearly defined in the aftermath of 1968 as they sometimes seemed decades later. Many radicals rejected electoral politics without being entirely clear what they might put in its place. In 1970, 1 million American students described themselves as 'revolutionaries'.[5]

The line between terrorism and politics might be a porous one. The Parti Socialiste Unifié in France was in many ways the incarnation of 'legitimate' politics. It contained – until 1968 – one former prime minister, Pierre Mendès France, and it was led by a future prime minister, Michel Rocard. There was, however, a moment in the aftermath of 1968 when Maoists and Trotskyists became powerful in the PSU and when Rocard worried that he was leading a movement of 'fifteen thousand potential terrorists'.[6]

Left-wing movements that were more or less peaceful in themselves often encompassed special units to defend demonstrations against the police or rival groups and this defence always involved the possibility of violence. Some militants recruited tough young men from the working class to act as guards. In Britain and America, this sometimes meant disastrous flirtations with the Hells Angels (see chap. 2). In Paris in 1968, the occupied Sorbonne was 'protected' for a time by 'Katangais' – members of the Paris lumpen proletariat. The Katangais, their name derived from the mercenaries fighting in Katanga, began to take the political ideas of their new friends with a seriousness that turned to tragicomedy. After the Sorbonne had been evacuated, and as it became clear that the students were not in fact enthusiastic about their company, a number of the Katangais took to the woods near Vienne. Apparently they believed that they were a new *maquis* preparing for the insurrection that would come with the resumption of the university term. After a while, they revealed to a priest that they had acted out their *maquisard* identity to the extent of executing one of their comrades, whom they suspected of treason. They were tried and received comparatively light sentences – it says something about the cult of the outlaw in the late 1960s that some members of the jury in a small provincial town appear to have sympathized with them.[7]

Surveys suggested that many who never came close to picking up a gun themselves were nonetheless reluctant to condemn those who did. The general suspicion of the police – strong in parts of continental Europe and among blacks in the United States even before the political upheavals of the 1960s – meant that many drew a distinction between support for terrorism and willingness to denounce it. In 1971 in West Germany, 40 per cent agreed that the violence of the Red Army Faction (RAF) was 'political', 20 per cent said that they would 'understand' the motives of someone who protected RAF fugitives and 6 per cent declared that they would do so themselves.[8] At the Santa Barbara campus of the University of California, students made similarly complicated distinctions: one in eight approved of bombing property and almost one in three approved of doing so 'in certain circumstances'; almost one in ten approved of kidnapping officials and almost one in five 'did not reject' this tactic.[9] In Northern Ireland, the number who planted bombs or fired guns ('volunteers' in Provisional IRA parlance) was probably just a few hundred, but it commanded a wider support that was only partly based on fear. The Provisional IRA eventually adopted a strategy of 'bullet and ballot box' that involved using violence while Sinn Fein, the political wing of republicanism, contested elections.

Political thinking about violence entailed elements of fantasy. Even student radicals who never came close to armed action found the figure of the guerrilla an attractive one. Colin Crouch, writing about his fellow students at the LSE, suggested that this was partly because guerrillas seemed so remote from the bureaucratic orderliness of

Western society: 'The guerrilla is thus virtually the ideal type of non-alienated man. It is through such an interpretation of guerrilla warfare that the revolutionary student in a western university is able to identify himself with the jungle warrior.'[10]

Both sides in France attributed a degree of violence to their opponents that bore little relation to reality. The Gaullist Jacques Chirac carried a revolver in May 1968 and believed that the trade unionist with whom he conducted secret meetings was similarly armed. The object in his interlocutor's pocket was actually a pipe. Strikers at the Lip factory in Besançon in the early 1970s had very different views about the CRS riot police. One, a woman of sixty-one, said that it was made up of ordinary men who had been driven to join by unemployment. Another striker, a man of nineteen, believed that recruits to the CRS were required to sign a paper saying that they would open fire on their own parents if ordered to do so.[11] However, the French left also sometimes fantasized about violence from its own side. Maoists recounted with relish that 'eight or nine' members of the French riot police had been killed at the Peugeot factory at Sochaux and their bodies dissolved in the acid tanks there.[12]

VARIETIES OF VIOLENCE

Some drew careful distinctions. Rioting was different from armed action. Joschka Fischer advised his contemporaries to 'put away your rifles and pick up your paving stones again'. Bernadette Devlin drew a similar distinction in Northern Ireland in 1968 – arguing that street violence was more 'democratic' than armed struggle: 'Everyone will defend a barricade but not everyone will shoulder a rifle.'[13] A group set up in support of the British Angry Brigade mocked the Jesuitical distinctions between 'legitimate' and 'illegitimate' violence: 'It's apparently OK to squat, attack police on a demo, hurl a CS gas canister in the House of Commons, picket, occupy etc. But as soon as you use a bomb (even against property solely) you forfeit, it seems, your identity as a socialist.'

As the quotation above suggests, the Angry Brigade themselves, or at least their supporters, distinguished between violence against people and that against property. The Brigade killed no one. Their bombs destroyed only property. The Spanish embassy was strafed with fire from a sub-machine gun but no one was hit – which suggests that either the guards were very lucky or the gunman was not trying to kill them. It is impossible to tell whether the members of the Brigade would have pulled back from murder if they had not been caught, as most left-wingers in France did, or spiralled into ever more extreme violence, as did some in Germany and Italy.

The first attack by the Italian Red Brigades simply involved burning a car – something that had happened hundreds of times during the student riots in Paris in May 1968. In the United States, there was large-scale violence mainly directed against property.[14] According to one estimate, there were 2,800 attacks (mostly bombings and arson) there between January 1969 and April 1970. Many of these were carried out by small groups, often acting in a single university campus.[15] The most notorious assault on property in the United States came in February 1970, when students from the University of California at Santa Barbara burned down the local branch of the Bank of America. This act helped radicalize the campus, and for a time many of those who had been associated with the attack seemed to flirt with something more extreme. David Carroll bought himself an M1 rifle and later recalled: 'a lot of my fantasies at the time were suicidal – trying to shoot a few politicians and take out as many as you could on the way out yourself'. Carroll, though, never fired a shot in anger and eventually became a Methodist minister. Warren Newhouser went underground after the fire, and was still living under a false identity when some determined researchers tracked him down almost twenty years later, but he never joined a revolutionary group.[16]

At the outset even attacks on people were relatively restrained. The first such attack conducted by the Red Brigades, in 1972, involved capturing a factory foreman and subjecting him to a brief period of ritual humiliation that did not involve physical harm. It was not very different from the sequestration of managers that had often happened during the strikes in France and Italy of 1968 and '69. The combat group of the Maoist Gauche Prolétarienne kidnapped a Renault manager. This was an alarming event for all concerned – including those members of the Gauche Prolétarienne who feared that they had come close to being accomplices to murder - but the group released their captive without conditions after two days. The Red Brigades in Italy and the Red Army Faction in Germany eventually moved from kidnapping to murder and particularly to the murder of captives – the Italian Christian Democrat politician Aldo Moro, in 1978, and the German employers' leader Hanns Martin Schleyer, in 1977.

Such killings aroused more disquiet among radicals than a shootout in the street or even the planting of a bomb. There was something about the ritual of execution – the blindfold, the terrified victim made to kneel – that recalled the agents of repression that guerrilla groups claimed to oppose. Cohn-Bendit interviewed one former Brazilian guerrilla who had kidnapped the American ambassador with horrified fascination: 'you could have put a bandage over his eyes and shot him?'[17] Some groups began to present themselves as a kind of alternative state and to use the language of the police – arrest, trial, provisional release.[18] Violence against people also sometimes set guerrilla groups against parts of the working class. This was especially true in Italy, where policemen often shared the impoverished southern origins of the least privileged factory workers and where the killing of Aldo Moro's five bodyguards, and of a Communist trade union leader in 1979, aroused particular distaste.

Some groups, notably the Black Panthers in the USA, emphasized the defensive quality of their violence. Carl Davidson, a white student leader who initially regarded himself as a supporter of non-violence, encountered black men in the South who admired Martin Luther King's pacifism, which they regarded as appropriate to a 'man of God', while they themselves carried weapons to his marches in case of attack by white racists. They believed that King knew about, and understood, their action.[19]

Some talked of symbolic or even 'ironic' violence. Benny Lévy of the Gauche Prolétarienne wrote, somewhat disingenuously: 'the violence that we used was symbolic: it did not aim to destroy the enemy physically. As a matter of principle we ruled out the death penalty.'[20] In 1967, German radicals prepared an elaborate attack on the visiting American vice president, which involved a custard pie. In 1970, the French Trotskyist Daniel Bensaïd developed a theory of such violence – arguing that it showed that militants would have been capable of causing real harm if they had chosen to do so and thus in a curious way underlining their restraint.[21] Some urban guerrillas became associated with a brooding solemnity and sense of their own importance, but there were times when violence was accompanied by a deliberate self-mockery. One movement in Germany produced American-style comic strips in which their own attempts to plant bombs were treated as objects of derision – in one a bearded 'freak' about to attack a bank is confused because he has never set foot in a bank; he asks whether he might attack a candy store instead.

THE CULTURE OF VIOLENCE

Violence went with a broader culture that often celebrated rebellion even if it was not explicitly political. The outlaw was a romantic figure in the late 1960s – partly because Hollywood had finally abandoned the orthodoxy of the 1950s that criminals should not be portrayed as attractive. *Cool Hand Luke* (1967), *Bonnie and Clyde* (1967), *Butch Cassidy and the Sundance Kid* (1969), *The Getaway* (1972) all showed criminals as romantic figures. The last broke the convention that criminals should always get their just desserts, though the first three, which finished with the unrepentant heroes dying in a hail of bullets, probably appealed more to young radicals. Valerio Morucci (an imprisoned former member of the Red Brigades who had repented of his crimes) told Daniel Cohn-Bendit that his own initiation into political violence happened as in cinema 'especially American cinema where people do not die for real'.[22] In Britain, the Angry Brigade signed some of their communiqués 'Butch Cassidy and the Sundance Kid'. Andreas Baader's favourite film was Sergio Leone's spaghetti western *Once Upon a Time in the West* (1968).[23]

The celebration of violence could take extraordinary forms. The 'family' gathered around Charles Manson in California carried out a series of murders (including that of the actress Sharon Tate) in 1968. Manson was mad, and, if his crimes had a political motive, it was certainly not a left-wing one: he talked of starting a race war. However, Michael 'Bommi' Baumann claims that he and his comrades in the German 2 June Movement admired Manson and sometimes affected to be devil worshippers. In Flint, Michigan in December 1969, at the last meeting of Students for a Democratic Society before their movement went underground, some of the Weathermen lauded Manson.[24] Susan Stern, a member of the Weathermen, later wrote: 'Charlie Manson was the death rattle of the children of the old movement, the decade of the SDS.'[25]

Criminals and prisoners often interested those who would eventually turn to political violence. Ulrike Meinhof worked with juvenile delinquents in the later 1960s. Radical students toyed with the language of armed robbery, as when Mark Rudd finished his letter to the president of Columbia University with the words, first given currency by the poet LeRoi Jones, 'Up against the wall Motherfucker; this is a stick up.' Prisoners – particularly violent ones serving long sentences – acquired a sinister mystique. This was true of the Glasgow gangster Jimmy Boyle – sentenced to life for murder in 1967 – and even more so of the London bank robber John McVicar, who escaped from a Durham jail in 1968 and remained at large for two years. The left-wing academic Laurie Taylor, who had befriended McVicar while teaching sociology to prisoners, warned his housemates that they might have to hide the fugitive – though McVicar, no doubt feeling that lentil bake and consciousness raising would be worse than prison, sought refuge with his criminal acquaintances.

In France, the Groupe d'Information sur les Prisons was founded in 1971 and succeeded in 1972 by the Comité d'Action des Prisonniers. These organizations secured reforms for French prisoners – often ones that involved extending privileges, such as that of receiving newspapers, from political to ordinary prisoners. They also inspired Michel Foucault's work on prison and punishment. The prison rebellion and/or breakout became an important feature of left-wing thinking. In France, some on the left were sympathetic to the men involved in a number of prison mutinies in the early 1970s – though the prisoners in question were not themselves political militants.

In West Germany, the Red Army Faction's leader had first escaped from prison and then, when locked up again more securely for more serious offences, conducted a public war of nerves with the authorities. In Italy, prison disturbances began at Le Nuove prison in Turin in 1969 and reached their climax with the rebellion at Alessandria in

May 1974, during which five hostages and two prisoners were killed. The occasion when Margherita Cagol rescued her husband Renato Curcio from prison became a part of the mythology of the Red Brigades. Italian prisons were brutal places and political prisoners were subjected to severe regimes in the 1970s but prison reform in the following decade sometimes eased the path of imprisoned guerrillas towards a renunciation of their violent past.[26] In the United States, the link between prison rebellion and political radicalism was more intimate – either because ex-prisoners joined radical groups, notably the Black Panthers,[27] or because imprisoned radicals joined prison mutinies. The most dramatic example was when Sam Melville was killed during a riot at Attica prison in 1971.

As political militants went underground, they often resorted to crime to fund their activities. Bank robbery was attractive to anti-capitalist groups. Pierre Goldman in France illustrated the blurred lines between political militancy, terrorism and common criminality. The son of a Polish Jew and a Resistance fighter, he fought alongside guerrillas in Venezuela before returning to France, where he was convicted of a killing during the armed robbery of a pharmacy. Having written an influential memoir in prison, he was freed when new evidence was produced, but then assassinated in mysterious circumstances in 1979. His funeral saw one of the last great gatherings of the *soixante-huitard* left. In the United States, a murderous and failed attempt to rob a Brinks armoured car in 1981 – carried out by the Black Liberation Army and the May 19th Communist Organization (the latter was a remnant of the Weather Underground) – marked the end of the cycle of political violence that had begun in the late 1960s.

TERRORISM AS INTERNATIONAL MOVEMENT

Terrorism came to seem shocking because it was the antithesis of democracy, but those who contemplated armed action often thought of themselves as part of an international movement that sought to overthrow autocratic regimes. Some of these regimes were in Latin America or Asia, but several West European countries had undemocratic governments in the late 1960s and early 70s. Spain was especially important partly because so many who had fled Francoism lived in other parts of Europe.

The politics of anti-Francoism could cut both ways. 'Alexandre' was a Spanish exile and member of the National Liberation Front in Paris. He recalled that many of his comrades understood that they themselves might be ministers after the fall of Franco and consequently distanced themselves from the denunciation of electoral politics that they associated with the French 68. Men, like Alexandre himself, who had only just acquired French nationality, were also keen to avoid trouble with the law, and a Spanish militant who was photographed throwing a paving stone at the French police had to be smuggled across the border into Belgium.[28] On the other hand, there were those in the French Basque Country who saw themselves as part of an armed struggle against the Spanish state. For them, the garrottings on the other side of the Pyrenees were the most important political events of the late 1960s and they justified violence on a scale that went beyond anything contemplated by most students in Paris. Christiane Etchalus, a French Basque militant who had already been imprisoned even before 1968, regarded the street violence of that year as amateurish: 'For me violence was synonymous with the armed struggle and thus with clandestinity.'[29] Even Britain was touched by the anti-Franco movement. Stuart Christie, who was accused of belonging to the Angry Brigade in Britain, had spent time in a Spanish prison.

Political violence changed its meaning in the course of the 1970s. The end of the war in Vietnam meant that the guerrilla fighters who had seemed most attractive to Western radicals were no longer at the centre of the world stage. Pinochet's *coup d'état* in Chile in 1973 made some on the left feel that violence was most likely to benefit the right and that even such an apparently stable country as Britain might be vulnerable to such violence. The international campaign against Pinochet was one that mainly emphasized democracy and opposition to torture rather than the possibility of violent insurrection.

The Provisional Irish Republican Army was the conspicuous exception to generalizations about the international quality of terrorism in the 1970s – and to many generalizations that one might make about guerrilla fighters of that decade. The Provisionals had emerged partly from the civil rights movement of 1968 in Northern Ireland and underwent their own version of 68 in the 1970s. Gerry Adams (born in 1948) and Martin McGuinness (born in 1950), who thought of themselves as having been influenced by the youth culture of the 1960s, rose up the hierarchy. 'Volunteers' who had left school at fifteen or sixteen used their time in the Maze prison to read the books that their more privileged contemporaries had encountered at Queen's University a few years earlier. The street murals of West Belfast sometimes presented the Provisional IRA as part of a global liberation struggle that also took in, say, the fight against apartheid in South Africa. There were, however, ways in which the Provisionals remained very un68ish. They meted out 'discipline' to delinquent youths, such as drug dealers. Their moral conservatism could produce odd results. One bomb-maker worried that the use of condoms in acid fuses might be at odds with the Pope's encyclical on the evils of birth control.[30]

ANTI-ZIONISM AND ANTI-SEMITISM

Increasingly, those who still praised guerrillas looked to the Palestinians. Indeed Palestinian-trained members of the Baader-Meinhof group and people sympathetic to the Palestinians – notably 'Carlos' – operated in Europe with the support of European militants. However, the various Palestinian guerrilla groups were more awkward allies that the Vietcong or freedom fighters of Latin America – partly because of the very fact that they were too close to home for Europeans. Visitors to Palestinian training camps could see that the most enthusiastic sponsors of the Palestinians were often Syria and Iraq – regimes that even the most deluded Europeans found hard to admire. Large numbers of left-wing militants – especially in France and the United States – were Jewish and sometimes conscious of anti-Semitism on the part of those who denounced them. Much of the militant left turned against Zionism for a time after the Six-Day War – in which Israel seized territory on the West Bank – but the possibility that anti-Zionism might turn into anti-Semitism made many uneasy.

There was, when it came to Israel, a difference between France and Germany. The German radical left talked obsessively about the legacy of Nazism but one obvious part of that legacy was that very few young Germans were Jewish. Furthermore, West Germany, as part of its attempt to atone for the crimes of the past and, in conspicuous contrast to Gaullist France, expressed almost unqualified support for Israel. Anti-Zionism was, therefore, particularly attractive to those who opposed the German state. Furthermore, some German radicals slid from anti-Zionism to positions that came to seem anti-Semitic. A synagogue was fire-bombed on the anniversary of Kristallnacht and one radical group marked this event with a pamphlet entitled 'Shalom and Napalm'. Sometimes this move was accompanied by a rewriting of German history, depicting the Third Reich in terms of class rather than race and occasionally suggesting that the supposed capitalist propensities of the Jews made them responsible for their own destruction. Horst Mahler – the left-wing lawyer associated with the Baader-Meinhof group – was eventually to move to the extreme right and to be convicted of Holocaust denial.

In France, by contrast, many on the radical left were Jewish and the word '*juif*' was an important part of *soixante-huitard* vocabulary. Demonstrators in Paris famously shouted – allegedly in response to anti-Semitic remarks about Daniel Cohn-Bendit – '*Nous sommes tous des juifs allemands.*' Pierre Goldman's autobiography was entitled *Souvenirs Obscurs d'un Juif Polonais Né en France*. References to Judaism in France were usually designed to evoke the Vichy past and few who made such references were religious or inclined to support Israel. Anti-Zionism rarely became anti-Semitism on the French left – partly because there was still anti-Semitism on the French right. Furthermore, some left-wing French Jews in 1968 were on a road that would eventually take them to Zionism and/or religious practice. Alain Geismar, one of the founders of the Gauche Prolétarienne, named the first of his sons, born in 1973, Pierre, after Pierre Overney, the Maoist militant killed by a security guard at a Renault factory in 1972. He named his second son, born in the 1980s, Elie, to mark his rediscovery of his Jewish roots. Even more spectacular was the transformation of Geismar's comrade Benny Lévy (alias Pierre Victor), an Egyptian Jew and the sinister *éminence grise* of French Maoism, who returned to Judaism in the 1970s and ended up a rabbi in Jerusalem.

The attack on the Munich Olympic Games of 1972 by a Palestinian Black September commando, which took part of the Israeli team hostage and killed some of its members, divided the radical left. Black September called for the release of leaders of the Red Army Faction as well as Palestinians imprisoned in Israel but the fact that their victims seemed to have been chosen on the basis of their nationality and race disturbed many. Lévy and Geismar both condemned the attack and it may have played a role in their decision to dissolve the Gauche Prolétarienne a year later.

PULLING BACK FROM THE BRINK

The dissolution of the Gauche Prolétarienne raises a question. What differentiated the various movements and individuals that had flirted with violence in the aftermath of 1968? Why did some of them pull back from the brink while others moved to ever more murderous acts? Violence was more prolonged and extreme in some countries than others. In mainland Britain there was no significant political violence after the arrest of the Angry Brigades in 1971. In France, there was little violence between the dissolution of the Gauche Prolétarienne in 1973 and the formation in 1979 of Action Directe – a group that never mobilized more than a few dozen members. In the late 1970s, the leaders of the Gauche Prolétarienne sometimes talked as though their most notable legacy was in fact the avoidance of violence. Sceptical observers pointed out that the movement had seriously discussed assassinating the former collaborator Paul Touvier and suggested that their peaceful dissolution was less inevitable than it was made to seem in retrospect. Former members of the Gauche Prolétarienne actually, carried out acts of violence after their group's dissolution. Meeting an old comrade from the organization in the 1980s, Daniel Rondeau did not dare ask him whether he had 'blood on his hands'.[31]

Germany and Italy saw much more violence in the 1970s – though it then declined, in Germany because leaders of the Red Army Faction were dead and in Italy because increasing numbers of former guerrillas turned away from violence. The United States witnessed a high level of violence – mainly against property rather than people – in the late 1960s and early 70s, but organized guerrilla movements subsided fast – partly because of the Nixon government's efforts to withdraw from the war in Vietnam, which had been the most important *casus belli* for the American radical left.

Radicalization and retreat could be two sides of the same coin. Those who reacted against violence often did so because they were horrified at the actions of the most extreme of those they might once have regarded as comrades. In 1968, the English historian Gareth Stedman Jones wrote sympathetically about political violence – 'identification with the example of the Vietnamese and Cubans resulted in an early awareness that in certain situations the use of non-violence is tantamount to political passivity'.[32] Though he did nothing to put his ideas into action or to arouse more than weary exasperation from the British authorities.[33]

Writing thirty years later, Stedman Jones reflected on the effects of his encounter with terrorism when he lived in Germany during the early 1970s:

> My distaste for groupuscule revolutionary politics was further enhanced by living in Frankfurt at a time when the Red Army Faction exercised considerable sway over the local Left. Their presence meant that even those who disagreed with the politics of revolutionary terror became reluctant to condemn it and unwilling to defend the democratic constitution of the Federal Republic. I became more than ever convinced that revolutionary and extra-parliamentary politics in Western Europe were intellectually frivolous and politically counter-productive.[34]

RETURN TO LEGALITY

How did those who had flirted with violence return to democratic politics? The gulf between terrorism and democratic politics was never, except perhaps in West Germany, quite as wide as it might have seemed. The British government carried on secret negotiations with the IRA for much of the 1970s. The intertwined world of the French intelligentsia and political elites made it surprisingly easy for those with the right connections to move from illegality to respectability. Benny Lévy was granted French citizenship by special dispensation of a right-wing president in 1975 – an extraordinary reward for someone who had only recently called for the overthrow of the French state. Régis Debray was extracted from a Bolivian prison with the help of the French government in 1970. During his absence Andreas Baader and Ulrike Meinhof, both on the run, had stayed at his Paris flat because they knew that his political connections would keep them safe from police raids. By 1981, Debray had an office in the Élysée Palace as an adviser to the newly elected President Mitterrand. Mitterrand himself never sympathized with terrorism or even very much with the radicalism of 1968, but he amnestied some members of Action Directe (who soon returned to their armed struggle) and more significantly refused to extradite people accused of terrorism in Italy. Even in the United States, people who had resorted to political violence were sometimes treated with remarkable leniency if and when they turned themselves in. Many involved in the Weather Underground served only a year or two in prison.

One curious legacy of the long 68 says much about violence. Many who had been radicalized in the late 1960s or 70s turned to writing works that were inspired by American crime fiction. Dominique Manotti, herself a historian and Communist activist before she became a writer of detective stories, remarked that May 1968 was the 'founding event' for authors such as herself.[35] Didier Daeninckx (born 1949) published *Meurtres pour Mémoire* in 1983 – a work based on the life and crimes of Maurice Papon, prefect of the Paris police between 1958 and 1967 – and *Le Géant Inachevé* (1984) which revolves around a man who looks back on his radical activism in the 1960s before 'the face of Pol Pot could be discerned behind the smile of Mao'. Cesare Battisti (born 1954) began to write *polars* while in exile in France after having been convicted of terrorist murder in Italy. Most famously, Stieg Larsson, the Swedish creator of the Millennium series, had been a very young 68er, campaigning against the Vietnam War when he was fourteen and joining a Trotskyist movement six years later.

The 68er authors sought to subvert conventional notions of 'classic literature' and to redefine notions of crime – in ways that concentrated attention on the powerful or on the state itself. However, their novels also often revealed a change in attitudes to crime and violence on the part of some 68ers. Left-wing movements were themselves held up to scrutiny or mockery – notably by Thierry Jonquet, a Trotskyist who published some of his novels under the pseudonym of Ramón Mercader, the name of Trotsky's assassin. The heroes of novels were less likely to be idealistic revolutionaries or heroic criminals. Increasingly, they were Chandleresque figures – disabused policemen or ex policemen. The hero of Jean-Patrick Manchette's *Morgue Pleine* (1973) was a private detective haunted by the fact that he had, as a gendarme, killed a demonstrator.

11

Defeat and Accommodation?

Jack Straw, president of the Students' Union at Leeds, dances with
the Duchess of Kent, chancellor of the university, in 1968.
Though on the left of the British student movement, Straw was not a
revolutionary, even before he began the long march that would take him to
being a minister in the Blair government of 1997.

In the short term, the protest movements of 68 were largely defeated. Indeed, the largest mobilizations of the period were often those in favour of the established order. This was true in Berlin where, in February 1968, a rally in support of US foreign policy attracted 150,000 people – several times the number who had demonstrated against the Americans a few days earlier. It was true in Milan when over 30,000 people attended the funeral of a policeman who had been killed in a conflict with demonstrators in November 1969.[1] It was true in Paris where the demonstration in favour of de Gaulle at the end of May was one of the largest, if not the largest, to be held in the whole of that month. In Britain, the novelist and Conservative politician Jeffrey Archer organized a petition to express support for the police after their confrontation with anti-Vietnam War protests.[2] It attracted 300,000 signatures – including some from Darby and Joan clubs (for old people), which puts one in mind of the old ladies in Elizabeth Taylor's novel *Mrs Palfrey at the Claremont* (1971) who worry about the 'poor police horses' confronting activists in Grosvenor Square.

The legislative election of June 1968 in France and the American presidential election in November of that year produced victories for the right. During his presidential campaign of 1968, Nixon coined the phrase 'silent majority' to describe those opposed to the noisy protests of that year. In France, Raymond Aron, a Jewish supporter of the Free French, attacked the student protests of May 1968 using the phrase *au nom des silencieux* that Alfred Fabre-Luce, a supporter of Vichy, had used to defend Pétainists in 1945. It says something about the political convulsions of 1968 that Aron and Fabre-Luce dined together in May and that Fabre-Luce was probably to the left of Aron by then.[3]

The most militant protesters of 68 often attacked the very idea of elections and put their faith in the 'direct democracy' of general assemblies. Jean-Paul Sartre wrote in 1972 that elections were a 'trap for fools'. Not surprisingly, the defenders of order favoured the more sedate form of politics that emerged from the secret ballot. This was seen everywhere from university politics to legislative elections. In Britain, Conservatives invested particular faith in the application of electoral democracy to trade unions, and one might argue that one of the last stands of 68 came in 1984–5 when Arthur Scargill, the most 68ish of British trade union leaders, took the National Union of Mineworkers without a ballot into a strike that was eventually crushed.

Relations between 68ers and the ballot box were more complicated than they looked. Some 68ers voted even at the height of their militancy. Some, like the French Trotskyist Alain Krivine, who ran for president in 1969, embraced elections as a means to further revolutionary aims, but others assumed that conventional democracy could bring real benefits. In Britain, many radicals voted for the Labour Party, even when they defined their politics in opposition to its leadership (see chap. 7). In France, some members of the PSU talked of overthrowing capitalism by force but the party's leader believed in electoral democracy.

In the USA, the Peace and Freedom Party put up a candidate for president on behalf of the radical left in 1968 and 1972. The Black Panther Party for Self-Defense had sometimes spoken the language of revolution in the late 1960s but in the early 70s, after Huey Newton's release from prison (see chap. 4), it invested much of its energy in fighting elections. Its achievements were relatively modest. Most of its efforts were now focused on Oakland, California. Bobby Seale and Elaine Browne failed to win the municipal elections of 1973. They did, however, mobilize a new electorate – some said that they registered 25,000 voters – and they did contribute to the victory of the black Democrat mayor Lionel Wilson in 1977.[4] One Black Panther explained their strategy in terms that suggested a world-weary realism: 'Our concept was that we can't change the world, we can't change every state, but if we can use Oakland as an example of how to go about garnering political power then people everywhere could see it, just like the breakfast program.'[5]

Sometimes those who had rejected the vote in the late 1960s embraced electoral politics in the 1970s and 80s. The change was most marked in Germany, where the conversions of first Daniel Cohn-Bendit and then Joschka Fischer attracted much attention. In the long term, it was hard for even the most committed anarchist to deny that the electoral victories of Thatcher (in 1979), Reagan (in 1980) and Mitterrand (in 1981) made a difference. By the early part of the twenty-first century 68ers often preserved their political engagement while abandoning their distaste for its electoral expression – so that they were actually more likely than the bulk of the population to vote and to do so even in the most unglamorous contests for local office. In France, one study showed that by 2004 82 per cent of *soixante-huitards*, against 45 per cent of the general population, voted in *all* elections.[6]

One curious feature of 68 was that extravagant revolutionary rhetoric co-existed with 'ordinary' politics – so that people could sometimes feel as though they were moving in two different worlds. Matters became even more complicated when militants recalled their actions at a time when 68's notion of 'democracy' seemed more questionable. At the University of Turin in 1968, radicals insisted that the 'general assembly' was the only legitimate expression of the will of the students but they agreed to a vote to show at least that they were not opposed by the majority. Maria Teresa Fenoglio was one of the militants who disliked the vote but, suspecting that the radicals might be defeated, she herself voted twice. The second time she did so dressed in expensive clothes. This garb concealed her identity but also appears to have gone with an odd sense that she had temporarily retrieved her identity as a respectable child of the bourgeoisie:

> We had a guilty conscience, because we said we were democratic, but we were very authoritarian, even in the mass meetings. We felt the greatest contempt for those who made up the famous silent majority, the sheep . . . so much that we assumed they would vote against it.
>
> Because of that I voted twice in the referendum. I put on two different outfits. In my history there has been the presence of another part of myself, that I profoundly despised, the girl from the good family, who had had the suitor, who had the fur coat given her by my mother and the strand of pearls. Because of that I probably identified with the

silent majority at the university. I went and dressed like them, exactly like them: 'Look, I've put on my fur, I've put on my last year's glasses.' I went to vote as a sixty-eighter, and then as a silent majoritarian.[7]

Sometimes it seemed that conventional politics, so bitterly denounced by 68ers, emerged triumphant after 68. In many countries, political parties increased their membership in the 1970s. The German Social Democratic Party had had 732,000 members in 1968; by 1976 this had increased to 1 million. In France, membership of all political parties doubled to just under 1 million between 1968 and 1976. Political parties expanded partly because they were seeking to counter 68 or benefiting from hostility to the forces that it had unleashed. Nicolas Sarkozy, who was to denounce 68 vehemently, rose up through the youth wing of the Gaullist party in the 1970s. However, 68ers themselves sometimes joined parties. Gérard Noiriel – a student at a teacher training college in a conservative part of provincial France – thought of himself as a *soixante-huitard*, but he expressed his politics by joining the Communist Party.[8] He was not alone. Membership of the Parti Communiste Français increased from just over 300,000 in 1967 to a little under 600,000 in 1978 and a particularly large proportion of these new recruits were young – for the first time, most party members were under the age of forty.[9] Many of these new members, felt, like Noriel, that, in spite of the hostility between party leaders and prominent *soixante-huitards*, the PCF was the best vehicle for *soixante-huitard* ideas. Communist trade unionists – in Britain, France and Italy – sought to translate the working-class agitation of 68 into concrete demands (see chap. 9).

In the late 1960s, many had been hostile to orthodox Communism because they associated it with bureaucratic inertia and, after 68, many former 68ers denounced the brutality of the Soviet regime. This denunciation was particularly marked in France and is often associated with the French publication of Solzhenitsyn's *Gulag Archipelago* in 1974 – though in fact the first number of the *Figaro Littéraire* after the interruption of publication caused by the strikes of May 1968 had carried extracts from Solzhenitsyn's *Cancer Ward*. In spite of this current of hostility, though, Communism in parts of Western Europe (or at least Communist Party membership) benefited from 68 partly because the explosion of left-wing groupuscules some-times made even those who were sympathetic to protest movements come to value the tough-mindedness that they associated with Com-munism. In Britain, David Triesman, the student leader from Essex University, joined the Communist Party in 1969, before moving to the more mainstream world of the Labour Party. At first he thought that the Communist Party would be the one agency capable of over-coming factional divisions on the left, of which he had become particularly conscious during a visit to the United States.[10] Even people who had left the Communist Party in disgust during the 1950s sometimes saw its virtues in the late 60s. The historian Maurice Agulhon was one of these and he worked with Communists as he sought to reform the University of Aix-en-Provence after 1968.

There were also ways in which Communism itself changed during the 1970s – sometimes as the party experienced its own delayed ver-sion of 1968. The official leaders of most West European Communist parties remained conformist and authoritarian but they found it increasingly hard to impose party orthodoxy, particularly support for the Soviet Union, on all their members. Even the usually loyal Parti Communiste Français expressed its disquiet about the Warsaw Pact invasion of Czechoslovakia in August 1968. One result of this was to open some chance for dissidents within each party to make themselves heard. This was true in Britain where Martin Jacques – born in 1945 – became an increasingly important figure in the party and eventually managed to transform one of its publications – *Marxism Today* – into an officially tolerated samizdat that often celebrated the memory of 68. It was also true in France, where Pierre Juquin, mocked by the Nanterre students as an exponent of the Communist Party line in 1968, became an opponent of his own party's official leadership.

Relatively young people who threw themselves into politics after 1968 often transformed parties (as the 'Polytechnic Trots' changed the British Labour Party) or helped create new ones – as people in France, some drawn from the *soixante-huitard* Parti Socialiste Unifié, worked in the new Parti Socialiste in the early 1970s, or as German 68ers helped build the Green Party. Former 68ers became increasingly important to conventional politics. In the United States, Tom Hayden, once leader of Students for a Democratic Society, became a member of the California legislature; in France, the former Trotskyist Henri Weber became a Socialist senator in the early 1980s. In 1998, when a Red/Green coalition brought Joschka Fischer among others into the German government, one newspaper described this as a posthumous victory for Rudi Dutschke, the student leader of 1968. At the same time, Tony Blair's government in Britain included Jack Straw – a student leader who had struck a delicate balance between protest and authority in 1968 – as well as David Triesman, who had been more radical in 1968 but who was now on his way to becoming Baron Triesman. The presence in the White House of Bill Clinton – who had joined in anti-Vietnam War marches during his time as a student at Oxford in 1968 – completed the sense that the Western world was run by 68ers.

FOREIGN POLICY

Had the 68ers, as their enemies sometimes complained, sold out? In two respects their position sometimes seemed incongruous. The first concerned foreign policy and particularly the defence of human rights. There had always been two aspects of 68. On the one hand, it opposed oppressive regimes; on the other hand, it opposed intervention by powerful Western democracies in the affairs of other countries. In the late 1960s and early 70s, this dual concern posed no problem because it seemed that – in Indochina, Pinochet's Chile and Franco's Spain – oppressive regimes were supported by the United States. Things began to change almost as soon as the last American helicopter flew out of Saigon. The fate of the 'boat people', those who fled Vietnam, engaged many who had once proclaimed their support for the Vietcong and produced in June 1979 a moment of apparent reconciliation between the two great enemies of 1968 – Jean-Paul Sartre and Raymond Aron. The campaign in favour of the boat people was directed in the first instance against Western governments that were reluctant to admit refugees. But those involved could hardly close their eyes to the reasons why so many Vietnamese people were willing to risk their lives on the South China Sea.

More awkward moments for 68ers came after the fall of the Soviet

Union. Until this point, the division between NATO and the Warsaw Pact had provided a moral alibi for sections of the left. They could denounce both blocs and call for the respect of human rights on both sides while knowing that they would not be asked to take any practical action. There was, however, a moment, between the fall of Gorbachev in 1991 and the consolidation of Vladimir Putin's power in 2000, during which Western powers could contemplate military intervention to defend the rights of minorities in other countries. This moment coincided with the period when former 68ers exercised most power in national governments and international organizations. The change was particularly dramatic in Germany, a country for which military intervention raised awkward memories.

Some 68ers justified intervention in terms of a transnational morality that they traced back to 1968. For them, intervention to protect threatened groups, as in Bosnia or Kosovo in the former Yugoslavia in the 1990s, or even to overthrow a tyrannical regime, as in Iraq in 2003, marked a break with the brutal *souverainisme* of Charles de Gaulle or the more nuanced Cold War realpolitik of Henry Kissinger. Tony Blair's Chicago speech of 1999 was one expression of this view. Some veterans of 68 participated in the various attempts at 'regime building' that followed the overthrow of governments by military force. The Brazilian Sérgio Vieira de Mello had been a student in Paris in 1968, and bore a scar from a police truncheon. He joined the United Nations Commission for Refugees and wrote a doctoral thesis on the notion of 'supranationality' before becoming UN High Commissioner in Kosovo. He was killed by an insurgent bomb in Iraq in 2003. Bernard Kouchner, who had gone from the Paris barricades to found Médecins sans Frontières, succeeded Sérgio Vieira de Mello in Kosovo in 1999. Among his aides were Tom Koenigs, a German 68er, and the Dutchman Dan Everts, who had been an anarchist.[11] NATO, once an object of bitter hostility from the left, looked more benign to some when it intervened in Yugoslavia. Jan Kavan – a participant in the Prague Spring who had, along with Cohn-Bendit, Karl-Dietrich Wolff and Tariq Ali, appeared in a BBC discussion of student power in 1968 – returned from exile to become the Czech Republic's minister of foreign affairs from 1998 to 2002. It was he who oversaw his country's entry into NATO.

Veterans of 68 were divided by questions of foreign policy. Régis Debray attacked French intervention in Kosovo, and even those who had not followed Debray in his shift to neo-Gaullism sometimes found distasteful the implication that powerful Western democracies had the right to expound international morality. Divisions became sharper after the American-led invasion of Iraq in 2003. Most politicians in continental Europe did not support that action. Some 68ers saw the demonstrations against the war as a rerun of those that had taken place against American policy in Vietnam. Mark Rudd, who had withdrawn from public life after his criminal conviction for his activities in the Weather Underground, felt at home in this new anti-war movement.[12]

68 AND THE SPIRIT OF CAPITALISM

Attitudes to capitalism were the second issue with regard to which 68ers were often accused of having sold out. The governments of Clinton and Blair were notable for the extent to which they believed that social reform could cohabit with private enterprise. Former *soixante-huitards* – notably Michel Rocard in France – sought to modernize socialism in ways designed to reduce its anti-capitalist component. More generally, 68ers in politics often concentrated on concerns – race, sex, environmentalism – that did not bring them into direct conflict with capitalism. Even when they talked a language of proletarian interest, many leaders of 68 were middle class, and a feature of the 1980s was the success of a largely middle-class left that focused on cultural issues alongside the defeat of a working-class left that emphasized social demands.

None of this makes 68 responsible for the success of Western capitalism. Middle-class 68ers may simply have adjusted to something that had been produced by forces beyond their control. But there are those who argue that 68 itself strengthened capitalism. This point was made by the French sociologists Luc Boltanski and Ève Chiapello, who argued that there were always two critiques of capitalism – an 'aesthetic' one that emphasized culture and a social one that emphasized more concrete matters of income and conditions.[13] They see 68 as marked by the predominance of the 'aesthetic' critique and argue that capitalism (by which they mean the management of large French companies) assimilated the aesthetic critique to develop a new kind of business practice that laid a heavier emphasis on personal freedom and creativity and that also produced higher levels of inequality. A cruder attack was made by Nicolas Sarkozy in the 2008 presidential campaign when he said that May 1968 had brought the unbridled and unscrupulous capitalism of 'short-term, money, speculation and . . . golden parachutes'.

In fact, the notion that 68 might have facilitated a certain kind of capitalism is a relatively old one. Even when they attacked it, 68ers were often fascinated by capitalism and in later life they were quick to observe the ways in which it had influenced their own former comrades. In a book published to mark the tenth anniversary of 1968, Régis Debray wrote: 'neo-capitalism advances masked with all the virtues of the counter-culture'.[14] A few years later, Daniel Cohn-Bendit noted that Bobby Seale, once of the Black Panthers, was selling barbeque sauce; Jerry Rubin, of the Yippies, was organizing meetings for businessmen in Manhattan; and Robert Stolk, of the Amsterdam Provos, emphasized that he was running a business not a cooperative.[15]

Traces of 68 are particularly visible in entertainment and the media – domains that themselves expanded and sometimes blended into other kinds of business in the decades after 1968. In the late 1970s, Susan Krieger coined the phrase 'hip capitalism' to describe the San Francisco rock radio station KPMX, which had flirted with the underground culture – at one point its staff were paid with 'muddy money' that had been dug up from a drug dealer's garden – before discovering the benefits of advertising deals.[16] Independent newspapers flourished around 1968 and the Underground Press Syndicate (founded in New York in 1967) came to have 200 members.[17] Most underground papers collapsed under the weight of debts and political disagreements but a few flourished. Richard Branson (born in 1950) began his business career in the late 1960s by producing a magazine called *The Student* – though his own studies had ceased when he dropped out of an expensive English school at the age of fifteen. Tony Elliott left Keele University in 1968 to found *Time Out*. His magazine celebrated the political rebellion as well as the cultural ferment of the late 1960s – though it was transformed in the early 1980s when Elliott broke with his own journalists to turn the magazine into a more aggressively commercial enterprise.

In 1973, Serge July returned from two years as a revolutionary agitator in the mining district in Bruay-en-Artois to be the first editor of the newspaper *Libération*, which was mainly staffed by members of the Maoist Gauche Prolétarienne and backed by patrons who included Sartre. The new paper was ferociously austere. It accepted no advertising and claimed to live on money provided by its readers, although it actually benefited from a finance director who inherited some money and an urbane banker who extended credit on the grounds that 'one does not refuse Sartre'.[18] Decisions were taken by 'general assemblies' and the paper had no hierarchy of salaries or power.

Over time, *Libération* became slicker and more stylish. It used photographs and cartoon strips to make itself distinctive and appealing, especially to the young. In the early 1980s, the paper underwent a sharp turn. It closed from February to May 1981 and reopened with new *éclat*. This *éclat* was partly due to the fact that François Mitterrand's election had brought the left to power for the first time since the 1950s – the new president took care to have himself photographed reading *Libération*. The paper's politics now moved towards a libertarian social democracy. In 1982, Serge July announced that it would accept advertising. However, he insisted that this was not because the paper had changed: 'It is advertising that has changed. It is an art. One can no longer say where culture begins and advertising finishes.' *Libération* itself became a brand – famous for its red logo that looked as though it might go equally well on a guerrilla's cap or at the head of a company report.

Advertising itself drew heavily on motifs and slogans from 1968 and these sometimes seemed to fit into a kind of capitalism in which brand image had become the most important form of property for many companies. The student leaders of 1968 were effective publicists. David Ogilvy (who combined a career in advertising with liberal political sympathies) remarked: 'Why shouldn't one give an advertising task to Red Dany [i.e. Cohn-Bendit] or Dutschke . . . he would be the right man for a Mercedes commercial. He knows how to sell things to young people.' It was rumoured that Dutschke had been offered 1,000 marks a month if he would ensure that photographs of him always featured a bottle of Pepsi Cola. Young radicals, who had grown up with television and colour magazines, were fascinated by advertising. In Germany, some of them turned a Johnnie Walker advertisement on its head. They produced a poster with the following words:

The Day is ending, time for Jonny Walker [sic]
An American soldier killed in Vietnam costs the USA 12 million dollars
A dead Vietcong costs 1.6 million
Because being particular in one's tastes always costs a bit more.[19]

Computers were another area in which the mark of 1968 seems obvious. Many protesters of the late 1960s would have said that IBM – a large, hierarchical corporation – stood for everything that they disliked. Students from Berkeley marched with IBM punch cards taped to their back to illustrate the conformity and utilitarianism that they believed to be imposed on them. A French student claimed that the Paris office of IBM, where his father was a manager, had sent its employees to join the right-wing rally in favour of de Gaulle at the end of May 1968.[20] But by the 1980s the fastest-growing computer companies were flexible and innovative ones that often presented themselves in conscious opposition to IBM and in alliance with the world of entertainment and design that had been so transformed by 1968. Steve Jobs (born in 1955) grew up on the west coast of America in the aftermath of 1968 and drew some of his style from the counter-culture – he lived on an Indian ashram for a time. His contemporary Bill Gates also admired the culture of the late 1960s and once offered millions of dollars to use a Rolling Stones song in his company's advertising. He had spent his youth programming computers and then devoted his middle years to philanthropy, which made him look as if he was living 68 backwards.

In some respects 68 helped resolve what Daniel Bell had called the 'cultural contradictions of capitalism'. The emphasis on production and investment had gone with a cult of hard work and self-denial but, if it was to survive, capitalism needed to produce consumers as much as goods. The hedonistic culture of the late 1960s encouraged consumption. Indeed those who thought of themselves as most strongly opposed to capitalism in 1968 were fascinated by the acquisition of luxury goods. Organized shoplifting was an important form of political protest – Maoists stole foie gras from Fauchon in Paris and distributed it to the bemused inhabitants of the *bidonvilles*.

Travel illustrated the new economy of hedonism. Organized holidays in the early twentieth century had often meant worthy trips that emphasized the benefits of fresh air or high culture. The quintessential travel company of the 1970s, by contrast, was Club Méditerranée. It was founded in 1950 and reconstituted in 1957 as an explicitly commercial organization, with its expansion underwritten by deals with American Express and investment from the Rothschild bank. Club Med did not present itself to its clients as a conventional business. Money did not change hands at the sites the company owned – guests swapped beads (which had of course been bought) for drinks. Club Med surfed on the same social waves as protest movements in the 1960s. Both celebrated an association with the non-European world – Club Med's self-presentation made much of Tahiti. Both involved the young and the educated – especially those drawn from the new middle classes produced by economic modernization. The complexity of relations between the two was illustrated in May 1968, when students attacked the Paris headquarters of Club Med and the company responded by offering some of them free holidays.[21]

Businesses, especially in America, had recognized that young people were a particularly attractive market since the 1950s and some of them treated the rise of a counter-culture in the late 1960s as another marketing opportunity. In October 1968, advertising agencies paid $300 per head to attend a conference on 'Selling to the American Youth Market'. Companies that sought to exploit the counter-culture sometimes did so in ways that involved gestures to political radicalism. The most notorious of these was the slogan used by Columbia records: 'The revolutionaries are on Columbia'. Columbia's advertising studiously avoided specific political statement and traded instead on a sense of rebellion encapsulated in slogans such as 'The man can't bust the music'. However, labels such as Columbia advertised in the alternative press, which also expounded radical politics. The FBI was so worried by this coexistence that it asked record companies to cease giving what the Bureau saw as a tacit subsidy for revolution.[22]

One can make too much of *soixante-huitard* capitalism. The fact that capitalism has flourished since 1968 does not mean that it has flourished *because* of 1968. A 68ish style eventually permeated some businesses, but most captains of industry remained conservative in both politics and culture after 1968. An emphasis on a few highly successful entrepreneurs and/or the self-presentation of some managers in large and modern companies is deceptive. The majority of those who had been politically active in 1968 did not embrace capitalism. Indeed those who had given much of their youth to political organization, or simply turned their back on conventional careers, were often poor in later life. Among a sample of students from a campus of the University of California, those who had been most active in protest movements around 1970 had incomes of less than $35,000 per year – some of them substantially less. Among those students who had not been active, six of fifteen had incomes of more than $70,000 – the highest was $150,000.[23] In the village of Cadenet in the South of France, Léa illustrated a *soixante-huitard* trajectory that was a long way from the clichés of former student radicals who had become entrepreneurs. The daughter of a shepherd, she had left the village to work as a typist in Marseilles but returned after being radicalized in 1968 to try her luck as an artist and then to support herself by raising goats. By the early part of the twenty-first century she was living in straitened circumstances.[24]

If 68ers had anything to do with business, then they worked in small enterprises, often ones that consciously turned away from the pursuit of profit. Many such ventures were dependent on public subsidy, especially provided at local level – thus, for example, when *Time Out* became a commercial operation in the early 1980s, many of its journalists helped found *City Limits*, which was backed by the Greater London Council. Some 68ers supported small, archaic operations. In France, Maoists allied with the movement to defend small shopkeepers and artisans that had been founded by Gérard Nicoud.[25]

If 68ers embraced conventional commercial methods at all, it was often because circumstances forced them to. The founders of the

Sunrise Communal Farm in Michigan in 1971 did not recognize private property. One of them, who had put up $7,500 of his money to make a down payment for the farm, was briskly told that his vote would count for no more than anyone else's in the conduct of the commune's business. The need to buy those commodities that could not be produced on the farm pushed commune members towards commerce. They opened shops to sell their handicrafts and in 1973 the farm was incorporated as a company in order to meet the requirements of a bank that granted it a business loan.[26]

Capitalism became more international after 1968, but the internationalism of capitalism was different from that of the student radicals. Roger Martin, a manager of the venerable industrial company Pont-à-Mousson, flew from Paris to New York, on the first Air France flight to leave after the strikes of 1968, to attend a meeting of the new international board of Morgan Stanley.[27] Martin did not belong to some *soixante-huitard* strand of neoliberalism or, indeed, to any variety of liberalism – he entitled his autobiography *Boss by Divine Right*. He was one of the founders of the Association des Grandes Entreprises Françaises, established in June 1969 to protect industry against flirtation with reform on the part of more soft-hearted business leaders.[28]

In any case, the internationalism of capitalism did not disguise the continuing importance of national differences and the extent to which this interacted with the consequences of 68. Régis Debray wrote in 1978 as though West German and American models of capitalism were almost the same,[29] but the economic debates of the 1980s often pitted German capitalism (with its relatively high degree of 'concerted action') against the lightly regulated American model. France has attracted particular attention from those who are interested in '*soixante-huitard* capitalism'. This is partly, perhaps, because it was the most explicitly dirigiste of the major Western economies. In France, more than anywhere else, commentators were conscious that the word 'liberalism' might refer to both the spread of freedom in the social sphere and the spread of the free market in the economic sphere.

However, the economic variety of liberalism did not seem to have advanced in the immediate aftermath of 1968 in France. Boltanski and Chiapello see the early 1970s as marked by an attempt to respond to the upheavals of 1968 with collective solutions – higher wages, more formal recognition for trade unions and the optimistic government policies characterized by Prime Minister Jacques Chaban-Delmas as 'La Nouvelle Société'. These initiatives were helped by the fact that the French economy, in conspicuous contrast to that of other Western states, grew quickly in the 1970s, more quickly than at any other time in French history. The period after 1974 was one of greater pessimism: the French economy, hit hard by the rise in oil prices, shrank and the government of Valéry Giscard d'Estaing, president from 1974 to 1981, applied more free-market policies. Scholars working on specific areas of economic policy have produced an even more complicated pattern of change after 1968. They see Chaban's resignation as prime minister in 1972 as marking a retreat from certain aspects of social, though not necessarily economic, liberalization. Some suggest that an economic liberalization that began in the mid-1960s was temporarily interrupted by 1968.[30]

As it turned out, it was the United States and Britain that saw the spread of free-market capitalism in the 1980s – though it was not obvious that this would be so at the beginning of the decade when many British Conservatives still looked to the relatively dirigiste economies of continental Europe for their models. Furthermore, the triumph of free-market ideas was associated with the political success of Margaret Thatcher and Ronald Reagan. For Reagan, denunciation of 68 was one of the most important components of his political identity. As for Thatcher, she made her first major political speech in the autumn of 1968 – using the occasion to mock student radicals: 'the student leader Daniel Cohn-Bendit has been awarded a degree . . . His examiners said that he had posed a series of most intelligent questions. Significant? I would have been happier if he had also found a series of intelligent answers'.[31]

Conclusion

Finnish students in May 1968.

Conclusion

The aftermath of 68 was a time of high confidence in the social sciences and many thought – like Howard Kirk, the radical sociologist anti-hero of Malcolm Bradbury's novel *The History Man* (1975) – that everything could be explained 'with a little Marx, a little Freud and a little social history'. Curiously, though, those who participated in 68 were reticent when it came to explaining their own past. When compiling their oral history of 1968, Ronald Fraser and his colleagues were struck by how much emphasis their interviewees placed on the local and the particular and by how few general themes emerged.[1] What, then, was 68 about? What were the causes and consequences of the wave of protest that marked the period?

REFORM AND REVOLUTION

The language of the time often suggested an absolute and unbridgeable divide between 68ers and the political systems of the countries in which they had grown up. Indeed, there is a danger that 68 is dismissed precisely because its achievements are judged against the most extravagant ambitions of its most flamboyant protagonists – those who said that they would transform society and levitate the Pentagon. Some protesters labelled their opponents as 'fascist', they attacked all major political parties and often even the very idea of electoral politics. But the gulf between mainstream politics and 68 was not always as wide as it seemed and the radicalism of the late 1960s often sprang out of reformism earlier in the decade. The radical left cooperated with more moderate progressive groups in the mid-1960s. Students for a Democratic Society summed up their wary relations with Lyndon Johnson with the words 'half the way with LBJ'. Lines of communication between radical and moderate left were rarely entirely broken – partly because so many young radicals were the children of leaders of the moderate left and because personal relations, for all the talk of generational conflict, sometimes remained cordial.

Two men – Pierre Mendès France in France and Robert Kennedy in the US – were in contact with sections of the radical left in 1968. Their ability to sustain this dialogue owed much to their attractive personal ities but also to the simple fact that they had been out of power for most of the 1960s, and had avoided the kind of precise political commitments that might have alienated supporters. Even in places where the radical left attacked the mainstream socialist parties most vigorously, there were some mainstream socialist leaders – Willy Brandt in Germany or Tony Benn in Britain – who felt private sympathy for aspects of student protest.

Often the reformism of the early 1960s acquired a momentum that eventually pushed beyond reform, or turned against institutions that had themselves pulled back from reform. Even the Catholic Church was affected by this process. The debates of the second Vatican Council (1962 to 1965) raised hopes among those who wanted a more open and politically engaged Church. In fact, especially after the death of John XXIII in 1963, reform exasperated conservatives without satisfying radicals. In 1968, the Archbishop of Milan complained that his diocese was now divided between 'Vatican I' - i.e. unreconstructed traditionalists – and 'Vatican III' – i.e. those who had gone way beyond the moderate reforms that the Catholic hierarchy had originally envisaged.[2]

The radicalization of 68 was not a one-way street. Movements that had begun as reformist became more extreme for a time but then returned to more modest conceptions of political change. This return was particularly visible at the end of the twentieth century – when 68ers were often in government. But the possibility that 68 might hold a reformist potential could be discerned even at the moment in the early 1970s when some 68ers were still prone to dismiss reform as betrayal. In late 1972, Le Mouvement Social, a historical journal that had been intimately associated with 68, planned a special edition on 'French reformism and reformers'. One of the moving spirits behind it recognized that they had drawn lessons from 68 'conceived as a real social movement and a false revolution'.[3]

THE TWO FACES OF AMERICA

The events of 68 revolved around the United States and it was with regard to America, more than anywhere else, that the reformism of the early 1960s both gave birth to, and came into conflict with, a new kind of radicalism. The civil rights movement that had begun in the 1950s in the American South influenced protest in Europe. The idea of a left that might be divorced from established parties, and perhaps even from the working class, owed much to America. European universities of the 1960s were frequently modelled on American ones, and so were European student protests. The US was a target for the most savage abuse but, at the same time, the rebellious movements of 68 were frequently American in their style. Joschka Fischer talked of America as having 'two faces' that made it an object of both contempt and emulation for his contemporaries in Germany.[4]

The 'two faces' of America can be traced back to 1945. The United States was the richest country in the world and generous in the largesse that it afforded to its allies. It was exuberantly capitalist and the leader of a global struggle against Communism but it was also often an object of admiration for the democratic left in Western Europe. Young American radicals believed passionately in the destiny of their own country, particularly in the early 1960s. The McCarthyism of the 1950s was over. Those who advocated progressive causes no longer feared being labelled as Communist. Many such people were, in fact, keen to escape from the sterile dichotomies of the Cold War and abstruse theological disputes that they associated with Marxism. They wanted to revive a distinctively American form of radicalism.

Oddly, America's role as the leading anti-Communist power was intertwined with the hopes that it aroused among some progressives. Cutting the right kind of figure on the international stage, especially after decolonization in Africa and Asia, meant talking a language of freedom and civil rights. More than anyone else, John F. Kennedy epitomized the contradiction of America in the early 1960s, a contradiction summed up in Michael Harrington's remark that Kennedy 'did not provide answers but had the merit of raising profound questions'.[5] Kennedy was a fierce exponent of Cold War thinking, but his early death, before the full consequences of his policies in Vietnam became apparent, meant that he went on being seen as the symbol of youthful hopes and that his brother Robert came to embody some of those hopes.[6] The largest live audience that John F. Kennedy ever addressed was not in Washington or Berlin but in Berkeley, California and Berkeley illustrated the hopes that many placed in America during the early 1960s. It provided more recruits for Kennedy's Peace Corps, founded in 1961, than any other university. The Free Speech movement at Berkeley in 1964 was emphatically not anti-American. One of those most active in the movement remarked that it drew its emotional power from the very fact that it seemed to bring to life the rhetoric of freedom on which he had been raised:

> It was like watching the mystery dramas come alive. No one could even say it because the words themselves had been so abused – 'democracy', 'Congress'. You know, it was like going to Church for years, then watching God walk on earth. You just realized, 'That's the meaning inside those dry terms.'[7]

The radicalization of the late 1960s in the United States was so violent that it shook all certainties. Much of the radical left seemed to turn against the American values they had once celebrated – though even this turn was sometimes expressed in ways that alluded to American traditions as, for example, when advocates of Black Power insisted on their right to bear arms. Nevertheless the radical left itself came to represent a face of America for much of the rest of the world. Student protest was one of the things that drew young Europeans to study at US universities. Parts of the European right were also influenced by a sense that America was the home of the counter-culture and even that it represented a new kind of dystopia. Angus Maude, a British Conservative who was to become a prominent supporter of Margaret Thatcher, wrote in 1972: 'As we try to grapple with our major imports from America – violence, drug taking, student unrest, the hippy cult and pornography – our own permissive leftists have been hailing them as signs of progress'.[8]

The American ruling class itself seemed shot through with self-doubt. Of course, internal protest was not the only reason for this. Failure to win in Vietnam, the loss of American economic leadership that went with the end of Bretton Woods and Watergate all contributed. For much of the 1970s, the United States was a confused, guilty and uncertain country. The Carter presidency of 1976 to 1980 epitomized this mood. It was haunted by the civil rights campaign and by Vietnam. Carter himself was, for all his folksy southern charm and Christian faith, a curiously 68ish figure – in his informality, his earnest moralizing about human rights and occasionally in his bursts of radicalism. He was also 68ish in that he sometimes looked more comfortable as an international campaigner after he had left the White House than he had done as a politician when he was in it. The victory of Reagan – who had fashioned his political identity in opposition to an imagined version of Berkeley – over Carter in 1980 was also a victory over 68.

VIETNAM

The single most important cause of change in the tone of politics in the 1960s was the Vietnam War. It was the escalation of US intervention in the mid-1960s that began to split radicals from the established left, and the Tet offensive of early 1968 was often recalled as the defining event of that year – a left-wing American teacher talked of 1968 as being 'the year of the Tet offensive and about 9,000 other cataclysmic events'.[9] Vietnam seemed to focus and incarnate all the other conflicts – about race, imperialism, militarism and capitalism – of the late 1960s. All sorts of rebellions could be tied to Vietnam. In Italy, Lotta Continua incited factory workers to chant 'Agnelli [the head of Fiat] Indochina is in your factory'.[10] Tom Fawthrop, a student who had come from back from Paris in the summer of 1968 to tear up his examination papers in Hull, talked of the road that led 'from the paddy fields of Vietnam to the examination hall'.[11]

There were strange paradoxes in all this. Some of the most

vociferous protesters in the United States – those at the most privileged universities – were the people least likely to be sent to fight.
Black Americans, who were, at least at first, more likely to be drafted,
seem to have been less likely than white ones to remember Vietnam
as an important historical episode.[12] Working-class white men were
sometimes hostile to anti-war protest, which did not necessarily mean
that they were in favour of the war. In Europe, there was protest in
Germany, where large numbers of American soldiers were stationed,
but which did not send it own soldiers abroad, and Britain, which
was an ally of the US but one that had refused to send troops to Vietnam; not to mention Sweden, whose government supported North
Vietnam by almost every means short of armed intervention.

References to Vietnam sometimes had a curiously abstract quality.
They seemed more to do with the romance of rebellion by the weak
against the strong than about any specific political project. In Paris in
1968, North Vietnamese and American delegates began negotiations
in the Majestic Hotel that was within walking distance of the Latin
Quarter where students were building their barricades. But formal
discussions between officials in suits were a world away from student
protests. The British ambassador to Paris noted: 'Suggestions that
there might be a connection between the student agitation and the
meeting in Paris on Vietnam were . . . rejected everywhere.'[13]

THE BABY BOOM

Vietnam mattered partly because it tied in with other changes in the
West. One of these resulted from the post-war baby boom and the
consequent increase in the number of people who reached the age of
eighteen in the second half of the 1960s. Demography does not
explain everything – birth rates did not go up in all West European
countries and not all 68ers were young. In particular, the workers
who went on strike in France and Italy and eventually Britain were
drawn from a wider age range than the students who demonstrated
at the same time. The baby boom was important for two reasons,
though. First, it provided the student movement with many of its foot
soldiers, if not its leaders. Second, there was a culture of youth that

accompanied 1968. It sprang partly from the sheer number of young people but also from the fact that prosperity and new means of communication created a new sense of what 'young' might mean. Not all protesters regarded themselves as part of a youth culture. Some thought in terms of ideologies that cut across generations and regarded an Americanized and commercial youth culture with active distaste. But many associated youth with rebellion and came to define 'the young' as though they were a new political entity, one that might provide an alternative to the working class.

All political parties – including those that defended the established order – felt that the young presented a special challenge that had to be addressed with co-option or control. The language of youth seeped through advertising, pop music and politics to touch the most unexpected people and institutions. In 1973, John Selwyn Gummer – an ambitious Conservative MP who had inherited the unctuous manner of his clergyman father – wrote a report on how his party might attract the support of the 'Pepsi Generation'.[14]

THE END OF THE POST-WAR?

Some observers believed that 68 marked the end of an era that had been overshadowed by the Second World War. An American report of 1967 put it thus: 'A new generation has come to maturity. Memories of war have faded, if they have been experienced at all. To increasing millions, the cataclysmic events of 1939–45 appear unreal.'[15] Those who most disliked student protest – Kissinger in the US, Mitterrand in France, Schmidt in Germany, Healey in Britain – often prided themselves on a tough-minded realism that they associated with wartime armies. War had a special meaning for the United States. It had brought the country into world affairs and had helped draw a partly immigrant population into a shared sense of national identity. Philip Roth's novel *American Pastoral* (1997) describes the confused horror of a successful Jewish businessman, Swede Levov, whose assimilation is epitomized by his wartime service in the Marine Corps, when his teenage daughter plants a bomb in protest about the Vietnam War in 1968.

There were many respects in which the world against which 68ers rebelled was one forged by the war. A Neapolitan student recalled: 'I remember at the mass meetings all the analyses used to start out, "After World War II ..." and half the crowd would leave because some guy was starting to go through the whole history of American imperialism.'[16] Students in Le Mans hauled down an American flag and replaced it with a North Vietnamese one on 8 May 1968 (the thirty-third anniversary of the day the Second World War ended in Europe).[17] War had not, however, been equally 'cataclysmic' in all the countries that were affected by 68. Many adult American men never left US soil and never came close to combat.

Memories of the war were more intense in much of continental Europe – no one could have claimed that the lives of Daniel Cohn-Bendit or Rudi Dutschke were not touched by the effects of war – and what often marked 68 there was the desire to recall particular aspects of the conflict. French, Italian and even German radicals celebrated the memory of the anti-Nazi resistance. Sometimes mockery and reverence were mixed together in the 68ish view of the Second World War. Radicals disliked the institutionalized piety of resistance memories while admiring what they took to be the 'real' resistance. Luisa Passerini remembered that her friends in northern Italy shocked their elders by talking about the 'mafia' of resistance veterans, while they also sought advice from former partisans – sometimes advice that extended to include the effective use of explosives.[18] Anti-Nazi resistance movements had a strange legacy in Britain because they had been sponsored by the Churchill government and the military establishment – though this sponsorship does not always seem to have left happy memories. The chief education officer of the Conservative Surrey County Council commented on student protest in the light of 'his experience with the partisans in Italy and ... the Balkans during the war ... he said he understood how the minds of such people worked'.[19]

AFFLUENCE

Western economies grew quickly in the twenty years before 1968. Increased prosperity had particular effects on young people. Their role as consumers with a high level of discretionary spending made them important to business. Governments built new universities partly to train those who would manage a new kind of economy, and parents were increasingly able to subsidize their children through long periods of study – though both governments and parents were sometimes disconcerted that students concentrated in large measure on subjects with little apparent economic utility.

There was a complicated relation between prosperity and political rebellion. Sometimes 68ers attacked consumerism and some were simply driven by a sense that there must be more to life than material well-being. Pierre Chanu – a historian who spent his life compiling statistics on trade and birth rates – said that he had learned from 1968 that 'one does not fall in love with an [economic] growth rate'.[20] Disdain for economic considerations sprang partly from the fact that young people took economic security for granted. One student at the LSE in the mid-1960s later recalled that he had not sought a conventional career because he had assumed that either full employment would allow him to survive with a succession of short-term jobs or capitalism itself would be overthrown.[21]

Prosperity was not, however, entirely secure in the 1960s. Some members of Students for a Democratic Society had reached out to the poor in the early years of the decade because they believed that the post-war boom was about to come to an end and that there would be an increase in unemployment in the winter of 1964. Their expectations were confounded partly because of increased government spending associated with the Vietnam War, but there was a downturn in many countries in 1968 itself. In the United States, a run on gold in March of that year marked the death throes of the 'growth liberalism' that had characterized the country for most of the period since 1945.[22] In Britain in June 1968, the philosopher Alasdair MacIntyre suggested that the government's willingness to tolerate unemployment of half a million marked a break with the Keynesianism that had dominated the country since 1945.[23]

These economic blips look small when compared to the troubles that were to beset Western economies during the 1970s. But downturn after a long period of growth could feel dramatic. Increases in unemployment were particularly likely to hit young people – partly because they were less well-established in jobs and partly because the post-war baby boom meant that there were many twenty-year-olds looking for work in and after 1968. The effects of unemployment were felt more quickly by the working classes than by students. Furthermore, one should remember that both prosperity and levels of unemployment varied sharply from one area to another. Even in West Germany, unemployment was sometimes high for a time in particular regions. In Northern Ireland, unemployment was high for much of the post-war period – especially among Catholics.

Extending the angle of vision to take in the 1970s makes the effects of economic downturn look more significant. Increasingly, student protest was intertwined with strikes, often directed against factory closures. The chronology of this process varied from country to country. In the United States, the number of strikes increased during the 1970s – although the student radicalism in the late 1960s had done much to break links between the trade unions and the broader left. In Britain, Germany and Italy, working-class mobilization peaked in the early 1970s – workers and employers struggled over the fruits of diminishing economic growth and governments sometimes made things worse in their attempts to regulate strikes with new legislation. In France, the general strike of 1968 was followed by a period in which the number of strikes was relatively low (very low indeed in 1969 and 1970) and in which economic growth rates were very high. This period came to an end only with the oil crisis of the mid-1970s.

Much analysis of 68 has revolved around seeking to identify one social cause. French sociologists confidently proclaimed that student rebels were children of the bourgeoisie who feared the *déclassement* that might spring from the modesty of their educational achievements or the fact that their qualifications were becoming less exclusive. At the same time, American sociologists argued that protests were led by the most academically able students from the most privileged institutions (see chap. 3). The truth is that multiple causes of dissatisfaction coexisted and rebellion drew together a coalition of disparate groups whose differences were often concealed by the effervescence of protest. In 1972, British university students (relatively privileged and educated individuals who often thought of themselves as belonging to a global movement) allied with striking coal miners, men who were poor even by the standards of the working class.

THE MEDIUM IS THE MESSAGE?

Some conservatives saw 68 as a product of the television age. British members of parliament believed that students at Essex University would ring Anglia Television to ensure that their most spectacular demonstrations were given appropriate attention.[24] It was certainly true that 68 provided opportunities for television. The Vietnam War had habituated a generation of television reporters to covering violent conflict and their coverage had itself done much to stimulate protest. Filming in Berlin or Berkeley could offer the same arresting images of violence without entailing the risk of real war. Television could flatten the contours of violence so that war, riot and boisterous demonstrations could appear the same.

Reporters were occasionally the target of attack. Dan Rather was knocked down by security men at the Democratic Convention in Chicago in 1968 – the episode was then replayed on broadcasts, as *Newsweek* put it, like footage of the boxer Sonny Liston being knocked out.[25] Generally, however, television crews were granted a kind of *de facto* neutrality that meant they could move easily around protest movements. A couple of radical film-makers attempting to record police behaviour in Paris in May 1968 simply announced that they were working for Dutch television.[26]

Television's relations with 68 were curious. An item of consumerist desire and one that was often used to diffuse a highly consensual notion of politics, television stood for things that protesters denounced, but the ubiquity of television sets helped link up different movements and fostered a, sometimes false, sense that people across the world were involved in the same kind of struggle. It encouraged displays that would look good when broadcast and everyone in 68 – including policemen and politicians – was conscious to some degree of playing to the camera. There were odd moments when it looked as if the whole of 68 had become a television performance, as when a Detroit couple were filmed for television watching a news broadcast of themselves looting during riots on the television set they had looted.[27]

Television was not the only medium of 68. Radio played a particularly important role in France in May 1968 and a more general one in the long 68 as the principal means by which rock music acquired an audience. Furthermore, some of the most important technologies of 68 were simple ones relating to printing and copying, which made possible the diffusion of posters. The posters produced by the collective operated in the school of fine art in Paris acquired particular importance, though it is a revealing illustration of the multiple forms of anti-authoritarianism in 68 that some of the most famous and valuable ones should have been those that never received the formal imprimatur of the radical students at this institution. Technology also helped promote the underground press and produced a curious culture in which experts scrutinized ephemeral publications for evidence of particular authors as a palaeographer might study the work of a particular medieval monk: 'the style, viewpoint and rhetoric show unmistakably the hand of Dr John of the 144 Piccadilly Squat'.[28]

68 was influenced by the fact that many of those involved in it had grown up in the age of mass media and had a particularly strong sense of how that media might be used. Radical students in Turin referred to their own journal as the 'Anti-Stampa', i.e. as the antithesis of the establishment newspaper of their town. Elsewhere radicals sometimes proved good at manipulating the established newspapers. *New Left Notes*, produced by the American Students for a Democratic Society, ran a column entitled 'We made the news today, oh boy'; the line was from a Beatles song, which was dedicated to the report of protest in the mainstream media.[29]

THE PERSONAL AND THE POLITICAL

Individualism was an important strand of 1968 – especially in the United States. Some invested their energy in ways to change their own lives as well as (or instead of) society. Sometimes there was a 68ish version of self-improvement – one that focused on health, physical beauty, the preservation of youth and spiritual or mental well-being. It looked as though a particular strand of the counter-culture, especially that associated with California, had evolved in ways that emphasized individualism, political quiescence and at least implicitly an acceptance of capitalism. Jerry Rubin, justifying his move away from political radicalism, remarked that he 'took care of his body as if it were a revolution'.

However, the new culture of the 1970s did not always go with an abandonment of political radicalism. Talking to Gaby Ceroni, a working-class Frenchman from St Nazaire who had made common cause with the Maoists in the late 1960s, Daniel Cohn-Bendit was struck by the way in which his friend had changed. Ceroni admitted that his life now revolved around yoga and jogging and that he had become interested in psychoanalysis – though not interested in under-going it himself. But none of this had blunted his political edge. He still worked at the factory and refused to accept the new hierarchies of pay – even ones that would have brought him advantages.[30]

Some 68ers felt that changing their personal lives might itself be a political act. Eric Hobsbawm, looking at 68 from the perspective of a 'congenitally pessimistic, middle-aged red', was struck by the fact that it raised questions about the frontiers between politics and per-sonal life: 'what if the "big things" were to be not the overthrow of capitalism, or even of some oppressive or corrupt political regimes, but precisely the destruction of traditional patterns of relations between people and personal behaviour *within existing society*?'[31]

Feminists in the 1970s were the most vocal advocates of blending the personal and the political. But, in fact, the emphasis on 'authen-ticity' was present in 1960s radicalism from the beginning – one thinks of Sandra Cason's suggestion that white participation in the desegregation campaigns in the American South would have been worthwhile even if they had achieved no concrete result.

IS 1968 OVER?

Interviewed in 2008, Daniel Cohn-Bendit insisted that '1968 is fin-ished'. It was a revealing remark – all the more so because, as he knew, he was echoing words that had once been used by the very *unsoixante-huitard* historian François Furet about the French Revolution.[32]

What, though, does it mean to say that 68 is over? The particular agitations associated with 68 generally ended in the second half of the 1970s, but this was a false twilight. In 1976, Willy Brandt wrote:

> I last heard of Cohn-Bendit in September 1975, when he and a few hundred young people were organizing a demonstration against a meeting of Frankfurt Social Democrats at which I appeared with Mário Soares, the leader of the Portuguese Socialists. The movement that had once flared into such potent life had dwindled to a wretched handful of purblind fanatics.[33]

Very few people would say that Cohn-Bendit had disappeared into obscurity now. Outside, and perhaps even inside, Germany, he is probably better known than Willy Brandt. Indeed, if 68 is primarily associated with the careers of its most famous leaders, then one might argue that the movement reached its peak in the late 1990s.

If 68 were to be seen in terms of ideas rather than individuals, then many would view the entry of its main exponents into government as a kind of defeat. In one sense, this argument is obviously right. Many 68ers rejected electoral politics and they would certainly have been astonished that some of their number would enter into government – let alone into governments that launched military interventions abroad or that cheerfully presided over prosperous capitalist economies. However, the pragmatism that many 68ers showed later in life did not always indicate a break with their youth. Some had always been marked by distaste for the ideological rigidity that they associated with the old left and sometimes by distaste for explicit ideology of any kind.

Action that involved working within the system, rather than trying to overthrow it, was particularly important to 68 as a working-class movement. There were workers who dreamed of destroying capitalism and there were moments – especially in France in May 1968 – when it looked as if they might do so. Generally, though, strikes were a means of surviving capitalism. Trade unions were never in total control of the agitations that emerged among their own members as a result of 68, but they did usually manage to channel protest into support for conventional demands revolving around pay and hours of work. Even the worker protests that attracted most middle-class attention – those that involved experiments in self-management – began with the unspoken assumption that the newly created companies would function within capitalism. Some of the most successful trade unionists of the period – Joe Gormley in Britain or Henri Krasucki in France – were extraordinarily conservative when judged by the standards of 68.

It is tempting to say that there were two different strands of 68. One involved the middle classes, especially students, and left a legacy concerned in large measure with non-economic issues. This strand continued to be influential in the 1980s and beyond. The second strand, most visible in the 1970s, involved the working classes and came to focus mainly on economic issues. The power that trade unions had acquired after 1968 was, however, largely broken in the 1980s and one might argue that governments turned to unions when they needed them to contain and channel labour agitation in the early 1970s, but then turned against them when they were able to do so in the 1980s. But there is no reason to suppose that the working-class defeats of the 1980s would have been any less severe if they had not been preceded by the victories of the 1970s – victories from which workers had drawn substantial material benefits.

Finally, most accounts of the long-term impact of 68 are deceptive in the emphasis that they place on a small number of high-profile leaders. The majority of those touched by the radicalism of the period were relatively obscure people and many of those who thought of themselves as 68ers were never full-time militants or even necessarily members of any political group. Many of them considered 68 as a spirit rather than an ideology. This does not mean that their involvement did not produce concrete results. The more puritanical militants of 68 sometimes denounced those who talked of changing their own lives rather than changing society but the two were not mutually exclusive and one might argue that the most important consequences of 68 came precisely from modest choices that individuals made with regard to their own lives. These choices were not always matters of self-indulgence. Changes in the ways parents regarded their children or women regarded themselves could have long-term implications.

There was also a change in personal behaviour that is hard to measure and hard to dismiss. Those who looked back on the protests of 68 often recalled that their most important feature was the new degree of openness with which they talked to other people. In the 1980s, two French people were interviewed about their experience of 1968. One had been a student at the agricultural college in Angers and the other at an elite Paris *lycée*, but they had similar memories. Both recalled spontaneous conversations and the sense that 'one really lived it, it was not bluff'. Later the Parisian recalled 'discussion groups formed everywhere' but he did not find the content of the conversations very interesting: 'The fact that one talks and what one says are two different things.'[34]

Some 68ers found that their years of militancy had excluded them from more lucrative occupations but others made a conscious choice to work in ways that they hoped would help people. Teaching was probably the single most common profession pursued by middle-class militants from 68. Even those who seemed most obviously bourgeois sometimes saw their work as a continuation of 68 by other means. Lawyers represented trade unions; doctors sought to promote an approach that focused on the patient. A few 68ers became hippies on communes, terrorists, government ministers or multimillionaires but the majority had unspectacular careers that often involved a degree of self-sacrifice. Dick Atkinson, a temporary lecturer in sociology who had recently finished a PhD at the LSE, played a small part in the student protests at Birmingham University in 1968. Interviewed about his life almost fifty years later, he recalled how he abandoned academic life and devoted himself to social activism in an unglamorous and impoverished area of Birmingham. Partly as a result of his political activities, he had lost his chance of a permanent lectureship and felt 'a bit disillusioned' with 'sociology in the ivory tower' but his move sprang mainly from the fact that local residents invited him. '[I] hadn't twigged that it would be sensible to be out there in the real world until people in the real world as it were found me, and said come and join us.'[35]

Date	USA	Europe	The Rest of the World
April 1960		Foundation of Parti Socialiste Unifié in France	
November 1960	John F. Kennedy elected president		
November 1961		In Germany SPD expels Sozialistischer Deutscher Studentenbund	
June 1962	Port Huron meeting marks new prominence for Students for a Democratic Society		
July 1962			Algeria gains independence after eight-year war
October 1962			Second Vatican Council opens
November 1963	President John F. Kennedy is assassinated. Vice president Lyndon Johnson succeeds him		
1964	Freedom Summer as students go south to help fight for civil rights		
July 1964	Civil Rights Act passed		

(continued)

Date	USA	Europe	The Rest of the World
September 1964	Free Speech movement begins at Berkeley	Nanterre campus of Paris University opened	
October 1964		Labour Party gains narrow victory in parliamentary elections. Harold Wilson becomes prime minister	
November 1964	Lyndon Johnson elected president		
February 1965			America begins bombing North Vietnam. Assassination of Malcolm X
April 1965	Demonstration in Washington against the Vietnam War		
June 1965			Overthrow of Algerian President Ben Bella by a coup
August 1965	Watts riots in Los Angeles	Campaign against Emergency Law in Germany unites unions and radical left	
December 1965		De Gaulle, opposed by Mitterrand, wins second round of presidential election in France	Second Vatican Council ends

January 1966	Student occupation at Trento in Italy		Tricontinental Conference, Havana
March 1966	Stokely Carmichael elected chairman of Students' Non-Violent Co-Ordinating Committee	Harold Wilson's Labour Party wins increased majority in parliamentary elections	
April 1965		Jeunesse Communiste Révolutionnaire founded in France	
May 1966		British government declares state of emergency in response to seamen's strike	Beginning of Cultural Revolution in China
July 1966	Stokely Carmichael uses phrase 'Black Power'		
September 1966			Speech by de Gaulle in Phnom Penh calling for peace in Vietnam
October 1966	Black Panther Party founded in California. Radical Student Alliance created in UK		
November 1966		Second student occupation at Trento	

(continued)

Date	USA	Europe	The Rest of the World
December 1966		Union des Jeunesses Communistes Marxistes-Léninistes founded in France. Grand Coalition brings SPD and Christian Democrats together in Germany	
February 1967		Creation of Comités Vietnam de Base in France. Strikes at Rhodiacéta in Besançon	
March 1967		Narrow victory for Gaullists in French legislative elections. Occupation of London School of Economics	
April 1967	Large demonstrations in New York and San Francisco against the Vietnam War	Formation of Northern Ireland Civil Rights Association. Coup by colonels in Greece	Régis Debray captured in Bolivia
June 1967		Policeman kills Benno Ohnesorg during demonstration against Shah of Iran in West Berlin. Michel Rocard becomes secretary of Parti Socialiste Unifié in France	

July 1967	Race riots in Newark and Detroit	Conference on Dialectics of Liberation in London	De Gaulle says 'Long live free Quebec'
October 1967			Che Guevara killed in Bolivia
December 1967		Creation of *comités d'action lycéens* in France	
January 1968		Confrontation between Daniel Cohn-Bendit and French minister of youth at Nanterre. Third student occupation at Trento	Tet offensive in Vietnam
February 1968		Demonstration against Vietnam War in West Berlin and counter-demonstration in favour of US	
March 1968	Johnson announces he will not seek re-election as president	Battle of Valle Giulia between police and militants in Rome. Anti-Vietnam War demonstration in London. Attack on American Express office in Paris. Formation of March 22 Movement at Nanterre	

(continued)

Date	USA	Europe	The Rest of the World
April 1968	Assassination of Martin Luther King – followed by riots in many cities. Occupation of Columbia University. Police kill Black Panther Bobby Hutton in Oakland, California	Enoch Powell's 'rivers of blood' speech. Rudi Dutschke shot and gravely injured in Berlin. Andreas Baader and others set fire to Frankfurt department store. Communist leader Pierre Juquin is forced off the Nanterre campus by *gauchiste* students	
May 1968		See chronology in chap. 5 for events in France	Negotiations between Americans and North Vietnamese in Paris
June 1968	Assassination of Robert Kennedy	Foundation of Revolutionary Socialist Students' Federation in UK. Emergency Law comes into force in West Germany – a defeat for the radical left	
July 1968			Violent suppression of demonstrations in Mexico
August 1968	Democratic National Convention in Chicago chooses Hubert Humphrey as candidate in presidential election. Violent suppression of demonstrators who have come to city	Warsaw Pact invasion of Czechoslovakia puts end to Prague Spring. Riots in Londonderry	Violence around Olympic stadium in Mexico City

(continued)

October 1968	Anti-Vietnam War demonstration in London. Formation of People's Democracy in Northern Ireland. Foundation of Maoist Gauche Prolétarienne in France	Large-scale massacre by police of protesters in Mexico City
November 1968	Strike at San Francisco State University, which lasts until following April. Election of Richard Nixon as president	
December 1968	Proposal 'Towards a Revolutionary Youth Movement' put to SDS national convention in Ann Arbor	
January 1969	LSE closed after student demonstrations	
April 1969	De Gaulle resigns after his proposal for decentralization is defeated in a referendum. Bernadette Devlin elected to British parliament. Jack Straw elected as president of National Union of Students	

Date	USA	Europe	The Rest of the World
May 1969	People's Park uprising in Berkeley		
June 1969	SDS splits into two factions – foundation of Weathermen	Pompidou wins French presidential election	
August 1969	Woodstock festival		
September 1969		Suicide of Gabrielle Russier in France. Beginning of 'Hot Autumn' of labour unrest in Italy	
October 1969	Days of Rage in Chicago	Social Democrat Willy Brandt becomes Chancellor in alliance with Liberals	
November 1969	Large demonstrations in Washington and San Franciso against Vietnam War		
December 1969	Police kill Black Panthers Fred Hampton and Martin Clark. At Flint Council, Weathermen decide to go underground	Provisional Irish Republic Army founded	
April 1970	Nixon announces invasion of Cambodia	Jean-Paul Sartre becomes editor of Maoist newspaper *La Cause du Peuple* after its editor Jean-Pierre Le Dantec is arrested	

May 1970	Killing of four students by National Guard during protest at Kent State University	Andreas Baader rescued from prison by a group including Ulrike Meinhof. Red Army Faction founded in Germany	
June 1970		Conservatives win general election in UK. Edward Heath becomes prime minister	
July 1970		Death of Salazar in Portugal	
September 1970	Weathermen help Timothy Leary escape from prison	Red Brigades founded in Italy	Salvador Allende becomes president of Chile
October 1970	Angela Davis arrested		
November 1970		Death of de Gaulle	
January 1971		Angry Brigade claim responsibility for bombing house of secretary of state for employment Robert Carr	
February 1971	Black Panthers split between supporters of Eldridge Cleaver and those of Huey Newton		
June 1971		Mitterrand becomes leader of newly formed Parti Socialiste	

(continued)

Date	USA	Europe	The Rest of the World
January 1972		Bloody Sunday: soldiers shoot thirteen unarmed demonstrators in Londonderry. Laws preventing radicals from holding state jobs in West Germany. Miners' strike begins in UK (ends following month)	
February 1972		Guard at Renault kills Maoist militant Pierre Overney – 200,000 attend his funeral the following month	
March 1972		Gauche Prolétarienne kidnaps Robert Nogrette (manager of Renault). He is released after two days	
June 1972	Acquittal of Angela Davis	Arrest of Andreas Baader and Ulrike Meinhof in Germany	
September 1972		Israeli athletes killed by Palestinian guerrillas at Munich Olympics	
November 1972	Nixon re-elected as president		

January 1973	Creation of French newspaper *Libération*	Signature of Paris accords on end of Vietnam War
April 1973	Beginning of strike at Lip at Besançon	
August 1973	Large-scale protests against expansion of French army camp at Larzac	
September 1973		Pinochet's coup in Chile. Salvador Allende is killed
November 1973	Protest at Athens Polytechnic against the military junta in Greece. Dissolution of Gauche Prolétarienne in France	
February 1974	Miners' strike in UK	
April 1974	Death of Pompidou. 'Carnation revolution' in Portugal. Fall of the dictatorship	
May 1974	Strike by Protestant Ulster Workers' Council prevents attempt at power-sharing in Northern Ireland. Valéry Giscard d'Estaing elected president of France	

(continued)

Date	USA	Europe	The Rest of the World
August 1974	Resignation of Nixon as president after Watergate scandal		
November 1974		First free elections after Junta in Greece	
February 1975		Thatcher becomes leader of British Conservative Pary	
April 1975			Saigon falls to North Vietnamese forces
November 1975		Death of Franco	
May 1976		Suicide of Ulrike Meinhof in prison	
September 1976			Death of Mao
September 1977	Mark Rudd (of Weather Underground) turns himself in	Hans-Martin Schleyer of German employers' association is kidnapped by Red Army Faction. His body is found in October	
October 1977		Andreas Baader and Gudrun Ensslin commit suicide in prison	

March 1978	Red Brigades kidnap Christian Democrat politician Aldo Moro in Rome. His body is found in May
May 1979	Conservative election victory in UK. Margaret Thatcher becomes prime minister
April 1980	Death of Sartre
July 1980	Cathy Wilkerson (of Weather Underground) resurfaces in New York
August 1980	Bomb planted by extreme right at Bologna railway station kills 85
November 1980	Ronald Reagan elected president
May 1981	François Mitterrand elected president of France
November 1992	Bill Clinton elected president
June 1994	Daniel Cohn-Bendit becomes a Green member of the European parliament

(continued)

Date	USA	Europe	The Rest of the World
May 1997		Labour Party victory in United Kingdom general election. Tony Blair becomes prime minister. Jack Straw is home secretary	
April 1998		German Red Army Faction announces its dissolution	
September 1998		Red/Green coalition rules Germany. Joschka Fischer is foreign minister	
April 2007		Nicolas Sarkozy, presidential candidate in France, talks of 'liquidating the legacy of May 68'	
May 2017		Emmanuel Macron (born 1977) is elected president of France. He is supported by Daniel Cohn-Bendit	

List of Illustrations

I. WORDS AND 'THE THING': DEFINING 68

'Beauty is in the street'. Poster, 1968. The most famous lithographs of 1968 were mainly produced by the collective at the Beaux Arts school in Paris. Generally, 2–3,000 copies of each were printed. This poster was produced in Montpellier and not much seen in 1968 itself. However, by the time of a sale in 2008, it had become the most valuable of all the *soixante-huitard* prints – partly perhaps because feminism had become an important part of the prism through which people looked back on 1968. It was sold at auction for over 3,000 euros. *Photo: Bibliothèque Nationale de France, Paris*

2. THE 68 GENERATION

Meeting of Students for a Democratic Society at Bloomington, Indiana in September 1963. The photo was taken by C. Clark Kissinger. He wrote: 'I asked everyone to raise a clenched fist salute just before I snapped the photo, as a symbol of the new resistance coming into being.' Note the conservative dress sense of most participants and the smiles – are they laughing at themselves for giving clenched fist salutes?
  From left to right, Tom Hayden, Don McKelvey, Jon Seldin, Nada Chandler, Nancy Hollander, Steve Max, Danny Millstone, Vernon Grizzard, Paul Booth, Carl Wittman, Mary McGroaty, Steve Johnson, Sarah Murphy, Lee Webb, Todd Gitlin, Dick Flacks, Mickey Flacks, Robb Burlage, Rennie Davis. *Photo: © C. Clark Kissinger*

3. UNIVERSITES

Malcolm X with members of the Oxford Union, 1964.

Malcolm X was invited to Oxford to debate the motion 'Extremism in the defence of Liberty is no vice; moderation in the pursuit of Justice is no virtue'. The phrase had been coined by the right-wing Republican senator for Arizona Barry Goldwater. Malcolm X, who was sceptical of white liberals, thought a Goldwater victory in the 1964 presidential election desirable because it would make political choices clearer. He spoke in favour of the motion. Malcolm X's own politics were evolving fast in 1964. He had recently left the Nation of Islam and was less enthusiastic about racial separation than he had sometimes seemed in the past.

The presence of a black revolutionary in the Oxford Union was less incongruous than it might first appear. Though Oxford students were primarily white, the university had never imposed the kind of racial segregation that would have been taken for granted at its namesake in Mississippi. The first non-white president of the Union had been elected in 1942 and Eric Abrahams, the president of the Union who invited Malcolm, was from Jamaica. His successor, Tariq Ali, was from Pakistan – though, as he told Malcolm, he was a Muslim 'in name only'. Both Ali and Abrahams had been 'gated', i.e. subject to a form of academic house arrest, for participation in demonstrations about the imprisonment of Nelson Mandela – they had special permission to leave their rooms to attend debates at the Union. Malcolm had probably encountered Oxford undergraduates before he came to Britain because debating teams from the university had visited the Norfolk Penal Colony in Massachusetts when he was incarcerated there.

In retrospect, the most striking feature of Oxford in 1964 concerned sex rather than race. Women had only been admitted to the Union in 1963, and only two of the eighteen officers of the Union (Suzanne Maiden and Prue Hyman) were women. The first female president of the Union (Geraldine Jones) was elected in 1968. Malcolm X often spoke in highly gendered terms (though his position on relations between the sexes was one of the areas in which his attitudes seemed to be changing fast). He referred in his speech to the 'castration' of black men in the United States. *Photo: Gillman & Soame, Oxford*

4. THE UNITED STATES

Robert Kennedy (left) and President Lyndon B. Johnson address the crowd during the presidential campaign, New York, 15 October 1964.

'Hey hey LBJ, how many kids have you killed today?'. Lyndon Johnson – old, ugly and vulgar – came to stand for everything that 68ers despised, especially during the Vietnam War. Robert Kennedy – young and idealistic – was one of the few politicians that some 68ers respected. The differences between the two men were, however, complicated. Kennedy was closely associated with the policies that his brother had initiated in Cuba and Vietnam. LBJ was, until the escalation of the war in Vietnam, sometimes seen with grudging admiration by the left – members of Students for a Democratic Society wore badges saying 'Half the way with LBJ'. *Photo: Cecil Stoughton/Lyndon Baines Johnson Presidential Library and Museum, The University of Texas at Austin*

5. FRANCE

Boy and girl on a bicycle, Avenue des Champs-Élysées, Paris, 1968.

Though this appears at first glance to be a photograph of student protest, it looks, on closer examination, as though these young people are attending the pro-Gaullist demonstration of 30 May 1968. *Photo: © Henri Cartier-Bresson/Magnum Photos*

6. WEST GERMANY

Demonstration on the Kurfürstendamm, Berlin, after the attempted assassination of Rudi Dutschke, April 1968. *Photo: Alex Waidmann, ullstein bild via Getty Images*

7. BRITAIN

Karl Dietrich Wolff (on the left), Tariq Ali (centre) and Daniel Cohn-Bendit at Karl Marx's tomb in Highgate Cemetery in mid-June 1968.

The three men had been brought to London to appear in a BBC documentary on student protest. Perhaps the French historian – and ex-Communist – Annie Kriegel was thinking of this photograph when she wrote that 1968 failed to produce any new ideology but rather, like flowers placed on graves on All Saints' Day, gave an appearance of life to old ones. *Private Eye* used the photograph for one of their covers and had the three men singing 'There's no business like show business'. Cohn-Bendit looks uncharacteristically subdued – perhaps because he was not really a Marxist. James Callaghan, the British home secretary, said that he had permitted Cohn-Bendit to enter the country so that he could teach him the words of the 'Internationale', 'as he does not seem to be too sure of them'. *Photo: Keystone-France/ Gamma-Keystone via Getty Images*

8. THE REVOLUTION WITHIN THE REVOLUTION: SEXUAL LIBERATION AND THE FAMILY

Rudi Dutschke with his baby son, April 1968.

Some argued that the political radicalism of the late 1960s went with macho posturing by men and that the women's liberation movement of the 1970s was, in part, a reaction against such behaviour. However, the attitudes of male radicals were sometimes more complicated than they first appeared. Beneath his lurid rhetoric, the German student leader Rudi Dutschke was a gentle person. Here he is with one of his children. His son was, inevitably, called Che. *Photo: Interfoto/Alamy*

9. WORKERS

Alfa Romeo workers in 1972. *Photo: Uliano Lucas/Alinari Archives*

IO. VIOLENCE

Wanted poster for members of the Weather Underground, issued 20 October 1972. The FBI, even more than police agencies in other countries, helped define the long 68. *Public domain*

II. DEFEAT AND ACCOMMODATION?

Jack Straw, president of the Students' Union at Leeds, dances with the Duchess of Kent, chancellor of the university, in 1968. Though on the left of the British student movement, Straw was not a revolutionary, even before he began the long march that would take him to being a minister in the Blair government of 1997. *Photo: The Yorkshire Post/ Reproduced with the permission of Special Collections, Leeds University Library*

CONCLUSION

Student protest touched almost every corner of the Western world in 1968. The photograph depicts a May Day demonstration in Jyväskylä in provincial Finland. Usually student and worker demonstrations were separate but on this occasion Socialist and Communist workers joined students. The demonstrators were asking for more democracy in the workplace and at the university. They were also protesting against plans to build a highway through a historic park in the city. Mikko Pyhälä has just thrown his student cap into the fire, as have Marjatta Pyhälä, Ismo Porna and his wife Virpi. The incident looks as though it is modelled on protests in Paris but it actually took place just before the Paris events. The confrontation with authority in Finland was less stark than in many other countries. The burning car was, in fact, a wreck that had been purchased by the students and burnt with the permission of the police. Most of the protesters' aims were achieved. Mikko Pyhälä, who became one of the first student representatives at the university in 1969, later served as an ambassador.

Erkki Liikanen, who repeated the cap-burning performance at Mikkeli in the following year, later became president of the Bank of Finland. *Photo: © Matti Salmi*

Every effort has been made to contact all copyright holders. The publishers will be happy to correct in future editions any errors or omissions brought to their attention.

Some Thoughts on Further Reading

Unless otherwise stated, place of publication for all books in English is London and for all books in French is Paris.

General books on 68 in the world include David Caute, *Sixty-Eight: The Year of the Barricades* (1988) and Mark Kurlansky, *1968: The Year That Rocked the World* (1998). Gerd-Ralner Horn's *The Spirit of '68: Rebellion in Western Europe and North America, 1956–1976* (Oxford, 2007) gives special attention to Mediterranean Europe. Arthur Marwick's *The Sixties: Cultural Revolution in Britain, France, Italy and the United States, c.1958–c.1974* (Oxford, 1998) has also been influential. Historians of France, in spite of their best intentions, tend to focus on their own country with brief references to the rest of the world. See Dominique Damamme, Boris Gobille, Frédérique Matonti and Bernard Pudal (eds.), *Mai–Juin 68* (2008) and Philippe Artières and Michelle Zancarini-Fournel (eds.), *68, Une Histoire Collective, 1962–1981* (2008). Historians of Germany have been more influenced by the turn to transnational history – see Martin Klimke, *The Other Alliance: Student Protest in West Germany and the United States in the Global Sixties* (Princeton, 2011), and Timothy S. Brown, *West Germany and the Global Sixties: The Anti-Authoritarian Revolt, 1962–1978* (Cambridge, 2013).

Though historians are increasingly prone to argue that 1968 was just the high point in a longer cycle of protest, their works (and mine) are still often published around anniversaries. The memorialization of 68 was already an object of satire in 1978 when Régis Debray published *Modeste Contribution aux Discours et Cérémonies Officielles du Dixième Anniversaire* and has now become a topic of historical study in itself. See

Jean-Pierre Rioux, 'À Propos des Célébrations Décennales du Mai Français', *Vingtième Siècle, Revue d'Histoire*, 23 (1989), pp. 49–58.

Works by 68ers started to appear almost as soon as the tear gas cleared. Hopeful publishers confined student radicals to country houses and Mediterranean islands with instructions not to emerge until they had a manuscript. Daniel Cohn-Bendit admitted in his own *Obsolete Communism: The Left-Wing Alternative* (1968) that editors had begged him to write 'anything . . . good or bad, exciting or dull'. Partly because there are so many memoirs and partly because so many 68ers went on to have academic careers, the frontier between primary and secondary sources is unusually blurred in writing on 68, and Daniel Bensaïd's *Une Lente Impatience* (2004), which would usually be regarded as a primary source, comments on a secondary one, Kristin Ross's *May 68 and its Afterlives* (Chicago, 2002).

Oral history has been particularly influential in the study of 1968. Ronald Fraser et al published *1968: A Student Generation in Revolt* in 1988. Robert Gildea, James Mark and Anette Warring's *Europe's 1968: Voices of Revolt* (Oxford, 2013) is more recent and perhaps even more committed to a collective approach among the authors and to scrupulous respect for the subjective experience of interviewees. Luisa Passerini's *Autobiography of a Generation: Italy, 1968* (Hanover, NH, 1996) combines academic research, mainly based on oral history, with personal reflection. Sometimes autobiography blends into polemic as old arguments are continued or new ones begun. Daniel Bensaïd and Alain Krivine published a book entitled *Mai Si!*. On the other side, Götz Aly's *Unser Kampf – ein irritierter Blick zurück* (2008) is a sharp denunciation of his own former comrades.

Some of the most influential writers on 68 now are the children of 68ers and as interested in their own contemporaries as in those of their parents. This is true of Julie Pagis, *Mai 68, un Pavé dans leur Histoire* (2014), and Virginie Linhart, *Volontaires pour l'Usine: Vies d'Établis (1967–1977)* (1994). Linhart has also written a more personal work, *Le Jour où Mon Père s'est Tu* (2008). Robert Linhart's *L'Établi* (first published in 1978) is probably the most famous work by an activist about his contacts with the working class – though Philip Cohen's *Reading Room Only: Memoir of a Radical*

Bibliophile (Nottingham, 2013) contains an interesting account of a career that involved, among other things, leaving Cambridge University to sign on as a cabin boy on a Grimsby trawler. There are relatively few accounts of 68 by workers themselves. Christian Chevandier's *La Fabrique d'une Génération: Georges Valero Postier, Militant et Écrivain* (2009) is a partial exception – though, admittedly, one that concerns an exceptional worker.

It is worth reading the periodicals of the period, many of which can be found online. London's *New Left Review* is an obvious example, as is *Esprit*, in which the radical Jesuit philosopher Michel de Certeau first advanced his interpretation of 68. Police reports are also interesting. FBI and CIA files can be found (often heavily redacted) online. One should remember, however, that even the French Renseignements Généraux could rarely keep track of the shifting sands of Maoist and Trotskyist groupuscules. The British Special Branch rarely bothered to distinguish between groups that they labelled 'anarchist'. The FBI believed at one point that Régis Debray's surname was De Bray.

The novels of authors such as Philip Roth and David Lodge say much about how 68 looked to those who observed from the sidelines. Édouard Balladur wrote a semi-fictional account – *L'Arbre de Mai: Chronique Alternée* (1978) – that was based partly on his own experiences as an aide to Pompidou. Robert Merle's novel *Derrière la Vitre* (1970) also blended fact and fiction as he drew on interviews with his own students at Nanterre. The diaries of influential figures reveal much about radical protest – partly because they show that there were long periods during which it barely impinged on establishment thinking. It is interesting, for example, that Arthur Schlesinger Jr could describe the Chicago Democratic Convention of 1968, which he attended, without mentioning the protests outside it – see his *Journals, 1952–2000* (2007). Matthew Brunwasser, 'Digging the Age of Aquarius', *Archaeology* 62, 4 (2009), pp. 30–33 describes excavating the remains of a hippy commune in California destroyed by fire in 1969.

Bibliography

PUBLISHED WORKS

Unless otherwise stated, place of publication for all books in English is London and for all books in French is Paris.

Aberbach, Joel D., and Walker, Jack L., 'The Meanings of Black Power: A Comparison of White and Black Interpretations of a Political Slogan', *American Political Science Review*, 64, 2 (1970)

Adam, Gérard, 'Étude Statistique des Grèves de Mai–Juin 1968', *Revue Française de Science Politique*, 20, 1 (1970)

Adams Moon, Penelope, ' "Peace on Earth: Peace in Vietnam": The Catholic Peace Fellowship and Antiwar Witness, 1964–1976', *Journal of Social History*, 36, 4 (2003)

Agulhon, Maurice, *De Gaulle: Histoire, Symbole, Mythe* (2000)

Ali, Tariq, *Street Fighting Years: An Autobiography of the Sixties* (2005)

Aly, Götz, *Unser Kampf – ein irritierter Blick zurück* (Frankfurt-am-Main, 2008)

Anderson, Perry, and Blackburn, Robin, *Towards Socialism* (1965)

Annan, Noel, *Report on the Disturbances in the University of Essex(1974)*

—, *Changing Enemies: The Defeat and Regeneration of Germany* (1995)

Anonymous, 'Students as an Anti-Parliamentary Opposition', *Minerva*, 6, 3 (1968)

Araiza, Lauren, ' "In Common Struggle Against a Common Oppression": The United Farm Workers and the Black Panther Party, 1968–1973', *The Journal of African American History*, 94, 2 (2009)

Ariès, Philippe, *Un Historien du Dimanche* (1980)

Aron, Raymond, *The Elusive Revolution: Anatomy of a Student Revolt* (1969)

—, *Mémoires: 50 Ans de Réflexion Politique* (this edn, 1990)

Artières, Philippe, and Zancarini-Fournel, Michelle (eds.), *68, Une Histoire Collective, 1962–1981* (2008)

Assayas, Olivier, interviewed in *Eye for Film* (March/April 2013)

Audigier, François, 'Le Malaise des Jeunes Gaullistes en Mai 68', *Vingtième Siècle, Revue d'Histoire*, 70 (2001)

—, 'Le Gaullisme d'Ordre des Années 68', *Vingtième Siècle, Revue d'Histoire*, 116 (2012)

Auron, Yair, *Les Juifs d'Extrême Gauche en Mai 68: Une Génération Révolutionnaire Marquée par la Shoah* (1998)

Balestrini, Nanni, and Moroni, Primo, *La Horde d'Or: La Grande Vague Révolutionnaire et Créative, Politique et Existentielle: Italie, 1968–1977* (2017, first published in Italy in 1988)

Balladur, Édouard, *L'Arbre de Mai: Chronique Alternée* (1978)

Bantigny, Ludivine, 'Le Temps Politisé: Quelques Enjeux Politiques de la Conscience Historique en Mai–Juin 68', *Vingtième Siècle, Revue d'Histoire*, 117 (2013)

Barnard, John, *American Vanguard: The United Auto Workers during the Reuther Years, 1935–1970* (Detroit, MI, 2004)

Barralis, Roger, and Gillet, Jean-Claude (eds.), *Au Coeur des Luttes des Années Soixante, les Étudiants du PSU: Une Utopie Porteuse d'Avenir?* (2010)

Baskir, Lawrence, and Strauss, William, *Chance and Circumstance: The Draft, the War and the Vietnam Generation* (New York, 1978)

Baumann, Michael (Bommi), *Terror or Love: The Personal Account of a West German Urban Guerrilla* (1979)

Becker, Jean-Jacques, *Un Soir de l'Été 1942 . . . Souvenirs d'un Historien* (2009)

Benin, Leigh David, *The New Labor Radicalism and New York City's Garment Industry: Progressive Labor Insurgents during the 1960s* (2000)

Benn, Tony, *Office without Power: Diaries, 1968–1972* (1988)

Bensaïd, Daniel, *Une Lente Impatience* (2004)

Bensaïd, Daniel, and Krivine, Alain, *Mai Si! 1968–1988, Rebelles et Repentis* (1988)

Berger, Ida, 'Une Avant-Garde Isolée: Les Étudiants Allemands', *Esprit*, 381 (May 1969)

—, 'Tiendront-ils? Étudiants Français et Allemands', *L'Homme et la Société*, 16 (1970)

Berlivet, Luc, and Sawicki, Frédéric, 'La Foi dans l'Engagement. Les Militants Syndicalistes CFTC de Bretagne dans l'Après-Guerre', *Politix*, 27 (1994)

Berman, Paul, *Power and the Idealists or the Passion of Joschka Fischer and its Aftermath* (2005)

Bertaux, Daniel, Linhart, Danièle, and Le Wita, Béatrix, 'Mai 1968 et la Formation de Générations Politiques en France', *Le Mouvement Social*, 143 (1988)

Beschloss, Michael R. (ed.), *Taking Charge: The Johnson White House Tapes, 1963–1964* (New York, 1997)

Biles, Roger, *Richard Daley: Race, Politics and the Governing of Chicago* (DeKalb, IL, 1995)

Blackledge, Paul, and Davidson, Neil (eds.), *Alasdair MacIntyre's Engagement with Marxism: Selected Writings, 1953–1974* (2008)

Blackstone, Tessa, and Hadley, Roger, 'Student Protest in a British University: Some Comparisons with American Research', *Comparative Education Review*, 15, 1 (1971)

Boag, Peter, ' "Does Portland Need a Homophile Society?" Gay Culture and Activism in the Rose City Between World War II and Stonewall', *Oregon Historical Quarterly*, 105, 1 (2004)

Boissieu, Alain de, *Pour Servir le Général, 1946–1970* (1982)

Boltanski, Luc, and Chiapello, Ève, *Le Nouvel Esprit du Capitalisme* (1999)

Bondu, Dominique, 'L'Élaboration d'une Langue Commune: LIP-la GP', *Les Temps Modernes*, 684–5 (2015)

Borstelmann, Thomas, *The Cold War and the Color Line: American Race Relations in the Global Arena* (Cambridge, MA, 2001)

Boudon, Raymond, 'Sources of Student Protest in France', *The Annals of the American Academy of Political and Social Science*, 395 (1971)

Bourdieu, Pierre, *Homo Academicus* (Stanford, CA, 1988)

Boyle, Kevin, *The UAW and the Heyday of American Liberalism, 1945–1968* (Ithaca, NY, 1995)

Brandt, Willy, *People and Politics* (1978)

Braungart, Margaret and Richard, 'The Effects of the 1960s Political Generation on Former and Left- and Right-Wing Youth Activist Leaders', *Social Problems*, 38, 3 (1991)

Brière-Blanchet, Claire, *Voyage au Bout de la Révolution: De Pékin à Sochaux* (2009)

Brillant, Bernard, *Les Clercs de 68* (2003)

Brown, Timothy S., 'Subcultures, Pop Music and Politics: Skinheads and "Nazi Rock" in England and Germany', *Journal of Social History*, 38, 1 (2004)

—, '1968 East and West: Divided Germany as a Case Study in Transnational History', *American Historical Review*, 114, 1 (2009)

—, *West Germany and the Global Sixties: The Anti-Authoritarian Revolt, 1962–1978* (Cambridge, 2013)

Brunwasser, Matthew, 'Digging the Age of Aquarius', *Archaeology*, 62, 4 (2009)

Bull, Anna Cento, and Cooke, Philip, *Ending Terrorism in Italy* (2013)

Burns, Jeffrey, 'Eugene Boyle, the Black Panther Party and the New Clerical Activism', *US Catholic Historian*, 13, 3 (1995)

Callu Agnès, (ed.), *Le Mai 68 des Historiens entre Identités Narratives et Histoire Orale* (2010)

Campagne, Juliette, 'Roubaix du Petit Livre Rouge aux Livres d'Images', *Les Temps Modernes*, 684–5 (2015)

Carr, Gordon, *The Angry Brigade* (1975)

Caute, David, *Sixty-Eight: The Year of the Barricades* (1988)

Caws, Mary Ann (ed.), *Maria Jolas, Woman of Action: A Memoir and Other Writings* (Columbia, SC, 2004)

Chemla, Éliane, 'Comme une Vraie Ouvrière à Nîmes', *Les Temps Modernes*, 684–5 (2015)

Chesneaux, Jean, and Nicholaus, Martin, 'Le Mouvement des "Radical Caucuses" dans les Sciences Humaines aux États-Unis', *L'Homme et la Société*, 16, 1 (1970)

Chevandier, Christian, *La Fabrique d'une Génération: Georges Valero Postier, Militant et Écrivain* (2009)

Ciernick, Helen M., 'A Matter of Conscience: The Selective Conscientious Objector, Catholic College Students, and the Vietnam War', *US Catholic Historian*, 26, 3 (2008)

Cleaver, Eldridge, *Soul on Ice* (this edn, 1969)

Coates, Ken, *Workers' Control: A Reply to Arthur Scargill* (Nottingham, 1977)

Cockburn, Alexander, and Blackburn, Robin (eds.), *Student Power: Problems, Diagnosis, Action* (1969)

Cohen, Habiba, *Elusive Reform: The French Universities, 1968–1978* (Boulder, CO, 1978)

Cohen, Paul, 'Happy Birthday Vincennes! The University of Paris-8 Turns Forty', *History Workshop Journal*, 69, 1 (2010)

Cohen, Philip (ed.), *Children of the Revolution: Communist Childhood in Post-War Britain* (1997)

Cohen, Philip, *Reading Room Only: Memoir of a Radical Bibliophile* (Nottingham, 2013)

Cohn-Bendit, Daniel, *Obsolete Communism: The Left-Wing Alternative* (1968)

—, *Nous l'Avons Tant Aimée, la Révolution* (1986)

Collins, Gail, *When Everything Changed: The Amazing Journey of American Women from 1960 to the Present* (2009)

Collins, Robert M., 'The Economic Crisis of 1968 and the Waning of the "American Century"', *American Historical Review*, 101, 2 (1996)

Cornils, Ingo, and Waters, Sarah (eds.), *Memories of 1968: International Perspectives* (Oxford, 2010)

Cotta, Michèle, *Cahiers Secrets de la Ve République*, vol. I: *1965–1977* (2007)

Cowie, Jefferson, 'Nixon's Class Struggle: Romancing the New Right Worker, 1969–1973', *Labor History*, 43, 3 (2002)

Crosland, Susan, *Tony Crosland* (1982)

Crossman, Richard, *The Diaries of a Cabinet Minister*, vol. II: *Lord President of the Council and Leader of the House of Commons, 1966–68* (1976)

Crouch, Colin, *The Student Revolt* (1970)

Crozier, Michel, *Ma Belle Époque: Mémoires, 1947–1969* (2002)

Dallek, Robert, *Flawed Giant: Lyndon Johnson and his Times, 1961–1973* (Oxford, 1998)

Damamme, Dominique, Gobille, Boris, Matonti, Frédérique, and Pudal, Bernard (eds.), *Mai–Juin 68* (2008)

Daum, Nicolas, *Mai 68: Des Révolutionnaires dans un Village Parisien, 20 Ans Après* (1988)

—, *Mai 68 Raconté par des Anonymes* (2008)

Davis, Angela, *An Autobiography* (this edn, 1990)

Davis, James K., *Assault on the Left: The FBI and the Sixties Anti-War Movement* (Westport, CT, 1997)

De Gaulle, Philippe, *Mémoires Accessoires, 1946–1982* (2000)

De Groot, Gerard (ed.), *Student Protest: The Sixties and After* (1998)

—, 'Ronald Reagan and Student Unrest in California, 1966–1970', *Pacific Historical Review*, 65, 1 (1996)

Debray, Régis, *La Révolution dans la Révolution* (1967)

—, *Modeste Contribution aux Discours et Cérémonies Officielles du Dixième Anniversaire* (1978)

—, *À Demain de Gaulle* (1993)

Decourt, Georges, *'Ils Gagnèrent le Large': Prêtres, Génération 68* (Villeurbanne, 2008)

Della Porta, Donatella, *Social Movements, Political Violence and the State: A Comparative Analysis of Italy and Germany* (Cambridge, 1995)

Delphy, Christine, 'Les Origines du Mouvement de Libération des Femmes en France', *Nouvelles Questions Féministes*, 16/18 (1991)

Deslippe, Dennis A., ' "Do Whites Have Rights?": White Detroit Policemen and "Reverse Discrimination" Protests in the 1970s', *Journal of American History*, 91, 3 (2004)

Devlin, Bernadette, *The Price of my Soul* (1969)

Doggett, Peter, *There's a Riot Going On: Revolutionaries, Rock Stars and the Rise and Fall of the 60s Counter-Culture* (2008)

Donoughue, Bernard, *Downing Street Diary: With Harold Wilson in No. 10* (2006)

Dressen, Marnix, *De l'Amphi à l'Établi: Les Étudiants Maoistes à l'Usine, 1967–1989* (2000)

Droit, Michel, *Les Feux du Crépuscule: Journal 1968–1969–1970* (1977)

Dubois, Mathieu, *Génération Politique: Les 'Années 68' dans les Jeunesses des Partis Politiques en France et en RFA* (2014)

Dudziak, Mary L., *Cold War Civil Rights: Race and the Image of American Democracy* (Princeton, 2000)

Duhé, Gregory, 'The FBI and Students for a Democratic Society at the University of New Orleans, 1968–1971', *Louisiana History: The Journal of the Louisiana Historical Association*, 43, 1 (2002)

Dutschke, Rudi, *Students and the Revolution* (1971)

Earl, Jennifer, Soule, Sarah A., and McCarthy, John D., 'Protest under Fire? Explaining the Policing of Protest', *American Sociological Review*, 68, 4 (2003)

Eley, Geoff, *A Crooked Line: From Cultural History to the History of Society* (Ann Arbor, MI, 2005)

Ellis, Richard J., 'Romancing the Oppressed: The New Left and the Left Out', *The Review of Politics*, 58, 1 (1996)

English, Richard, *Armed Struggle: The History of the IRA* (Oxford, 2003)

Epistémon (pseudonym for Didier Anzieu), *Ces Idées qui ont Ébranlé la France: Nanterre, Novembre 1967–Juin 1968* (1968)

Ergas, Yasmine, '1968–79. Feminism and the Italian Party System: Women's Politics in a Decade of Turmoil', *Comparative Politics*, 14, 3 (1982)

Eribon, Didier, *Michel Foucault (1926–1984)* (1989)

Eynon, Bret, 'Community in Motion: The Free Speech Movement, Civil Rights, and the Roots of the New Left', *The Oral History Review*, 17, 1 (1989)

Fabre-Luce, Alfred, *J'ai Vécu Plusieurs Siècles* (1974)

Fairfield, Richard, *Communes USA* (New York, 1972)

Falcon, Priscilla, 'Only Strong Women Stayed: Women Workers and the National Floral Workers Strike, 1968–1969', *Frontiers: A Journal of Women's Studies*, 24, 2/3 (2003)

Farrell, James, *The Spirit of the 60s: Making Postwar Radicalism* (New York, 1997)

Farrell, Michael et al, 'Discussion on the Strategy of People's Democracy', *New Left Review*, 1, 55 (May–June 1969)

Favretto, Ilaria, 'Rough Music and Factory Protest in Post-1945 Italy', *Past and Present*, 228, 1 (2015)

Ferguson, Niall, *Kissinger, 1923–1968: The Idealist* (2015)

Ferry, Luc, and Renaut, Alain, *La Pensée 68: Essai sur l'Anti-Humanisme Contemporain* (1985)

Flacks, Richard, 'Social and Cultural Meanings of Student Revolt: Some Informal Comparative Observations', *Social Problems*, 17, 3 (1970)

Foccart, Jacques, *Le Général en Mai: Journal de l'Élysée*, vol. II: *1968– 1969* (1998)

Foley, Michael S., *Confronting the War Machine: Draft Resistance during the Vietnam War* (Chapel Hill, NC, 2003)

Foot, Paul, *The Rise of Enoch Powell* (1969)

Fouchet, Christian, *Mémoires d'Hier et de Demain*, vol. I: *Au Service du Général de Gaulle: Londres 1940, Varsovie 1945, Alger 1962, Mai 1968* (1971)

Fraser, Ronald, with Bertaux, Daniel, Eynon, Bret, Grele, Ronald, Le Wita, Béatrix, Linhart, Danièle, Passerini, Luisa, Staadt, Jochen and Tröger, Annemarie, *1968: A Student Generation in Revolt* (1988)

Freeman, Jo, *The Politics of Women's Liberation: A Case Study of an Emerging Social Movement and its Relation to the Policy Process* (1975)

Freeman, Joshua B., 'Hardhats: Construction Workers, Manliness, and the 1970 Pro-War Demonstrations', *Journal of Social History*, 26, 4 (1993)

—, *American Empire: The Rise of a Global Power, the Democratic Revolution at Home, 1945–2000* (New York, 2012)

Frey, Matthias, *Postwall German Cinema: History, Film History and Cinephilia* (2013)

Furlough, Ellen, 'Packaging Pleasures: Club Méditerranée and French Consumer Culture, 1950–1968', *French Historical Studies*, 18, 1 (1993)

Gales, Kathleen E., 'A Campus Revolution', *British Journal of Sociology*, 17, 1 (1966)

Gastaut, Yvan, 'Les Bidonvilles, Lieux d'Exclusion et de Marginalité en France durant les Trente Glorieuses', *Cahiers de la Méditerranée*, 69 (2004)

Geismar, Alain, *Mon Mai 1968* (2008)

Georgi, Frank, ' "Le Pouvoir est dans la Rue": 30 Mai 1968 la Manifestation Gaulliste des Champs-Élysées', *Vingtième Siècle, Revue d'Histoire*, 48 (1995)

—, 'Jeux d'Ombres: Mai, le Mouvement Social et l'Autogestion (1968– 2008)', *Vingtième Siècle, Revue d'Histoire*, 98 (2008)

Gerassi, John, *Talking with Sartre: Conversations and Debates* (New Haven, CT, 2009)

Germain, Rosie, 'Reading the Second Sex in 1950s America', *Historical Journal*, 56, 4 (2013)

—, 'The British and American Reception of French Existentialism, 1939–1972' (PhD, Cambridge University, 2013)

Giesbert, Franz-Olivier, *Jacques Chirac* (1987)

Gildea, Robert, Mark, James, and Warring, Anette (eds.), *Europe's 1968: Voices of Revolt* (Oxford, 2013)

Gildea, Robert, Mark, James, and Pas, Niek, 'European Radicals and the "Third World": Imagined Solidarities and Radical Networks, 1958–73', *Cultural and Social History*, 8, 4 (2011)

Ginsborg, Paul, *A History of Contemporary Italy: Society and Politics, 1943–1980* (1990)

Goldman, Pierre, *Souvenirs Obscurs d'un Juif Polonais Né en France* (1975)

Gordon, Daniel A., 'A Mediterranean New Left? Comparing and Contrasting the French PSU and the Italian PSIUP', *Contemporary European History*, 19, 4 (2010)

Gorman, Robert, *Michael Harrington: Speaking American* (New York, 1995)

Gormley, Joe, *Battered Cherub* (1982)

Goupil, Romain, interview, *Esprit*, 242 (1998)

Graham, Gael, *Young Activists: American High School Students in the Age of Protest* (DeKalb, IL, 2006)

Granberg, Donald, and Campbell, Keith E., 'Certain Aspects of Religiosity and Orientations toward the Vietnam War among Missouri Undergraduates', *Sociology of Religion*, 34, 1 (1973)

Grappin, Pierre, *L'Île aux Peupliers. De la Résistance à Mai 68: Souvenirs du Doyen de Nanterre* (Nancy, 1993)

Grimaud, Maurice, *En Mai, Fais ce qu'il te Plaît: Le Préfet de Police de Mai 68 Parle* (1977)

Gruel, Louis, *La Rébellion de 68: Une Relecture Sociologique* (Rennes, 2004)

Guilhaumou, Jacques, 'Mémoires d'un Étudiant en Mai 1968: Le Flux des Manifestations et le Protagoniste de l'Événement', *Le Mouvement Social*, 233 (2010)

Hale, Christopher, *Massacre in Malaya: Exposing Britain's My Lai* (2013)

Hall, Eric Allen, ' "I Guess I'm Becoming More and More Militant": Arthur Ashe and the Black Freedom Movement, 1961–1968', *Journal of African American History*, 96, 4 (2011)

Hall, Stuart, 'The Great Moving Right Show', *Marxism Today*, January 1979

Hall, Stuart, Critcher, Chas, Jefferson, Tony, Clarke, John, and Roberts, Brian (eds.), *Policing the Crisis: Mugging, the State and Law and Order* (this edn, 2013)

Halliwell, Martin, and Withan, Nick (eds.), *Reframing 1968: American Politics, Protest and Identity* (Edinburgh, 2018)

Halsey, A.H., and Marks, Stephen, 'British Student Politics', Daedalus, 97, 1 (1968)

Hamilton, Scott, *The Crisis of Theory: E.P. Thompson, the New Left and Postwar British Politics* (Manchester, 2011)

Hammond, Phillip E., and Mitchell, Robert E., 'Segmentation of Radicalism: The Case of the Protestant Campus Minister', *American Journal of Sociology*, 71, 2 (1965)

Haworth, Rachel, 'Representations of 1968 in French Popular Music: The Case of Dominique Grange', *Modern and Contemporary France*, 16, 2 (2008)

Hay, Roy, and McLauchlan, John, 'The Oral History of Upper Clyde Shipbuilders: A Preliminary Report', *Oral History*, 2, 1 (1974)

Hayden, Tom, *Reunion: A Memoir* (this edn, 1989)

—, *Radical Nomad: C. Wright Mills and his Times* (Boulder, CO, 2006)

Hazareesingh, Sudhir, *In the Shadow of the General: Modern France and the Myth of de Gaulle* (Oxford, 2012)

Healey, Denis, *The Time of My Life* (this edn, 1990)

Heffer, Simon, *Like the Roman: The Life of Enoch Powell* (1998)

Heineman, Kenneth J., *Campus Wars: The Peace Movement at American State Universities in the Vietnam Era* (New York, 1993)

HMSO, Report from the Select Committee on Education and Science, Session 1968–69, *Student Relations*, 7 vols. (1969)

Hobsbawm, Eric, *Interesting Times: A Twentieth-Century Life* (2002)

Hoch, Paul, and Schoenbach, Vic, *LSE: The Natives Are Restless: A Report on Student Power in Action* (1969)

Hocquenghem, Guy, *Lettre Ouverte à Ceux qui Sont Passés du Col Mao au Rotary* (1986)

—, *L'Amphithéâtre des Morts* (1994)

Hoefferle, Caroline, 'Just at Sunrise: The Sunrise Communal Farm in Rural Mid-Michigan, 1971–1978', *Michigan Historical Review*, 23, 1 (1997)

—, *British Student Activism in the Long Sixties* (2012)

Horn, Gerd-Rainer, *The Spirit of '68: Rebellion in Western Europe and North America, 1956–1976* (Oxford, 2007)

—, *The Spirit of Vatican II: Western European Progressive Catholicism in the Long Sixties* (Oxford, 2015)

Horowitz, Daniel, 'Rethinking Betty Friedan and the Feminine Mystique: Labor Union Radicalism and Feminism in Cold War America', *American Quarterly*, 48, 1 (1996)

Huff, Christopher A., 'Radicals Between the Hedges: The Origins of the New Left at the University of Georgia and the 1968 Sit-In', *The Georgia Historical Quarterly*, 94, 2 (2010)

Hulsether, Mark, '"Christianity and Crisis" in the 1950s and Early 1960s: A Case Study in the Transformation of Liberal Protestant Social Thought', *The Journal of Presbyterian History*, 79, 2 (2001)

Isserman, Maurice, *The Other American: The Life of Michael Harrington* (New York, 2001)

Ives, Eric, Drummond, Diane K., and Schwarz, Leonard (eds.), *The First Civic University: Birmingham, 1880–1980* (Birmingham, 2000)

Jacka, Keith, Cox, Caroline, and Marks, John, *The Rape of Reason: The Corruption of the Polytechnic of North London* (Enfield, 1975)

Jackson, Julian, *Living in Arcadia: Homosexuality, Politics and Morality in France from the Liberation to Aids* (Chicago, 2009)

Jacobs, Ron, *The Way the Wind Blew: A History of the Weather Underground* (1997)

Jeffreys-Jones, Rhodri, *Peace Now!: American Society and the Ending of the Vietnam War* (New Haven, CT, 1999)

Jeffries, Hasan Kwame, 'SNCC, Black Power, and Independent Political Party Organizing in Alabama, 1964–1966', *Journal of African American History*, 91, 2 (2006)

Jeffries, Judson L. (ed.), *On the Ground: The Black Panther Party in Communities across America* (Jackson, MI, 2010)

Jenkins, Roy, *A Life at the Centre* (1991)

Joffrin, Laurent, *Mai 68: Histoire des Événements* (1988)

Johnson, Roberta Ann, 'The Prison Birth of Black Power', *Journal of Black Studies*, 5, 4 (1975)

Jones, Thai, *A Radical Line: From the Labor Movement to the Weather Underground, One Family's Century of Conscience* (New York, 2004)

Joseph, Peniel E., 'The Black Power Movement, Democracy and America in the King Years', *American Historical Review*, 114, 4 (2009)

Julia, Dominique, 'Le Mouvement Étudiant', *Études* (June–July, 1968)

Julliard, Jacques, interview with Patrick Fridenson, *Le Mouvement Social*, 223 (2008)

Kane, John J., 'Civil Rights in Northern Ireland', *The Review of Politics*, 33, 1 (1971)

Kasinsky, Renée, *Refugees from Militarism* (New Brunswick, NJ, 1976)

Keane, John, *Vaclav Havel: A Political Tragedy in Six Acts* (1999)

Kenny, Anthony, *A Path from Rome* (Oxford, this edn, 1986)

Kissinger, Henry, *The White House Years* (1979)

Klarsfeld, Beate and Serge, *Mémoires* (2015)

Klimke, Martin, *The Other Alliance: Student Protest in West Germany and the United States in the Global Sixties* (Princeton, 2010)

Kornetis, Kostis, *Children of the Dictatorship: Student Resistance, Cultural Politics, and the 'Long 1960s' in Greece* (2013)

Kriegel, Annie, *Ce que j'ai Cru Comprendre* (1991)

Krieger, Susan, *Hip Capitalism* (1979)

Krivine, Alain, *Ça te Passera avec l'Âge* (2006)

Kundnani, Hans, *Utopia or Auschwitz: Germany's 1968 Generation and the Holocaust* (2009)

Kurlansky, Mark, *1968: The Year that Rocked the World* (1998)

Kusch, Frank, *Battleground Chicago: The Police and the 1968 Democratic National Convention* (Chicago, 2004)

Kutschke, Beate and Norton, Barley (eds.), *Music and Protest in 1968* (Cambridge, 2013)

Laing, Adrian, *R.D. Laing: A Biography* (1994)

Lallement, Bernard, *'Libé', l'Oeuvre Impossible de Sartre* (2004)

Landron, Olivier, *À la Droite du Christ: Les Catholiques Traditionnels en France depuis le Concile Vatican II, 1965–2015* (2015)

Lang, Clarence, 'Between Civil Rights and Black Power in the Gateway City: The Action Committee to Improve Opportunities for Negroes (Action), 1964–1975', *Journal of Social History*, 37, 3 (2004)

Langeois, Christian, *Henri Krasucki, 1924–2003* (2012)

Layerle, Sébastien, 'En l'Autre Bord: Filmer les Forces de l'Opposition à Mai 68', *Le Mouvement Social*, 223 (2008)

Le Dantec, Jean-Pierre, 'D'où Vient l'Établissement', *Les Temps Modernes*, 684–5 (2015)

Le Garrec, Jean, *Une Vie à Gauche* (2006)

Le Goff, Jean-Pierre, *La Fin du Village: Une Histoire Française* (2012)

Lever, Janet, and Schwartz, Pepper, *Women at Yale: Liberating a College Campus* (New York, 1971)

Levine, Donald, 'Sociology Confronts Student Protest', *The School Review*, 78, 4 (1970)

Levy, Peter B., *The New Left and Labor in the 1960s* (Urbana, IL, 1994)

Lichter, Robert S., and Rothman, Stanley, 'Jews on the Left: The Student Movement Reconsidered', *Polity*, 14, 2 (1981)

Lieberman, Robbie, *Prairie Power: Voices of 1960s Midwestern Student Protest* (Columbia, MO, 2004)

Linhart, Robert, *L'Établi* (1978/1981)

Linhart, Virginie, *Volontaires pour l'Usine: Vies d'Établis, 1967–1977* (1994, 2010)

—, *Le Jour où Mon Père s'est Tu* (2008)

Logan, R.F.L., and Goldberg, E.M., 'Rising Eighteen in a London Suburb: A Study of Some Aspects of the Life and Health of Young Men', *British Journal of Sociology*, 4, 4 (1953)

Long, Imogen, 'Writing Gaullist Feminism: Françoise Parturier's Open Letters, 1968–1974', *Modern and Contemporary France*, 19, 3 (2011)

Lougarot, Gisèle, *Pays Basque Nord: Mai 68 en Mémoires* (Bayonne, 2008)

Lumley, Robert, *States of Emergency: Cultures of Revolt in Italy from 1968 to 1978* (1990)

Lyons, Paul, *The People of this Generation: The Rise and Fall of the New Left in Philadelphia* (Philadelphia, PA, 2003)

Maeda, Darryl J., 'Black Panthers, Red Guards, and Chinamen: Constructing Asian American Identity through Performing Blackness, 1969–1972', *American Quarterly*, 57, 4 (2005)

Mammone, Andrea, 'The Transnational Reaction to 1968: Neo-Fascist Fronts and Political Cultures in France and Italy', *Contemporary European History*, 17, 2 (2008)

Maney, Gregory, 'Transnational Mobilization and Civil Rights in Northern Ireland', *Social Problems*, 47, 2 (2000)

Mankoff, Milton, and Flacks, Richard, 'The Changing Social Base of the American Student Movement', *The Annals of the American Academy of Political and Social Science*, 395 (1971)

Manotti, Dominique, 'Roman Noir', *Le Mouvement Social*, 219–20 (2007)

Marcellin, Raymond, *L'Ordre Public et les Groupes Révolutionnaires* (1969)

Margairaz, Michel, and Tartakowsky, Danielle (eds.), *1968, entre Libération et Libéralisation: La Grande Bifurcation* (Rennes, 2010)

Markovits, Andrei, *The Politics of West German Trade Unions: Strategies of Class and Interest Representation in Growth and Crisis* (Cambridge, 1986)

Martin, Roger, *Patron de Droit Divin* (1984)

Marwick, Arthur, *The Sixties: Cultural Revolution in Britain, France, Italy and the United States, c.1958–c.1974* (Oxford, 1998)

Massu, Jacques, *Baden 68: Souvenirs d'une Fidélité Gaulliste* (1983)

Maurin, Eric, and McNally, Sandra, 'Vive la Révolution! Long-Term Educational Returns of 1968 to the Angry Students', *Journal of Labor Economics*, 26, 1 (2008)

McAdam, Doug, 'The Biographical Consequences of Activism', *American Sociological Review*, 54, 5 (1989)

McGrogan, Manus, 'Vive la Révolution and the Example of Lotta Continua: The Circulation of Ideas and Practices Between the Left Militant Worlds of France and Italy Following May '68', *Modern and Contemporary France*, 18, 3 (2010)

McLaughlin, Malcolm, *The Long Hot Summer of 1967: Urban Rebellion in America* (2014)

McMillian, John, ' "Our Founder, the Mimeograph Machine": Participatory Democracy in Students for a Democratic Society's Print Culture', *Journal for the Study of Radicalism*, 2, 2 (2009)

Mercer, Ben, 'The Paperback Revolution: Mass Circulation Books and the Cultural Origins of 1968 in Western Europe', *Journal of the History of Ideas*, 72, 4 (2011)

Mercier, Charles, 'René Rémond à Nanterre en 1968', *Vingtième Siècle, Revue d'Histoire*, 104 (2009)

Merle, Robert, *Derrière la Vitre* (1970)

Mershon, Carol A., 'Between Workers and Union: Factory Councils in Italy', *Comparative Politics*, 21, 2 (1989)

Mewes, Horst, 'The German New Left', *New German Critique*, 1 (1973)

Milkis, Sidney M., and Mileur, Jerome M. (eds.), *The Great Society and the High Tide of American Liberalism* (Amherst, MA, 2005)

Miller, James, *Democracy is in the Street: From Port Huron to the Siege of Chicago* (New York, 1987)

Minces, Juliette, 'Réflexions Autour du "Journal de la Commune Étudiante"', *L'Homme et la Société*, 16, 1 (1970)

Mitterrand, François, *Lettres à Anne, 1962–1995* (2016)

Mohandesi, Salar, ' "Becoming One with the People": L'Établi Américain Hier et Aujourd'hui', *Les Temps Modernes*, 684–5 (2015)

Morazé, Charles, *Un Historien Engagé: Mémoires* (2007)

Morin, Edgar, *Autocritique* (1959)

—, *Journal, 1962–1987* (2012)

Nelson, Alondra, *Body and Soul: The Black Panther Party and the Fight Against Medical Discrimination* (Minneapolis, MN, 2013)

Neville, Richard, *Hippie Hippie Shake* (1995)

Neville Brown, L., 'Student Protest in England', *The American Journal of Comparative Law*, 17, 3 (1969)

Nicolet, Claude, *Pierre Mendès France ou le Métier de Cassandra* (1959)

Nivet, Philippe, 'Maurice Grimaud et Mai 1968', *Histoire@Politique*, 27 (2015)

Noiriel, Gérard, *Penser Avec, Penser Contre: Itinéraire d'un Historien* (2003)

Nora, Pierre (ed.), *Essais d'Ego-Histoire* (1987)

Norman, Philip, *The Stones* (this edn, 1985)

Olmi, Jean-Claude, 'Les Lycéens contre l'Armée', *Esprit*, 424 (1973)

Paget, Karen M., 'From Stockholm to Leiden: The CIA's Role in the Formation of the International Student Conference', *Intelligence and National Security*, 18, 2 (2003)

—, *Patriotic Betrayal: The Inside Story of the CIA's Secret Campaign to Enroll American Students in the Crusade against Communism* (New Haven, CT, 2015)

Pagis, Julie, 'La Politisation d'Engagements Religieux: Retour sur une Matrice de l'Engagement en Mai 68 ', *Revue Française de Science Politique*, 60, 1 (2010)

—, *Mai 68, un Pavé dans leur Histoire* (2014)

Passerini, Luisa, *Autobiography of a Generation: Italy 1968* (Hanover, NH, 1996)

Passerini, Luisa, and Aymard, Anne-Marie, 'Le Mouvement de 1968 Comme Prise de Parole et Comme Explosion de la Subjectivité: Le Cas de Turin', *Le Mouvement Social*, 143 (1988)

Paulson, Darryl, and Stiff, Janet, 'An Empty Victory: The St Petersburg Sanitation Strike, 1968', *Florida Historical Quarterly*, 57, 4 (1979)

Payne, Cril, *Deep Cover: An FBI Agent Infiltrates the Radical Underground* (New York, 1979)

Pereira, N., and Schär, R. 'Soixante-Huitards Helvétiques: Étude Prosopographique', *Le Mouvement Social*, 239 (2012)

Perrot, Jean-Claude and Michelle, Rebérioux, Madeleine and Maitron, Jean, 'La Sorbonne par Elle-Même: Mai–Juin 1968', *Le Mouvement Social*, 64 (1968)

Peyrefitte, Alain, *C'était de Gaulle* (2002, first published 1994)

Phillips-Fein, Kim, *Invisible Hands: The Businessmen's Crusade Against the New Deal* (2009)

Piaget, Charles, *Lip. Charles Piaget et les Lip Racontent* (1973)

Pitt, Malcolm, *The World on our Backs: The Kent Miners and the 1972 Miners' Strike* (1979)

Pizzolato, Nicola, ' "I Terroni in Città": Revisiting Southern Migrants' Militancy in Turin's "Hot Autumn" ', *Contemporary European History*, 21, 4 (2012)

Porhel, Vincent, *Ouvriers Bretons: Conflits d'Usines, Conflits Identitaires en Bretagne dans les Années 1968* (Rennes, 2008)

Posner, Charles (ed.), *Reflections on the Revolution in France: 1968* (1970)

Power, Lisa, *No Bath but Plenty of Bubbles: An Oral History of the Gay Liberation Front, 1970–73* (1995)

Prazan, Michaël, *Pierre Goldman: Le Frère de l'Ombre* (2005)

Prince, Simon, 'The Global Revolt of 1968 and Northern Ireland', *Historical Journal*, 49, 3 (2006)

Prochasson, Christophe, *François Furet: Les Chemins de la Mélancolie* (2013)

Rae, John, *The Old Boys' Network: A Headmaster's Diaries, 1972–1986* (this edn, 2009)

Raguénès, Jean, *De Mai 68 à LIP: Un Dominicain au Coeur des Luttes* (2008)

Raskin, Eleanor, letter 10 May 1968, *Journal of American Studies*, 19, 2 (1985)

Raskin, Jonah, *Out of the Whale: Growing up in the American Left* (New York, 1974)

Rauch, Marie-Ange, *Le Théâtre en France en 1968: Crise d'une Histoire; Histoire d'une Crise* (2008)

Rauzy, Antoine, 'L'Apparition et l'Extension des Comités de Soldats en France dans les Années 70 (Mai 1974–Mars 1976)', History MA (Paris, 1999)

Reeves, Michelle, ' "Obey the Rules or Get Out", Ronald Reagan's 1966 Gubernatorial Campaign and the "Trouble in Berkeley" ', *Southern California Quarterly*, 92, 3 (2010)

Reichard, Richard, 'We Can't Hide and They Are Wrong: The Society for Homosexual Freedom and the Struggle for Recognition at Sacramento State College, 1969–1971', *Law and History Review*, 28, 3 (2010)

Reid, Donald, ' "Établissement": Working in the Factory to Make Revolution in France', *Radical History Review*, 88 (2004)

Reynolds, Chris, 'Understanding 1968 – the Case of Brest', *Modern and Contemporary France*, 16, 2 (2008)

—, *Sous les Pavés ... The Troubles: Northern Ireland, France and the European Collective Memory of 1968* (Frankfurt, 2014)

Reynolds, Sian, 'Dijon in May 1968: Local Politics, the Spectre of Anarchy and the "Silent Majority" ', *Modern and Contemporary France*, 16, 2 (2008)

Richard, Gilles, and Sainclivier, Jacqueline (eds.), *Les Partis à l'Épreuve de 68: L'Émergence de Nouveaux Clivages, 1971–1974* (Rennes, 2012)

Rioux, Jean-Pierre, 'Tombeau pour Mendès France', *Vingtième Siècle, Revue d'Histoire*, 2 (1984)

—, 'À Propos des Célébrations Décennales du Mai Français', *Vingtième Siècle, Revue d'Histoire*, 23 (1989)

Ritterband, Paul, 'Ethnic Power and the Public Schools: The New York City School Strike of 1968', *Sociology of Education*, 47, 2 (1974)

Rivenc, François, 'Quelques Réflexions sur l'Établissement en Usine', *Les Temps Modernes*, 684–5 (2015)

Robert, Frédéric, 'The Rhetoric of Social Movements: Differential Images of the Recruitment in Students for a Democratic Society (SDS), 1960–1965', *Revue Française d'Études Américaines*, 99 (2004)

Rocard, Michel, 'intervention', 'Table Ronde: Pierre Mendès France et Mai 68', *Matériaux pour l'Histoire de Notre Temps* 63, 1 (2001)

—, *Si la Gauche Savait: Entretiens avec Georges Marc Benamou* (2005)

Rogers, Bethany L., 'Teaching and Social Reform in the 1960s: Lessons from National Teacher Corps Oral Histories', *The Oral History Review*, 35, 1 (2008)

Rolin, Olivier, *Tigre en Papier* (2002)

Rondeau, Daniel, *L'Enthousiasme* (1988)

Rooke, Margaret, *Anarchy and Apathy: Student Unrest, 1968–1970* (1971)

Roos, Philip, 'A Comment on Student Protest', *American Sociological Review*, 35, 3 (1970)

Rorabaugh, W.J., *Berkeley at War: The 1960s* (Oxford, 1989)

—, *Kennedy and the Promise of the Sixties* (Cambridge, 2002)

Ross, Kristin, *May 68 and its Afterlives* (Chicago, 2002)

Rossinow, Doug, *The Politics of Authenticity: Liberalism, Christianity and the New Left in America* (New York, 1998)

Rouède, André, 'La Révolte des Lycéens', *Esprit*, 372 (1968)

Roussel, Éric, *Georges Pompidou* (1984)

—, *Pierre Mendès France* (2007)

Rowbotham, Sheila, *Promise of a Dream: Remembering the Sixties* (this edn, 2001)

—, 'Cleaners' Organizing in Britain from the 1970s: A Personal Account', *Antipode: A Radical Journal of Geography*, 38, 3 (2006)

Rudd, Mark, *Underground: My Life with SDS and the Weathermen* (New York, 2009)

Russier, Gabrielle, *Lettres de Prison* (1970)

Salper, Roberta, 'U.S. Government Surveillance and the Women's Liberation Movement, 1968–1973: A Case Study', *Feminist Studies*, 34, 3 (2008)

Saville, John, *Memoirs from the Left* (2003)

Scargill, Arthur, and Kahn, Peggy, *The Myth of Workers' Control* (Leeds, usually described as published in 1980 though obviously earlier than this)

Schelsky, Helmut, *Die skeptische Generation: Eine Soziologie der deutschen Jugend* (Cologne, 1957)

—, 'The Wider Setting of Disorder in the German Universities', *Minerva*, 10, 4 (1972)

Schilling, Britta, *Postcolonial Germany: Memories of Empire in a Decolonized Nation* (Oxford, 2014)

Schlesinger, Arthur M., Jr, *The Crisis of Confidence: Ideas, Power and Violence in America* (Boston, 1969)

—, *Robert Kennedy and His Times*, vol. II (Boston, 1978)

—, *Journals, 1952–2000* (2007)

Schnapp, Alain, and Vidal-Naquet, Pierre, *Journal de la Commune Étudiante: Textes et Documents, Novembre 1967–Juin 1968* (1969)

Schuman, Howard, and Scott, Jacqueline, 'Generations and Collective Memories', *American Sociological Review*, 54, 3 (1989)

Schuyler, Michael W., 'Ghosts in the White House: LBJ, RFK and the Assassination of JFK', *Presidential Studies Quarterly*, 17, 3 (1987)

Schwartz, Thomas Alan, *Lyndon Johnson and Europe: In the Shadow of Vietnam* (Cambridge, MA, 2003)

Sedgwick, Peter, 'Pseud Left Review', *International Socialism*, 25 (1966)

—, 'Victory for the Vietcong. Is it the Right Slogan?' *Labour Worker*, 5 August 1966

Sedlmaier, Alexander, and Malinowski, Stephen, '"1968": A Catalyst of Consumer Society', *Cultural and Social History*, 8, 2 (2011)

Seidman, Michael, 'Workers in a Repressive Society of Seductions: Parisian Metallurgists in May–June 1968', *French Historical Studies*, 18, 1 (1993)

Seiffert, Jeanette *'Marsch durch die Institutionen?': Die '68er' in der SPD* (Bonn, 2009)

Self, Robert, '"To Plan Our Liberation": Black Power and the Politics of Place in Oakland, California, 1965–1977', *Journal of Urban History*, 26, 6 (2000)

Seligmann, Françoise, *Liberté, Quand tu nous Tiens . . .* vol. II: *L'Espoir et la Honte: Mendès, l'Algérie, Mai 68* (2003)

Serenelli, Sofia, 'Private 1968 and the Margins: The Vicolo Cassini's Community in Macerata, Italy', *Memory Studies*, 6, 1 (2013)

Shepherd, Robert, *Enoch Powell* (1996)

Shesol, Jeff, *Mutual Contempt: Lyndon Johnson, Robert Kennedy and the Feud that Defined a Decade* (New York, 1997)

Shey, Thomas, 'Sex and Family Planning in Denmark and in Danish Communes', *International Journal of Sociology of the Family*, 7, 1 (1977)

Short, Philip, *Mitterrand: A Study in Ambiguity* (2013)

Simon, Catherine, *Algérie, les Années Pieds-Rouges: Des Rêves de l'Indépendance au Désenchantement (1962–1969)* (2009)

Sjøli, Hans Peter, 'Maoism in Norway', *Scandinavian Journal of History*, 33, 4 (2008)

Skardhamar, Laura P., '"Real Revolution" in Kana Commune', *Scandinavian Journal of History*, 33, 4 (2008)

Small, Melvin, *Johnson, Nixon and the Doves* (New Brunswick, NJ, 1988)

Sommier, Isabelle, 'Mai 68: Sous les Pavés d'une Page Officielle', *Sociétés Contemporaines*, 20 (1994)

Stedman Jones, Gareth, interview with Eric Hobsbawm, *Marxism Today* (November 1986)

—, 'History and Theory: An English Story', *Historein*, 3 (2001)

Stern, Susan, *With the Weathermen: The Personal Journey of a Revolutionary Woman* (1975)

Stryker, Sean D., 'Knowledge and Power in the Students for a Democratic Society, 1960–1970', *Berkeley Journal of Sociology*, 38 (1993)

Sugrue, Thomas J., 'Affirmative Action from Below: Civil Rights, the Building Trades, and the Politics of Racial Equality in the Urban North, 1945–1969', *Journal of American History*, 91, 1 (2004)

—, *Sweet Land of Liberty: The Forgotten Struggle for Civil Rights in the North* (New York, 2008)

Supple, Barry, *Doors Open* (Cambridge, 2009)

Suran, Justin David, 'Coming Out Against the War: Antimilitarism and the Politicization of Homosexuality in the Era of Vietnam', *American Quarterly*, 53, 3 (2001)

Tarrow, Sidney, *Democracy and Disorder: Protest and Politics in Italy, 1965–1975* (Oxford, 1989)

Taylor, J.D., 'The Party's Over? The Angry Brigade, the Counter-Culture and the British New Left, 1967–1972', *Historical Journal*, 58, 3 (2015)

Taylor, Peter, *Behind the Mask: The IRA and Sinn Fein* (1997)

Thompson, E.P., *Writing by Candlelight* (1980)

Thompson, Ruth Anne, ' "A Taste of Student Power": Protest at the University of Tennessee, 1964–1970', *Tennessee Historical Quarterly*, 57, 1 (1998)

Todd, Olivier, *Malraux: Une Vie* (2001)

Tolomelli, Marica, '1968: Formen der Interaktion zwischen Studenten- und Arbeiterbewegung in Italien und der Bundesrepublik', *Geschichte und Gesellschaft*, Sonderheft 17 (1998)

—, 'De l'Universités |sic| à l'Usine: Italie et Allemagne (1968–1973)', *Les Temps Modernes*, 684–5 (2015)

Tröger, Annemarie, 'Les Enfants du Tertiaire: Le Mouvement Étudiant en RFA de 1961 à 1969', *Le Mouvement Social*, 143 (1988)

Turpin, Frédéric, *Jacques Foccart: Dans l'Ombre du Pouvoir* (2015)

Tyler May, Elaine, *Homeward Bound: American Families in the Cold War Era* (this edn, 2008)

Varon, Jeremy, *Bringing the War Home: The Weather Underground, the Red Army Faction and Revolutionary Violence in the Sixties and Seventies* (Berkeley, CA, 2004)

Veyne, Paul, *Et dans l'Éternité je ne m'Ennuierai Pas: Souvenirs* (2014)

Vigna, Xavier, 'Les Ouvriers de Denain et de Longwy Face aux Licencie-ments (1978–1979)', *Vingtième Siècle, Revue d'Histoire*, 84 (2004)

—, *L'Insubordination Ouvrière dans les Années 68: Essai d'Histoire Poli-tique des Usines* (Rennes, 2007)

—, 'Préserver l'Ordre Usinier en France à la Fin des Années 68', *Agone*, 50 (2013)

Vigna, Xavier, and Zancarini-Fournel, Michelle, 'Les Rencontres Improba-bles dans "les Années 68"', *Vingtième Siècle, Revue d'Histoire*, 101 (2009)

Vincendeau, Ginette, *Jean-Pierre Melville: An American in Paris* (2003)

Von der Goltz, Anna, 'Generations of 68ers: Age-Related Constructions of Identity and Germany's "1968"', *Social and Cultural History*, 8, 4 (2011)

Waldegrave, William, *A Different Kind of Weather: A Memoir* (2015)

Wallace, Christine, *Germaine Greer: Untamed Shrew* (1997)

Wallach, Jennifer Jensen, 'Replicating History in a Bad Way? White Activ-ists and Black Power in SNCC's Arkansas Project', *Arkansas Historical Quarterly*, 67, 3 (2008)

Waters, Rob, 'Black Power on the Telly: America, Television, and Race in 1960s and 1970s Britain', *Journal of British Studies*, 54, 4 (2015)

Wells, Tom, *The War Within: America's Battle over Vietnam* (Berkeley, CA, 1994)

Whalen, Jack, and Flacks, Richard, *Beyond the Barricades: The Sixties Generation Grows Up* (Philadelphia, PA, 1989)

Wiazemsky, Anne, *Une Année Studieuse* (2012)

Widgery, David (ed.), *The Left in Britain, 1956–1968* (1976)

Williams, Shirley, *Climbing the Bookshelves* (2009)

Wood, James L., 'Remembering the Free Speech Movement: Notes of an Observer', *Sociological Focus*, 13, 3 (1980)

Wright Mills, C., *Letters and Autobiographical Writings*, edited by Kath-ryn Mills and Pamela Mills (2000)

Wyatt, David, *When America Turned: Reckoning with 1968* (Amherst MA, 2014)

Zantovsky, Michael, *Havel: A Life* (2014)

Ziegler, Philip, *Wilson: The Authorized Biography* (1993)

WEBSITES

'Back to Rudi Dutschke's Pram' in *Sightandsight*: 'Let's talk European', 7 January 2008, http://www.signandsight.com/features/1633.html

http://www.margaretthatcher.org

www.leeds.ac.uk/reporter/may68/protest.htm

https://www.cia.gov/library/readingroom/document/0002987248

Interview with Karsten Voigt by Harry Kreisler, 2001, http://globetrotter
.berkeley.edu/people/Voigt/voigt-cono.html

http://www.birmingham.ac.uk/Documents/college-artslaw/history/cccs/
Interview-Transcripts/Dick-Atkinson.pdf

ARCHIVES

London National Archives
CAB 128/44/51
CRIM 1/5256
DPP 2/4379
DPP 2/5018/4
DPP 2/4548
ED 207/125
FCO 7/863
FCO 13/58
FCO 21/215
FCO 9/252
FCO 33/85
FCO 68/128
FO 1042/125
FO 1042/126
HO 325/104
MEPO 2/10962
MEPO 2/10986
MEPO 26/73
PREM 13/2653

Cambridge, Churchill College
Hailsham papers, HLSM 2/42/2/57 and HLSM 2/22/17

Cambridge University Library
Needham papers, K 323

London, King's College
Archives of King's College Students' Union
KU/M2/7

Stafford, Staffordshire Public Record Office
D 4490/48

Warwick University, Modern Records Centre
Archives of National Union of Students, MSS 280/51/3

Paris, Institut d'Études Politiques
Archives of Maurice Grimaud

Notes

INTRODUCTION

1. Olivier Assayas, interviewed in *Eye for Film* (March/April 2013).
2. Daniel Rondeau, *L'Enthousiasme* (1988).
3. Jonah Raskin, *Out of the Whale: Growing up in the American Left* (New York, 1974); Thai Jones, *A Radical Line: From the Labor Movement to the Weather Underground, One Family's Century of Conscience* (New York, 2004).
4. Daniel Bertaux, Danièle Linhart, and Béatrix Le Wita, 'Mai 1968 et la Formation de Générations Politiques en France', *Le Mouvement Social*, 143 (1988), pp. 75–89.
5. Marica Tolomelli, '1968: Formen der Interaktion zwischen Studenten- und Arbeiterbewegung in Italien und der Bundesrepublik', *Geschichte und Gesellschaft*, Sonderheft 17 (1998), pp. 82–100.
6. Luisa Passerini, *Autobiography of a Generation: Italy, 1968* (Hanover, NH, 1996), p. 60.

1. WORDS AND 'THE THING': DEFINING 68

1. Stafford, Staffordshire Public Record Office (Staff), D4490/48, letter from J.C.H., 20 November 1970.
2. Ibid., Powell to Patricia S., 12 April 1972.
3. Stuart Hall, 'The Great Moving Right Show', *Marxism Today*, January 1979.
4. Sean D. Stryker, 'Knowledge and Power in the Students for a Democratic Society, 1960–1970,' *Berkeley Journal of Sociology*, 38 (1993), pp. 89–138.
5. Charles Morazé, *Un Historien Engagé: Mémoires* (2007), p. 305.

6. Intervention by Michel Rocard, 'Table Ronde: Pierre Mendès France et Mai 68', *Matériaux pour l'Histoire de Notre Temps*, 63, 1 (2001), pp. 161–79.

7. Régis Debray, *Modeste Contribution aux Discours et Cérémonies Officielles du Dixième Anniversaire* (1978), p. 49.

8. Publisher's introduction, Michael (Bommi) Baumann, *Terror or Love: The Personal Account of a West German Urban Guerrilla* (1979), p. 12.

9. Jeremy Varon, *Bringing the War Home: The Weather Underground, the Red Army Faction and Revolutionary Violence in the Sixties and Seventies* (Berkeley, CA, 2004), p. 46.

10. Richard Crossman, *The Diaries of a Cabinet Minister*, vol. II: *Lord President of the Council and Leader of the House of Commons, 1966–68* (1976), p. 700, entry for 10 March 1968.

11. Sheila Rowbotham, *Promise of a Dream: Remembering the Sixties* (this edn, 2001), p. 162.

12. Lisa Power, *No Bath but Plenty of Bubbles: An Oral History of the Gay Liberation Front, 1970–73* (1995).

13. Martin Klimke, *The Other Alliance: Student Protest in West Germany and the United States in the Global Sixties* (Princeton, 2010), p. 14.

14. Tom Hayden, *Reunion: A Memoir* (this edn, 1989), p. 93.

15. https://www.cia.gov/library/readingroom/document/0002987248

16. Pierre Grappin, *L'Île aux Peupliers. De la Résistance à Mai 68: Souvenirs du Doyen de Nanterre* (Nancy, 1993), p. 281.

17. Luisa Passerini, *Autobiography of a Generation: Italy, 1968* (Hanover NH, 1996), p. 109.

18. Richard Fairfield, *Communes USA* (New York, 1972), p. 3.

19. *The Times*, 31 October 1968.

20. Daniel Cohn-Bendit, *Nous l'Avons Tant Aimée, la Révolution* (1986).

21. John Gerassi, *Talking with Sartre: Conversations and Debates* (New Haven, CT, 2009), p. 236. Sartre said of Cohn-Bendit: 'He was far from being brilliant, I didn't like him very much.'

22. Anna Cento Bull and Philip Cooke, *Ending Terrorism in Italy* (2013), p. 75.

23. Ron Jacobs, *The Way the Wind Blew: A History of the Weather Underground* (1997), p. 94.

24. Alain Schnapp and Pierre Vidal-Naquet, *Journal de la Commune Étudiante: Textes et Documents, Novembre 1967–Juin 1968* (1969); Jean-Claude and Michelle Perrot, Madeleine Rebérioux and Jean Maitron, 'La Sorbonne par Elle-Même: Mai–Juin 1968', *Le Mouvement Social*, 64 (1968).

25. One journal devoted an issue largely to its own role in 1968, *Le Mouvement Social*, 223 (2008).

26. Geoff Eley, *A Crooked Line: From Cultural History to the History of Society* (Ann Arbor, MI, 2005), pp. 4, 53.

27. London National Archives (NA) HO 325/104, Metropolitan Police, Special Branch Reports dated 22 and 26 February 1968.

28. Sudhir Hazareesingh, *In the Shadow of the General: Modern France and the Myth of de Gaulle* (Oxford, 2012), p. 185.

29. Marc Ferro, *Mes Histoires Parallèles: Entretiens avec Isabelle Veyrat-Masson* (2011), p. 338.

30. Eric Hobsbawm, *Interesting Times: A Twentieth-Century Life* (2002), p. 250.

31. Scott Hamilton, *The Crisis of Theory: E.P. Thompson, the New Left and Postwar British Politics* (Manchester, 2011), p. 125.

32. Julie Pagis, *Mai 68: Un Pavé dans Leur Histoire* (2014), p. 81.

33. Robbie Lieberman, *Prairie Power: Voices of 1960s Midwestern Student Protest* (Columbia, MO, 2004), p. 76.

34. Pagis, *Mai 68*, p. 31.

35. Nicolas Daum, *Mai 68: Des Révolutionnaires dans un Village Parisien, 20 Ans Après* (1988). This book was published in a slightly revised version, which threw more light on the long-term careers of some of its interviewees in *Mai 68 Raconté par des Anonymes* (2008).

36. Myriam Chermette and Anne-Sophie Lechevallier, 'Des Droites: Postures et Récits de Réactions', in Agnès Callu (ed.), *Le Mai 68 des Historiens: Entre Identités Narratives et Histoire Orale* (2010), pp. 159–68, p. 164.

37. Annie Kriegel, *Ce que j'ai Cru Comprendre* (1991), p. 710.

38. Jean-Jacques Becker, *Un Soir de l'Été 1942 . . . Souvenirs d'un Historien* (2009), pp. 284–305.

39. Paul Veyne, *Et dans l'Éternité je ne m'Ennuierai Pas: Souvenirs* (2014), p. 176.

40. Maurice Agulhon, 'Vu des Coulisses', in Pierre Nora (ed.), *Essais d'Ego-Histoire* (1987), pp. 9–59, p. 37.

41. Alain Krivine, *Ça te Passera avec l'Âge* (2006), p. 142.

42. Robert Linhart, *L'Établi* (1978/1981), p. 83.

43. Virginie Linhart, *Le Jour où Mon Père s'est Tu* (2008); for her aunt's comments see *Le Monde*, 16 May 2008.

44. Antoine de Baecque, 'Reprise d'Hervé le Roux', in Philippe Artières and Michelle Zancarini-Fournel (eds.), *68, Une Histoire Collective, 1962–1981* (2008), pp. 271–5.

45. William Waldegrave, *A Different Kind of Weather: A Memoir* (2015), pp. 71–84.

46. *The Times*, 25 April 1970.

47. Churchill College, Cambridge, HLSM 2/22/17, Waldegrave to Hailsham, 11 June 1968.

48. Thatcher Foundation website, 111380, Minutes of the Authority of Government Policy Group, 22 October 1975.

49. *The Times*, 20 March 1968.

50. Colin Crouch, *The Student Revolt* (1970), p. 68.

51. Anna von der Goltz, 'Generations of 68ers: Age-Related Constructions of Identity and Germany's "1968"', *Social and Cultural History*, 8, 4 (2011), pp. 473–91.

52. Andrea Mammone, 'The Transnational Reaction to 1968: Neo-Fascist Fronts and Political Cultures in France and Italy', *Contemporary European History*, 17, 2 (2008), pp. 213–36.

53. François Audigier, 'Le Malaise des Jeunes Gaullistes en Mai 68', *Vingtième Siècle, Revue d'Histoire* , 70 (2001), pp. 71–88.

54. Penelope Adams Moon, ' "Peace on Earth: Peace in Vietnam": The Catholic Peace Fellowship and Antiwar Witness, 1964–1976', *Journal of Social History*, 36, 4 (2003), pp. 1033–57.

55. Robert Gildea, James Mark and Niek Pas, 'European Radicals and the "Third World": Imagined Solidarities and Radical Networks, 1958–73', *Cultural and Social History*, 8, 4 (2011), pp. 449–71.

56. Julie Pagis, 'La Politisation d'Engagements Religieux: Retour sur une Matrice de l'Engagement en Mai 68', *Revue Française de Science Politique*, 60, 1 (2010), pp. 61–89.

57. Jean-Pierre le Goff, *La Fin du Village: Une Histoire Française* (2012), p. 182.

58. Olivier Landron, *À la Droite du Christ: Les Catholiques Traditionnels en France depuis le Concile Vatican II, 1965–2015* (2015).

59. NA CRIM 1/5256, summing up by Humphreys in trial of Paul Hoch and others for riot, 20 July 1970.

60. Beate Kutschke, 'In Lieu of an Introduction' in Beate Kutschke and Barley Norton (eds.), *Music and Protest in 1968* (Cambridge, 2013), pp. 1–11, p. 4, and Kailin R. Rubinoff, 'A Revolution in Sheep's Wool Stockings: Early Music and 1968', in ibid., pp. 237–54.

61. Kostis Kornetis, *Children of the Dictatorship: Student Resistance, Cultural Politics, and the 'Long 1960s' in Greece* (2013).

62. Yasmine Ergas, '1968–79. Feminism and the Italian Party System: Women's Politics in a Decade of Turmoil', *Comparative Politics*, 14, 3 (1982), pp. 253–79.

63. NA FCO 7/863, minute by Braithwaite, 20 June 1968.

64. NA FCO 9/252, report by Halford-MacLeod, 28 March 1968.

65. NA FCO 68/128, report on conference on 'Youth in Revolt' held in Trinidad and Tobago in 1969.

66. Staff, D4490/48, Powell to E., 17 May 1972.

67. Raymond Marcellin, *L'Ordre Public et les Groupes Révolutionnaires* (1969).

68. I am grateful to Lisa Bald for showing me her unpublished work on this topic.

69. NA PREM 13/2563, Reilly to FO, 29 May 1968.

70. Ibid., Reilly to FO, 22 May 1968.

71. Peter B. Levy, *The New Left and Labor in the 1960s* (Urbana, IL, 1994), p. 90.

72. NA FCO 13/58, memorandum on losses to the British Institute in Paris, Francis Scarfe, 22 June 1968.

73. NA MEPO 2/10962, statement by Sergeant Terry Kelley to Metropolitan Police, 22 August 1967.

74. Gareth Stedman Jones, 'History and Theory: An English Story', *Historein*, 3 (2001), pp. 103–24.

75. Laurent Chollet, 'Le LSD, les Hippies et la Californie', in Philippe Artières and Michelle Zancarini-Fournel (eds.), *68, une Histoire Collective, 1962–1981* (2008), pp. 80–85.

76. Guy Hocquenghem, *L'Amphithéâtre des Morts* (1994), p. 53.

77. Tony Benn, *Office without Power: Diaries, 1968–1972* (1988), p. 151, entry for 25 February 1969.

78. Crouch, *The Student Revolt*, p. 57.

79. NA PREM 13/2653, Reilly to FO, 22 May 1968.

80. Yair Auron, *Les Juifs d'Extrême Gauche en Mai 68: Une Génération Révolutionnaire Marquée par la Shoah* (1998).

81. Catherine Simon, *Algérie, les Années Pieds-Rouges: Des Rêves de l'Indépendance au Désenchantement (1962–1969)* (2009).

82. Hayden, *Reunion*, p. 207.

83. John Keane, *Vaclav Havel: A Political Tragedy in Six Acts* (1999), p. 184.

84. Michael Zantovsky, *Havel: A Life* (2104), p. 109.

85. Richard Neville, *Hippie Hippie Shake* (1995), p. 151.

86. Edgar Morin, *Journal, 1962–1987* (2012), pp. 852–3.

87. Gerassi, *Talking with Sartre*, p. 68.

88. Rosie Germain, 'The British and American Reception of French Existentialism, 1939–1972' (PhD, Cambridge University, 2013).

89. NA FCO 21/215.

90. Crouch, *The Student Revolt*, p. 72.

2. THE 68 GENERATION

1. Guy Hocquenghem, *Lettre Ouverte à Ceux qui Sont Passés du Col Mao au Rotary* (1986), p. 15.
2. Nancy Mitford, *The Spectator*, 30 May 1968.
3. Robert Gorman, *Michael Harrington: Speaking American* (New York, 1995), pp. xviii, xxi.
4. Adrian Laing, *R.D. Laing: A Biography* (1994), p. 140.
5. Alain Schnapp and Pierre Vidal-Naquet, *The French Student Uprising, November 1967–June 1968* (Boston, 1971).
6. Mary Ann Caws (ed.), *Maria Jolas, Woman of Action: A Memoir and Other Writings* (Columbia, SC, 2004). For Jolas's action see also London National Archives (NA) HO 325/104, report by Special Branch, 26 February 1968.
7. Gael Graham, *Young Activists: American High School Students in the Age of Protest* (DeKalb, IL, 2006), p. 5.
8. Sidney Tarrow, *Democracy and Disorder: Protest and Politics in Italy, 1965–1975* (Oxford, 1989), pp. 88–9.
9. Alain Peyrefitte, *C'était de Gaulle* (this edn, 2002), p. 1289. De Gaulle addressing ministers on 11 May 1966.
10. Philip Short, *Mitterrand: A Study in Ambiguity* (2013), p. 248.
11. Juliette Minces, 'Réflexions Autour du "Journal de la Commune Étudiante"', *L'Homme et la Société*, 16, 1 (1970), pp. 149–59.
12. Timothy S. Brown, *West Germany and the Global Sixties: The Anti-Authoritarian Revolt, 1962–1978* (Cambridge, 2013), p. 80.
13. Sheila Rowbotham, *Promise of a Dream: Remembering the Sixties* (this edn, 2001), p. 166.
14. Luisa Passerini, *Autobiography of a Generation: Italy, 1968* (Hanover, NH, 1996), pp. 23, 28.
15. Sheila Rowbotham, 'Cleaners' Organizing in Britain from the 1970s: A Personal Account', *Antipode: A Radical Journal of Geography*, 38, 3 (2006), pp. 608–25.
16. Nicholas Hatzfeld, 'Les Morts de Flins et Sochaux: De la Grève à la Violence Politique', in Philippe Artières and Michelle Zancarini-Fournel (eds.), *68, Une Histoire Collective, 1962–1981* (2008), pp. 322–5.
17. Nicolas Daum, *Mai 68: Des Révolutionnaires dans un Village Parisien, 20 Ans Après* (1988), interview with Michel, pp. 89–104.
18. Nuno Pereira and Renate Schär, 'Soixante-Huitards Helvétiques: Étude Prosopographique', *Le Mouvement Social*, 239 (2012), pp. 9–23.

19. Anna von der Goltz, 'Generations of 68ers: Age-Related Constructions of Identity and Germany's "1968"', *Social and Cultural History*, 8, 4 (2011), pp. 473–91.

20. Agnès Callu, 'La Socialisation des Historiens de l'Intra-Histoire au Profil Scientifique', in Agnès Callu (ed.), *Le Mai 68 des Historiens: Entre Identités Narratives et Histoire Orale* (2010), pp. 69–88, p. 74.

21. R.F.L. Logan and E.M. Goldberg, 'Rising Eighteen in a London Suburb: A Study of Some Aspects of the Life and Health of Young Men', *British Journal of Sociology*, 4, 4 (1953), pp. 323–45.

22. Interview with Romain Goupil, *Esprit*, 242 (1998), pp. 141–7.

23. *The Times*, 29 May 1968.

24. L. Neville Brown, 'Student Protest in England', *The American Journal of Comparative Law*, 17, 3 (1969), pp. 395–402.

25. Von der Goltz, 'Generations of 68ers'.

26. Michaël Prazan, *Pierre Goldman: Le Frère de l'Ombre* (2005), p. 31.

27. Elaine Tyler May, *Homeward Bound: American Families in the Cold War Era* (this edn, New York, 2008).

28. Yvan Gastaut, 'Les Bidonvilles, Lieux d'Exclusion et de Marginalité en France Durant les Trentes Glorieuses', *Cahiers de la Méditerranée*, 69 (2004), pp. 233–50.

29. Habiba Cohen, *Elusive Reform: The French Universities, 1968–1978* (Boulder, CO, 1978), p. 240.

30. Robert Linhart, *L'Établi* (1978/1981), p. 15.

31. It was reckoned that about a third of the 450,000 Portuguese workers who arrived in France between 1962 and 1968 were fleeing military service. See Gisèle Lougarot, *Pays Basque Nord: Mai 68 en Mémoires* (Bayonne, 2008), pp. 80–90.

32. Antoine Rauzy, 'L'Apparition et l'Extension des Comités de Soldats en France dans les Années 70 (Mai 1974–Mars 1976)', History MA (Paris, 1999).

33. Jean-Claude Olmi, 'Les Lycéens contre l'Armée', *Esprit*, 424 (1973), pp. 1201–10.

34. *The Times*, 20 December 1968.

35. Nicolas Daum, *Mai 68: Des Révolutionnaires dans un Village Parisien, 20 Ans Après* (1988), pp. 263–78.

36. Jean-Daniel Bénard, 'Les Relations entre le BN de l'UNEF et les Forces de Police en 1967–1968', in Roger Barralis and Jean-Claude Gillet (eds.), *Au Coeur des Luttes des Années Soixante, les Étudiants du PSU: Une Utopie Porteuse d'Avenir?* (2010), pp. 235–41, p. 41.

37. Eric Allen Hall, ' "I Guess I'm Becoming More and More Militant": Arthur Ashe and the Black Freedom Movement, 1961–1968', *Journal of African American History*, 96, 4 (2011), pp. 474–502.

38. Jacques Foccart, *Le Général en Mai: Journal de l'Élysée*, vol. II: 1968–1969 (1998), p. 215, entry for 20 June 1968.

39. Neville Brown, 'Student Protest in England'.

40. Mick Jagger expressed 'guarded' support for the Maoist Richard Deshayes who called for the 'liberation of pop'. Manus McGrogan, 'Vive la Révolution and the Example of Lotta Continua: The Circulation of Ideas and Practices Between the Left Militant Worlds of France and Italy Following May '68', *Modern and Contemporary France*, 18, 3 (2010), pp. 309–28.

41. Philip Norman, *The Stones* (this edn, 1985), p. 341.

42. Alan F. Moore, 'British Rock: The Short "1968" and the Long', in Beate Kutschke and Barley Norton (eds.), *Music and Protest in 1968* (Cambridge, 2013), pp. 154–70.

43. Virginie Linhart, *Volontaires pour l'Usine: Vies d'Établis, 1967–1977* (this edn, 2010), pp. 53, 115.

44. Rachel Haworth, 'Representations of 1968 in French Popular Music: The Case of Dominique Grange', *Modern and Contemporary France*, 16, 2 (2008), pp. 181–94.

45. Timothy S. Brown, 'Subcultures, Pop Music and Politics: Skinheads and "Nazi Rock" in England and Germany', *Journal of Social History*, 38, 1 (2004), pp. 157–78.

46. NA MEPO 26/73, transcript of John Moffatt's statement made to the press on 18 September 1969 and subsequent interrogation of Moffatt by Superintendent Cas, 21 September 1969.

47. Édouard Balladur, *L'Arbre de Mai: Chronique Alternée* (1978), p. 95.

48. Doug Rossinow, *The Politics of Authenticity: Liberalism, Christianity and the New Left in America* (New York, 1998), p. 166.

49. Tom Wells, *The War Within: America's Battle over Vietnam* (Berkeley, CA, 1994), p. 109.

50. Tessa Blackstone and Roger Hadley, 'Student Protest in a British University: Some Comparisons with American Research', *Comparative Education Review*, 15, 1 (1971), pp. 1–19.

51. Michael S. Foley, *Confronting the War Machine: Draft Resistance during the Vietnam War* (Chapel Hill, NC, 2003), p. 352.

52. Pereira and Schär, 'Soixante-Huitards Helvétiques'.

53. Henry Kissinger, *The White House Years* (1979), p. 510.

54. Linhart, *Volontaires pour l'Usine*, p. 180.

55. Philip Cohen, 'Red Roots from Lenin to Lennon', in Philip Cohen (ed.), *Children of the Revolution: Communist Childhood in Post-War Britain* (1997), pp. 21–9, p. 62.

3. UNIVERSITIES

1. Cited in James K. Davis, *Assault on the Left: The FBI and the Sixties Anti-War Movement* (Westport, CT, 1997), p. 40.
2. Cambridge University Library, Needham Papers, K 323, *Socialists in Higher Education Bulletin*, 4.
3. On the Anti-University, see London National Archives (NA) HO 325/104, report by Metropolitan Police, 26 February 1968.
4. Rosie Germain, 'The British and American Reception of French Existentialism, 1939–1972' (PhD, Cambridge University, 2013), p. 79.
5. Anthony Kenny, *A Path from Rome* (Oxford pbk, 1986), p. 162.
6. Barry Supple, *Doors Open* (Cambridge, 2009), p. 228.
7. Bernard Donoughue, *Downing Street Diary: With Harold Wilson in No. 10* (2006), pp. 8–9.
8. Gerard de Groot, 'The Culture of Protest: An Introductory Essay', in Gerard de Groot. (ed.), *Student Protest: The Sixties and After* (1988), pp. 3–11.
9. HMSO, Report from the Select Committee on Education and Science, Session 1968–69, *Student Relations* (1969), memorandum by Roy Cox and Ernest Rudd, pp. 299–310, p. 301.
10. Raymond Boudon, 'Sources of Student Protest in France', *The Annals of the American Academy of Political and Social Science*, 395 (1971), pp. 139–49. Pierre Bourdieu, *Homo Academicus* (Stanford, CA, 2000), pp. 159–93. Richard Flacks was one of the few American sociologists who referred to a specific French school of interpretation of student protest (though he did not name Bourdieu or Boudon) and contrasted it with the apparent situation in the United States. See Richard Flacks, 'Social and Cultural Meanings of Student Revolt: Some Informal Comparative Observations', *Social Problems*, 17, 3 (1970), pp. 340–57.
11. Tessa Blackstone and Roger Hadley, 'Student Protest in a British University: Some Comparisons with American Research', *Comparative Education Review*, 15, 1 (1971), pp. 1–19.
12. Philip Rieis, 'A Comment on Student Protest', *American Sociological Review*, 35, 3 (1970), p. 528.
13. HMSO, *Student Relations*, vol. VI, sub-committee C, Evidence and Appendices, memorandum by the Guildford School of Art Student

Union, pp. 1–4, p. 2. See also ibid., memorandum by ATTI, pp. 23–9, p. 23.

14. Louis Gruel, *La Rébellion de 68: Une Relecture Sociologique* (Rennes, 2004); Julie Pagis, *Mai 68, un Pavé dans leur Histoire* (2014).

15. Philippe de Gaulle, *Mémoires Accessoires, 1946–1982* (2000), p. 189.

16. Richard Crossman, *The Diaries of a Cabinet Minister*, vol. II: *Lord President of the Council and Leader of the House of Commons, 1966–68* (1976), entry for 10 March 1968, p. 700.

17. Milton Mankoff and Richard Flacks, 'The Changing Base of the American Student Movement', *The Annals of the American Academy of Political and Social Science*, 395 (1971), pp. 54–67.

18. Eric Maurin and Sandra McNally, 'Vive la Révolution! Long-Term Educational Returns of 1968 to the Angry Students', *Journal of Labor Economics*, 26, 1 (2008), pp. 1–33.

19. HMSO, *Student Relations*, Bell speaking on 5 May 1969, vol. V, p. 337.

20. Jean Chesneaux and Martin Nicholaus, 'Le Mouvement des "Radical Caucuses" dans les Sciences Humaines aux États-Unis', *L'Homme et la Société*, 16, 1 (1970), pp. 3–26.

21. Habiba Cohen, *Elusive Reform: The French Universities, 1968–1978* (Boulder, CO, 1978), p. 23.

22. HMSO, *Student Relations*, vol. VII, memorandum by British Sociological Association, pp. 195–6.

23. Kathleen E. Gales, 'A Campus Revolution', *British Journal of Sociology*, 17, 1 (1966), pp. 1–19.

24. Blackstone and Hadley, 'Student Protest in a British University'.

25. Kenneth J. Heineman, *Campus Wars: The Peace Movement at American State Universities in the Vietnam Era* (New York, 1993), p. 13.

26. Eric Ives, 'The Events of 1968', in Eric Ives, Diane K. Drummond and Leonard Schwarz (eds.), *The First Civic University: Birmingham, 1880–1980* (Birmingham, 2000), p. 369.

27. Donald Levine, 'Sociology Confronts Student Protest', *The School Review*, 78, 4 (1970), pp. 529–41.

28. Ibid.

29. Chesneaux and Nicholaus, 'Le Mouvement des "Radical Caucuses"'.

30. Levine, 'Sociology Confronts Student Protest'.

31. Daniel Cohn-Bendit, Jean-Pierre Duteuil, Bertrand Gérard and Bernard Granautier, 'Why Sociologists?', in Alexander Cockburn and Robin Blackburn (eds.), *Student Power: Problems, Diagnosis, Action* (1969), pp. 373–8.

32. Michel Crozier, *Ma Belle Époque: Mémoires, 1947–1969* (2002), p. 347.

33. Philip Cohen, *Reading Room Only: Memoir of a Radical Bibliophile* (Nottingham, 2013), p. 99.

34. Crozier, *Ma Belle Époque*, p. 314.

35. London National Archives, CRIM 1/5256, Mr Platt-Mills referring to the qualifications of Paul Hoch, p. 6.

36. Cambridge University Library, Needham Papers, K 323, report on Socialists in Higher Education, 12 April 1969

37. Jonah Raskin, *Out of the Whale: Growing up in the American Left* (New York, 1974).

38. Luisa Passerini and Anne-Marie Aymard, 'Le Mouvement de 1968 Comme Prise de Parole et Comme Explosion de la Subjectivité: Le Cas de Turin', *Le Mouvement Social*, 143 (1988), pp. 39–74.

39. Supple, *Doors Open*, p. 300.

40. Lara P. Skardhamar, ' "Real Revolution" in Kana Commune', *Scandinavian Journal of History*, 33, 4 (2008), pp. 441–63.

41. Frédéric Robert, 'The Rhetoric of Social Movements: Differential Images of the Recruitment in Students for a Democratic Society (SDS), 1960–1965', *Revue Française d'Études Américaines*, 99 (2004), pp. 85–102.

42. Ben Mercer, 'The Paperback Revolution: Mass Circulation Books and the Cultural Origins of 1968 in Western Europe', *Journal of the History of Ideas*, 72, 4 (2011), pp. 613–36.

43. Epistémon, *Ces Idées qui ont Ébranlé la France: Nanterre, Novembre 1967–Juin 1968* (1968).

44. Paul Cohen, 'Happy Birthday Vincennes! The University of Paris-8 Turns Forty', *History Workshop Journal*, 69, 1 (2010), pp. 206–24.

45. Tom Hayden, *Radical Nomad: C. Wright Mills and his Times* (Boulder, CO, 2006).

46. Doug McAdam, 'The Biographical Consequences of Activism', *American Sociological Review*, 54, 5 (1989), pp. 744–60. In the control comparison group 18 per cent had become professors.

47. Jack Whalen and Richard Flacks, *Beyond the Barricades: The Sixties Generation Grows Up* (Philadelphia, PA, 1989), p. 151.

4. THE UNITED STATES

1. Niall Ferguson, *Kissinger, 1923–1968: The Idealist* (2015), p. 788.

2. Cited in Joshua B. Freeman, *American Empire: The Rise of a Global Power, the Democratic Revolution at Home, 1945–2000* (New York, 2012), p. 251.

3. Daniel Matlin, 'On Fire: the City and American Protest in 1968', in Martin Halliwell and Nick Whitham (eds.), *Reframing 1968: American Politics, Protest and Identity* (Edinburgh, 2008), pp. 107–29.

4. Ferguson, *Kissinger*, p. 788.

5. James Miller, *Democracy is in the Streets: From Port Huron to the Siege of Chicago* (New York, 1987), p. 16.

6. Tom Hayden, *Reunion: A Memoir* (this edn, 1989), p. 464.

7. Ibid., p. 504.

8. Letter from Eleanor Raskin, 10 May 1968, *Journal of American Studies*, 19, 2 (1985), pp. 255–60.

9. Tom Hayden, *Radical Nomad: C. Wright Mills and his Times* (Boulder, CO, 2006), p. 56.

10. Maurice Isserman, *The Other American: The Life of Michael Harrington* (New York, 2000), p. 249.

11. Hayden, *Radical Nomad*, p. 59.

12. Isserman, *The Other American*, p. 183.

13. Hayden, *Reunion*, p. 41.

14. John McMillian, ' "Our Founder the Mimeograph Machine": Participatory Democracy in Students for a Democratic Society's Print Culture', *Journal for the Study of Radicalism*, 2, 2 (2009), pp. 85–110.

15. Hayden, *Reunion*, p. 114.

16. Sean D. Stryker, 'Knowledge and Power in the Students for a Democratic Society, 1960–1970', *Berkeley Journal of Sociology*, 38 (1993), pp. 89–138.

17. Karen M. Paget, *Patriotic Betrayal: The Inside Story of the CIA's Secret Campaign to Enroll American Students in the Crusade against Communism* (New Haven, CT, 2015), p. 375.

18. Ferguson, *Kissinger*, pp. 284, 286.

19. Mary L. Dudziak, *Cold War Civil Rights: Race and the Image of American Democracy* (Princeton, 2000).

20. Cited in Thomas Borstelmann, *The Cold War and the Color Line: American Race Relations in the Global Arena* (Cambridge, MA, 2001), p. 1.

21. Cited in Mark Hulsether, ' "Christianity and Crisis" in the 1950s and Early 1960s: A Case Study in the Transformation of Liberal Protestant Social Thought', *The Journal of Presbyterian History*, 79, 2 (2001), pp. 151–71.

22. Martin Klimke, *The Other Alliance: Student Protest in West Germany and the United States in the Global Sixties* (Princeton, 2010), p. 148.

23. Paget, *Patriotic Betrayal*, p. 233.

24. Donald Granberg, and Keith E. Campbell, 'Certain Aspects of Religiosity and Orientations toward the Vietnam War among Missouri Undergraduates', *Sociology of Religion*, 34, 1 (1973), pp. 40–49.

25. Robert S. Lichter and Stanley Rothman. 'Jews on the Left: The Student Movement Reconsidered', *Polity*, 14, 2 (1981), pp. 347–66.

26. Doug Rossinow, *The Politics of Authenticity: Liberalism, Christianity and the New Left in America* (New York, 1998).

27. Phillip E. Hammond and Robert E. Mitchell, 'Segmentation of Radicalism: The Case of the Protestant Campus Minister', *American Journal of Sociology*, 71, 2 (1965), pp. 133–43.

28. Penelope Adams Moon, ' "Peace on Earth: Peace in Vietnam". The Catholic Peace Fellowship and Antiwar Witness, 1964–1976', *Journal of Social History*, 36, 4 (2003), pp. 1033–57. Helen M. Ciernick, 'A Matter of Conscience: The Selective Conscientious Objector, Catholic College Students, and the Vietnam War', *US Catholic Historian*, 26, 3 (2008), pp. 33–50.

29. Richard J. Ellis, 'Romancing the Oppressed: The New Left and the Left Out', *The Review of Politics*, 58, 1 (1996), pp. 109–54.

30. Robbie Lieberman, *Prairie Power: Voices of 1960s Midwestern Student Protest* (Columbia, MO, 2004).

31. Michael W. Schuyler, 'Ghosts in the White House: LBJ, RFK and the Assassination of JFK', *Presidential Studies Quarterly*, 17, 3 (1987), pp. 503–18.

32. Sidney Milkis, 'Lyndon Johnson, the Great Society, and the "Twilight" of the Modern Presidency', in Sidney Milkis and Jerome Mileur (eds.), *The Great Society and the High Tide of Liberalism* (Amherst, MA, 2005), pp. 1–50, p. 9.

33. Hayden, *Reunion*, p. 125.

34. Jeremy Varon, *Bringing the War Home: The Weather Underground, the Red Army Faction and Revolutionary Violence in the Sixties and Seventies* (Berkeley, CA, 2004), p. 139.

35. Conversation between Daley and Lyndon Johnson, 16 January 1964 in Michael R. Beschloss (ed.), *Taking Charge: The Johnson White House Tapes, 1963–1964* (New York, 1997), p. 168.

36. Jeff Shesol, *Mutual Contempt: Lyndon Johnson, Robert Kennedy and the Feud that Defined a Decade* (New York, 1997), p. 242.

37. Robert Dallek, *Flawed Giant: Lyndon Johnson and his Times, 1961–1973* (Oxford, 1998), p. 331.

38. Gregory Duhé, 'The FBI and Students for a Democratic Society at the University of New Orleans, 1968–1971', *Louisiana History: The Journal of the Louisiana Historical Association*, 43, 1 (2002), pp. 53–74.

39. Lauter and Howe, cited in Renée Kasinsky, *Refugees from Militarism* (New Brunswick, NJ, 1976), p. 6.

40. Lawrence Baskir and William Strauss, *Chance and Circumstance: The Draft, the War and the Vietnam Generation* (New York, 1978), p. 14.
41. James Farrell, *The Spirit of the 60s: Making Postwar Radicalism* (New York, 1997).
42. Kenneth J. Heineman, *Campus Wars: The Peace Movement at American State Universities in the Vietnam Era* (New York, 1993), p. xi.
43. Peter B. Levy, *The New Left and Labor in the 1960s* (Urbana, IL, 1994), p. 46.
44. Kevin Boyle, *The UAW and the Heyday of American Liberalism, 1945–1968* (Ithaca, NY, 1995), p. 233.
45. Jennifer Earl, Sarah A. Soule and John D. McCarthy, 'Protest under Fire? Explaining the Policing of Protest', *American Sociological Review*, 68, 4 (2003), pp. 581–606. The authors are in fact slightly sceptical about the theory that the American police were very violent – though their case study (of New York in the years after 1968) may be unusual.
46. Bourricaud, cited in Alain Peyrefitte, *C'était de Gaulle* (2002, first published 1994), p. 1693, entry for 8 May 1968.
47. Charles E. Jones, 'Arm Yourself or Harm Yourself: People's Party II and the Black Panther Party in Houston, Texas' in Judson L. Jeffries, *On the Ground: The Black Panther Party in Communities Across America* (Jackson, MS, 2010), pp. 3–40.
48. Heineman, *Campus Wars*, p. 254.
49. Roberta Salper, 'U.S. Government Surveillance and the Women's Liberation Movement, 1968–1973: A Case Study', *Feminist Studies*, 34, 3 (2008), pp. 431–55.
50. Duhé, 'The FBI and Students for a Democratic Society at the University of New Orleans, 1968–1971'.
51. Cril Payne, *Deep Cover: An FBI Agent Infiltrates the Radical Underground* (New York, 1979), pp. 41, 33.
52. W.J. Rorabaugh, *Berkeley at War: The 1960s* (Oxford, 1989), p. 173.
53. Peniel E. Joseph, 'The Black Power Movement, Democracy and America in the King Years', *American Historical Review*, 114, 4 (2009), pp. 1001–16.
54. Hasan Kwame Jeffries, 'SNCC, Black Power, and Independent Political Party Organizing in Alabama, 1964–1966', *The Journal of African American History*, 91, 2 (2006), pp. 171–93.
55. Robert Self, ' "To Plan Our Liberation": Black Power and the Politics of Place in Oakland, California, 1965–1977', *Journal of Urban History*, 26 (2000), pp. 759–92.
56. Rossinow, *The Politics of Authenticity*, p. 195.

57. Jennifer Jensen Wallach, 'Replicating History in a Bad Way? White Activists and Black Power in SNCC's Arkansas Project', *Arkansas Historical Quarterly*, 67, 3 (2008), pp. 268–87.

58. Joel D. Aberbach and Jack L. Walker, 'The Meanings of Black Power: A Comparison of White and Black Interpretations of a Political Slogan', *American Political Science Review*, 64, 2 (1970), pp. 367–88.

59. Angela Davis, *An Autobiography* (this edn, 1990), p. 164.

60. Darryl J. Maeda, 'Black Panthers, Red Guards, and Chinamen: Constructing Asian American Identity through Performing Blackness, 1969–1972', *American Quarterly*, 57, 4 (2005), pp. 1079–1103.

61. Jones, 'Arm Yourself or Harm Yourself', in Jeffries (ed.), *On the Ground*, pp. 3–40.

62. Davis, *An Autobiography*, p. 164.

63. Lauren Araiza, ' "In Common Struggle Against a Common Oppression": The United Farm Workers and the Black Panther Party, 1968–1973', *The Journal of African American History*, 94, 2 (2009), pp. 200–223.

64. Jeffrey Burns, 'Eugene Boyle, the Black Panther Party and the New Clerical Activism', *US Catholic Historian*, 13, 3 (1995), pp. 137–58.

65. Alondra Nelson, *Body and Soul: The Black Panther Party and the Fight Against Medical Discrimination* (Minneapolis, MN, 2013).

66. Arthur M. Schlesinger, Jr, *The Crisis of Confidence: Ideas, Power and Violence in America* (1969), p. 23.

67. Thomas J. Sugrue, *Sweet Land of Liberty: The Forgotten Struggle for Civil Rights in the North* (New York, 2008), p. 335.

68. John Barnard, *American Vanguard: The United Auto Workers during the Reuther Years, 1935–1970* (Detroit, MI, 2004), p. 434.

69. Edgar Morin, *Journal, 1962–1987* (2012), p. 857.

70. Gerard de Groot, 'Ronald Reagan and Student Unrest in California, 1966–1970', *Pacific Historical Review*, 65, 1 (1996), pp. 107–29.

71. Michelle Reeves, ' "Obey the Rules or Get Out": Ronald Reagan's 1966 Gubernatorial Campaign and the "Trouble in Berkeley"', *Southern California Quarterly*, 92, 3 (2010), pp. 275–305.

72. Régis Debray, *La Révolution dans la Révolution* (1967), pp. 8–9.

73. Arthur M. Schlesinger, Jr, *Robert Kennedy and his Times*, vol. II (Boston, MA, 1978), p. 805.

74. Hayden, *Reunion*, p. 102.

75. Arthur M. Schlesinger, Jr, *Journals, 1952–2000* (2007), p. 260, entry for 13 May 1967.

76. Ibid., p. 278, entry for 19 February 1968.

77. David Wyatt, *When America Turned: Reckoning with 1968* (Amherst, MA, 2014), pp. 232–3.

78. Roger Biles, *Richard Daley: Race, Politics and the Governing of Chicago* (DeKalb, IL, 1995), p. 150.

79. Christopher A. Huff, 'Radicals Between the Hedges: The Origins of the New Left at the University of Georgia and the 1968 Sit-In', *The Georgia Historical Quarterly*, 94, 2 (2010), pp. 179–209.

80. Joshua B. Freeman, *American Empire: The Rise of a Global Power. The Democratic Revolution at Home, 1945–2000* (New York, 2012), p. 250.

81. Melvin Small, *Johnson, Nixon and the Doves* (New Brunswick, NJ, 1988).

5. FRANCE

1. Dominique Julia, 'Le Mouvement Étudiant', *Études* (June–July, 1968), pp. 8–28.

2. Alain Peyrefitte, *C'était de Gaulle* (2002, first published 1994), p. 1648, entry for 25 March 1968.

3. Michel Crozier, *Ma Belle Époque: Mémoires, 1947–1969* (2002), p. 343.

4. Raymond Aron, *The Elusive Revolution: Anatomy of a Student Revolt* (1969).

5. Didier Eribon, *Michel Foucault (1926–1984)* (1989), p. 192.

6. Luc Ferry and Alain Renaut, *La Pensée 68: Essai sur l'Anti-Humanisme Contemporain* (1985).

7. Crozier, *Ma Belle Époque*, p. 328.

8. Peyrefitte, *C'était de Gaulle*, pp. 1707–8, entry for 10 May 1968.

9. Charles Mercier, 'René Rémond à Nanterre en 1968', *Vingtième Siècle, Revue d'Histoire*, 104 (2009), pp. 141–52.

10. Cited in Laurent Joffrin, *Mai 68: Histoire des Événements* (1988), p. 26.

11. Alain de Boissieu, *Pour Servir le Général, 1946–1970* (1982), p. 186.

12. Daniel Bensaïd, *Une Lente Impatience* (2004), p. 83.

13. Jacques Foccart, *Le Général en Mai: Journal de l'Élysée*, vol. II: *1968–1969* (1998), p. 105.

14. Michèle Cotta, *Cahiers Secrets de la Ve République*, vol. I: *1965–1977* (2007), p. 121, entry for 21–22 May.

15. Olivier Todd, *Malraux: Une Vie* (2001), p. 534.

16. Michel Droit, *Les Feux du Crépuscule: Journal 1968–1969–1970* (1977), p. 25, entry for 15 May.

17. Jean-Daniel Benard, 'Les Relations entre le BN de l'UNEF et les Forces de Police en 1967–1968', in Roger Barralis and Jean-Claude Gillet

(eds.), *Au Coeur des Luttes des Années Soixante, les Étudiants du PSU: Une Utopie Porteuse d'Avenir?* (2010), pp. 235–41, p. 237.

18. Maurice Grimaud, *En Mai, Fais ce qu'il te Plaît. Le Préfet de Police de Mai 68 Parle* (1977), p. 333.

19. Alain Geismar, *Mon Mai 1968* (2008), p. 150. Grimaud claimed that the 'dialogue' between himself and the student leaders was a 'myth'. He had never spoken on the telephone to either Geismar or Cohn-Bendit (interview with Grimaud in *Liaisons*, May 2008, in Grimaud Archives, Paris, Institut d'Études Politiques). However, Kean Pinon, the police photographer who sometimes accompanied Grimaud in May 1968, recalled having photographed him talking to Jacques Sauvageot and Daniel Cohn-Bendit at the entrance to the Sorbonne (ibid.).

20. Philippe Nivet, 'Maurice Grimaud et Mai 1968', *Histoire@Politique*, 27 (2015), pp. 18–32.

21. Christian Fouchet, *Mémoires d'Hier et de Demain*, vol. I: *Au Service du Général de Gaulle: Londres 1940, Varsovie 1945, Alger 1962, Mai 1968* (1971), p. 227.

22. Frédéric Turpin, *Jacques Foccart: Dans l'Ombre du Pouvoir* (2015).

23. Peyrefitte, *C'était de Gaulle*, p. 1645, entry for 23 March 1968.

24. Jean-Jacques Becker, *Un Soir de l'Été 1942 ... Souvenirs d'un Historien* (2009), p. 286.

25. London National Archives (NA) PREM 13/2653, Reilly to Foreign Office, 20 May 1968.

26. Maurice Agulhon, 'Vu des Coulisses', in Pierre Nora (ed.), *Essais d'Ego-Histoire* (1987), pp. 9–59.

27. Maurice Agulhon, *De Gaulle: Histoire, Symbole, Mythe* (2000).

28. Régis Debray, *À Demain de Gaulle* (1993).

29. Alain Geismar, *Mon Mai 1968* (2008), pp. 37, 129.

30. Ginette Vincendeau, *Jean-Pierre Melville: An American in Paris* (2003), p. 78.

31. Tickell met Rocard 'at the moment of greatest excitement for his party' and was struck by his 'sang froid and grip on events' (NA FCO 13/58 Tickell to Lush, 5 June 1968).

32. Peyrefitte, *C'était de Gaulle*, p. 1638, entry for 14 February 1968.

33. NA PREM 13 /2653, Reilly to FO, 30 May 1968, reporting meeting between member of embassy staff and Ballanger.

34. Peyrefitte, *C'était de Gaulle*, p. 1638, entry for 14 February 1968.

35. Charles Morazé, *Un Historien Engagé: Mémoires* (2007), p. 305.

36. Debray, *À Demain de Gaulle*, pp. 13–14.

37. Peyrefitte, *C'était de Gaulle*, pp. 1237–9.

38. Virginie Linhart, *Volontaires pour l'Usine: Vies d'Établis, 1967–1977* (this edn, 2010), p. 39.

39. Godard was taken aback when Madame Pompidou offered him and his sick wife a lift home from Paris airport in 1968. See Anne Wiazemsky, *Une Année Studieuse* (2012), p. 253.

40. Édouard Balladur, *L'Arbre de Mai: Chronique Alternée* (1978), p. 74.

41. Éric Roussel, *Georges Pompidou* (1984), p. 246.

42. Pompidou explained his thinking in a private letter to Raymond Aron that was written in July 1968. The fact that he should write a letter to an academic critic says much about Pompidou – Raymond Aron, *Mémoires: 50 Ans de Réflexion Politique* (this edn, 1990), pp. 659–61.

43. Roussel, *Pompidou*, p. 247.

44. Gérard Adam, 'Étude Statistique des Grèves de Mai–Juin 1968', *Revue Française de Science Politique*, 20, 1 (1970), pp. 105–19.

45. PREM 13/2653, Reilly to FO, 29 May 1968.

46. Xavier Vigna, *L'Insubordination Ouvrière dans les Années 68: Essai d'Histoire Politique des Usines* (Rennes, 2007), p. 29.

47. Christian Chevandier, *La Fabrique d'une Génération: Georges Valero Postier, Militant et Écrivain* (2009), p. 151.

48. Vigna, *L'Insubordination Ouvrière*, p. 81.

49. Ibid., p. 59.

50. Ludivine Bantigny, 'Le Temps Politisé: Quelques Enjeux Politiques de la Conscience Historique en Mai–Juin 68', *Vingtième Siècle, Revue d'Histoire*, 117 (2013), pp. 215–29.

51. Adam, 'Étude Statistique des Grèves de Mai–Juin 1968'.

52. Michael Seidman, 'Workers in a Repressive Society of Seductions: Parisian Metallurgists in May–June 1968', *French Historical Studies*, 18, 1 (1993), pp. 255–78. Seidman points out that 58 per cent of strikes in metallurgy were started by workers in their thirties; only 8 per cent were begun by those under twenty.

53. Vigna, *L'Insubordination Ouvrière*, p. 45.

54. Gisèle Lougarot, *Pays Basque Nord: Mai 68 en Mémoires* (Bayonne, 2008), p. 195.

55. NA PREM 13/2653, Morgan to Hood, 20 May 1968.

56. Becker, *Un Soir de l'Été 1942*, p. 268.

57. Michèle Cotta, *Cahiers Secrets de la Ve République*, vol. I, p. 117, entry for 15 May.

58. Seidman, 'Workers in a Repressive Society of Seductions'.

59. Marie-Ange Rauch, *Le Théâtre en France en 1968: Crise d'une Histoire; Histoire d'une Crise* (2008), p. 200.

60. Chris Reynolds, 'Understanding 1968 – the Case of Brest', *Modern and Contemporary France*, 16, 2 (2008), pp. 209–22.

61. Chevandier, *La Fabrique d'une Génération*, p. 148.

62. Lougarot, *Pays Basque Nord*, pp. 156–8.

63. Rauch, *Le Théâtre en France en 1968*, dedication.

64. Vincent Porhel, *Ouvriers Bretons: Conflits d'Usines, Conflits Identitaires en Bretagne dans les Années 1968* (Rennes, 2008), p.13.

65. On the implantation of Christian trade unionism in Brittany, see Luc Berlivet and Frédéric Sawicki, 'La Foi dans l'Engagement: Les Militants Syndicalistes CFTC de Bretagne dans l'Après-Guerre', *Politix*, 27 (1994) , pp. 111–42.

66. Peyrefitte, *C'était de Gaulle*, p. 1695, entry for 8 May 1968.

67. NA PREM 13/2653, Reilly to FO, 22 May 1968.

68. Sian Reynolds, 'Dijon in May 1968: Local Politics, the Spectre of Anarchy and the "Silent Majority"', *Modern and Contemporary France*, 16, 2 (2008), pp. 195–208.

69. Lougarot, *Pays Basque Nord*, p. 172.

70. Jean-Pierre Le Goff, *La Fin du Village: Une Histoire Française* (2012), p. 165–6.

71. Rauch, *Le Théâtre en France en 1968*, p. 193.

72. Lougarot, *Pays Basque Nord*, pp. 116, 95. There were 2,650 candidates in 1968; the previous year that had been just 1,147.

73. NA PREM 13/2653, Reilly to FO, 28 May 1968, reporting lunch of business leaders at the Suez Group.

74. NA PREM 13/2653, notes by Palliser, 24 May 1968.

75. Franz-Olivier Giesbert, *Jacques Chirac* (1987), p. 130.

76. Cotta, *Cahiers Secrets de la Ve République*, vol. I, p. 123, entry for 25 May 1968.

77. Claude Nicolet, *Pierre Mendès France ou le Métier de Cassandra* (1959).

78. Éric Roussel, *Pierre Mendès France* (2007), p. 469.

79. Jacques Massu, *Baden, 68: Souvenirs d'une Fidélité Gaulliste* (1983), p. 96.

80. NA FCO 13/58, report, dated 5 June 1968, on meeting between Tickell and Rocard, 29 May 1968.

81. Jean-Pierre Rioux, 'Tombeau pour Mendès France', *Vingtième Siècle, Revue d'Histoire*, 2 (April 1984), pp. 43–54.

82. Roussel, *Pierre Mendès France*, p. 480.

83. Françoise Seligmann, *Liberté, Quand tu nous Tiens*, vol. II: *L'Espoir et la Honte: Mendès, l'Algérie, Mai 68* (2003), p. 271.

84. Cotta, *Cahiers Secrets de la Ve République*, vol. I, p. 117, entry for 15 May 1968. At the same time, Cohn-Bendit said that the Communists were 'Stalinist toads'.

85. Droit, *Les Feux du Crépuscule*, p. 39, entry for 27 May 1968.

86. Aron, *Mémoires*, p. 657.

87. Michel Rocard, *Si la Gauche Savait: Entretiens avec Georges-Marc Benamou* (2005), p. 136.

88. François Mitterrand, *Lettres à Anne, 1962–1995* (2016), p. 715, Mitterrand to Anne Pingeot, 26 August 1970.

89. Philip Short, *Mitterrand: A Study in Ambiguity* (2013), p. 251.

90. *Le Monde*, 17 May 1968.

91. Fouchet, *Mémoires d'Hier et Demain*, vol. II, p. 23.

92. Philippe de Gaulle, *Mémoires Accessoires, 1946–1982* (2000), p. 202.

93. Massu, *Baden 68*, p. 32.

94. NA PREM 13/2653, Reilly to FO, 22 May 1968.

95. Ibid., Reilly to FO, 20 May 1968.

96. Peyrefitte, *C'était de Gaulle*, p. 1711, entry for 11 May 1968.

97. NA PREM 13/2653, BAOR to MOD, 29 May 1968.

98. Ibid., Reilly to FO, 30 May 1968.

99. Ibid., Reilly to FO, 28 May 1968.

100. Ibid., Reilly to FO, 28 May 1968.

101. Ibid., Reilly to FO, 29 May 1968.

102. Ibid., Reilly to FO, 29 May 1968.

103. Foccart, *Le Général en Mai*, p. 178.

104. Peyrefitte, *C'était de Gaulle*, pp. 1775–6, entry for 30 May 1968.

105. Philippe Ariès with Michel Winock, *Un Historien du Dimanche* (1980), p. 184.

106. YL, 'The May Movement at the Lycée Pasteur, Neuilly', in Charles Posner (ed.), *Reflections on the Revolution in France: 1968* (1970), pp. 128–42, p. 139.

107. Foccart, *Le Général en Mai*, p. 28, entry for 14 May, and p. 125, entry for 23 May 1968.

108. François Audigier, 'Le Gaullisme d'Ordre des Années 68', *Vingtième Siècle, Revue d'Histoire*, 116 (2012), pp. 53–68.

109. Frank Georgi, ' "Le Pouvoir est dans la Rue": 30 Mai 1968 la Manifestation Gaulliste des Champs-Élysées', *Vingtième Siècle, Revue d'Histoire*, 48 (1995), pp. 46–60.

110. Jacques Guilhaumou, 'Mémoires d'un Étudiant en Mai 1968: Le Flux des Manifestations et le Protagoniste de l'Événement', *Le Mouvement Social*, 233 (2010), pp. 165–81.

111. André Rouède, 'La Révolte des Lycéens', *Esprit*, 372 (1968), pp. 1003–14.

112. Rocard, *Si la Gauche Savait*, pp. 149–51.

113. Epistémon (pseudonym for Didier Anzieu), *Ces Idées qui ont Ébranlé la France: Nanterre, Novembre 1967–Juin 1968* (1968).

6. WEST GERMANY

1. https://www.cia.gov/library/readingroom/document/0002987248

2. John Rae, *The Old Boys' Network: A Headmaster's Diaries, 1972–1986* (this edn, 2009), p. 65, entry for 12 July 1974.

3. Noel Annan, *Changing Enemies: The Defeat and Regeneration of Germany* (1995).

4. London National Archives (NA) FO 1042/125, Gladstone, 'Students in West Berlin', 30 June 1967.

5. Helmut Schelsky, *Die skeptische Generation: Eine Soziologie der deutschen Jugend* (Cologne, 1957).

6. Hans Kundnani, *Utopia or Auschwitz: Germany's 1968 Generation and the Holocaust* (2009), p. 66.

7. Ida Berger, 'Tiendront-ils? Étudiants Français et Allemands', *L'Homme et la Société*, 16 (1970), pp. 173–84. Berger attributed the relative youth of female students to the fact that families were less willing to fund the education of girls and that, consequently, those women who did get to university tended to be more able than their male counterparts.

8. Article in the *Neue Zürcher Zeitung*, 8 February 1968, cited in 'Students as an Anti-Parliamentary Opposition', *Minerva*, 6, 3 (1968), pp. 448–57.

9. Annemarie Tröger, 'Les Enfants du Tertiaire: Le Mouvement Étudiant en RFA de 1961 à 1969', *Le Mouvement Social*, 143 (1988), pp. 13–38.

10. Berger, 'Tiendront-ils?'

11. Ida Berger, 'Une Avant-Garde Isolée: Les Étudiants Allemands', *Esprit*, 381 (May 1969), pp. 790–805.

12. Martin Klimke, *The Other Alliance: Student Protest in West Germany and the United States in the Global Sixties* (Princeton, 2011), p. 25.

13. Florian Havemann cited in James Mark and Anne von der Goltz, 'Encounters', in Robert Gildea, James Mark and Anette Warring (eds.), *Europe's 1968: Voices of Revolt* (Oxford, 2013), pp. 131–63, p. 150.

14. Kundnani, *Utopia or Auschwitz*, p. 33.

15. Rudi Dutschke, *Students and the Revolution* (1971), p. 14. This is a version of a speech first given at Uppsala in 1968.

16. Alain Krivine, *Ça te Passera avec l'Âge* (2006), p. 96.

17. Britta Schilling, *Postcolonial Germany: Memories of Empire in a Decolonized Nation* (Oxford, 2014), p. 134.
18. Timothy S. Brown, '1968 East and West: Divided Germany as a Case Study in Transnational History', *American Historical Review*, 114, 1 (2009), pp. 69–96.
19. Thomas Alan Schwartz, *Lyndon Johnson and Europe: In the Shadow of Vietnam* (Cambridge, MA, 2003), p. 87.
20. Cited in Robert Dallek, *Flawed Giant: Lyndon Johnson and his Times, 1961–1973* (Oxford, 1998), p. 87.
21. 'Back to Rudi Dutschke's Pram', in *Sightandsight*: 'Let's talk European', 7 January 2008; http://www.signandsight.com/features/1633.html. The interview involving Aly and Katharina Rutschky was originally conducted by *Tageszeitung*.
22. 'Students as an Anti-Parliamentary Opposition', *Minerva*, 6, 3 (1968), pp. 448–57.
23. Wolfgang Kraushaar, 'Hitler's Children? The German 1968 Movement in the Shadow of the Nazi Past', in Ingo Cornils and Sarah Waters (eds.), *Memories of 1968: International Perspectives* (Oxford, 2010), pp. 79–102, p. 84.
24. Anna von der Goltz, 'Generations of 68ers: Age-Related Constructions of Identity and Germany's "1968"', *Social and Cultural History*, 8, 4 (2011), pp. 473–91.
25. Piotr Osęka, Polymeris Voglis and Anna von der Goltz, 'Families', in Gildea et al, *Europe's 1968*, pp. 46–71.
26. Kundnani, *Utopia or Auschwitz*, p. 81.
27. Rebecca Clifford, Robert Gildea and James Mark, 'Awakenings', in Gildea et al, *Europe's 1968*, pp. 21–45.
28. Interview with Karsten Voigt by Harry Kreisler, 2001, http://globetrotter.berkeley.edu/people/Voigt/voigt-cono.html
29. Beate and Serge Klarsfeld, *Mémoires* (2015), p. 182.
30. NA FO 1042/125, report on quadripartite consultations held in Bonn, 19 July 1967.
31. Brown, '1968 East and West: Divided Germany as a Case Study in Transnational History'.
32. https://www.cia.gov/library/readingroom/document/0002987248
33. Helmut Schelsky, 'The Wider Setting of Disorder in the German Universities', *Minerva*, 10, 4 (1972), pp. 614–26.
34. Von der Goltz, 'Generations of 68ers'.
35. Brown, '1968 East and West: Divided Germany as a Case Study in Transnational History'.

36. NA FO 1042/126, note by H.A. Stephenson, 28 September 1967.
37. https://www.cia.gov/library/readingroom/document/0002987248.
38. Willy Brandt, *People and Politics* (1978), p. 198.
39. Horst Mewes, 'The German New Left', *New German Critique*, vol. 1 (1973), pp. 22–41.
40. Jeanette Seiffert, '*Marsch durch die Institutionen?*': *Die '68er' in der SPD* (Bonn, 2009).

7. BRITAIN

1. HMSO, Report from the Select Committee on Education and Science, Session 1968–69, *Student Relations* (1969), vol. II, pp. 81.
2. L. Neville Brown, 'Student Protest in England', *The American Journal of Comparative Law*, 17, 3 (1969), pp. 395–402.
3. A Trotskyist wrote a parody of a *Private Eye* parody to mock Perry Anderson. Peter Sedgwick, 'Pseud Left Review', *International Socialism*, 25 (1966), pp. 18–19.
4. *Private Eye*, 7 June 1968.
5. Philip Cohen, *Reading Room Only: Memoir of a Radical Bibliophile* (Nottingham, 2013), p. 39.
6. Gareth Stedman Jones, 'History and Theory: An English Story', *Historein*, 3 (2001), pp. 103–24.
7. Leeds University website, www.leeds.ac.uk/reporter/may68/protest.htm
8. Sheila Rowbotham, *Promise of a Dream: Remembering the Sixties* (this edn, 2001), p. 179.
9. Richard Neville, *Hippie Hippie Shake* (1995), p. 111.
10. London National Archives (NA) FCO 33/85, note by Palisser, 18 June 1968.
11. On Americans in Britain and the role of the anti-Vietnam War movement in Britain, see NA HO 325/104.
12. NA DPP 2/4379, note by Heatherington, 11 May 1967.
13. HMSO, *Student Relations*, vol. I, p. 50.
14. Ibid., vol. II, p. 201, evidence of Marie Jahoda, 18 March 1969.
15. NA ED 207/125, Report by 'Security Service', 18 May 1972.
16. Neville, *Hippie Hippie Shake*, p. 151.
17. John Rae, *The Old Boys' Network: A Headmaster's Diaries, 1972–1986* (this edn, 2009), pp. 33–4, entry for 25 June 1973.
18. A.H. Halsey and Stephen Marks, 'British Student Politics', *Daedalus*, 97, 1 (1968), pp. 116–36.
19. John Saville, *Memoirs from the Left* (2003), p. 158.

20. HMSO, *Student Relations*, vol. VII, memorandum from sub-committee D on visit to Paris, 11–12 June 1969, pp. 180–82, p. 181.

21. Karen Paget, 'From Stockholm to Leiden: The CIA's Role in the Formation of the International Student Conference', *Intelligence and National Security*, 18, 2 (2003), pp. 134–67.

22. Warwick University, Modern Records Centre MSS 280/51/3, undated manifesto. Ibid., MacCallum to Savage, 26 October 1966.

23. Caroline Hoefferle, *British Student Activism in the Long Sixties* (2013), pp. 68, 90.

24. Jack Straw, 'In the Year of Student Rebellion: How I See the Future', Leeds University website, www.leeds.ac.uk/reporter/may68/protest.htm

25. *The Times*, 10 April 1969. Note that there are two different articles on this topic in this issue.

26. Margaret Rooke, *Anarchy and Apathy: Student Unrest, 1968–1970* (1971), p. 15.

27. Stafford, Staffordshire Public Record Office, D 4490/48, letter from George B., 25 June 1972.

28. Perry Anderson and Robin Blackburn, *Towards Socialism* (1965).

29. Cited in Tony Benn, *Office without Power: Diaries, 1968–1972* (1988), p. 247, entry for 8 March 1970.

30. Halsey and Marks, 'British Student Politics'.

31. Paul Hoch and Vic Schoenbach, *LSE: The Natives Are Restless: A Report on Student Power in Action* (1969), p. viii.

32. Philip Ziegler, *Wilson: The Authorized Biography* (1993), p. 221.

33. Shirley Williams, *Climbing the Bookshelves* (2009), p. 35.

34. Ibid., pp. 183–4.

35. Roy Jenkins, *A Life at the Centre* (1991), p. 251.

36. Benn, *Office without Power*, p. 87, entry for 26 June 1968.

37. Ibid., p. 82, entry for 14 June 1968.

38. Bernard Crick, cited in Susan Crosland, *Tony Crosland* (1982), p. 70.

39. Gareth Stedman Jones, *Marxism Today* (November 1986).

40. HMSO, *Student Relations*, vol. V, memorandum by Roy Cox and Ernest Rudd, pp. 299–310, pp. 307, 309.

41. Colin Crouch, *The Student Revolt* (1970), p. 15.

42. HMSO, *Student Relations*, vol. II, memorandum by the Federation of Conservative Students, signed Ian Taylor, pp. 325–7, p. 325.

43. Ibid., evidence of Stephen Keppel, Chairman of the Federation of Conservative Students, p. 332, 13 May 1969.

44. Hoefferle, *British Student Activism*, p. 108.

45. Tariq Ali, *Street Fighting Years: An Autobiography of the Sixties* (this edn, 2005), p. 261.

46. NA DPP 2/4548, statement by Superintendent Leslie Garrett.

47. Bernadette Devlin, *The Price of my Soul* (1969), p. 53.

48. John J. Kane, 'Civil Rights in Northern Ireland', *The Review of Politics*, 33, 1 (1971), pp. 54–77.

49. Simon Prince, 'The Global Revolt of 1968 and Northern Ireland', *Historical Journal*, 49, 3 (2006), pp. 851–75. Chris Reynold, *Sous les Pavés . . . The Troubles: Northern Ireland, France and the European Collective Memory of 1968* (Frankfurt, 2014).

50. Michael Farrell in 'Discussion on the Strategy of People's Democracy', *New Left Review*, 1, 55 (May–June 1969).

51. Cyril Toman in ibid.

52. Eamonn McCann in ibid.

53. Ibid.

54. Devlin, *The Price of my Soul*, p. 13.

55. Ronald Fraser with Daniel Bertaux, Bret Eynon, Ronald Grele, Béatrix Le Wita, Danièle Linhart, Luisa Passerini, Jochen Staadt and Annemarie Tröger, *1968: A Student Generation in Revolt* (1988), p. 220.

56. Peter Taylor, *Behind the Mask: The IRA and Sinn Fein* (1997), p. 61.

57. Gregory Maney, 'Transnational Mobilization and Civil Rights in Northern Ireland', *Social Problems*, 47, 2 (2000), pp. 153–79.

58. Kane, 'Civil Rights in Northern Ireland'.

59. Maney, 'Transnational Mobilization and Civil Rights in Northern Ireland'.

60. Rob Waters, 'Black Power on the Telly: America, Television, and Race in 1960s and 1970s Britain', *Journal of British Studies*, 54, 4 (2015), pp. 947–70.

61. Paul Foot, *The Rise of Enoch Powell* (1969), p. 95.

62. Simon Heffer, *Like the Roman: The Life of Enoch Powell* (1998), pp. 461–3.

63. Robert Shepherd, *Enoch Powell* (1996), p. 355.

64. Christopher Hale, *Massacre in Malaya: Exposing Britain's My Lai* (2013).

65. In October 1968, *The People* ran an article entitled: 'If the word "student" makes you feel sick'. See Rooke, *Anarchy and Apathy*, p. 10.

66. Denis Healey, *The Time of My Life* (1990), p. 228.

67. Peter Sedgwick, 'Victory for the Vietcong. Is it the Right Slogan?', *Labour Worker*, 5 August 1966.

68. *The Times*, 17 April 1968.

69. *Guardian*, 18 October 1968.

70. Williams, *Climbing the Bookshelves*, p. 185.

71. Hansard, House of Commons, 13 June 1968.
72. See Keith Jacka, Caroline Cox and John Marks, *The Rape of Reason: The Corruption of the Polytechnic of North London* (Enfield, 1975).
73. Churchill College, Cambridge, HLSM 2/42/2/57, Conservative Party Research Department, August 1976, 'The Communist Party and Left-Wing Extremist Groups'. The Research Department reckoned that membership of the IMG had declined to 1,000 by 1976. The largest Maoist group in Britain had 300 members.

8. THE REVOLUTION WITHIN THE REVOLUTION: SEXUAL LIBERATION AND THE FAMILY

1. Gregory Duhé, 'The FBI and Students for a Democratic Society at the University of New Orleans, 1968–1971', *Louisiana History: The Journal of the Louisiana Historical Association*, 43, 1 (2002), pp. 53–74.
2. Alain Peyrefitte, *C'était de Gaulle* (2002, first published 1994), p. 1638, entry for 14 February 1968.
3. Cited in David Widgery (ed.), *The Left in Britain, 1956–1968* (1976), pp. 354–8.
4. Gail Collins, *When Everything Changed: The Amazing Journey of American Women from 1960 to the Present* (2009), p. 184.
5. Jo Freeman, *The Politics of Women's Liberation: A Case Study of an Emerging Social Movement and its Relation to the Policy Process* (1975), p. ix.
6. Tom Hayden, *Reunion: A Memoir* (this edn, 1989), p. 300.
7. Cited in Christine Wallace, *Germaine Greer: Untamed Shrew* (1997), p. 162.
8. Janet Lever and Pepper Schwartz, *Women at Yale: Liberating a College Campus* (New York, 1971).
9. Alexander Cockburn and Robin Blackburn (eds.), *Student Power: Problems, Diagnosis, Action* (1969).
10. King's College London archives, King's College Union Society, KU/M2/7, report by Mary Dunne, external affairs officer for summer of 1973, and ibid., Carolyn Jones, Annual Report of the Last Lady Vice President, 1972–1973, 16 March 1973. The establishment of the Gaysoc was reported to the executive committee of the union by Mary Dunne on 16 May 1973, at which point one of her male colleagues proposed that 'the Executive congratulate Miss Dunne for her endeavours and that such should be minuted'.
11. Nuno Pereira and Renate Schär, 'Soixante-Huitards Helvétiques: Étude Prosopographique', *Le Mouvement Social*, 239 (2012), pp. 9–23.

12. Dominique Bazire, 'Les Filles aux ESU', in Roger Barralis et Jean-Claude Gillet (eds.), *Au Coeur des Luttes des Années Soixante, les Étudiants du PSU: Une Utopie Porteuse d'Avenir?* (2010), pp. 189–90.

13. Noel Annan, *Report of the Disturbances in the University of Essex* (1974), p. 10.

14. Ibid.

15. Warwick University, Modern Records Centre, MSS 280/51/3, speech by Geoff Martin, 30 March 1967.

16. Luisa Passerini and Anne-Marie Aymard, 'Le Mouvement de 1968 Comme Prise de Parole et Comme Explosion de la Subjectivité: Le Cas de Turin', *Le Mouvement Social*, 143 (1988), pp. 39–74.

17. Pereira and Schär, 'Soixante-Huitards Helvétiques'.

18. Roger Barralis, 'ESU et PSU au Féminin: Quelques Données Chiffrées', in Barralis and Gillet (eds.), *Au Coeur des Luttes des Années Soixante*, p. 191.

19. Luisa Passerini, *Autobiography of a Generation: Italy 1968* (Hanover, NH, 1996), p. 71.

20. Colin Crouch, *The Student Revolt* (1970), p. 57.

21. Kenneth J. Heineman, *Campus Wars: The Peace Movement at American State Universities in the Vietnam Era* (New York, 1993), p. 35.

22. Rosie Germain, 'Reading the Second Sex in 1950s America', *Historical Journal*, 56, 4 (2013), pp. 1041–62.

23. Peyrefitte, *C'était de Gaulle*, p. 1639, entry for 14 February 1968.

24. Imogen Long, 'Writing Gaullist Feminism: Françoise Parturier's Open Letters, 1968–1974', *Modern and Contemporary France*, 19, 3 (2011), pp. 313–27.

25. Shirley Williams, *Climbing the Bookshelves* (2009), p. 191.

26. Anne Wiazemsky, *Une Année Studieuse* (2012), p. 120.

27. Sheila Rowbotham, *Promise of a Dream: Remembering the Sixties* (this edn, 2001), p. 96.

28. Laurent Besse, 'Un Ministre et les Jeunes: François Missoffe, 1966–1968', *Histoire@Politique*, 4 (2008).

29. Mark Rudd, *Underground: My Life with SDS and the Weathermen* (2009), pp. 164–5.

30. HMSO, Report from the Select Committee on Education and Science, Session 1968–69, *Student Relations*, vol. I (1969), p. 50.

31. Raymond Jean preface to Gabrielle Russier, *Lettres de Prison* (1970), p. 61.

32. Christine Delphy, 'Les Origines du Mouvement de Libération des Femmes en France', *Nouvelles Questions Féministes*, 16/18 (1991), pp. 137–48.

33. Xavier Vigna, *L'Insubordination Ouvrière dans les Années 68: Essai d'Histoire Politique des Usines* (Rennes, 2007), p. 43.

34. Daniel Horowitz, 'Rethinking Betty Friedan and the Feminine Mystique: Labor Union Radicalism and Feminism in Cold War America', *American Quarterly*, 48, 1 (1996), pp. 1–42.

35. Michel Rocard, *Si la Gauche Savait: Entretiens avec Georges-Marc Benamou* (2005), p. 147.

36. *Coventry Evening Telegraph*, 5 February 1971, cited on Thatcher Foundation website, 101815.

37. Angela Davis, *An Autobiography* (this edn, 1990), p. x.

38. Eldridge Cleaver, *Soul on Ice* (this edn, 1969).

39. C. Wright Mills, 'Letter to the New Left', *New Left Review*, 1/5 (September/October 1960).

40. C. Wright Mills, *Letters and Autobiographical Writings*, edited by Kathryn Mills and Pamela Mills (2000), p. 254.

41. Ibid., p. 333.

42. Robbie Lieberman, *Prairie Power: Voices of 1960s Midwestern Student Protest* (Columbia, MO, 2004), p. 91.

43. Passerini, *Autobiography of a Generation*, p. 148.

44. Gabrielle in Nicolas Daum, *Mai 68: Des Révolutionnaires dans un Village Parisien, 20 Ans Après* (1988), pp. 115–27.

45. Rhodri Jeffreys-Jones, *Peace Now!: American Society and the Ending of the Vietnam War* (New Haven, CT, 1999), pp. 157–62.

46. Ruth Anne Thompson, ' "A Taste of Student Power": Protest at the University of Tennessee, 1964–1970', *Tennessee Historical Quarterly*, 57, 1 (1998), pp. 80–97.

47. Justin David Suran, 'Coming Out Against the War: Antimilitarism and the Politicization of Homosexuality in the Era of Vietnam', *American Quarterly*, 53, 3 (2001), pp. 452–88.

48. Passerini and Aymard, 'Le Mouvement de 1968 Comme Prise de Parole'.

49. Peter Boag, ' "Does Portland Need a Homophile Society?" Gay Culture and Activism in the Rose City Between World War II and Stonewall', *Oregon Historical Quarterly*, 105, 1 (2004), pp. 6–39.

50. Julian Jackson, *Living in Arcadia: Homosexuality, Politics and Morality in France from the Liberation to Aids* (Chicago, IL, 2009).

51. Richard Reichard, ' "We Can't Hide and They Are Wrong": The Society for Homosexual Freedom and the Struggle for Recognition at Sacramento State College, 1969–1971', *Law and History Review*, 28, 3 (2010), pp. 629–74.

52. Lisa Power, No Bath but Plenty of Bubbles: An Oral History of the Gay Liberation Front, 1970–73 (1995), p. 41.

53. Hayden, Reunion, p. 161.

54. Guy Hocquenghem, L'Amphithéâtre des Morts (1994). Daniel Bensaïd, Une Lente Impatience (2004).

55. Matthew Brunwasser, 'Digging the Age of Aquarius', Archaeology, 62, 4 (2009), pp. 30–33.

56. John Davis and Juliane Fürst, 'Drop-outs', in Robert Gildea, James Mark and Anette Warring (eds.), Europe's 1968: Voices of Revolt (Oxford, 2013), pp. 193–210.

57. Laura P. Skardhamar, ' "Real Revolution" in Kana Commune', Scandinavian Journal of History, 33, 4 (2008), pp. 441–63.

58. Susan Stern, With the Weathermen: The Personal Journey of a Revolutionary Woman (1975).

59. Richard Fairfield, Communes USA (New York, 1972), p. 65.

60. Sofia Serenelli, 'Private 1968 and the Margins: The Vicolo Cassini's Community in Macerata, Italy', Memory Studies, 6, 1 (2013), pp. 91–104.

61. Thomas Shey, 'Sex and Family Planning in Denmark and in Danish Communes', International Journal of Sociology of the Family, 7, 1 (1977), pp. 15–24.

62. Skardhamar, ' "Real Revolution" in Kana Commune'.

63. Caroline Hoefferle, 'Just at Sunrise: The Sunrise Communal Farm in Rural Mid-Michigan, 1971–1978', Michigan Historical Review, 23, 1 (1997), pp. 70–104.

64. Georges Decourt, 'Ils Gagnèrent le Large': Prêtres, Génération 68 (Villeurbanne, 2008), p. 62.

65. Gerd-Rainer Horn, The Spirit of Vatican II: Western European Progressive Catholicism in the Long Sixties (Oxford, 2015).

66. Julie Pagis, 'Déscolarisons l'École', in Dominique Damamme, Boris Gobille, Frédérique Matonti and Bernard Pudal (eds.), Mai–Juin 68 (2008), pp. 370–82.

67. Hayden, Reunion, p. 426.

9. WORKERS

1. Charles Piaget, Lip. Charles Piaget et les Lip Racontent (1973), p. 10.

2. Marie Černá, John Davis, Robert Gildea and Piotr Osęka, 'Revolutions', in Robert Gildea, James Mark and Anette Warring (eds.), Europe's 1968: Voices of Revolt (Oxford, 2013), pp. 107–30, p. 111.

3. John Saville, Memoirs from the Left (2003), p. 159.

4. Xavier Vigna, 'Les Ouvriers de Denain et de Longwy Face aux Licenciements (1978–1979)', *Vingtième Siècle, Revue d'Histoire*, 84 (2004), pp. 129–37.

5. Éliane Chemla, 'Comme une Vraie Ouvrière à Nîmes', *Les Temps Modernes*, 684–5 (2015), pp. 286–97.

6. American figures included electricity, gas and sanitary services while European ones appear to have been confined to mining, manufacture, construction and transport.

7. The *Annuaire Statistique* gives the figures as monthly averages for each year. I have simply multiplied by twelve to give these figures, except for 1970, where the individual monthly totals (cited in chap. 5) give a slightly different total, which I have used here.

8. Raymond Aron, *The Elusive Revolution: Anatomy of a Student Revolt* (1969), pp. 28–9.

9. Robert Poujade cited in Sian Reynolds, 'Dijon in May 1968: Local Politics, the Spectre of Anarchy and the "Silent Majority"', *Modern and Contemporary France*, 16, 2 (2008), pp. 195–208.

10. Ilaria Favretto, 'Rough Music and Factory Protest in Post-1945 Italy', *Past and Present*, 228, 1 (2015), pp. 207–47.

11. Paul Ginsborg, *A History of Contemporary Italy: Society and Politics, 1943–1980* (1990), p. 518.

12. Jean Le Garrec, *Une Vie à Gauche* (2006), p. 69.

13. François Rivenc, 'Quelques Réflexions sur l'Établissement en Usine', *Les Temps Modernes*, 684–5 (2015), pp. 24–33.

14. Paiget, *Lip. Charles Piaget et les Lip Racontent*, p. 151.

15. Dominique Bondu, 'L'Élaboration d'une Langue Commune: LIP-la GP', *Les Temps Modernes*, 684–5 (2015), pp. 69–80.

16. Frank Georgi, 'Jeux d'Ombres: Mai, le Mouvement Social et l'Autogestion (1968–2008)', *Vingtième Siècle, Revue d'Histoire*, 98 (2008), pp. 29–41.

17. London National Archives (NA) FCO 13/58, record of conversation between Rocard and Crispin Tickell on 29 May 1968, 5 June 1968.

18. Roy Hay and John McLauchlan. 'The Oral History of Upper Clyde Shipbuilders: A Preliminary Report', *Oral History*, 2, 1 (1974), pp. 45–58.

19. Arthur Scargill and Peggy Kahn, *The Myth of Workers' Control* (Leeds, usually described as published in 1980 though obviously earlier than this) and Ken Coates, *Workers' Control: A Reply to Arthur Scargill* (Nottingham, 1977).

20. Paul Lyons, *The People of this Generation: The Rise and Fall of the New Left in Philadelphia* (Philadelphia, PA, 2003), p. 216.

21. Leigh David Benin, *The New Labor Radicalism and New York City's Garment Industry: Progressive Labor Insurgents during the 1960s* (2000).

22. Marica Tolomelli, 'De l'Universités [*sic*] à l'Usine: Italie et Allemagne (1968–1973)', *Les Temps Modernes*, 684–5 (2015), pp. 96–119.

23. Salar Mohandesi, ' "Becoming One with the People": L'Établi Américain Hier et Aujourd'hui', *Les Temps Modernes*, 684–5 (2015), pp. 120–46.

24. Marnix Dressen, *De l'Amphi à l'Établi: Les Étudiants Maoïstes à l'Usine, 1967–1989* (2000), pp. 169, 11.

25. Juliette Campagne, 'Roubaix du Petit Livre Rouge aux Livres d'Images', *Les Temps Modernes*, 684–5 (2015), pp. 254–65.

26. Donald Reid, ' "Établissement": Working in the Factory to Make Revolution in France', *Radical History Review*, 88 (2004), pp. 83–111.

27. Dressen, *De l'Amphi à l'Établi*, p. 18.

28. Ibid., p. 283.

29. Jean-Pierre Le Dantec, 'D'où Vient l'Établissement', *Les Temps Modernes*, 684–5 (2015), pp. 16–23.

30. Virginie Linhart, *Volontaires pour l'Usine: Vies d'Établis, 1967–1977* (this edn, 2010), pp. 227–31.

31. NA CAB 128/44/51, Cabinet Conclusions, 23 October 1969.

32. Tolomelli, 'De l'Universités à l'Usine'.

33. Andrei Markovits, *The Politics of West German Trade Unions: Strategies of Class and Interest Representation in Growth and Crisis* (Cambridge, 1986), p. 223.

34. Michael Seidman, 'Workers in a Repressive Society of Seductions: Parisian Metallurgists in May–June 1968', *French Historical Studies*, 18, 1 (1993), pp. 255–78.

35. Christian Langeois, *Henri Krasucki, 1924–2003* (2012).

36. Carol A. Mershon, 'Between Workers and Union: Factory Councils in Italy', *Comparative Politics*, 21, 2 (1989), pp. 215–35.

37. Margaret and Richard Braungart, 'The Effects of the 1960s Political Generation on Former and Left- and Right-Wing Youth Activist Leaders', *Social Problems*, 38 (1991), pp. 297–315.

38. Linhart, *Volontaires pour l'Usine*, p. 193.

39. Hans Peter Sjøli, 'Maoism in Norway', *Scandinavian Journal of History*, 33, 4 (2008), pp. 478–90.

40. Nicola Pizzolato, ' "I Terroni in Città": Revisiting Southern Migrants' Militancy in Turin's "Hot Autumn" ', *Contemporary European History*, 21, 4 (2012), pp. 619–34.

41. Malcolm Pitt, *The World on our Backs: The Kent Miners and the 1972 Miners' Strike* (1979), p. 100.

42. Ibid., p. 97.
43. Thatcher Foundation website, 130177, 'The National Union of Mineworkers', Armstrong minute to Thatcher, 20 October 1981.
44. Joe Gormley, *Battered Cherub* (1982), p. 186.
45. E.P. Thompson, *New Society*, 24 February 1972, reprinted in *Writing by Candlelight* (1980), pp. 65–76, p. 70.
46. Tolomelli, 'De l'Universités à l'Usine'.
47. Nicolas Hatzfeld, 'Les Morts de Flins et Sochaux: De la Grève à la Violence Politique', in Philippe Artières et Michelle Zancarini-Fournel, *68: Une Histoire Collective, 1962–1981* (2008), pp. 322–5.
48. Xavier Vigna, 'Préserver l'Ordre Usinier en France à la Fin des Années 68', *Agone*, 50 (2013), pp. 115–33.
49. Ibid.
50. Vincent Porhel, *Ouvriers Bretons: Conflits d'Usines, Conflits Identitaires en Bretagne dans les Années 1968* (Rennes, 2008), p. 69.
51. Priscilla Falcon, 'Only Strong Women Stayed: Women Workers and the National Floral Workers Strike, 1968–1969', *Frontiers: A Journal of Women's Studies*, 24, 2/3 (2003), pp. 140–54.
52. Darryl Paulson and Janet Stiff, 'An Empty Victory: The St Petersburg Sanitation Strike, 1968', *Florida Historical Quarterly*, 57, 1 (1979), pp. 421–33.
53. Peter B. Levy, *The New Left and Labor in the 1960s* (Urbana, IL, 1994), p. 54.
54. Jefferson Cowie, 'Nixon's Class Struggle: Romancing the New Right Workers, 1969–1973', *Labor History*, 43, 3 (2002), pp. 257–83.
55. Kim Phillips-Fein, *Invisible Hands: The Businessmen's Crusade Against the New Deal* (2009), p. 153.
56. Paul Ritterband, 'Ethnic Power and the Public Schools: The New York City School Strike of 1968', *Sociology of Education*, 47, 2 (1974), pp. 251–67.
57. Dennis A. Deslippe, ' "Do Whites Have Rights?": White Detroit Policemen and "Reverse Discrimination" Protests in the 1970s', *The Journal of American History*, 91, 3 (2004), pp. 932–60.
58. Joshua B. Freeman, 'Hardhats: Construction Workers, Manliness, and the 1970 Pro-War Demonstration', *Journal of Social History*, 26, 4 (1993), pp. 725–44.
59. Thomas J. Sugrue, 'Affirmative Action from Below: Civil Rights, the Building Trades, and the Politics of Racial Equality in the Urban North, 1945–1969', *The Journal of American History*, 91, 1 (2004), pp. 145–73. Clarence Lang, 'Between Civil Rights and Black Power in the

Gateway City: The Action Committee to Improve Opportunities for Negroes (Action), 1964–1975', *Journal of Social History*, 37, 3 (2004), pp. 725–54.

60. Phillips Fein, *Invisible Hands*, p. 153.

10. VIOLENCE

1. Daniel Cohn-Bendit, *Nous l'Avons Tant Aimée, la Révolution* (1986), p. 127.

2. Ludivine Bantigny, 'Le Temps Politisé: Quelques Enjeux Politiques de la Conscience Historique en Mai–Juin 68', *Vingtième Siècle, Revue d'Histoire*, 117 (2013), pp. 215–29.

3. J.D. Taylor, 'The Party's Over? The Angry Brigade, the Counter-Culture and the British New Left, 1967–1972', *Historical Journal*, 58, 3 (2015), pp. 877–900. Taylor argues that it is not clear that the Angry Brigade was a coherent group in the way that some of its communiqués suggested.

4. Donatella della Porta, *Social Movements, Political Violence and the State: A Comparative Analysis of Italy and Germany* (Cambridge, 1995).

5. Ronald Fraser et al, *1968: A Student Generation in Revolt* (1988), p. 260.

6. Michel Rocard, *Si la Gauche Savait: Entretiens avec Georges-Marc Benamou* (2005), p. 146.

7. Jean Raguénès, *De Mai 68 à LIP: Un Dominicain au Coeur des Luttes* (2008), p. 87.

8. Jeremy Varon, *Bringing the War Home: The Weather Underground, the Red Army Faction and Revolutionary Violence in the Sixties and Seventies* (Berkeley, CA, 2004), p. 199.

9. Jack Whalen and Richard Flacks, *Beyond the Barricades: The Sixties Generation Grows Up* (Philadelphia, PA, 1989), p. 79.

10. Colin Crouch, *The Student Revolt* (1970), p. 24.

11. Charles Piaget, *Lip. Charles Piaget et les Lip Racontent* (1973), pp. 66–7.

12. On this rumour see *Libération*, 28 December 2002. See also Olivier Rolin, *Tigre en Papier* (2002), p. 176.

13. Fraser et al, *1968: A Student Generation in Revolt*, p. 110.

14. Varon, *Bringing the War Home*, p. 3.

15. Ibid.

16. Whalen and Flacks, *Beyond the Barricades*, p. 72.

17. Cohn-Bendit, *Nous l'Avons Tant Aimée, la Révolution*, p. 112.

18. Nanni Balestrini and Primo Moroni, *La Horde d'Or: La Grande Vague Révolutionnaire et Créative, Politique et Existentielle: Italie, 1968–1977* (2017, first published in Italy in 1988).

19. Robbie Lieberman, *Prairie Power: Voices of 1960s Midwestern Student Protest* (Columbia, MO, 2010), p. 46.

20. Isabelle Sommier, 'Mai 68: Sous les Pavés d'une Page Officielle', *Sociétés Contemporaines*, 20 (1994), pp. 63–82.

21. Daniel Bensaïd, *Une Lente Impatience* (2004), p. 218.

22. Cohn-Bendit, *Nous l'Avons Tant Aimée, la Révolution*, p. 156.

23. Matthias Frey, *Postwall German Cinema: History, Film History and Cinephilia* (2013), p. 79.

24. Varon, *Bringing the War Home*, p. 151.

25. Susan Stern, *With the Weathermen: The Personal Journey of a Revolutionary Woman* (1975), p. 205.

26. Anna Cento Bull and Philip Cooke, *Ending Terrorism in Italy* (2013).

27. Roberta Ann Johnson, 'The Prison Birth of Black Power', *Journal of Black Studies*, 5, 4 (1975), pp. 395–414.

28. Nicolas Daum, *Mai 68: Des Révolutionnaires dans un Village Parisien, 20 Ans Après* (1988), pp. 105–14.

29. Lougarot, Gisèle, *Pays Basque Nord: Mai 68 en Mémoires* (Bayonne, 2008), p. 275.

30. Richard English, *Armed Struggle: The History of the IRA* (Oxford, 2003), p. 131.

31. Daniel Rondeau, *L'Enthousiasme* (2006), pp. 140–44.

32. Gareth Stedman Jones, 'The Meaning of Student Revolt', in Alexander Cockburn and Robin Blackburn (eds.), *Student Power: Problems, Diagnosis, Action* (1969), pp. 25–56, p. 44.

33. Stedman Jones's views were reported in HMSO, Report from the Select Committee on Education and Science, Session 1968–69, *Student Relations* (1969), vol. I, p. 136.

34. Gareth Stedman Jones, 'History and Theory: An English Story', *Historien*, 3 (2001), pp. 103–24.

35. Dominique Manotti, 'Roman Noir', *Le Mouvement Social*, 219–20 (2007), pp. 107–9.

11. DEFEAT AND ACCOMMODATION?

1. Robert Lumley, *States of Emergency: Cultures of Revolt in Italy from 1968 to 1978* (1990), p. 234.

2. London National Archives MEPO 2/10986, press release from Greater London Council, 4 November 1968.

3. Alfred Fabre-Luce, *J'ai Vécu Plusieurs Siècles* (1974), p. 337.

4. Robert Self, ' "To Plan Our Liberation": Black Power and the Politics of Place in Oakland, California, 1965–1977', *Journal of Urban History*, 26, 6 (2000), pp. 759–92.

5. Bill Jennings, cited in Jeffrey Burns, 'Eugene Boyle, the Black Panther Party and the New Clerical Activism', *US Catholic Historian*, 13, 3 (1995), pp. 137–58.

6. Julie Pagis, *Mai 68, un Pavé dans leur Histoire* (2014), p. 128.

7. Luisa Passerini, *Autobiography of a Generation: Italy, 1968* (Hanover, NH, 1996), p. 64.

8. Gérard Noiriel, *Penser Avec, Penser Contre: Itinéraire d'un Historien* (2003).

9. Mathieu Dubois, *Génération Politique: Les Années 68 dans les Jeunesses des Partis Politiques en France et en RFA* (2014), p. 281.

10. Caroline Hoefferle, *British Student Activism in the Long Sixties* (2012), p. 101.

11. Paul Berman, *Power and the Idealists or the Passion of Joschka Fischer and its Aftermath* (2005).

12. Mark Rudd, *Underground: My Life with SDS and the Weathermen* (New York, 2009).

13. Luc Boltanski and Ève Chiapello, *Le Nouvel Esprit du Capitalisme* (1999).

14. Régis Debray, *Modeste Contribution aux Discours et Cérémonies Officielles du Dixième Anniversaire* (1978), p. 60.

15. Cohn-Bendit, *Nous l'Avons Tant Aimée, la Révolution*, pp. 35, 57.

16. Susan Krieger, *Hip Capitalism* (1979).

17. Michaël Rolland, '*Actuel* (1970–1975) et les Contre-Cultures des Années 1968 en France', in Michel Margairaz and Danielle Tartakowsky (eds.), *1968, entre Libération et Libéralisation: La Grande Bifurcation* (Rennes, 2010), pp. 149–62.

18. Bernard Lallement, '*Libé*', *l'Oeuvre Impossible de Sartre* (2004).

19. Alexander Sedlmaier and Stephen Malinowski, ' "1968" – A Catalyst of Consumer Society', *Cultural and Social History*, 8, 2 (2011), pp. 255–74.

20. Jacques Guilhaumou, 'Mémoires d'un Étudiant en Mai 1968: Le Flux des Manifestations et le Protagoniste de l'Événement', *Le Mouvement Social*, 233 (2010), pp. 165–81.

21. Ellen Furlough, 'Packaging Pleasures: Club Méditerranée and French Consumer Culture, 1950–1968', *French Historical Studies*, 18, 1 (1993), pp. 65–81.

22. Peter Doggett, *There's a Riot Going On: Revolutionaries, Rock Stars and the Rise and Fall of the '60s Counter-Culture* (2007), p. 221.

23. Jack Whalen and Richard Flacks, *Beyond the Barricades: The Sixties Generation Grows Up* (Philadelphia, PA, 1989).

24. Jean-Pierre Le Goff, *La Fin du Village: Une Histoire Française* (2012), pp. 170–82.

25. On Maoist relations with Nicoud's movement, see Claire Brière-Blanchet, *Voyage au Bout de la Révolution: De Pékin à Sochaux* (2009).

26. Caroline Hoefferle, 'Just at Sunrise: The Sunrise Communal Farm in Rural Mid-Michigan, 1971–1978', *Michigan Historical Review*, 23, 1 (1997), pp. 70–104.

27. Roger Martin, *Patron de Droit Divin* (1984), p. 267.

28. Danièle Fraboulet, 'Le CNPF et les Mutations de la Vie Politique et Sociale de l'Après Mai 68', in Gilles Richard and Jacqueline Sainclivier (eds.), *Les Partis à l'Épreuve de 68: L'Émergence de Nouveaux Clivages, 1971–1974* (Rennes, 2012), pp. 97–108.

29. Debray, *Modeste Contribution*, p. 59.

30. Margairaz and Tartakowsky (eds.), *1968, entre Libération et Libéralisation*.

31. Thatcher Foundation website, 101632, 'What's Wrong with Politics', 11 October 1968.

CONCLUSION

1. Ronald Fraser et al, *1968: A Student Generation in Revolt* (1988).

2. Gerd-Rainer Horn, *The Spirit of Vatican II: Western European Progressive Catholicism in the Long Sixties* (Oxford, 2015), p. 123.

3. Jacques Julliard, interview with Patrick Fridenson, *Le Mouvement Social*, 223 (2008), pp. 21–5.

4. Martin Klimke, *The Other Alliance: Student Protest in West Germany and the United States in the Global Sixties* (Princeton, 2010), p. 235.

5. Maurice Isserman, *The Other American: The Life of Michael Harrington* (New York, 2001), p. 206.

6. W.J. Rorabaugh, *Kennedy and the Promise of the Sixties* (Cambridge, 2002).

7. Bret Eynon, 'Community in Motion: The Free Speech Movement, Civil Rights, and the Roots of the New Left', *The Oral History Review*, 17, 1 (1989), pp. 39–69.

8. Quoted in Stuart Hall, Chas Critcher, Tony Jefferson, John Clarke and Brian Roberts (eds.), *Policing the Crisis: Mugging, the State and Law and Order* (this edn, 2013), p. 29.

9. Cited in Bethany L. Rogers, 'Teaching and Social Reform in the 1960s: Lessons from National Teacher Corps Oral Histories', *The Oral History Review*, 35, 1 (2008), pp. 39–67.

10. Manus McGrogan, 'Vive la Révolution and the Example of Lotta Continua: The Circulation of Ideas and Practices Between the Left Militant Worlds of France and Italy Following May '68', *Modern and Contemporary France*, 18, 3 (2010), pp. 309–28.

11. Pamphlet of the Radical Student Alliance quoted in Colin Crouch, *The Student Revolt* (1970), pp. 72–3.

12. Howard Schuman and Jacqueline Scott, 'Generations and Collective Memories', *American Sociological Review*, 54, 3 (1989), pp. 359–81.

13. London National Archives PREM 13/2653, Reilly to FO, 22 May 1968.

14. Henry Penfold, 'Far-Fetched Resolutions: The Evolution of the Labour Party, 1976–1981' (undergraduate dissertation, King's College London, 2016).

15. Klimke, *The Other Alliance*, p. 151.

16. Luisa Passerini, *Autobiography of a Generation: Italy, 1968* (Hanover, NH, 1996), p. 128.

17. Xavier Vigna and Michelle Zancarini-Fournel, 'Les Rencontres Improbables dans "les Années 68"', *Vingtième Siècle, Revue d'Histoire*, 101 (2009), pp. 163–77.

18. Passerini, *Autobiography of a Generation*, pp. 52, 57.

19. HMSO, Report from the Select Committee on Education and Science, Session 1968–69, *Student Relations* (1969), vol. VI, memorandum by Tony Heath, member of Surrey County Council, 11 December 1968, pp. 121–3.

20. Pierre Chanu, 'Le Fils de la Morte', in Pierre Nora (ed.), *Essais d'Ego-Histoire* (1987), pp. 61–107.

21. Ronald Fraser et al, *1968: A Student Generation in Revolt* (1988), p. 66.

22. Robert M. Collins, 'The Economic Crisis of 1968 and the Waning of the "American Century"', *American Historical Review*, 101, 2 (1996), pp. 396–422.

23. Paul Blackledge and Neil Davidson (eds.), *Alasdair MacIntyre's Engagement with Marxism: Selected Writings, 1953–1974* (2008), pp. 361–7.

24. HMSO, *Student Relations*, vol. II, evidence of Brian Connell, pp. 247–59, 15 April 1969, p. 250, question from Mr Bell.

25. Quoted in Frank Kusch, *Battleground Chicago: The Police and the 1968 Democratic National Convention* (Chicago, 2004), p. 147.

26. Sébastien Layerle, 'En l'Autre Bord: Filmer les Forces de l'Opposition à Mai 68', *Le Mouvement Social*, 223 (2008), pp. 7–12.

27. Thomas J. Sugrue, *Sweet Land of Liberty: The Forgotten Struggle for Civil Rights in the North* (New York, 2008), p. 348.

28. Hall et al, *Policing the Crisis*, p. 418.

29. Peter B. Levy, *The New Left and Labor in the 1960s* (Urbana, IL, 1994), p. 118.

30. Daniel Cohn-Bendit, *Nous l'Avons Tant Aimée, la Révolution* (1986), pp. 35, 95–6.

31. Eric Hobsbawm, *Interesting Times: A Twentieth-Century Life* (2002), p. 251.

32. Cohn-Bendit would have been aware of Furet's work because he had been on a jury that awarded him a prize. See Christophe Prochasson, *François Furet: Les Chemins de la Mélancolie* (2013), p. 444.

33. Willy Brandt, *People and Politics* (1978), p. 204.

34. Cited in Daniel Bertaux, Danièle Linhart and Béatrix Le Wita, 'Mai 1968 et la Formation de Générations Politiques en France', *Le Mouvement Social*, 143 (1988), pp. 75–89.

35. http://www.birmingham.ac.uk/Documents/college-artslaw/history/cccs/Interview-Transcripts/Dick-Atkinson.pdf

Acknowledgements

I am grateful to my editor Simon Winder and to James Pullen – my agent at The Wylie Agency, whose contribution to this book went much beyond the call of duty. Ruth Pietroni and Richard Duguid saw it through the press. Bela Cunha, the queen of copy-editors, agreed to emerge from partial retirement to work – with her characteristic mixture of rigour and sympathy – on my behalf. Cecilia MacKay was extremely helpful in finding the pictures. I also owe particular thanks to C. Clark Kissinger and Matti Salmi, who not only granted me permission to use photographs they had taken but also went out of their way to provide information. Mikko Pyhälä amd Juho Saksholm gave valuable help in locating a photograph.

Stuart Aveyard, James Bjork, Chris Dillon, Sarah Howard, Tom Kelsey, Dan Matlin, Chris Machut, Helen Parr and Maggie Scull read all or parts of this book and I am grateful for the useful advice that they gave, as I am grateful for the insights that have come from the students I have taught over the last twenty-five years at Kings's College London. Lisa Bald and Rosie Germain let me read their important unpublished work.

Most of all, I am grateful to my family – to my parents, my sister Katie, my brother-in-law Richard, and to my children Emma and Alexander. Alison Henwood read the whole book in draft but my debts to her, as ever, extend to matters way beyond this practical help and beyond anything that I could put into words.

Index

Page references in *italic* indicate illustrations and tables.